Use Foreclosure Law!

Use Foreclosure Law!

Keep Your Home

(Or, Walk Away Under <u>Your</u> Terms)

Second Edition – 2012

(1/13/12)

Ken "Postman" Kappel

Sun Light Press

Use Foreclosure Law!
Keep Your Home

Second Edition – 2012

Published by: Sun Light Press, LLC

The purpose of this book is to remove the fear of the unknown for underwater homeowners through education; and, introduce current and future homeowners and residential investors to economic fundamentals they <u>must</u> be aware of, particularly regarding Wall Street's world of Structured Finance. All of the material herein is provided for informational purposes only. In the event of incidental or consequential damages in connection with, or arising out of, the furnishing of facts, opinion, ideas and an array of action options; the author, editors and pub-lisher express no warranties, and are not liable for any actions or non-actions taken by read-ers.

Always obtain legal, investment and tax advice from a professional before acting.

Library of Congress Cataloging-in-Publication Data:
ISBN-10: 0-615-59282-1
ISBN-13: 978-0-615-59282-4 (Paperback)
1. Author // Title: Ken "Postman" Kappel // Use Foreclosure Law: Keep Your Home
Bibliography and Index
1. Real Estate; 2. Economics; 3. Self-Help
Cover illustration ©2008 Justin Robertson.

Printed in the USA by Create Space, a DBA, of On-Demand Publishing, LLC, part of the Amazon group of companies.

10 9 8 7 6 5 4 3 2 1

Dedicated To:

Homeowners who discover that their mortgage is "<u>underwater</u>" aka "<u>upside-down</u>."

Those wishing to own – some day.

Homeowners who <u>do not realize</u> that they were <u>victims of fraudulent</u> Predatory Lending and Securities Law violations.

Using Foreclosure Law they have the <u>legal right and obligation</u> to turn their situation strongly to the advantage of their families by Confronting Fraudulent Housing Debt

Debt is Real

(You can believe it.)

Equity is Merely Opinion

(Believe what you will – first – be informed.)

Dump *Your* Debt

(Banks Dumped Their Debt – On You!!!)

Acknowledgement

Special thanks to Mike Vego, my very best friend of thirty six years. Mike has been an advisor and trusted Consigliore. As a Real Estate Broker he brought a special insight to this work.

Over time, initially struggling against slowly accumulating, yet, compelling evidence, precipitated by the Housing Bubble, which makes up the core of this work, we came to understand that there was significant evidence that the lack of regulation and oversight of Mortgage Backed Securities (MBS), derivatives, CDS, hedge funds, multi-etceteras, was going to lead to a major collapse of our financial system. It has come to pass. The collapse is in. The moribund corpse has been mummified by infusions of Federal Reserve fiat money, money printing, it cannot continue too much longer before foreign nations will not accept the dollar. It only survives because the dollar is "reserve currency" of the world. This too shall pass. Ask the Chinese, Russians, Saudis, the list goes on.

Borrower's were in many − if not most cases − systematically defrauded as the Bubble soared out of sight.

- Do anything – make the loan.
- Say anything – make the loan.
- Fudge the numbers − make the loan.
- Toxic or not – make the loan.
- Liable to fail into default – make the loan.

That was the Mandate, the Siren's Songs from Wall Street.

Without Mike's willingness to suspend disbelief (and, as über-editor, he challenged, always challenged), his sharing of insight and strong suggestions for moderation, this book would no doubt be even more strident than what some may come to believe it now is. In mild defense we suggest that we've been generally correct about these issues since 2005. The evidence for Systemic Fraud leading to Systemic Crash mounts higher. Those who think that we're likely to muddle through economically this time − yet once again − may come around. Or not. We don't hold our breath. Denial is a fabled and wondrous enabler.

We were all systemically defrauded. Greenspan was the enabler. He refused to regulate Wall Street, as he was legally bound to do. Worse he enabled Wall Street to "create money" (leverage). Wall Street created a lot of money, which was/is actually debt. They gambled recklessly with that money to line their pockets. They now want taxpayer's to pay that (unpayable) debt, and, also, *continue* to line *their* pockets. Enough!

CAVEAT

"All the perplexities, confusion and distress in America arise not from defects in their Constitution or Confederation, nor from want of honor or virtue, so much as downright <u>ignorance</u> of the nature of coin, credit and circulation." Former U.S. President, John Adams [Emphasis added.]

"... and if the national bills issued, be bottomed (as is indispensable) on pledges of specific taxes for their redemption within certain and moderate epochs, and be of proper denomination for circulation, <u>no interest on them would be necessary or just</u>, because they would answer to every one of the purposes of the metallic money withdrawn and replaced by them." Former US President Thomas Jefferson. [Emphasis Added.]

"... and gave to the people of this Republic The Greatest Blessing They Ever Had − <u>Their Own Paper To Pay Their Own Debts</u>." Former US President Abraham Lincoln. [Emphasis Added.]

"The Congress shall have the power: To <u>coin money, regulate the value thereof</u> and of foreign coin and to fix the standards of weights and measures." Constitution of the United States, Article I Legislative Department, Section 8, page 5. George Washington. President and Deputy from Virginia.

Presidential Power. We cite these former Presidents to set a tone for this book. Moreover, to indicate that all Americans must understand the nature of money if they are to have a deeper sense of empowerment, which comes from education. Our Founding Fathers well knew what they were about. We sincerely hope that we stay strong to our course, which in part calls for − begs for − readers to accept a willingness to suspend political biases − even if only temporarily. The Greater Task is to learn from our Founding Fathers who had arrived on these shores in order to escape Unjust Tyranny. They left behind systems of governance and control often exercised by European Despots, based on antiquated inherited privilege and acquiesce to previously accumulated wealth taken on the death of those unable to defend themselves against the raw power of sharp steel wielded significantly from Greed and Power Lust.

Yet, ultimately,. *The People United Can Never Be Defeated.* At this point, January 2012, utilization of the Rule of Law is what we have left to defend our *families and our homes.*

Information Is Power. We disagree with John Adams, but *only* in the sense that he used the word *"ignorance"* when we think he might have better said: "lack of information." For us − *ignorance* means to *know* the facts – and *ignore* them. Whereas, in adverse conditions, lack of information leads to fear, denial and often − loss. This book has been written to explain what happened in the housing market − in the economy − and to *outline a course of action* that can bring control and optimism back in your life. This can only happen through direct action − direct action by you. In a word − it begins with − *education.*

Rather than being paralyzed – in denial. Rather than continuing to pay on a loan, which is larger than the actual value of the home – being underwater. Rather than allowing foreclosure – to be taken against your family's best interest – you need to *take action* in order to control the situation in the interest of security and happiness for your family. This applies to those who are facing foreclosure, and, frankly, moreover and particularly, for those who are underwater – who will assuredly be going deeper – underwater.

Currently there are approximately 72 million homes in America. Fifty-six million of those homes have mortgages. We allege and will attempt to prove to your satisfaction that nearly 90% of all mortgages issued after 2000 were illegally and fraudulently securitized – immediately after – if not simultaneously upon execution at the Close of Escrow (COE).

Further – as of this writing in late December 2011, 29% to 35%, if not more, of *all mortgages* are underwater right now. (See, Zillow.com). Zillow reports the underwater number as 28.9% of total homes with mortgages – 14.4 million homes. Yet, if a family had to sell, they must add in transaction costs running approximately 7%. Adding that 7% to 28.9%, means that <u>35% of all homes with mortgages are underwater</u>. Most of the folks who think their debt equals the amount owed – and they are not underwater – are frankly kidding themselves.

This means that over 18 million mortgages are underwater. This is a condition precedent for massive Strategic Defaults (aka "walking away) over the next few years. Never ever do that. Never strategically default. By educating yourself with this book and our blog <u>www.useforeclosure.com</u>, you can empower yourself to Confront Fraudulent Housing Debt and bring about Forced Debt Reorganization. Basically a mod with principal reduction to – or slightly below – current market value. If that is a mortgage you could live with, read on.

If you gain information – learn the facts – then you *know what you are doing,* and can start *doing what you are knowing.*

Chuck Prince was the CEO of Citigroup, which is subject to allegations in the financial press that it may be insolvent. Mr. Prince was quoted in the *Financial Times*, stating:

> **"As long as the music is playing, you've got to get up and dance.**
> **We're still dancing."**

The music has stopped. They're not dancing any more. In fact, Mr. Prince was asked to leave the dance floor by Citigroup's Board of Directors. They sat him down and terminated him. Citigroup and many depository banks around the world are in significant trouble because of a lack of liquidity (a lack of nearly free money which the Fed still passes out to them, and tries to hide that fact from all of us). Balance sheets are being tampered with in order to not have to show the world (and their shareholders) that actually many of them are insolvent. Their total financial liabilities exceed their total financial assets. Generally cause for bankruptcy declaration.

It's a familiar refrain these days. Yet, not often reported in the Main Stream Media (MSM). Overall there are many reports that bank regulators, primarily the Federal Reserve System (Fed), is allowing banks to fudge their numbers, while the Securities Exchange Commission (SEC) also looks away. Of late, this seems to be Fed practice. Reward and protect the financial elites, to the detriment of the taxpayers. Remember, the SEC willfully ignored evidence presented to them over years that Bernie Madoff was running a Ponzi scheme.

We were pleased to see that they sometimes (rare enough) *get it* across the Pond in Great Britain. Mr. Prince's remarks from March, 2008, were commented on by a major player in world finance.

> *"If banks feel they must keep on dancing while the music is playing and that at the end of the party the central bank will make sure everyone gets home safely, over time the parties will become wilder and wilder. That might not matter were the consequences limited to the partygoers. But they are not."* Governor of the Bank of England, Mervyn King. Bloomberg. June, 2008.

"Fed actions only effect the economy accidentally. Their total focus is on protecting banks." James Rickards, widely quoted world class economics analyst, 12/19/2011.

"Housing Doom. "Experts already know that when mortgage holders have 'negative equity' they are much more inclined to put their keys in the mailbox…. Hence, the name for this *increasingly common practice* 'jingle mail.' Secretary of the Treasury Henry Paulson is desperately trying to put together a national "rate freeze" to avoid, what could be, the most devastating surge of foreclosures the world has ever seen. Paulson's rate freeze does not offer 'New Hope' as promised, but rather, a lifetime of servitude paying off an asset of decreasing value." Mike Whitney.

"What we are witnessing right now is not just a collapse of faith in one single institution. Instead, it stems from a loss of trust in the whole style of modern finance, with all its complex slicing and dicing of risk into ever-more opaque forms." Gillian Tett, *Financial Times.*

We want to be very clear; and have you understand that throughout this book you will find repetition. A lot of repetition. In literature they call it "echoing." All well and good. At the bottom line:

Repetition is the Mother of Memory.

Table of Contents

PREFACE

"We've given you a Republic – if you can keep it."
Benjamin Franklin.

We have *not kept it.*

Our democratic Republic has been usurped by a rapacious Financial Monetary Apparatus – wrapped and operating as one – yet, going by many names:

- Rothschild's Centuries Old War-Based Central Banking;
- Deep Domestic and Global Generational Wealth;
- Entrenched Capital;
- The Cabal;
- The Powerz That Be (TPTB);
- Financial Elites;
- Financial Engineering;
- Structured Finance;
- Wall Street;
- Federal Reserve System (Fed);
- Wall Street Investment Banks (IBs);
- Too Big to Fail Banks (TBTF);
- Banksters.

The latter term – Banksters – is our frivolous – yet deeper – favorite name for *all* of the above.

They are all from *Bankistan.* In the U.S., generally located near the street named: *Wall,* in lower Manhattan. In 1685, Dutch settlers built a wall there to protect themselves from an Indian tribe called the Lenape People, who, after earlier selling Manhattan to these early America Settlers for a pittance, decided they wanted it back. A wall was constructed (east to west) from the East River to the Hudson River to protect the settlers who believed they had a *valid legal claim,* and who wanted to keep the land and their lives.

Some *walls* are well designed to keep people safely inside, while keeping potentially unruly people outside. Like – Occupiers and Tea Partiers.

Wall Street wants and intends to keep you:

- out of the loop;
- out of being in the know;
- generally dumbed down;
- most of all obedient; and,
- oh-so quiet.

Yet, now comes a wild card – a very loud – *Occupy Movement* – repping for the (sometimes reluctant) 99%. Wall Street – the Banksters – seem to be concerned. Why not? Smart Tea Party folks are also showing up and Ron Paul made some nice comments re the Occupy Movement. *We'll* not head off into wild Conspiracy *Theories,* regarding Economic and/or Martial Law (see below), though over decades we've proudly become Conspiracy *Therapists.*

These Banksters have successfully evoked Fiscal (government) and Monetary (Fed) Policy and Practice that worked for their personal enrichment, particularly their bonuses − ridiculous bonuses − awarded in the face of failure by their beholden − captured − Board's of Directors, courtesy of still generous taxpayer bailouts, authorized by the Young President and freely given by the Fed. Can you say: Enough!!! Will you?

No state or nation can long endure if Financial Elites − clever and ruthless people acting in concert − who possess and share unconscious aberrant sociopathic and/or psychopathic tendencies and urges − conspire in unison (with "willing political accomplices") to suborn, take and control a nation for their own purposes through creation of enormous and unpayable debt. Ultimately, an (insolvent) U.S. Financial Elite Dominated Global Economic Empire, even though supported by F-18s and drones will ultimately be defeated by Mr. Market.

Particularly, if Mr. Market is aided by Americans standing up to protect their families who utilize the Rule of Law to protect and take back their underwater homes by Confronting Fraudulent Housing Debt in order to achieve a Forced Debt Reorganization.

Today, the *"willing accomplices"* mentioned above, are the most part of the American Congress, which today, 12/23/11, enjoys only an 11% approval rating by the American People. This is in no way intended to absolve the *Young "captured(?)" President.* (We really try to give benefit of doubt − if at all possible − even if a stretch.)

What ails the U.S.? To mention a few items:

- Illegal foreclosures are rampant.

- Our Banks, which are falsely considered Too Big To Fail (TBTF), are insolvent.

- Inflation actually runs at 7.5%, not 3.6%, falsely reported by the Fed; (http://www.shadowstats.com).

- Unemployment runs at 23%; not 9%, falsely reported by the Fed; (http://www.shadowstats.com).

- GDP is closer to -1.3, not +2.1, falsely reported by the Fed; (http://www.shadowstats.com).

- Central Banking has gone berserk.

- American taxpayers bailing out the European Union, and their TBTF Banksters, so they don't (at least not until summer, 2012) take our TBTF Banksters down with them.

- Big Oil, Pharma, Agra, Nuclear etc., are poisoning people and the environment − while destroying the American Way of Life.

- The wide spread <u>nuclear fallout</u> and <u>contamination</u> of the Japanese People from the accident in Fukushima, Japan is suppressed by the media. *Nothing to see here. Move along.* **False.**

- NIHONMATSU, Fukushima -- Anger and anxiety are spreading here after highly radioactive gravel from inside the Fukushima nuclear disaster evacuation zone was traced on Jan. 17, 2012 to several construction projects in the city, including at local schools. The contaminated gravel, quarried in the town of Namie, was first discovered in the concrete at a new apartment block.

  http://mdn.mainichi.jp/mdnnews/news/20120118p2a00m0na012000c.html.

- Talk of "recovery" is mere cheer leading by the Fed, designed to boost confidence for the stock market, etc., in our "consumer economy."

- Black Friday retail sales:. 2011 − $41.2 billion; 2008 − $64 billion http://www.adviscrone.com/

- Christmas 2011 retail sales up a robust 4.5% over 2010. Yet retailers gloomy re 2012. http://retailindustry.about.com/od/statisticsresearch/ http://www.rte.ie/news/2011/1229/retail-business.html

- FBI reported record-breaking firearm sales over the holidays. Gun dealers requested more than 1.5 million background checks − highest single-month topping November 2011, CNN reported. Allegedly 10,800,000 guns sold in US in 2011. Yet, crime is down. Go Figure. http://nssf.org/newsroom/.

- "Squeezed by rising living costs, a record number of Americans — nearly 1 in 2 — have fallen into poverty or are scraping by on earnings that classify them as low income." www.npr.org

- Currently 49 million Americans receive food stamps; and, college loan debt exceed $1 Trillion, now higher than all outstanding credit card debt.

- Our National Debt is unsustainable and unpayable. See below.

- The National Defense Authorization Act of 2011 enables the President or the military to declare any American a "suspected" terrorist and be detained indefinitely without arraignment, formal charge of crime, right to counsel, due process, or enabled to bring a Writ of Habeas Corpus, long a pillar of our Constitution. A prelude to Martial Law? Congress allegedly debated this issue <u>for one hour</u>. Initially, it took

Jon Stewart to put the matter forward strongly. And, of course the ACLU has now taken notice. Great Good Luck.

- The US Senate voted 86 - 14 to pass the National Defense Authorization Act of 2011 which allows for the indefinite military detention of American citizens without charge or trial. "*Montanans have announced the launch of recall campaigns against Senators Max Baucus and Jonathan Tester, who voted for the bill.*" www.Salem-News.com."

- In response − 99% are emerging.

- Alternatively, did 99% emerging force the NDAA?

- Recently discovered in December, 2011 is that the National Association of Realtors (NAR) has *"inadvertently"* been overstating the actual number of home sales for the last three years. Their numbers are widely used as an economic gauge. Can you say: *"It's a Great Time To Buy."*

- *"Throughout the foreclosure crisis, Washington has done little to help people hang on to their homes. All those programs that were supposed to help — HAMP, HARP, Hope for Homeowners — have mostly failed.*" Gretchen Morgenson, NY Times, 12/24/11.

- Lloyd Blankfein, CEO of Goldman Sachs, told a reporter for the *Sunday Times* of London that he's just a banker *"... doing God's work."* Thereby invoking the ultimately discredited _Divine Right_ Of Kings, which, in part, our Founding Father's fought off to establish our democratic Republic. A perfect example − beyond arrogance − demonstrating the avaricious nature and ethos of the unscrupulous − if not psychotic trader − following a war-based business model that slaughters millions of innocents. He unconsciously claims divinity? Makes a joke? More like a Fraudian slip!

- Again: illegal foreclosures are rampant ; and,

- More homeowners are underwater every month. From 29-33% are actually underwater − with no equity, 1/2/11. Yet, *44% believe* they are underwater.

Ownership Society? That is not the current condition. It is no "ownership society;" and the center can not − nor will not − hold much longer. If you consider the "center" to be the Middle Class, then face it. It's over. The center has not held. Breath. Feels good to step through the "looking glass," and come to terms with reality. Then, we can get to work. Let's do it! Let's go!

If you enter this place − please − leave your politics outside the door. We get way too much of that in the Main Stream Media (MSM).

Left(?) − Middle(?) − Right(?)

Give us a break. We speak those languages, have enjoyed "feeling good" being in and proudly −of − those Belief Systems − over time − as we grew up. Finally − we had to put away childish things. Here's your first homework assignment. Google: *"Hegelian Dialect,"* and you'll understand exactly what we're trying to say. We'll try again: Powerz wisely pit left v. right − against one another − in endless circus-like non-consequential finger pointing electoral debates and so much more. This presidential electoral circus collectively costs several billion dollars − to buy office − and now takes place for 18 months before each Presidential election. Please.

This work − our/your − journey here − is about families and their homes. So forget about blaming anybody − no time for that. Well − we can and do blame Banksters and their hired politicians. If you didn't before − by the time you finish this book − you likely will as well. Let's get to work.

The Good News. Here − with this book and our blog − we offer you information that if studied − becomes knowledge − called education. If you do the work, you will be empowered and disposed towards Confronting Fraudulent Housing Debt.

Those with fortitude, resolution and determination to protect and defend their family and their home by reading this book and our blog (see, www.UseForeclosureLaw.com), will subsequently be offered "tools," which will enable you to take affirmative and proactive legal action. Will empower underwater homeowners − by removing the fear of the unknown.

Our Story? That's it. And, were sticking to it. <g> Capiche?

Another Point of View. Gerald Celente is founder and director of The Trends Research Institute, author of <u>Trends 2000</u> and <u>Trend Tracking</u> (Warner Books), and publisher of The Trends Journal. He has been forecasting trends since 1980.

Below is what Gerald recently wrote on December 22, 2011. Oh, but wait, first, understand this. You see − Gerald is widely regarded by many as the top Trend analyst around. He was recently personally economically burned. A six figure investment he had placed in MF Global, which recently went down, was "confiscated." Some think it may have been a "controlled take-down," such as what many people think is what happened to former venerated Investment Bank, Lehman Brothers. Some say Henry Paulson, was the engineer of that debacle as the Treasury Secretary in the 2008 Crash. We remind you that Mr. Paulson had recently been Chairman of Goldman Sachs, and killing Lehman Brothers certainly did reduce the competition.

At any rate, Gerald, as a result of his recent experience, has recently surmised in other articles and interviews, that they've ripped the face off of the Rule of Law; and that *no investments* are safe any longer. Many others have chimed in, and a consensus of deep systemic fraud is emerging. We're just saying: be very careful where you have your money – your retirement funds – your investments.

The theory goes that under a second oncoming (since the prior one in 2008) historically unprecedented Crunch; if the Banksters need your money to prop themselves up and avoid bankruptcy – and they certainly do – they're just liable to take it. Witness: MF Global. Over $2 Billion client money initially disappeared. Though, guess what? Some believe that JP Morgan who sits on the Bankruptcy Court *Creditor's* Committee, has got all that "missing money" tidied up in *their* London office. And very recent reports show Goldman Sachs also played a hand just two months before MF Global filed for bankruptcy. Well whadda ya know!

If you missed it, just Google: "MF Global," and you'll be up to speed.

This just in, on 1/5/12, Gerald announced on CoasttoCoastAM.com radio that he has received 70% of his purloined funds. Where's the rest of it?

Gerald wrote:

"Hold onto your hat, your wallet, and your wits."

"After a tumultuous 2011 in which many of the trends we had forecast became headline news around the world, we are now forewarning of an even more tumultuous year to come."

"While it would give us great pleasure to forecast a 2012 of joy and prosperity – all brought about by the wisdom and benevolence of our fearless leaders – since we are not running for office or looking to profit by gulling the people, we tell it as we see it in our: **12 Top Trends 2012.**"

"One megatrend looms on the near horizon. And we forecast that when it strikes, it will be a shock felt around the world. Hyperbole it's not! Our research has revealed that at the very highest levels of government this megatrend has been seriously discussed. Read on:"

"**1. Economic Martial Law:** Given the current economic and geopolitical conditions, the central banks and world governments already have plans in place to declare economic martial law … with the possibility of military martial law to follow."

"**2. Battlefield America:** With a stroke of the Presidential pen, language was removed from an earlier version of the National Defense Authorization Act, granting the President authority to act as judge, jury and executioner. Citizens, welcome to "Battlefield America.""

"**3. Invasion of the Occtupy:** 15 years ago, Gerald Celente predicted in his book *Trends 2000* that prolonged protests would hit Wall Street in the early years of the new millennium and would spread nationwide. The "Occtupy" is now upon us, and it is like nothing history has ever witnessed."

"**4. Climax Time:** The financial house of cards is collapsing, and in 2012 many of the long-simmering socioeconomic and geopolitical trends that Celente has accurately forecast will come to a climax. Some will arrive with a big bang and others less dramatically … but no less consequentially. Are you prepared? And what's next for the world?"

5. Technocrat Takeover: "Democracy is Dead; Long Live the Technocrat!" A pair of lightning-quick financial coup d'états in Greece and Italy have installed two unelected figures as head of state. No one yet in the mainstream media is calling this merger of state and corporate powers by its proper name: Fascism, nor are they calling these "technocrats" by their proper name: Bankers! Can a rudderless ship be saved because a technocrat is at the helm?"

6. Repatriate! Repatriate!: It took a small, but financially and politically powerful group to sell the world on globalization, and it will take a large, committed and coordinated citizens' movement to "un-sell" it. "Repatriate! Repatriate!" will pit the creative instincts of a multitude of individuals against the repressive monopoly of the multinationals."

7. Secession Obsession: Winds of political change are blowing from Tunisia to Russia and everywhere in between, opening a window of opportunity through which previously unimaginable political options may now be considered: radical decentralization, Internet-based direct democracy, secession, and even the peaceful dissolution of nations, offering the possibility for a new world "disorder."

8. Safe Havens: As the signs of imminent economic and social collapse become more pronounced, legions of New Millennium survivalists are, or will be, thinking about looking for methods and ways to escape the resulting turmoil. Those "on-trend" have already taken measure to implement Gerald Celente's 3 G's: Gold, Guns and a Getaway plan. Where to go? What to do? Top Trends 2012 will guide the way."

9. Big Brother Internet: The coming year will be the beginning of the end of Internet Freedom: A battle between the governments and the people. Governments will propose legislation for a new "authentication technology," requiring Internet users to present the equivalent of a driver's license and/or bill of health to navigate cyberspace. For the general population it will represent yet another curtailing of freedom and level of governmental control."

10. Direct vs. Faux Democracy: In every corner of the world, a restive populace has made it clear that it's disgusted with "politics as usual" and is looking for change. Government, in all its forms – democracy, autocracy, monarchy, socialism, communism – just isn"t working. The only viable solution is to take the vote out of the hands of party politicians and institute Direct Democracy. If the Swiss can do it, why can't anyone else?"

11. Alternative Energy 2012: Even under the cloud of Fukushima, the harnessing of nuclear power is being reinvigorated by a fuel that is significantly safer than uranium and by the introduction of small, modular, portable reactors that reduce costs and construction time. In addition, there are dozens of projects underway that explore the possibility of creating cleaner, competitively priced liquid fuels distilled from natural sources. Plan to start saying goodbye to conventional liquid fuels!"

"**12. Going Out in Style:** In the bleak terrain of 2012 and beyond, "Affordable sophistication" will direct and inspire products, fashion, music, the fine arts and entertainment at all levels. US businesses would be wise to wake up and tap into the dormant desire for old time quality and the America that was."

In the event that you have lingering doubts regarding the veracity of indictments of high finance herein, we offer the following by Michael M. Thomas, whose Wall Street career spanned some thirty years. He retired as a partner at Lehman Brothers, directly in the belly-of-the-beast. In retirement years he wrote the brilliant "Midas Touch" column at the *New York Observer*.

He makes it clear that the Wall Street − including the Investment Banks that were all partnerships back in the day − was a kinder, gentler and much more ethical place. Starting in the seventies, *traders* began their intrusion into management, and by the time the Investment Banks went public in the nineties, any focus on ethical conduct was lost to a hand over fist "personal profit mania," heedless of any value added. Except to their increasingly unethical − which morphed to now − clearly fraudulent daily practice − designed to exclusively enrich themselves. We give you: **The 1%.**

"At the end of the day, the convulsion to come won't really be about Wall Street's derivatives malefactions, or its subprime fun and games, or rogue trading, or the folly of banks. It will be about this society's final opportunity to rip away the paralyzing shackles of corruption or else dwell forever in a neo-feudal social order. You might say that 1384 has replaced 1984 as our worst-case scenario. I have lived what now, at 75, is starting to feel like a long life."

"If anyone asks me what has been the great American story of my lifetime, I have a ready answer. It is the corruption, money-based, that has settled like some all-enveloping excremental mist on the landscape of our hopes, that has permeated every nook of any institution or being that has real influence on the way we live now."

Quote above comes from Mr. Thomas' article called: The Big Lie posted at The Daily Beast. (Hat tip May S, via Yves Smith).

National Debt. To put another brick in the wall − to alert you to the certainty of our oncoming domestic economic demise − below are comments from John Williams speaking at KingWorldNews.com. Mr. Williams is widely considered the leading if not single economic analyst that tracks and publishes *real numbers based on current statistics* in direct contradiction to the lies and obfuscations released by the Fed. His web is located at ShadowStats.com, http://www.shadowstats.com/. "

His 12/29/11, commentary was titled: *"Annual Deficits of $5 Trillion Are Not Sustainable."*

"Significant space was taken up in the government's latest financial statements to assess the sustainability of the current system. Most of the material covered was overly misleading nonsense."

"Those looking at the current $80 trillion of government debt and obligations, who think such is stable, need to consider that the circumstance is getting worse each year by at least $5 trillion. Taxes cannot be raised enough to bring the system into balance for one year, let alone for the ongoing future."

"Every penny of government spending—except for Social Security and Medicare—could be cut and the system still would be in annual deficit. Massive cuts have to be put in place (an absolute necessity with the social insurance), if there is to be any hope of restoring long-term solvency for the United States government...."

"There is no political will apparent among those currently controlling the White House and Congress to do so. Accordingly, the U.S. will be doomed to an eventual hyperinflation, as the government prints money to meet its obligations. That process already has started. There is little time."

"The next Fed action to help the economy (a.k.a. prop-up banking system liquidity), easily could be the one that pushes the U.S. dollar into the abyss. Much greater detail, again, will follow with the new hyperinflation report...."

———————————

Not looking too good. It's a big job to fix it right up. Yet, we're up to it. *You* can do it!!!

Remember, your job is to protect and defend your family and your home. If enough of you do so − significant numbers − the rest of it will fall into place, albeit with a great gnashing of teeth and extreme pushback from "Banksters." Imagine − what would happen if the 99% moved their checking accounts from TBTF Banks into local and regional banks, credit unions and savings and loan entities? That'll be the day! Read on.

INTRODUCTION – SECOND EDITION

(December, 2012)

Much has occurred since we closed out the First Edition of this book in June, 2009. That is frankly a very very mild understatement. We have seen the further erosion of the Middle Class (the engine of our Consumer Economy); rampant unemployment; a government in Washington D.C. that is in a near perpetual adolescent gridlock; and, moreover, in relation to the focus of this book, continuing destruction of housing values, leaving perhaps, 17 million homeowners underwater – virtual lessees – indentured debt slaves in their very own homes.

Why would Powerz That Be, allow this to occur?

The Powerz simply do not care. They are the Financial Elites that have merged with the National Security State – the War Machine – and through the genius of Central Banking (a wretched spawn of the Centuries-old Rothschild Banking System) are busy practicing Empire on the Global Financial Stage. Worse, they've destroyed that as well. How?

It's quite simple. If a nation issues excessive debt-based fiat money (which is the definition of "inflation") then such debt – *liquidity* as it's called by Financial Powerz – ultimately destroys the value of all currencies, which results in "price inflation that you see at the pump, the grocery store, which leads to hyperinflation, which is arguably on the way.

Above, we say "all currencies" because today most nations are controlled in some way by Central Banking issuance of fiat currency. (Individual Sovereign European governments are constrained in that they can not issue Euros.) Nonetheless, it has now *metastasized* and all nations and people are victims of the Banksters.

We discuss this throughout the book, and will leave it to that. However, we are on the verge of destruction of the dollar, and a Greater Depression than what the world experienced in the 1930s. No one can say with certainty, *when* that will happen, but, most realistic economic analysts assert that it is not a matter of *if,* it is a matter of *when.*

We will touch on – rather expose – the oncoming Global Financial Crash later in the book – count on it. But, to touch briefly; we all read that Europe is falling down, their nations and major banks are insolvent. And, the European Central Bank is borrowing money from the Federal Reserve and a few other central banks to prop up the Euro. Etcetera. Well, Europe and the Euro *are* falling. This drags down *their* banks, AND, *our* intertwined, so-called Too Big To Fail banks who are heavily invested in the major European banks, generally through derivative exposure (big un-backed insurance type gambling). In this case they are not holding cash reserves to pay off on bank default claims. The AIG bailout is an example. The Fed pumped $180 billion into AIG, which immediately passed out $12 billion to Goldman Sachs. How nice of the taxpayers.

In reality several financial entities are *Too Big To Survive* because – as they have proven – they threaten to destroy the U.S. and World economies with their reckless creation of debt. This can never be allowed to happen again. Well, not for 50 to 80 years or so when a new business cycle is upon us largely because people who remember what happened have passed on. So history repeats itself. Evermore. We have an entire chapter on Business Cycles.

Our Mission is to remove the Fear of The Unknown for underwater homeowners through education, enabling them to:

Confront Fraudulent Housing Debt.

By reading and studying this book, which contains the fundamentals − the foundation of your education; and, our blog: UseForeclosureLaw.com, which contains breaking news, particularly, near daily updates on the emerging legal context; and, then telling us you have done so, we can offer "tools," legal information, not legal advice, to enable you to use what remains of the Rule of Law in order to:

Confront Fraudulent Housing Debt.

This book exists to inform underwater homeowners that by Using Foreclosure Law to Keep Their Homes, average Americans can use existing laws (based generally on *fraudulent inducement* and *failure to legally disclose* in loan origination) to legally leverage control away from "lenders," and ultimately rebalance the economy. We can drive the Young President's release from capture by Financial Elites, led in public, by Tim-Boy "Tax Dodger" Geithner. He of the AIG bailout when Mr. Geithner was President of the New York Federal Reserve Bank. Though Geithner is Treasury Secretary (his predecessors were Robert Rubin and Henry Paulson), they all arguably worked as *double agents* for the Banking Cartel. Witness: all three are wretched spawn of Goldman Sachs.

Mr. Geithner played a number of interesting roles through his early career; first, as a protégé of Henry Kissinger. His Master ultimately became Robert Rubin, former Co-Chairman of Goldman Sachs, and subsequently Bill Clinton's Treasury Secretary, where Rubin played a principal role in the mid-nineties in setting in place a scheme that would successfully blow up − *Housing Bubble Boom* − then blow out − *Housing Bubble Bust* − the housing market while he and his friends on Wall Street, *took* historically unprecedented fortunes, through executive bonuses and stock options.

Word has it that Rubin is *still* the ultimate owner of Obama's left ear, while the irascible Jamie Dimon, CEO of JP Morgan Chase, owns Obama's right ear. Today the instrument − the ear-holder − the gate keeper − is the Young President's Chief of Staff, Bill Daley, arguably No. 3 man to Mr. Dimon. Rahm Emanuel, former Chief of Staff, was long on Goldman's Sach's "consultancy" payroll before he was appointed Chief of Staff to control the ears, eyes and gate to the White House.

Whoops. This just-in, 1/11/12. There is yet another change in Whitehouse Gatekeepers.. Daley going back to Chicago to spend more time with his grandchildren. Hope they're young enough to appreciate it.

The New New Guy. Jack Lew is now in as the Young President's Chief of Staff, Chief Gatekeeper. Here's his background according to the <u>Wall Street Journal</u>.

"Age-Birth Date-Location: 56; Aug. 29, 1955; New York City.

"Education: Graduated with bachelor's degree from Harvard in 1978 and a law degree from Georgetown University in 1983.

"Experience: Served in Obama administration as Deputy Secretary Of State from 2009-2010 and as Budget Director from Nov. 2010 to present. Served as Budget Director in Clinton administration from 1998-2001. Began career in Washington in 1973 as Legislative Aide on Capitol Hill, including stint as Domestic Policy Adviser to House Speaker Thomas P. O'Neill, Jr. Private sector experience includes serving as Managing Director and Chief Operating Officer of Citi's Global Wealth Management Branch. Also served as Chief Operating Officer and Executive Vice President of New York University."

So this gentleman has been a Government Apparatchik for most of his career until he slipped out for a bit to take Banking Cartel training at Citibank. But, there's more. At Citibank he headed a branch that invested in John Paulson's Advantage Plus LP, which in partnership with, yes, you guessed it, Goldman Sachs. Paulson bet that housing would destruct, and worked closely with Goldman, in what amounted to them selling Mortgage Backed Securities to their Institutional Investors clients, while at the same time – without disclosure to their *own* clients, betting with Paulson that these investments in MBS would fail.

Lawsuits and even the government's case against Goldman Sachs continue. So – Lew has been trained at Citibank and indirectly by Goldman Sachs on how to sack the American People. His salary that one year at Citi was $1.1M. Handsome pay!!! And, to think of the pay cut he has willingly endured to control who gets to speak to the President. Guess, he'll make the money back on the back end. You can't make this stuff up.

Questions Abound: In lieu of law - Jack Lew? Has JP Morgan Chase truly lost the Young President's ear due to in-fighting? Or, is it mere passing of the baton? Has Bob Rubin (originally of: Goldman Sachs (the Mother Ship), then Treasury Secretary, closing out his *public* career at Citibank overseeing the housing debacle that in part he designed) brought in his man once again? Does he not own Geithner - and New Man: Jack Lew? Is Jack Lew the creature of Bank Lobbying's highest art form? Beyond campaign funding money control, would it not be logical to make certain that the Young President continues to only see and listen to folks vetted by the Banking Cartel? Is it: "Yes" to all of the above? We're just saying.

Some still wonder *why* the Young President seems to be so effectively "captured" by banking interests – the Banking Cartel. Looking back a couple of years ago; their clear and continuing power was exhibited the week ending May

3, 2009, the very day this book (First Edition) was closed out and submitted for publication.

That week Republican Senators stopped a provision in a Bankruptcy Bill – that would have enabled a Bankruptcy Judge to order a home owner "cramdown" (principal reduction) to current market value. "Cramdown" in that context simply meant "principal reduction." These would be achieved with what we call a *"legitimate loan modification,"* but, the banks will not go there.

We believe that principal reductions to current market value will only be achieved through: Forced Debt Reorganization. Those words are our construct, and simply mean a *legitimate* loan mod; brought about through the threat of, or, in fact – litigation – whereby the underwater homeowner is able to prove up Securitization (and other) Fraud in the loan origination process.

Don't try that at home. Only very few professionals are able to achieve that on behalf of underwater homeowners, and we know some of them. We'll be glad to make introductions, IF, you educate yourself. You're already reading the book. You must also read the blog thoroughly. By becoming a knowledgeable and *professional client,* you can work with professionals, and not slow them down. Better yet, they won't have to bill you for the time it takes to educate you. You come to the dance already educated – ready to dance – ready to rock.

Then you work with a professional who can provide proper legal pleadings, buttressed with an "Affidavit" by a legally qualified "expert witness." This qualifies as "evidence" in a court proceeding, because in fact without such an Affidavit, a Securitization Audit is only a "report." More below.

We've pulled two articles from our blog that set the tone, offer some bits critical to your understanding – how you were defrauded at the beginning – when you set your signature to your Promissory Note. .

Homeowner's Econ 101
First and foremost this is an education site.

We're trying to show you, educate you, so that you'll understand what the Banksters did, AND, how they did it. Frankly, it was illegal and fraudulent. Far beyond "Predatory Lending."

We always say: if you know what you're *doing*, you can do what you're *knowing*. We'll bet you more than five cents that you have an illegal loan, if you obtained it between 2002 and 2008. We intend to help you do something about it — offer you real "tools" and "processes" to confront your lender, servicer, whatever you call them, they are Banksters all.

However, you need to read our book and ALL the posts on the blog in order to understand what happened, what happened to you, what happened with your (likely illegal and predatory) loan docs. If you do, we'll offer tools to help you obtain your desired outcome; and prepare you to: *Confront Fraudulent Housing Debt.*

But, homework first.

Think on it, the average home buyer spends nearly fifty hours to locate the right home, make an offer, obtain financing and Close Escrow. We're suggesting you spend twenty bucks and thirty hours.

Twenty bucks (or less) to buy the book. Ten hours to read it.

Thirty hours to read all the articles on the blog.

Twenty bucks and thirty hours. Frankly, that is a heck of a deal!

OK – time for the Next Step. We've written a summary – call it a study guide – to show you to how to read the blog quickly, and with impact. Impact on your brain that is. It will grow through the addition of new brain cells. That's really what learning is: growth of new brain cells, which we call memory.

Next step:

Use Foreclosure Law – University
How To Read This Education Blog
To Achieve Your Desired Outcome

As you may know – throughout the blog – we say to underwater homeowners and folks with foreclosure issues:

read our book ($20, or less);

read the blog (all of it. it's free);

tell us you have done steps 1 & 2 (soon we'll have a form to fill out on the blog);

if you do your homework, tell us by filling out and electronically sending us the form; then;

we'll share "tools" enabling you to Confront Fraudulent Housing Debt.

Bottom line – you must become informed – educated – must understand:

- what has gone <u>on</u>,
- what has gone <u>wrong</u> – with our economy; and,
- moreover, WHY.

You must do your homework. When you do that you are in a position to be:

Doing **what you are now** *Knowing* **...**

Aware of <u>how to</u>;

Confront Fraudulent Housing Debt

Deeper, is that you must become an informed, *Professional Client.* If you are underwater, you face a battle ahead, and will require the assistance of professionals. We are not attorneys and do not provide legal advice. However, we know attorneys and other facilitating professionals who we believe are: honest, knowledgeable, experienced and committed as consumer rights advocates. After all, we've been searching for such individuals for four years.

After you've done your homework, when you begin to work with professionals − you'll understand exactly your role in the process − and won't need them to hold your hand − not so much. Hand holding costs counsel time, thus − money. You want to be able to assist counsel, not drag them through educating you, and having to bill you for what you can do on your own; right here, at virtually no charge. Do your homework.

Lecture over. The steps to effectively read and understand the blog − a Magazine-Style Web / Blog − are below. We've enabled pretty darn intuitive navigation on the blog in order to make it easy to read quickly − yet − get it.

First, on the left sidebar, click on MONTHLY ARCHIVES. You'll get a drop down. Start by clicking on December, 2010, on the bottom. All December article headlines will drop down on the left side (the main window), like a magazine Table of Contents. Take your time, read the Titles as you scroll all the way down. Then, go to January, 2011. When you've done them all, by working your way up, month by month, maybe thirty minutes tops, you'll have read the Title of every posting on the blog. Now, you're literally beginning to build memory and setting up to actually create new brain cells − again, memory. (This IS brain science, but don't worry about it. <g>)

Second, now from the top of the blog go to: HOME. This drops down the most recently posted articles in chronological order. As you scroll down, you'll see all the Titles again, with a snippet of introductory text. Like before, scroll down through the Titles, but, take a couple of seconds to read the short bit of text below the Title.

Third. When you scroll down to the bottom of the first screen, on the left, click on "← Previous Entries." Up pops the next set of articles. Scroll slowly now, keep scrolling until you've read through the article Titles and text snippets from the present − back through January, 2010. Whew. You might take an hour to do this, but, it's worth it.

The Great News, is that by then you've read ever article Title twice, and have also read a short text snippet about each article. Truly now, you are building new brain cells − they call it memory. The key is repetition. Each time you read a Title, synapses (thread like tiny molecular structure thingies) are formed in your brain. As you read them a second time, due to repetition, synapses magnetize together into atoms, and, miracle, form new brain cells. Literally growing your brain. We used to teach computer networking technology, so, we learned a bit of brain science related to learning.

Repetition is the Mother of Memory

Fourth. Take a break.

Fifth. Next, read all of the articles (not many) in the Must Read section in the left sidebar. The large picture is presented in there − "critical information" − you'll be turning into knowledge.

Sixth. Now you will go deeper in terms of "critical information," which will give you fundamental understanding. Directly below the MONTHLY ARCHIVES section is the CATEGORY ARCHIVES section, click on that, it will give you a drop down, scroll down to MUST READ. Click on that and a list of approximately 25 files will drop down in the left column. These documents are the core – documents we've placed under the MUST READ category over time. You really need to read all of these. Some are long. Those who've become inspired by what they've read through the Steps above – students who bit the bullet – will print all of these postings, and study over time, sharing some with family and friends. *This it the real deal*.

Seventh. You are now a much more knowledgeable person. Next, go back and repeat step Two above. But, this time, open articles of particular interest to you and read them. Again you'll start in December, 2010 and move forward to the present.

Remember, this book has the background, the fundamentals, explanations of historic trends, as well as pertinent predatory and fraud law; and much, much more. The <u>contents of the book</u> will form the <u>foundation</u> of your new knowledge.

Whereas, <u>the blog</u> contains <u>breaking news and critical information</u> regarding current litigation potentials and process, based on real time current events. The blog is a <u>real-time</u> extension of the book; call it: the Digital Second Edition.

That's almost the whole deal. Does it take time? Of course, but, it is doing your homework. And, with your new knowledge, you'll be good and darned mad. You'll understand what the banks have done to not only *your* family, but, also, the American People over time. It's called Financial Engineering, and they are very good at it. But, they've committed fraud. Literally a Fraud on you and on Foreclosure Courts. Many state judges (though comprised by the fact that their pensions are caught up in the situation, and, are at risk, some of these invested in MF Global) are just now understanding – and angry about it as well. Not only that, but, other actions are going forward to bring to the attention of the world, how and why the judges are compromised.

"Oh what a tangled web we weave when first we practice to deceive."
William Shakespeare

Deeper. The Glass-Steagall Act, created in 1933, which kept financial entities separate in their functions, was partially repealed as a result of the Gramm-Leach-Billey Act in 1998. This was engineered by Wall Street Investment Banks, and certain Government Officials (Rubin, Paulson and Geithner) who were alumni of, or, beholden to Wall Street Investment Banks (Goldman Sachs). It could be well argued that figuratively and literally – at the brain trust helm were – again, Wall Street Investment Banks. They of course ~~bought~~ brought Congress along with them. Numbers below are from 2011. See, Open Secrets.

- Total spent by lobbyists in Washington D.C. for Finance, Insurance & Real Estate: $237,633,878.

- Total Number of Lobbyists in Washington D.C.: Finance, Insurance & Real Estate: 2,247.

From the *New York Times:*

"The Glass-Steagall Act restored public confidence in banking practices during the Great Depression. ....Some legislators and bank reformers argued that the act was never necessary, or that it had become outdated and should be repealed."

"Congress responded to these criticisms in passing the Gramm-Leach-Bilely Act of 1999, which made significant changes to Glass-Steagall. The 1999 law did not make sweeping changes in the types of business that may be conducted by an individual bank, broker-dealer or insurance company. Instead, the act repealed the Glass-Steagall Act's restrictions on bank and securities-firm affiliations. It also amended the Bank Holding Company Act to permit affiliations among financial services companies, including banks, securities firms and insurance companies. The new law sought financial modernization by removing the very barriers that Glass-Steagall had erected." [Emphasis Added.]

Yet, this very revealing information is only the tip of the iceberg. After legal restrictions were removed, Financial Engineers established a scheme including the now infamous Mortgage Electronic Registration System (MERS), and consciously, intentionally and fraudulently subverted centuries of Legal Property Law embedded in the laws of every state. This was a malicious end-run that was an intentional Fraud on the Court(s); all U.S. Counties; and, you – the homeowner. The law is that the Promissory Note and the Mortgage/Deed of Trust cannot be separated, they must stay together throughout the life of the loan. (More below.)

The next step of these Financial Elites – these Financial Engineers – was to create the Global Housing Bubble. (This followed on the dot.com Bubble, which they also created – for their profit – from Wall Street; while Greenspan turned a blind eye.) State Foreclosure Judges are just now beginning to wake up to this, and are (repeat) decidedly not happy about it. We are all waking up as well. Witness: *Occupy Wall Street.* Which will grow every day – until it doesn't – or forces radical change such as enacted in Glass Steagall. But, will Congress defer to their Wall Street Masters – or – to the voters who elect them to office? We'll be watching. Hopefully you will also, because it directly effects your life. Now and going forward.

When you've read – book and blog – as suggested in the steps above:

Congratulations – you'll be a Graduate of Use Foreclosure Law University. You'll be ready to move on for your Master's Degree.

Moreover, you're now a professional client, and we can work with you. Offer you "tools," which are actually resources and processes to Confront Predatory/Fraudulent Housing Debt. You'll choose what you want to do based on your intended outcome, and, the real facts regarding your loan documents.

Sorry, but, we don't have time to individually talk you through the learning curve. That's why we wrote the book and keep writing the blog – enabling you to discover and read information which becomes *knowledge certain.* Do your homework and you'll be able to take professional responsibility for your future actions in this regard. The banks have been and continue front-running a gigantic con game. They want to own everything. We don't think so.

Sure, they own the Young President; they also own: Congress; the Main Stream Media (MSM); and more.

However, they don't own you, and frankly, they don't own your Promissory Note, Deed-of-Trust/Mortgage, or Title to your home, even though they think they've got you convinced that they do. If your mortgage was one of 90% of all loans written between 1998 and 2007 – they likely don't. And, that's what you're going to prove to them, and, the court if your "matter" does not settle before trial. *It likely will*

Very few free houses will *be given* away. You've got to *take them back* – using Forced Debt Reorganization. But, don't let them confuse the fraud perpetuated against you with the hollow argument that you would be getting a "free" house. Your house is bought and paid for, yes, already paid for.

By who? By you.

How? The Promissory Note you GAVE THEM.

Some folks will want to go. Walk away, relinquishing the house; yet, leaving a perfected Title for a subsequent owner; no future debt; with fraud and RICO based monetary damages from a Settlement in their pockets; and, process and attorney fees (in order to get there) paid by the lender. This can be facilitated by combining the Federal Administrative Process Act of 1947 with a Securitization Audit, which proves the actual fraud in the securitization process of the Promissory Note. Robo-Signing is but the tip of the iceberg.

Some folks will want to stay. With a clean, unclouded "Quiet Title" in their name, significant principal reduction to current market value, and an affordable 5% fixed rate, thirty year amortizing loan, potentially some fraud and RICO monetary damages in their pocket, and all process and attorney fees (in order to get there) paid by the lender. This, also, can be facilitated by combining the Federal Administrative Process Act of 1947; with a Securitization Audit, which proves the actual fraud in the securitization process of the Promissory Note. Robo-Signing is but the tip of the iceberg.

Too Good Too Be True? Not necessarily so. While these are "best case" outcomes − at the bottom line − the loan docs were fraudulent from the day you signed them. The Deed of Trust and Promissory Note were Null and Void, when you executed them − set your signature to them.

Proof? Dig out your Promissory Note. Near the top you will find language similar to the following: *"... promise to pay for a loan I have received."* No − you hadn't! Did you ever see a deposit in your bank account for the amount of the loan? The monies that were paid to the seller came from you − you created the money, the loan, not the bank. Slow down.

You didn't allegedly receive the loan until after you signed the note. This is important − critically important.

When you signed the Note, it was not true you were promising to pay for a loan *"I have received."* "you had *not "received" the loan* prior to your signature, because clearly you had not received a loan prior to your signing. The bank knew this, understood this, but, you did not. In fact what they did − after the fact − was endorse it (typically in blank), then deposit your Promissory Note in their bank, as a cash item − just like a check. From that deposit, which they logged on their balance sheet as an "asset," they wrote a check to pay off the property seller − with the money they logged as an "asset" − that you created with your signature. You created the money to pay the seller. Astonishing. But, wait − there is much more.

They then filed a copy of your Promissory Note with the Federal Reserve System. Due to "fractional reserve" banking they could take your − credit worthy − signature on your $500,000 Promissory Note, and literally loan an additional $4,500,000 into existence. They were able to loan this extra money, and at the same time, your Promissory Note was recorded as an "asset" a deposit on their books. Astonishing.

So, you see, they were already paid, and you loaned them the money with your signature to do it. This is one of the dirty little secrets maintained by the Federal Reserve and the banks that actually own the Fed. It is not the Federal Government that owns the Fed, it is privately owned. And, the owners − Banksters − are not your friends. Beyond wanting your money − your house − and anything else of value they can take from you, they simply view you as chattel − uneducated indentured servants. Frankly, slaves − formerly wage slaves − now debt serfs − with a few privileges.

Did they offer − or did you ask for − a receipt when you signed and gave them the Promissory Note? Why not? It is a "Security" you created by your signature, a Negotiable Instrument − similar to a personal check. They later, if not immediately, sold it to Wall Street as a Security that you created, and got paid *again*. You, in fact, created the asset (Promissory Note) upon which the "loan" was created, they did not. This is your credit. The fact that they withheld this information from you when you went through this process is also illegal and a breach of any contract (Trust agreement) that you entered into with them (Fraudulent Inducement). Additionally, there was not a "meeting of the minds," therefore, under contract law, that contract was/is null and void. But, you must prove it.

Further, they did not sign the Note, which would also indicate a meeting of the minds − which did not occur. Proof being their "missing" signature. Do understand, this is not legal advice − purely legal information.

Looking directly at the law and the facts, because it was not true − that you *had received* a loan before signing − under contract (trust) law the Promissory Note was null and void the instant you signed it. So, for additional and different reasons, is the Deed of Trust/Mortgage Trust contract. There is a lot more to this than we're sharing right now. A lot more that you need to understand. If you do your homework, we'll explain this and much more to you, and make referrals, enabling you to work with professionals.

After you've done your homework − educated yourself − and filled out and returned the online form found on our blog, which begins the conversation − and are ready to Confront Fraudulent Housing Debt, assisted by professionals, you may understand why, at some point, you may choose to stop making payments. *Stop making payments?* We're *not* saying you should − we're *not* giving you legal or investment advice − yet, that's exactly what "Too Big To Fail" Banks tell folks who want to apply for a HAMP Loan Modification. They tell many of them to stop making payments − *basically instructing them to default* − if they want to qualify for a Loan Mod. Then they penalize them later for doing it − damaging their credit by stopping payments − then foreclosing anyway! Many readers have heard these and similar stories of the nightmare, house of mirrors that honest folks are put through seeking the Holy Grail of a loan mod. And, still they never get a "legitimate loan mod," with principal reduction.

You must institute a *Forced Debt Reorganization.* Are you ready to *Confront Fraudulent Housing Debt?* When you are thoroughly educated you likely will be.

You'll be able to start building your future nest egg and have some cash in hand to facilitate a process, which normally begins with your obtaining a Securitization Audit. Why? That audit will document − legally verify − if in fact your Promissory Note that you GAVE the bank was illegally Securitized by the banks. Meaning, that it was illegally placed into a Servicing and Pooling (SAP) agreement with other (illegal) Promissory Notes held within (generally) a New York State Trust that was organized by the Investment Banks; and, subsequently (if not fraudulently beforehand) sold to Institutional Investors all over the world as Residential Mortgage Backed Securities (RMBS). These Investors were/are: major insurance companies, pension funds, municipalities, other entities, and even foreign Central Banks.

Securitization of the Promissory Note is illegal if the Promissory Note was separated from the Deed of Trust / Mortgage. It broke the Chain of Title. In most cases it *was* broken, and, the Securitization Audit and other documents prove that fact. The Promissory Note became a non-securitized note. Thus not legal to be sold as: *"Mortgage Backed."* More to the point for your benefit, No

Party has the legal standing in which to foreclose on you. This is why some judges, who've been brought to understand (as you are being right now) what really happened, are angry and have stated in recent decisions, that foreclosure matters brought forward in their current form: *"... are a fraud upon this court."* You'll find articles supporting this point as you read current postings on the blog.

A Securitization Audit works for your legal purposes. And frankly – as incredible as it seems – if your loan was securitized: <u>no party has the legal right to foreclose on you</u>. Certainly not the Auctioneer on the Courthouse steps, or, the "Servicing Company" that they represent, or the purported "lender", or, the Trustee they may purport to represent. This is a major part of your legal leverage. Without it you're just talking. With it, the Bankers are forced to the table.

You will learn about bifurcation, conversion, re-conveyance and how these can apply to your "loan." A hint, Google: *Administrative Procedure Act of 1946.* Later, we'll tell you more on that. Nutshell: by closely adhering to exacting standards of procedure, of process, you can remove and replace the lender, and have the property recorded at the County Recorder's office in your name, removing any other parties or entities that have, or may make claims to any rights on your property. This is not trivial, but, once you've become educated – you will see the light.

Yet, this does not alter the fact that *until dealt with* – the Promissory Note, is a lien on the property. This must be taken into consideration before you begin a Title Reconveyance Process.

There are a number of different ways to proceed for the educated underwater homeowner – entirely dependent on your actual loan documents; your economic situation; and, your intentions. To repeat, you must educate yourself. Being up front – we seek to build and earn your trust – through the education process.

Final Note: If you <u>will</u> not or <u>can</u> not take the time to protect your family and your home by educating yourself, we wish you well, and regret that we have not adequately shown you a path to removing the fear of the unknown – bringing you a logical solution to your pain; and thereby, obtaining your desired outcome.

Disclaimer: Neither this document nor our blog contain legal advice. They are designed to offer information, for educational, and, even some *ironic* entertainment purposes for those who wish to *seriously understand* housing markets. We attempt to show how, and, why, homeowners must take the initiative to protect and defend their families themselves. Very rarely does anything of real value come easily. No "owned" public or private "officials" will do it for you. The word "Hope" in some of the Government foreclosure "programs" (and the Young President's electoral magic) was nothing but a cruel joke.

Neither this writing, nor the blog offer legal, accounting or investment advice. See a qualified and licensed professional for such services. We can and will help with that, but, only <u>after</u> you've educated yourself. Remember –

through education – you can become a knowledgeable and empowered Professional Client. You'll be very proud of that, and, inject the possibility of _opportunity_ into your family dynamic. A very good – if not one of the _best things_.

To _walk_ the talk while _walking_ the walk,
you must first learn to _talk_ the talk.

In the end, positivity will carry the day. That's why we offer you information becoming knowledge certain. This is – _only is_ – if you do your homework – which can lead to the courage to Confront Fraudulent Housing Debt. Make that decision and quick as can be, we'll be there to back up your play.

In our calm moments, we sometimes think that life is all a game. You choose. Decide which game, which part of the Master Game you want to play. And remember:

Losers are stuck.

Winners grow their brains and move forward – by taking Action.

Like in the end of the film, _"The Matrix."_ The People did and will ultimately prevail – even if only for brief periods of time. We're all One family. Occupy Your Home, one family at a time.

Last two lines of _"The Matrix."_

"Did you always know?"

"No – but I believed – I believed," said the Oracle.

Of course this concept – fairy tales, or, oft ordained over time as a folk tales – arguably goes to the whoo whoo. But, yet, deeper now, merely echo similar construct brought forward into the current cultural lexicon by such films as Peter Jackson's interpretation of Tolkien's, _"Lord of the Rings;"_ James Cameron's _"Avatar;"_ even, in the extremely non-fiction and extraordinary documentary recently presented by Foster Gamble, titled, _"Thrive."_

We are all touched at a spiritual level by art that attempts to croon, as good mother's have done through the ages, "Don't worry honey – everything's going to be all right." This is the human condition. It feel's good. Yet, looked at another way there is more than good intention embodied in mythology, even in slogans. "The People United can Never Be Defeated," comes to mind. Rah Rah, and Yeah Yeah!!! We call our guarded optimism post post modernism, a term we thought we invented in the early nineties – simply meaning, for us – irony on irony.. Now we discover that Academe has swarmed over that term, and we'll let it go at that. Gladly.

Finally here – we have work to do – let's get to it.

INTRODUCTION – FIRST EDITION

In August, 2008, we published a similar book titled: *Choose Foreclosure: The Case For Walking Away*, that book had a different theme than this one. The *anonymous* author of that book was: *"The Postman."*

Much changed since August 2008. Consequently, we've re-titled and *significantly* updated that book to reflect what we've learned in the last six months. The previous and current author is, Ken "Postman" Kappel, a licensed real estate agent in California, with a background in major media, as well as years working on Wall Street has come forward. He originally published on this topic on the web starting in 2004, at: The Home Owner's Economist.

He stopped writing that blog, in 2006 because no one could or would believe what was coming. Alas, Ignore the Messenger. Now that his predictions have finally come true, magically all the arrows in his back – popped out. Great Relief. Yet, folks still have enormous and great difficulty accepting what is sure to come over the next several years. It is not a pretty picture. Unless you educate, prepare and defend yourself, Structured Finance – Wall Street – will continue to have it's way with you, as so many millions who have been illegally foreclosed on, and those underwater who have attempted in good faith to arrange a loan modification have discovered. Much much more on this below.

Housing is crashing with no end in sight for at least three more years. Finance has continued its downward spiral – propped up – bailed-out – by appropriately angry taxpayers.

It Isn't About Politics. As much as possible we've kept politics out of this book, which is basically about money – for purposes herein – *mortgage money*. Come along for several hours of reading, lose rose colored glasses, partisan political identity and hearts worn on sleeves of partisan rigor. Dropping what you may come to see – as former childish ways – may not feel good right away. However, it will make sense when you focus on the single issue which unites nearly everyone reading this book – those with mortgage payment issues and/or those underwater in home loans.

Routinely throughout the book (and on the blog) we reveal in plain-speak language why and how Financial Elites – now called Banksters in the common parlance – have destroyed our housing market. In particular, they set upon a scheme in the mid-nineties that has proven to be successful for Wall Street and destructive for Main Street.

Yet, ultimately, the banker's hegemony – their control of America – is not sustainable. Over time, Grand Schemes have taken control, yet, they ultimately lose control when the people act in concert. Notably Charles Hughes Smith (and other Bloggers writing from the increasingly respected margins), have suggested that the President may have a deeper end game that he is *forced* to play. (Though perhaps quite willingly and astutely – in a "good" Machiavellian way.)

If the bankers are given (actually they <u>take</u> it) all the rope they can swing on, an aroused and very angry public, led by underwater homeowners with "mortgage issues" may force the President to *reluctantly* go back on the road prior to the 2012 elections and solemnly declare that he gave the bankers the opportunity to fix the problems with the economy – they could not do it. So he must take action. [Writing from December 2011, clearly he did no such thing.]

Hope for Change. Clearly campaign rhetoric, which did not play out.

––––––––––––––––

Why The Postman? The 1987 science fiction novel, *The Postman,* was written by Eric Brin. In 1997 Kevin Costner both directed and starred in a film adaptation. The Internet Movie Data Base wrote of the film: "It is 2013. War has crippled the Earth. Technology has been erased….." Regarding the plot they wrote: "Post-apocalyptic America. What begins as a con game becomes one man's quest to rebuild civilization by resuming postal service."

The Postman came into existence as a result of travels by a loner who traveled the West merely trying to survive. He wished neither to join the violent Survivalists, or, any of the local communities of ordinary people who clung together for mutual support, while being regularly and violently dominated and exploited by Survivalists acting like time immemorial War Lords. Feudal Lords, who treated them as indentured servants – as serfs.

By accident, the Postman came into possession of the uniform and mail bags of a deceased U.S. postman. He discovered that as he went from one local community-village to another in rural Oregon (hoping for a bowl of soup), people were given a new sense of hope because he claimed to represent the *Restored United States of America,* and moreover, he was *The Postman.* He brought mail to them and would deliver mail for them. The Postman brought the news – moreover, he brought Hope and Information to those who were in a similar condition.

––––––––––––––––

Today our society bears grim comparison to this dreadful scenario. Acting out the role of Survivalists who were nothing more than Feudal Lords, *dominating* their serfs, we have Structured Finance – run amuck. The U.S. has devolved from a prosperous Industrial Capitalism with a vibrant middle-class that led a (debt based) "consumer economy" to a failed-state Finance Capitalism under the name of Globalization, or, The New World Order. (They wish.)

In similar form that economic deep debt-based scenario has occurred for the last several Centuries. Every time – including this time – it implodes. In the U.S. alone, the Crash of 1895, The Crash of 1907, The Crash of 1929, which led to the Great Depression, are significant examples. Always for the same reason – excessive debt funding to financial entities (called leverage) which leads to financial speculation (betting). History is now repeating itself.

We truly wish to avoid politics in this book. It is not about Liberals or Libertarians, or people somewhere in-between. This leads us to squarely placing the blame on Entrenched Capital, which has captured not only the American People, the Congress; but, has decimated formerly great industrial and manufacturing entities. They sent our industry, the heart – the key – to creating National Wealth – National Treasure, off-shore. Got a job? If so, keep it.

Entrenched Capital, or the Banking Cartel, literally controls the lives of ordinary Americans. As Banking Elites' *political power* increased significantly in the last ten years – regarding home ownership – they created a system dominated by Systemic Predatory Lending and violation of Securities Law. In a word: Fraud.

In 2009 in Tucson, President Obama announced his Homeowners Affordability and Stability Plan (HAMP) … another *new* plan. This was backed by Treasury Secretary, Tim-Boy Geithner and the Financial System. Too big to fail? Not necessarily – but, it did fail. Why? Another false dream, a fake-out to underwater homeowners, who were promised a life-line, only to receive threads that failed, never a serious PLAN, which would include principal reduction. Much more on that to come, and particularly in the blog UseForeclosureLaw.com.

They used the media to focus the people's anger on AIG bonuses which are a mere trifle – nothing – in relation to the real debt piled on the taxpayers. Those bonuses represent less than 1 percent of the money awarded to AIG, which they immediately passed through to seven major financial entities. Investment Bank, Goldman Sachs received the most, in excess of $12 Billion. A representative from Goldman Sachs was a member of the "group" that made the decision to award the taxpayers money to failed – insolvent – institutions. Self dealing? The hand of Goldman Sachs is never far from the surface.

It continued getting worse. Witness: the brand new Obama/Geithner Private Public Partnership Plan. That was announced March 30, 2009, in time for the G20 meetings in London. They couldn't wait two more days to announce it on April Fool's Day. Guess who is getting fooled?

This new plan rewarded the very financial institutions that created the problem. It allowed them through various shell entities, such as hedge funds (which they often control through funding and extension of liquidity), to purchase (and profit therefrom) toxic mortgages they hold in Mortgage Backed Securities. Thus removing them from the books of the malefactors and enabling their friends (actually *themselves)* to profit from this now nearly worthless paper mortgage paper. When they Dump their Debt, who pays the bill? Taxpayers. Who profits? Banks. Who is the Greater Fool? We are. So far.

Hold that thought. Below we'll show you how American families can turn this around to their benefit.

What You Can Do. In a single word, you must do your own: "cramdown," or in three words, what we call a *Forced Debt Reorganization.* Thus, what we call a *legitimate* loan modification. Meaning, a loan modification that reduces the principal amount owed on the house to current market value. We write a great deal and (in detail) about this in subsequent chapters, and more so in the blog at: UseForeclosureLaw.com.

Cramdown – Gone – Down! The Obama/Geithner loan modifications allowing for cramdown in bankruptcy failed because the Banking Cartel controlled the Senate and blocked the cramdown provision for principal reduction on April 30, 2009. Yet, and another continuing travesty, if the Senate had allowed the cramdown provision, homeowners would only qualify if they filed for bankruptcy.

> **The path to "cramdown" Principal Reduction, better called "Forced Debt Reorganization" is through legal leverage utilizing Predatory Lending and Securities Law violations and issues, only discoverable through a Forensic Loan Audit; combined with a Securitization Audit. The latter is the key.**

Forced Debt Reorganization. The bottom line is that you must do your own cramdown using legal leverage obtained through a Forensic Loan Audit and, moreover, a Securitization Audit, and then work with an attorney to Use Foreclosure Law to Keep Your Home.

Democratic Senator Dick Durbin nailed it on the floor of the Senate with an astonishing assessement of the the cramdown failure. He said,

> *"And the banks – hard to believe in a time when we're facing a banking crisis that many of the banks created – are still the most powerful lobby on Capitol Hill. And they frankly own the place." [Emphasis Added.]*

That is what we're talking about throughout this book, *"the banks – frankly own the place."* The *place:* Congress. We argue that the Young President is in a terrible dilemma. Go along with the banks that have been in charge for the last ten years, actually longer; or, as suggested above, pull an end run, truly represent the American People; and, face the Consequences. Either way: Very Serious Business.

The most alarming trend in this financial crisis hasn't simply been the shift of costs onto the taxpayer when financial entity (Investment Banks and Too Big To Fail Banksters) bondholders and stockholders should be taking the hit. It can be well argued, and is being done by many analysts, that this Administration is clearly violating both the Spirit and the Letter of the Law. Even the *Washington Post* has recently described how the Administration and Treasury are circumventing bailout legislation. One method is through funneling funds through various entities that they declare don't have to conform to legal restraints put on by Congressional requirements. That's great. They end run Congress who can loudly claim they were innocent, and hope to keep their jobs in 2012. It will be interesting.

Why Do Banks Have Such Political Power? They bought and paid for it! Over the last decade, the financial and insurance industries have pumped $5 Billion dollars through direct campaign contributions and feet on the ground lobbying to influence Congress.

That does not include the additional $7.7 Trillion that the Fed finally reported [in December 2011] it had put into the banks beyond the $800 Billion TARP program that they told us about. And, while it was a law suit by Bloomberg Financial that forced the Fed to give up this information; we've seen where New York City Mayor Michael Bloomberg's sympathies lay. Fully a 1%'er he's disparaged the Occupy Movement and authorized his cops to beat on them. So, it's not hard to see why the 99% say:

"They Got Bailed Out. We Got sold out."

The overall travesty – forced on sold out homeowner-borrowers and taxpayers alike – is designed to do one thing. That *thing* is to enable insolvent banks to retain their hegemony – continuing control – over the American People. Tragically, homeowners are losing their homes every day (2 million in 2007-2008). This is projected by Credit Suisse to grow to 2.5 million families *every year* for the next four years.

The Intent. This book, *Use Foreclosure Law! Keep Your Home,* is designed to bring you *Real Hope For Real Change.* However, you must do it yourself. Help will not come from our Government. Later we'll show you step by step how to Use Foreclosure Law to Keep Your Home and protect your family.

Ours is not a *Hope Now* plan, or any other hopie-changie "plans" brought forward by the Treasury Department to *"keep people in their homes."* Their plans are actually designed to save their precious and insolvent Investment Banks and other major banks – at the expense of all taxpayers. Their intent and "best practice" is to *keep people in their homes as indentured servants* to the Banking Cartel. A bit strong? We'll present evidence below to prove it to you beyond a reasonable doubt.

Remember our Mission is to <u>remove the fear of the unknown from defrauded underwater homeowners through education.</u> If you do the work – you'll gain the reward.

The Postman in the original book by Eric Brin, claimed to represent the Restored United States of America. This author offers a vision and practical framework to enable and obtain the Restored American Dream Of Affordable Homeownership, while rebalancing the economy and putting America back to work. (World Peace will be desert.)

Jobs must come home, we must rebuild our infrastructure through our manufacturing base, or, we defile the actual intentions of our Founding Fathers, many of whom left their birth nations – to escape the very tyranny that has been brought back to life in 2012. They founded a democratic Republic, which is a form of government embodying democratic principles and where a monarch is not the head of state. Clearly, that has failed. As Benjamin Franklin said: "We've given you a Republic, if you can keep it." What we've lost are "democratic principles." Elections are bought and paid for. Voting counts are electronically tampered with. And, while the Young President is not a "monarch," his claim to detain Americans without filing a formal charge or indictment, no right to an attorney, or right to due process, smacks of the actions of a Despot, an Oligarch, a Dictator. And Congress backs his play. We ask now discredited Senator John McCain (who introduced this part of the Bill), have you become a traitor to the very nation you nearly gave your life for, as you trample the Constitution?

While many millions see – and many more will soon see – their mortgage payments increasing, all American homeowners see the value of their homes decreasing. The value of millions of homes is becoming less (in some areas much less) than what is owed. This puts you underwater and in an involuntary servitude. Paying on debt that is higher than the value of the asset.

Mortgages and Deeds of Trust provide that if you do not make payments, the lender can take the home back through foreclosure. In this book we will show you and your family that to *Use Foreclosure Law* and take power from your lender is a rational and legal and ethical response to the conditions that have been imposed by the Financial System for their benefit – to the detriment of homeowners – the Middle Class – all Americans.

Debt Primer. Too much debt, excess debt combined with fear, the condition that has frozen the banks since August, 2007 (called the Credit Crunch – which is really a *Debt Crunch)* sets in motion severe negative consequences:

1. The act of debt liquidation [foreclosure] forces individuals [and lenders] into distressed selling of assets.

2. As a result of debt liquidation the money stock starts shrinking and this in turn slows down the velocity of money. Ultimately the turn of events is slowed – if not frozen.

3. A fall in money values leads to a decline in the price level [of real estate].

4. The value of people's assets [homes] falls while the value of their liabilities [home loan] remains intact, which precipitates bankruptcies [and/or foreclosure].

We thank noted economist Frank Shostak, adjunct scholar of the Mises Institute and who is also Chief Economist of M.F. Global for the points above, which we [added to in brackets] for specificity.

Clearly we have too much debt in our economy. The banks feel the pinch as more and more people than ever before in history are defaulting on home loans.

Often as a result of Predatory Lending, enhanced by the fraudulent home loan Securitization Process. Witness: creation of Mortgage Backed Securities (MBS).

Consequently, as the inevitable four steps above are unfolding, we ask: why would anyone not Use Foreclosure Law to obtain a reduction in principal amount owed, in order to remain in their home when its value is rapidly decreasing? Under current government offered "Plans" and "Loan Modifications," the amount owed remains the same (increases for many), even though the value of the home is decreasing.

Deep researcher Sharon-Brigitte Kayser-Scherman who publishes incisive and deeply ironic editorials on AmericanChronicle.com, writes on the overall economic situation. She recently wrote."David Ignatius of the Washington Post wrote a piece that tells us why the system is screeching to a halt. Here is an excerpt:

> "Frightened financiers are pulling back from credit markets – going on strike, if you will – to escape the unraveling daisy chain of securitized assets and promissory notes that binds the global financial system. As each financier tries to protect against the next one's mistakes, the whole system begins to sag. That's what we're seeing now, as credit market troubles spread from bundles of subprime residential mortgages to bundles of other kinds of debt – from student loans to retailers' receivables to municipal bonds."

Ms. Kayser-Scherman went on to say:

> "Most people dislike economics because of its convoluted jargon. If they only knew that it was a trick to deter them from learning. So, why hide terms such as collateralized debt obligations (CDOs) or structured investment vehicle (SIV)? If you do not have a clue and are about to start scratching your head, here is what Richard Sylla, professor of economics and financial history at NYU's Stern School of Business says in a report titled 'The Black Box Economy,' by Stephen Mihm last January."

> "'A lot of financial innovation is designed to get around regulation. The goal is to make more money, and you can make more money if you <u>don't have to keep capital</u> to back up your investments.'" [Emphasis added.]

Homeowner's Economics 101. Inside this book you can learn enough about economics so that you will understand how the cards have been stacked against you and your family. Written in plain English, not economic jargon, you will learn about various options available to you to correct the situation to your benefit, rather than to the benefit of financial entities that have fraudulently deceived you through a general pattern of Predatory Lending and Securitization Fraud.

The Key. In order to enable you to understand how this book can make a difference in your life – how you can protect your family – we offer a guide and some specific suggestions in the latter chapters.

The following Chapters have been assembled in a particular order to bring you information that is not taught in schools nor available in the media. What we offer you is a basic and specific focused course in *Homeowner's Economics*

101 in order for you to understand how and why the U.S. Economy is in desperate straits as a result of *deliberate action* by financial powers. To undo their power *you* must take *deliberate action*. We will explain how to do that.

The California Legislature passed a Financial Literacy Bill. Consider this book your any-state home study *Homeowner's Economics 101* course in Financial Literacy. Particularly as it may affect future decisions that you must make as your mortgage payments reset higher, or your mortgage loan increasingly puts you underwater.

To the Point. This book was explicitly written as a guide for millions of homeowners who have discovered that they cannot afford their house payments after the payment resets upward, or, for any reason, household income has been reduced. Millions more homeowners have discovered that their property is not worth the amount that they owe – they are underwater. We will give you the data, the information and explain why the situation is only going to become worse. We strongly believe that you must have and understand this information in order to make an informed decision to take action which will protect your family. Contrary to some Realtor's opinions, we are nowhere near the bottom of the housing market. This is documented throughout the book and particularly in the Appendices.

Don't look for a housing bottom until we reach 2015. Serious. Even then it will remain on the bottom for an indeterminate number of years. In Japan they are yet to fully recover from their market top in 1990. Twenty-two years!!!

Using Foreclosure Law to Keep Your Home is a major decision. You must clearly understand *why* it is legally and ethically appropriate – *why* it is a rational act that in itself will begin to balance the economy – if enough people *Use Foreclosure Law*. When you understand – you are no longer a victim. Rarely in history do normal people – above-average citizens – have the opportunity to actually change the world – the way things are done. That opportunity is available today.

This book was written to give you information you need to understand in order to make an *informed* decision. To enable you to understand that you have every right (if not an obligation to family), to legally *Confront Fraudulent Housing Debt* that was placed in a majority of cases based on Systemic Fraudulent Predatory Lending practices by major players in the U.S. Financial Industry.

Below is a brief synopsis of the contents of following chapters. We believe that if you have an initial overview, an early sense of direction for the book you will be better prepared to understand some relatively complex issues. Always when we can – we avoid technical financial industry and economic jargon. When we can't – we define those terms in clear language as we first introduce them to you.

Chapter 1. Opening Statement. Here we give you an overview of what has transpired in the housing market over the last ten years. Included are various terms and definitions you need to understand that pertain to the housing fiasco.

Chapter 2. Smoking Guns. This chapter identifies various acts by some national lending institutions that are clear violations of the law, and point to certain prosecutions that are under way, which will be to the advantage of all homeowners. It also documents the actual lending process beginning on the ground with Mortgage Brokers and traces the loans through the financial system where they were aggregated into Securities and sold to Institutional Investors as Mortgage Backed Securities (MBS).

They were. Now the Securitization Market – aka the commercial Secondary Market – is dead. Today, in excess of 80% of all home loans are backed by FHA and/or the GSE's – Fannie Mae and Freddie Mac (who are still acquiring "conforming" loans from private originators). This is the only remaining market, for MBS's. The existing "toxic assets" we've read about, and which the financial elites, backed by our Young President, are in the process of being dumped on all taxpayers, to keep the major banks from collapsing. Dumping them into Fannie/Freddie, and some are used as "dead" collateral for further bailout money from the Fed.

Chapter 3. The Political Economy. We introduce the fact that all economies are political in nature, and the corresponding fact that all politics are grounded in the economic system or process in place. We offer a first look at the Federal Reserve System, it's interactions with various Administrations; and explain why the world wide banking system is now at risk, teetering on disaster, in large part due to two "G's" – Globalization and Greenspan.

Chapter 4. Greenspan's Boom – Bernanke's Bust. As the title indicates, we briefly look at the how and why of booms and busts. Frankly we indict those who have fraudulently brought us a busted housing bubble. We explain the nuance regarding inflation and deflation with a passing view to manipulated government statistics that are released to an unsuspecting public. We show that even the accounting system utilized by the Fed is designed to keep the American People from actually understanding what really goes on in the world of manipulated high finance. That is only one of *their* dirty secrets.

Chapter 5. A Brief Analysis of Business Cycles. In this overview chapter we provide you with information that is vital for you to understand regarding Mania-Cycles, where entire societies come to believe in a false premise that this or that asset will continue up in value. We also document how over time the Fed has given a free pass to lending institutions and Investment Banks, which enables taxpayer bailouts for these entities after they throw caution to the winds. When they ignore and subvert responsible risk assessment – by making inappropriate loans to those who have no chance of paying them back. They knew it, yet they proceeded – certain – that the Fed and Treasury would bail them out at the expense of all taxpayers. Arguably *they are* the Fed and Treasury. We too have been captured.

Chapter 6. Their Legal Issues. We look at a flood of early litigation against so-called reputable financial institutions brought by the FBI, SEC, various State Attorney Generals; and also civil suits brought by all the parties in this fiasco who all seem to be suing each other. Really. Further, we show how appraisers were pressured to deliver home price valuations that were often higher than they should have been in order to "make the deal work." This guaranteed higher fees for Mortgage Brokers and so-called "lenders" up through the chain. Note: the place to discover the current and future action breaking on the litigation front is on our blog. UseForeclosureLaw.com

---

The next several chapters are what you've been waiting for. They're about you and what you can do to solve your own problems. But, first we had to give you enough information for you understand that Using Foreclosure Law is perhaps the most rational, ethical, legal and maybe the best business decision you may make in your life. Read the chapters in order, you'll be better off.

Chapter 7. Fraud. This short chapter is an extensive definition of fraud courtesy of The "Lectric Law Library." This chapter bears reading twice – it's legalese – there will be no quiz. Yet, you must begin to understand what likely was done to you through the loan origination process. This information will enable you to begin to understand what you can do about it, and, give you a glimmer of understanding that you might be able to receive a monetary "award" for damages you have already suffered.

Chapter 8. Predatory Lending. Here we present many specific illegal and fraudulent practices that may have been perpetrated on you – victimized you. These are within the category of Predatory Lending. We give you enough information so that you can gather your own loan origination documents and seek out a Forensic Loan Audit and a Securitization Audit. This may lead you to bring an action or stop foreclosure by working through an attorney. Repeat, working with an attorney.

We are not attorneys and do not anywhere in this book
offer legal, investment or tax advice.

However, when you have read this book and our blog, and let us know you have done so, see our blog: www.UseForeclosureLaw.com, where we will provide you access to "tools," which will enable you to move forward with the confidence of an educated person. Fear of the unknown removed.

Chapter 9. Your Legal Issues. We show the general process of foreclosure. We give you information and links to enable you determine the basics of foreclosure law in your state. Based on the two preceding chapters, you may have enough information to make a preliminary determination as to whether or not you have been the victim of Predatory Lending and Securitization Fraud. We close with some possible scenarios, which enable you (working with your own legal counsel) to control the process in your situation.

Chapter 10. Choose – Action. Here we attempt to show you that you are not alone, and that in Using Foreclosure Law, first and foremost you are making a business decision. Hopefully the information in the preceding chapters have convinced you that there is nothing at all emotional in making a business decision. We include articles and opinion to buttress the fact that you need to take action to protect *your* family – not wealthy Wall Street – Bankster Elites.

Chapter 11. Closing Statement. In summation we remind you of historical elements – of events that have occurred in economies over centuries when the greedy have exploited those who did not possess the information or power of the Financial Elites. We look at the effect of Using Foreclosure Law on your future credit, and how you might workout or seek Forced Debt Reorganization (resulting in a significant principal – amount owed – reduction) with legal leverage on your side.

Chapter 12. Use Foreclosure Law! Here we evoke the book's title and bring forward the specifics involving Predatory Lending and Securities Law violations that you, working with an attorney, can use to legally leverage your desired outcome – if the violations of law are significant. We explain in detail what a Forensic Loan Audit and a Securitization Audit is, and why you must obtain them as the mandatory first step to take before obtaining legal counsel to press your claim against the lender.

Appendices. In the Appendix Sections we present some basic information; and, moreover, "testimony" by nationally recognized "expert witnesses," in their own words that we believe buttress the argument to Use Foreclosure Law to Keep Your Home.

Appendix A: Sample Notice Of Default ("NOD")
Appendix B: Sample Notice Of Trustee's Sale
Appendix C: Sample Quit Claim Deed
Appendix D: Questions To Ask An Attorney
Appendix E: Ellen Brown: Esq. – Wall Street Likes Your Amnesia
Appendix F: James Kunstler – 2012 Forecast
Appendix G: Nye Lavalle – Fraudulent … Assignments
Appendix H: Michael M. Thomas – The Big Lie
Appendix I: Chaz Valenaza – Middle Class Is Dead
Appendix J: Nassim Taleb – The Black Swan
Appendix K: State By State Foreclosure Laws

Ken *"Postman"* Kappel

FORWARD

With the exception of:

- long time home owners who have paid off their mortgage and hold fee simple title in their name;
- people who buy their homes "all cash" and possess fee simple title; and,
- those that have inherited fee simple title homes without mortgage debt;

the rest of us are *really renters*.

Lenders *really own* the houses. They merely rent the house to us, and allow us to record the Title and Deed under our names. This gives us the *illusion* that we own a house, which we turn into a home for our families.

True, this arrangement gives us a right to enjoy the appreciation in value. Of course you remember *"house prices always go up,"* and, *"its a great time to buy."* The point is that we pay interest for the right to enjoy appreciation of our homes. Yet, as millions of families are discovering today, the hoped for (in some cases "promised" by some unscrupulous Mortgage Brokers), and, by other professionals such as real estate agents, appreciation has reversed and houses are "losing" significant value across the nation.

Worse, when the market inevitably turns, as it has, appreciation turns into depreciation, and home values go down. This puts homeowners in a terrible bind. Particularly so for those with Adjustable Rate Mortgages (ARMs), and now increasingly for those who are "underwater," owing more on the mortgage than the house is worth.

Some say that the "American Dream" is the *independence of home ownership*. Fine, but, that is *not* a right – or a guarantee – to windfall unearned gains in house values! In the long run, on average, home value gains are modest at best. Historically they've gone up near the rate of *inflation* increases. This has historically been 1%. Yet, you need to understand that the Government measure rate of inflation, CPI, is restrained, rather gamed.

Economic Lesson: *Inflation* is the increase in the money supply. When they increase the money supply that is "inflation. When that occurs, soon thereafter, we receive *"price inflation,"* which we see at the gas pump and when shopping.

In the last ten years home values decoupled from inflation and doubled, tripled in value in some areas. Is that value here today? No. Long gone.

The actual value of a house is what a ready, willing and able buyer will pay for a given house *today*. With lending frozen and markets flooded with foreclosed properties – buyers are not willing – or able – to pay anywhere near the amount that is actually owed on the house. Leaving the average homeowner under stress with <u>no way to sell</u> (without taking a loss and literally bringing money to the closing table in an underwater situation) and move on. Consequently, we feel it appropriate to say that these distressed families are indentured to – trapped by – the financial system.

They are debt serfs, basically only leasing their homes, and, are paying a much higher monthly payment than if they rented a similar house in the same neighborhood. Is this you? In addition they/you are solely responsible for often significantly expensive home maintenance.

Decreasing Values. Relying on statistical models and real numbers, many experts (presented throughout this book) have concluded that values will continue to decrease for several years into the future. Some experts provide evidence to support their conclusions that based on the current situation, values will decrease until at least 2015. Some say longer.

A research paper out of USC's School of Policy Planning by Professor of Urban Planning, Dowell Myers and doctorial candidate Sungho Rru points to the fact that Boomers are retiring and downsizing their living requirements in 2012, thus placing even more housing inventory on the market for sale. Lew Sichelman, celebrated syndicated columnist on real estate was quoted in the *San Francisco Chronicle* reporting on their findings, and said,

> "The USC researchers don't expect the generational correction to begin until 2011 or so. That's just about the time the most pessimistic prognosticators suggest the American housing market will finally return to normal after spending five years or so on the rocks. [Emphasis Added.]

> "But it's also when the first wave of Boomers reaches age 65, the traditional dividing point between seniors and working adults. And once that tipping point is reached, Myers and Ryu say they will put more houses up for sale than the market will be able to absorb. 'After 2010, the leading edge of the Boomers will pass age 65 and growth among the elderly population will substantially exceed that of younger adults, an unprecedented social and economic development,' they argue."

What a joke, "... finally return to normal...." Push that out for five more years. While you may grit your tee and want to believe we're near the bottom – we're not. Read on.

Getting Worse. Herb Greenberg writing in Seeking Alpha.com, wrote an article titled: "Mortgage Resets: Subprime May Be Ending, Option ARMS Have Just Begun." He wrote,

> "Paul Jaber, a portfolio manager at the Perpetual Value Fund: 'The option ARM loan was very popular through Q1'07 – so take 40 months from that date, plus 3 months for them to go 90 days late and then and only then will you see foreclosures start to level off... The reason why Countrywide Financial, Washington Mutual, Wachovia Bank, Downey Financial and First Fed Financial are all imploding is because the 2003-2004 pay option ARM loans are all recasting and then going 90 days late... Pay option ARM loans have a teaser payment that will last until the loan goes 110%-125% of original value and then the loan RECASTS to a fully amortizing loan. That is how a payment skyrockets.'"

What to Do. The right cause of action for your family rests on a matter of factual evidence – not opinion – nor hopes and dreams. Acting rationally – when irrational behavior surrounds you – is not only a courageous act, it is an affirmative action – even – as we'll show in the book, an act of leadership. The overriding imperative is to protect your family.

Whether Democrats, Conservatives, Independents, Liberals, Liberaltarians, Libertarians or Republicans (so many labels), politicians can't save you. Arguably they've been forced, due to the cost of election campaigns, to cede power to those who give them money to purchase their political fiefdoms. Politicians from both sides of the aisle appear (to us) to have sold their integrity – their principles – and denied any character they may have learned as children. (We're not blaming their parents.) Today in 2012 – Congress has a 20% approval rating. So that point is clear. We refuse any pronunciation for the oncoming 2012 election.

Today's politicians are forced into a Faustian Bargain in order to gain access to campaign funds. *They go along to get along.* When pigs fly we'll see meaningful campaign finance reform. Spoils go to victors, and victors utilize spoils to their personal advantage – first. Human Nature? Or the result of a particular historical cycle that we are in? But, this is not that book. See economist, Dr. Ravi Batra's excellent book, *The New Golden Age: The Coming Revolution Against Political Corruption and Economic Chaos.*

As we'll show below, financial system Banksters bolstered by *unprecedented liquidity* (debt "money" made available to them to lend and/or invest), colluded to keep you in indentured servitude – indentured to a system that is front-loaded against homeowners. Current wide-spread litigation argues that Investment Bankers, bond Rating Agencies, local lenders, Mortgage Banks, Mortgage Brokers, and Appraisers in many cases worked together to fraudulently inflate the value of houses beyond their real value in order to claim fees and grow profits. This is not surprising.

Lack of Regulation. The lack of regulation was initially surprising to us when we began our education process in 2005. We discovered over time that the game is entirely fixed. We've become deeply cynical and now perceive that a continuing *coup d'état* occurred. Some argue that began with Jack Kennedy's assignation in 1963. While that may – or may not be so – the money game changed radically in the mid-nineties. It was radically transformed when Robert Rubin, former chairman of Goldman Sachs became Treasury Secretary, and the game was on.

Below we'll show how and why regulation was either removed from our system through Legislative initiatives over the last 25 years, and, particularly, since the mid-nineties. Clearly regulations in place were simply not enforced by those entrusted to ensure that our Financial System operated legally and ethically – on the up and up. Well it actually did. Up and up in profits for them, and up and up in untenable, unpayable debt for the rest of us.

Some argue that lenders did not and do not set prices. That the market – the actual buyer – sets the price, the value. In a normal market, a historical market, this is true. However, due to excess liquidity and the fact that many home buyers made no down payment, did not disclose source of income, etc., clearly shows that the financial markets were no longer concerned over the risk involved in dubious non-standard loans. They had access to cheap money (debt), and told the chain below them, *"Make the loan, get the deal done. We're all making fees. The (naive) Institutional Investors are given the increased risk on exotic loans."*

Those arguably damaged the most are from both top and bottom tiers. At the top tier are Institutional Investors who invested in Mortgage Backed Securities (bonds, made up of aggregated home loans), securitized on the face value of Promissory Notes given by home buyers to home lenders. Institutional Investors, such as: pension funds, insurance companies, banks, hedge funds, foreign central banks, and others, discovered that their investments in Mortgage Backed Securities (MBS) have lost huge amounts of money (some becoming worthless), as more and more mortgages default into foreclosure.

These are the "toxic" assets you read about in the paper. Behind them are the real threat, derivatives (basically insurance bets) you read about, that few actually understand, which are the real threat to the financial industry – to the Global Economy right here, right now as we write on December 21, 2012. Yet, all that the various Central Banks can do is to print more money, create more unpayable debt, as they kick the can down the road, because there can be no political solution.

Politicians don't have the nerve, because they would immediately lose office if they legislated appropriate correctives, which would take time to work the magic – return to economic equilibrium. Leading us to conclude that when you think of the Great Depression in the Thirties, imagine that what faces all of us will be worse. We'll explain all of this in straight-forward language below.

At the bottom tier are new and refinanced ARM mortgage holders who discover they cannot pay higher reset payments. At the same time, because house values are going down, they can not refinance out of harm's way, as many were clearly told they would be able to do by Mortgage Brokers and real estate agents, before the ARMs would reset and the payment increased. An ever larger group estimated in the multi-millions are those borrowers who have discovered that their home is worth less than the amount of money they owe on it. We estimate this represents 33% of all mortgage holders. Below is part of an article from our blog that is titled:

"33% Underwater — Radical But We're Sorta Sticking To It — Another Point of View."

"Well well well. Numbers are light in the chart below, compared to recent Zillow reporting of 28.9, underwater. What we really like in this very graphic report is that they show numbers for folks who are NEARLY underwater. And, we'll bet, there numbers are light there as well. Meaning more **Nearly Underwater** than they report.

"Overall, this is important. What is great is that you can drill down to your state for the real story. Our point is that when you see nearly across the board reporting of another 4% of homeowners being **Nearly Underwater**, and, then you factor in an additional cost of 7% for sales transaction fees if they sold soon, well, that pumps up the number of "functionally underwater" homes, we think, to over 33%. Looked at another way. Nearly 33% of 52 million homes with mortgages, or, **17.4 million families** are likely underwater. That's our call, and we're sticking to it."

Should You *Use Foreclosure Law*? The message or mission of this book, combined with our blog, is to remove the fear of the unknown from underwater homeowners through education. Enabling you to Confront Fraudulent Housing Debt and protect your family. Don't be a serf nor an indentured slave. Take control of your life. Don't let others, some of whom may have fraudulently deceived you, control your life.

Price Discovery. Below we present The case for Using Foreclosure Law to Keep Your Home as a non-emotional business decision. However, before we do that we want to introduce a critical concept – in two words – Price Discovery.

In its simplest definition, Price Discovery is a method of determining the price for a specific commodity or security or product through basic supply and demand factors related to the market. In addition, Price Discovery is the general process used in determining prices. Prices are dependent upon market conditions, which affect demand. For example, if the demand for a house is higher than the supply, the price will typically increase, and vice versa. Yet, if the money available to purchase houses is greatly increased and loan standards are loosened – risk is ignored, rather passed on to a Greater Fool (Institutional Investors) – the result will always be a Housing Bubble.

Price Discovery for the Federal Reserve and the U.S. Treasury is discovering various "Plans" to *"keep people in their homes"* (to bailout Investment Banks) have failed. [They have.]

Price Discovery for Investment Banks is discovering that Mortgage Backed Securities are marketable at 30 cents or less on the dollar; and Institutional Investors are suing you to buy them back at face value. [They are.]

Price Discovery for local, regional and national home lending institutions is discovering that 30-50% of your privately held "portfolio" properties have been vacated (foreclosed by you, or more and more often, foreclosed after being "strategically defaulted" on by the borrower); and you further discover that you can only sell them at 50-70% of the note value because there are so many similarly distressed properties on the market that prices have dropped dramatically. [They have. Dropped dramatically.]

Price Discovery for Realtors and other housing and mortgage professionals is discovering that the real estate market has returned to a normal and balanced market. You can once again do business assisting sellers to sell and buyers to buy homes that now have *affordable* prices based on historical Loan to Value and Income to Debt ratios. [Not yet. Not for a long time.]

Price Discovery *for residential investors* who've been priced out of the market is discovering that lenders have given up and are selling Real Estate Owned (REO) properties at absolute auctions (no minimum bid). Once again you can purchase properties at auction for "buy and hold," meaning that rentals will enable the deals to cash flow. [We are not even close to being there yet.

Price Discovery *for homeowners living in underwater homes* is waking up every morning for the next 3-4 years (if lucky) to discover that your home continues to decrease in value, yet your house payment increases, or remains the same.

Price Discovery *for homeowners who "strategically defaulted" (walked away) from underwater homes* is discovering that a home very similar to the one you bought from 2005-07 at $400,000 (and walked away from at $320,000), can be purchased *by you* with the down payment you saved (over the last few years) for $275,000 – and you do it.

Price Discovery brings you *back* to an affordable home – the *Restored American Dream.*

Price Discovery then may ultimately be evidenced by house values returning to their pre-bubble prices from as far back as 1992. Not so shocking when you consider we are likely entering a Second – or – Greater Depression. Thus, *reversion to the mean,* which occurs in nearly every bubble throughout history. Thus, ultimately, homes become affordable once again.

This will happen. Every bubble in history crashes as has this one. We've only begun to see the down-side. If you are underwater, how deep is the water? How *long* does it take to get to the bottom before you go back up and resurface. We believe and will attempt to prove in this book that the more people who Use Foreclosure Law – and the *sooner they do it* – the sooner the bottom will be achieved in housing, A bottom that induces potential buyers to come back into the market. The longer it takes – the deeper the bottom. What is the point of staying underwater – of drowning – with unrelenting financial and emotional stress on your family?

In *Use Foreclosure Law,* we will explain this. But, please, remember what Price Discovery *really is* and how it applies to you. Think of Price Discovery as the underlying or sub-theme for this book, and how, ultimately Price Discovery is your friend – but only *if* you've taken action and used legal leverage to protect your family by Using Foreclosure Law to Keep Your Home, or, using it to withdraw from the market while it is resetting.

In general, most people do not see the world *as it is* because there is too much information and never enough time. Consequently, we see the world *as we wish it to be.* Therefore to be an effective agent on behalf of your family, you need to possess information not readily available in the media. Information that gives a wider and historical view of the landscape. In this book, we present information that documents how and why most homeowners have been placed in an untenable position – frankly – been placed at risk.

We offer the opportunity to make an informed decision by suggesting a roadmap, based on what has previously occurred, and how information might enable action. Please remember, maps and roads only clarify and expedite journeys – they do not guarantee arrival at your intended destination. The safe harbor, the destination is achieved by taking action through an unemotional business decision to protect your family and your long term financial position.

Another Opinion. Writing in *Barron's*, excellent columnist, 2008, Randall Forsyth said,

"An estimated 8.8 million American households owe more on their mortgages than their home is worth. To be sure, that's also because of the miniscule down payment required on houses in recent years, which left an insignificant margin of safety. And with little skin in the game, these homebuyers who took a page from the playbook of private-equity or hedge-fund speculators have little to lose when they vacate their houses in foreclosure. Many are cynically walking away from obligations they are well able to meet. …

"For other homebuyers – who innocently believed in the free-lunch loans with no collateral or income verification and that were based on the bet that house prices only went up – the prospect of being thrown out of their homes is traumatic. … [Emphasis Added.]

"Only when the median-income household can afford the median-price home will the crisis end. With lenders tightening loan terms and incomes not rising rapidly, the affordability gap will likely have to be closed by house prices falling further." [Emphasis added.]

He wrote that in 2008. This gives us some indication of the reality – that until we return to *historical actual gross housing debt to actual gross income ratios* – houses simply won't be affordable. Incomes are decreasing against true "price inflation," leaving less cash to make mortgage payments.

Here We Are. We found it interesting that widely read and respected blogger Mike "Mish" Shedlock, writing from his blog, Global Economic Trend Analysis, made the following comments:

"Many stuck in ARMs will not be able to refinance. Those in ARMs *seem* poised to benefit anyway. However for the "truly stuck" it is all a mirage. Mortgage lending standards, fees, down payments, etc, are much different than a year ago. On a comparable basis, mortgage rates are way higher for most than they were a year ago.

"Treasury yields will have to drop much further for those in ARMs with rates tied to treasuries to benefit much. More than likely it will be too little, too late for most struggling homeowners. Rising unemployment will exacerbate this problem. <u>Heaven help us</u> if it becomes *socially acceptable* for those severely under water on their mortgage, yet still able to make payments, to simply hand over the keys and say goodbye. With that in mind, I am wondering: <u>How long will it take for a book to come out, advocating just that strategy</u>?" [Emphasis added.]

It took several months for us to do that. And, since then – nearly a year from the start – to re-write the original book based on new significant information we learned in the last four months. That information is based on using legal leverage, and you will rarely find it in the press.

We first heard that it was becoming *socially acceptable* for people to *walk away* from noted real estate economic statistician and author of *Timing The Real Estate Market,* Robert Campbell. He was giving a presentation to residential investors. The following morning the light bulb went on, and we saw the title: *Choose Foreclosure: The Case For Walking Away* in our mind's eye. That is what we understood at that time. Having researched this very issue for several years, that gave us a theme and a message to bring forward.

Soon after we discovered that Mish had been writing about it for more than a month, and we had missed his initial articles.

Our overall interpretation at that time was that walking away – as many had begun to do – might generate a financial Tsunami that would not only sweep away Wall Street as we've known it – as it has become in the last decade – but, that also, millions of lives would be severely disrupted as a direct result. This has happened.

As you'll read in a latter chapter, even those who have already been foreclosed-on, who have waked away in defeat, have another chance. We'll detail it later, but the bottom line is that *illegal loans* are and *were – illegal loans.* Current fraud law enables individuals to bring a fraud-based law suit for monetary damages for at least one year after the fraud is discovered by the defrauded party.

In the past year we have learned much more about this entire fiasco. Enough to realize that people don't have to walk away if they don't wish to. That's why we've updated and added significantly to the book – this book. We gave it a more meaningful and specific title:

Use Foreclosure Law!
Keep Your Home
Or, Walk Away Under <u>Your</u> Terms.

Because we made comments above regarding President Obama being *captured* by the financial elites – by Wall Street, we though it appropriate to give Mish the update comment on this subject from April 15, 2009.

"Week in and week out, the best two reads on Bloomberg are Caroline Baum and Jonathan Weil. Please consider Weil's article: **Obama Stakes His Fortunes on Failed Banksters**.

"Now that we have a rough idea how President Barack Obama and his lieutenants plan to prop up insolvent financial institutions using taxpayers' money, we're left with a more difficult question: Why?

"Why doesn't the Obama administration force insolvent banks and insurance companies to come clean about their losses first? It's the "why" that's so vexing. The who, what, when, and how are mere details, by comparison.

"More than anyone else's, it should be in Obama's political self-interest to accelerate the worst of the financial crisis and get as much of the inevitable pain behind us as quickly as possible. Every day he waits is one less day he will have between the time we hit rock bottom and the next election. And yet, Obama and his minions are doing all they can to delay the reckoning, which only will make it worse.

"When publicly owned companies change management, often the smartest thing a new chief executive officer can do is clear the decks and take a "big bath" charge to earnings. In other words, the company writes off all its worthless assets and reports huge losses, pushing every conceivable drop of red ink into the past. The new CEO gets to blame his predecessor's dumb mistakes. The company gets a fresh start with the investing public.

"Obama could have taken the same approach with the banks the moment he took office, while he still had standing to blame the financial crisis on George W. Bush's administration, stupid regulators, and corrupt lawmakers -- that is, everyone but himself.

"Obama didn't do that. And now, six months into the government's Troubled Asset Relief Program, his administration's approach to the financial crisis is largely indistinguishable from its predecessor's. The only objective, it seems, is to buy time, in hopes that an economic recovery somehow will materialize and lift the financial system back to health. ....

"Whatever the case, as long as the government refuses to remove the cancer of zombie banks from our financial system, there's little hope the U.S. will return to robust economic growth anytime soon. And the longer our wounded banks are allowed to stagger along with no end-game in sight, the greater the risk for Obama that voters will conclude he's as responsible for blowing the cleanup as others were for causing the crisis."

"He'd better act soon. Time may not be our side any longer.

"It's tough arguing with Weil, so I make it a point not to. Indeed I am with him on the zombification of banks, having written about zombie banks for what seems like forever. A good example is **Night of the Living Fed** from March of 2008 although that was by no means my first post about **Zombification**.

"The key question is "why?" There are many conspiracy theories circulating on this, the most prevalent of which is these actions are all part of a planned grand scheme for (take your choice) the Fed, Goldman Sachs, or the **Bilderberg Group** to rule the world. I dismiss such theories and instead offer misguided belief in Keynesian claptrap. Bernanke and Krugman are also believers in Keynesian claptrap. Krugman even won a Nobel prize."

OK, Mish. Thank you very much. Two and ½ years later and it's getting worse.

U.S. DECLARATION OF INDEPENDENCE

In Congress, July 4, 1776.

A Declaration

By the REPRESENTATIVES of the
UNITED STATES OF AMERICA,
In GENERAL CONGRESS assembled.

When in the Course of human events, it becomes necessary for one people to dissolve the political bands which have connected them with another, and to assume among the powers of the earth, the separate and equal station to which the – Laws of Nature and of Nature's God entitle them, a decent respect to the opinions of mankind requires that they should declare the causes which impel them to the separation.

We hold these truths to be self-evident, that all men are created equal, that they are endowed by their Creator with certain unalienable Rights, that among these are Life, Liberty and the pursuit of Happiness. – That to secure these rights, Governments are instituted among Men, deriving their just powers from the consent of the governed, – That whenever any Form of Government becomes destructive of these ends, it is the Right of the People to alter or to abolish it, and to institute new Government, laying its foundation on such principles and organizing its powers in such form, as to them shall seem most likely to effect their Safety and Happiness.

Prudence, indeed, will dictate that Governments long established should not be changed for light and transient causes; and accordingly all experience hath shewn, that mankind are more disposed to suffer, while evils are sufferable, than to right themselves by abolishing the forms to which they are accustomed. But when a long train of abuses and usurpations, pursuing invariably the same Object evinces a design to reduce them under absolute Despotism, it is their right, it is their duty, to throw off such Government, and to provide new Guards for their future security. – Such has been the patient sufferance of these Colonies; and such is now the necessity which constrains them to alter their former Systems of Government. The history of the present King of Great Britain is a history of repeated injuries and usurpations, all having in direct object the establishment of an absolute Tyranny over these States. To prove this, let Facts be submitted to a candid world.

He has refused his Assent to Laws, the most wholesome and necessary for the public good.

He has forbidden his Governors to pass Laws of immediate and pressing importance, unless suspended in their operation till his Assent should be obtained; and when so suspended, he has utterly neglected to attend to them.

He has refused to pass other Laws for the accommodation of large districts of people, unless those people would relinquish the right of Representation in the Legislature, a right inestimable to them and formidable to tyrants only.

He has called together legislative bodies at places unusual, uncomfortable, and distant from the depository of their public Records, for the sole purpose of fatiguing them into compliance with his measures.

He has dissolved Representative Houses repeatedly, for opposing with manly firmness his invasions on the rights of the people.

He has refused for a long time, after such dissolutions, to cause others to be elected; whereby the Legislative powers, incapable of Annihilation, have returned to the People at large for their exercise; the State remaining in the mean time exposed to all the dangers of invasion from without, and convulsions within.

He has endeavoured to prevent the population of these States; for that purpose obstructing the Laws for Naturalization of Foreigners; refusing to pass others to encourage their migrations hither, and raising the conditions of new Appropriations of Lands.

He has obstructed the Administration of Justice, by refusing his Assent to Laws for establishing Judiciary powers.

He has made Judges dependent on his Will alone, for the tenure of their offices, and the amount and payment of their salaries.

He has erected a multitude of New Offices, and sent hither swarms of Officers to harrass our people, and eat out their substance.

He has kept among us, in times of peace, Standing Armies without the Consent of our legislatures.

He has affected to render the Military independent of and superior to the Civil power.

He has combined with others to subject us to a jurisdiction foreign to our constitution, and unacknowledged by our laws; giving his Assent to their Acts of pretended Legislation:

For Quartering large bodies of armed troops among us:

For protecting them, by a mock Trial, from punishment for any Murders which they should commit on the Inhabitants of these States:

For cutting off our Trade with all parts of the world:

For imposing Taxes on us without our Consent:

For depriving us in many cases, of the benefits of Trial by Jury:

For transporting us beyond Seas to be tried for pretended offences

For abolishing the free System of English Laws in a neighbouring Province, establishing therein an Arbitrary government, and enlarging its Boundaries so as to render it at once an example and fit instrument for introducing the same absolute rule into these Colonies:

For taking away our Charters, abolishing our most valuable Laws, and altering fundamentally the Forms of our Governments:

For suspending our own Legislatures, and declaring themselves invested with power to legislate for us in all cases whatsoever.

He has abdicated Government here, by declaring us out of his Protection and waging War against us.

He has plundered our seas, ravaged our Coasts, burnt our towns, and destroyed the lives of our people.

He is at this time transporting large Armies of foreign Mercenaries to compleat the works of death, desolation and tyranny, already begun with circumstances of Cruelty & perfidy scarcely paralleled in the most barbarous ages, and totally unworthy the Head of a civilized nation.

He has constrained our fellow Citizens taken Captive on the high Seas to bear Arms against their Country, to become the executioners of their friends and Brethren, or to fall themselves by their Hands.

He has excited domestic insurrections amongst us, and has endeavoured to bring on the inhabitants of our frontiers, the merciless Indian Savages, whose known rule of warfare, is an undistinguished destruction of all ages, sexes and conditions.

In every stage of these Oppressions We have Petitioned for Redress in the most humble terms: Our repeated Petitions have been answered only by repeated injury. A Prince whose character is thus marked by every act which may define a Tyrant, is unfit to be the ruler of a free people.

Nor have We been wanting in attentions to our British brethren. We have warned them from time to time of attempts by their legislature to extend an unwarrantable jurisdiction over us. We have reminded them of the circumstances of our emigration and settlement here. We have appealed to their native justice and magnanimity, and we have conjured them by the ties of our common kindred to disavow these usurpations, which, would inevitably interrupt our connections and correspondence. They too have been deaf to the voice of justice and of consanguinity. We must, therefore, acquiesce in the necessity, which denounces our Separation, and hold them, as we hold the rest of mankind, Enemies in War, in Peace Friends.

We, therefore, the Representatives of the United States of America, in General Congress, Assembled, appealing to the Supreme Judge of the world for the rectitude of our intentions, do, in the Name, and by Authority of the good People of these Colonies, solemnly publish and declare, That these United Colonies are, and of Right ought to be Free and Independent States; that they are Absolved from all Allegiance to the British Crown, and that all political connection between them and the State of Great Britain, is and ought to be totally dissolved; and that as Free and Independent States, they have full Power to levy War, conclude Peace, contract Alliances, establish Commerce, and to do all other Acts and Things which Independent States may of right do. And for the support of this Declaration, with a firm reliance on the protection of divine Providence, we mutually pledge to each other our Lives, our Fortunes and our sacred Honor.

The unanimous Declaration of the thirteen United States of America.

Signed by Order and Behalf of the Congress,

JOHN HANCOCK, President

Attest.

CHARLES THOMSON, Secretary

U.S. HOMEOWNER'S DECLARATION OF INDEPENDENCE

In America, January 12, 2009
(1/2/12)

A Declaration
For United States Homeowners

WHEN IN THE COURSE OF HUMAN EVENTS, it becomes necessary for individual American Citizen Homeowners, within the Jurisdiction of current United States and State laws, and, moreover, acting for the Benefit and Security of their Families, to take a unilateral decision to Revoke and/or Adjudicate fraudulent property contracts, they have the right if not the Obligation to Family to do so.

Operating under current Civil Law, Laws of Nature and of Nature's God have entitled them with fair respect to the Opinions of Mankind, and makes it necessary to Declare the causes which impel them to take such decision.

WE HOLD THESE TRUTHS TO BE SELF-EVIDENT, that all men and women are created equal, that they are endowed by their Creator with certain unalienable Rights, that among these are Life, Liberty and the pursuit of Happiness.

IN ORDER TO SECURE these rights under Democracy, Governments are instituted among Men and Women, deriving their just powers from the consent of the governed. That whenever any Form of Government, or, in concert with Wall Street Investment Banking Broker-Dealer Agents, or other Financial Entities is party to destruction of these ends, it is not only the Individual and Collective Right of the People, but, moreover, the Duty of Individual Citizens to take unilateral actions to Confront and seek to Furthermore, Abolish Avaricious, Illicit and moreover, Fraudulent Practice. Yet, it must be made clear that there is no intent herein to seek to alter Government Authority. Actions of a Resolute People can, and in this instance, will, enable Adjustment and Balance to be Restored through Enforcement of Existent Written Laws and Regulations and Actions by themselves, utilizing the Rule of Law, as indicated and outlined by our Founding Fathers.

We Hold that various Broker-Dealers: including Investment Banks, Depository Banks; Mortgage Banks, and other Financial Entities, as, Agents of, or operating with consent and within an Alleged Regulatory Framework or Apparatus, of the Federal Reserve System, OCC, FHFA, CFTC and SEC, organized within or condoned by the U.S. Federal Government have arguably:

Placed the currency of the United States at great peril and risk.

Placed U.S. Treasury Bonds at great peril and risk.

Placed the United States Financial System at great peril and risk.

Placed the Global Financial System at great peril and risk.

Placed millions of American Homeowners at great peril and risk.

We argue that these Abominations are a result of Dereliction of Duty, moreover, a Coerced and Witting Malfeasance by the Administration, U.S. Supreme Court; Congress and the Department of Justice, forced to bend their Collective Knee(s), to the Avaricious Power of previously cited Financial Entities; and, directly resulting therefrom, have exhibited recent Specific Behaviors, Legislative Enactments and Actions (and/or lack thereof) that clearly do not have intent to regard the Best Interest in heart and mind of 99% of Americans, nor, Specifically as recognized herein, for U.S. Homeowner's. Further and in Specificity, the U.S. Department of Justice with Standing above all other Legal and Enforcement Entities, has Abandoned it's Prime Directive by Willfully Failing to Investigate and Indict specific Fraudulent Commercial Malefactors as outlined above.

ALL OF THE ABOVE, has caused Millions of American (and World-Wide) Citizen-Homeowners to live in Daily Concern, in Fear over the Very Security of their Castles – their Homes. And, therefrom, many have lost the Right to Private Enjoyment of their property. Over the last several years Millions have been illegally foreclosed on and been illegally evicted from their Homes.

Such Depredations have and continue to effect at various degrees our Rights. Among these Rights are Life, Liberty, and, in Particular in this regard, the pursuit of Happiness, within the very walls of our Respective Homes.

IN ORDER TO PUT AN END to Capricious and Fraudulent Behavior by said Financial Entities, and because said Fraudulent Behaviors tear at the Very Fabric of the Republic of the United States of America, beholden to a Constitution; and operating under a representative electoral Democracy; –

WE DECLARE that acting under existing the Rule of Law, we will henceforth, acting within remedies specified generally at Law and Contract Law, as Codified in the Universal Commercial Code as enacted and regulated by the Federal Government and Various States, Use Foreclosure Law in order to Confront Fraudulent Housing Debt, and thereby and when appropriate, Defend Our Homes, utilizing, when required, Securitization Audits; subsequently retain counsel; and, vigorously stand for our rights under the Rule of Law and thereby defend our Families.

WE FINALLY DECLARE that if Equitable Settlements cannot be negotiated, we will Utilize and Occupy the Courts to exercise our legal rights: to litigate against any and all Parties that knowingly and willfully Committed Fraud against Our Person(s) and Our Family's Person(s); and fully Publicize our Litigious Acts throughout our Neighborhoods and Communities, Simultaneously entreating Media to focus their attention on Our Righteous Causes of Actions, now Contemplated to be made part and parcel of Moving Papers before the Courts.

Signed,
For All Wish to Join:

// Kenneth R. Kappel

Dated: January 12, 2012

PRE RAMBLE

"The unlimited emission of bank paper has banished all [Great Britain's] specie, and is now, by a depreciation acknowledged by her own statesmen, carrying her rapidly to bankruptcy, as it did France, as it did us, and will do us again, and every country permitting paper to be circulated, other than that by public authority." Thomas Jefferson, 1813.

The Founding Fathers were arguably more than anything else, rebelling against *financial* servitude. Not merely a few isolated taxes and tariffs, but due to the fact that King George III eliminated the colonist's right to coin their own money. And even more so than against the King, they were specifically rebelling against the Bank of England and the entire banking cartel in that country. They were rebelling against a central banking system that was held and operated by the banks themselves. Below we'll present a great deal of information you need to understand.

And indeed, more than a century later, Great Britain was in so much financial pain and under siege, that the once Great Empire was relying on U.S. support to defend its currency, and literally defend its sovereignty during two World Wars. After World War II Britain completely relinquished its former monetary hegemony to the United States of America.

Well after Jefferson's words and fifty years *after* the War of 1812, the simmering contempt from our former Masters in Great Britain was palpable:

"If this mischievous financial policy, which has its origin in North America, shall become endurated down to a fixture, then that Government will furnish its own money **without cost**. It will pay off debts and **be without debt**. It will have all the money necessary to carry on its commerce. It will become prosperous without precedent in the history of the world. The brains and wealth of all countries will go to North America. That country must be destroyed or it will destroy every monarchy on the globe." (*London Times*, 1865) [Emphasis added.]

This was a clear and naked defense of Rothschild based − war based − Central Banking. We would issue our own currency through the Treasury, and not pay interest to a central bank for the privilege. President's Lincoln and Kennedy did exactly that. RIP.

Clearly, as long as the British Empire endured, they did not want to let us go. World War II was the ultimate end of their hegemony over America. On the other hand from a deeper monetary point of view based on a forensic analysis of the actual ownership of the Federal Reserve System − don't be too sure. However, that would be a different book.

Throughout early American history (until a capitulation in 1913 with the formation of the Federal Reserve System), Patriotic Americans struggled against central banking which was used throughout Europe. The Great European Rothschild Banking Empire (that often financed *both* sides of European Wars over time) was often the force, the power behind the scenes of European Central Banking origination, as it was, with the formation of the U.S. Federal Reserve System (the Fed). The Rothschild American agent, Paul Warburg was their instrument here. He drove the process of initiating the Federal Reserve System from 1908 through 1913. At the origin of our great nation, and for some time thereafter, Thomas Jefferson, Benjamin Franklin, James Madison, Andrew Jackson and many others were particularly strident against having a central bank controlled and owned by bankers.

Fellow Founding Father Alexander Hamilton took, a Federalist position, moreover, a Royalist position – the other side of the coin and always struggled for a central bank along British lines. He was accused by some contemporaries of being a Royalist – of wishing to bow to the Queen or King of England. Over time Hamilton's struggles for a central bank would go one step forward and two steps back.

Currency in the form of notes that are issued by sovereign governments or authorized central banks as legal tender, is also known as *coin of the realm.* Today we have Federal Reserve *Notes.* These are in fact, Federal Reserve bank currency authorized and issued on behalf of the government – not *by* the government. In other words they are not *Sovereign Nation* currency issued by the government itself, which are generally not subject to taxpayers making interest payments to the Fed, as we do, to thank them for printing the legal tender – the "money" we must use by law.

Why does this continue? In the U.S. the central bank (owned by regional banks) creates huge fortunes for itself from interest paid ultimately by the government's taxpayers. Moreover, government rulers enjoy such a system, which is never made public, never reported in main stream media nor taught in schools, because it enables the government to borrow money for their preferred needs, and then simply tax citizens who do not clearly understand what is happening to them. Never will you see any statements as to the Fed's actual profitability and who it actually distributes those profits to.

Above we offered the Declaration of Independence in order to allow you to see and remind you that our nation was carved out of the grasping claws of King George III and his bankers. When Benjamin Franklin was asked by the British government how it was that the Colonies were beginning to prosper he replied:

"That is simple. In the colonies we issue our own money. It is called 'Colonial Script'. We issue it in proper proportion to the demands of trade and industry to make the products pass easily from the producers to the consumers... In this manner, creating for ourselves our own paper money, we control its purchasing power, and we have no interest to pay to no one."

Britain said little, yet immediately passed laws to stop the Colonials from issuing their "script."

"In one year, the conditions were so reversed that the era of prosperity ended, and a depression set in, to such an extent that the streets of the Colonies were filled with unemployed." Benjamin Franklin.

A great deal more ensued, but Young America had finally had enough and subsequently the Boston Tea Party occurred, as a direct action against the British East India Company, which demanded and received monopolies from the King which were to the disadvantage to the Colonists. Outraged, the Brits came down hard and finally the War of Independence, aka the Revolutionary War began.

We will not review the ensuing actions, finally culminating in the War of 1812, but for the most part they revolved around the issue of who would control the banking system – particularly the creation and control of money. Would it be: privateers and banks with a *private* central bank for *their* profit; or, a government owned and operated central bank for the benefit of its *citizens*. Such an entity, operated by and through the Treasury department, would charge no interest to its citizens. Meaning we would not have a huge national debt. This is tricky as both Abraham Lincoln and Jack Kennedy discovered after they had instituted such a program. RIP.

The struggle raged over time culminating in the Panic of 1907, which some have argued was really a significant market dislocation (crash) engineered by himself, J.P. Morgan, the leading industrialist and one of the wealthiest men in the U.S. He had a deep relationship with British banking. Over a hundred years later in 2008 he is arguably *still* one of the Rulers of Wall Street through the existing Morgan Banking Empire, which plays the most prominent role in American Banking through various entities we'll visit below. In 1907 J.P.'s goal was to bring the American People, moreover, the politicians, to finally allow/accept a central bank. It took six more years – yet – it was done. This gave *the banks* power to control the People's Money.

"If you squeeze them hard enough – they will squeal." The Postman

Without rehearsing their methods in detail, they got the job done in 1913. Prior to 1913, Woodrow Wilson had accepted an offer to sign such a bill for a central bank if they would give him the funds to run for President. They did. He did. And the Federal Reserve System was enacted by Congress in voting (after midnight), and signed very early the following day by Wilson in 1913. A *Fait Accompli.*

This Bill took control of the money supply away from Congress (as <u>defined in the U.S. Constitution</u>) and gave it to private banking elites. Here we are, in 20012, perched on a Greater Depression (contrary to the Fed, we're already in a deepening recession), that may bring down the financial system as we know it right now. As over 48 million Americans are on food stamps it is not likely that we'll soup lines, which were common in the 1930's.

Later in 1913, another significant event occurred. Private forces pushed through the Sixteenth Amendment to the U.S. Constitution, and in a stroke of the pen <u>*the Internal Revenue Service (IRS) was created so the government could collect income taxes to pay off the interest that would be due on the notes issued by the Federal Reserve System*</u>. Point. Game. Set. Match.

Prior to this time, foreign tariffs on imported goods nearly *funded* the entire U.S. Government. Now the bankers and politicians would have an income tax. This enabled bankers to create and ultimately control the "people's money." Naturally politicians listened very closely when the bankers spoke or whispered.

Fed Not Federal. There is nothing "Federal" about the Federal Reserve System. The word "Federal" was used to allow the citizens to think it was Federally owned and operated – a Government entity. It is not a government entity. It is a government chartered privately owned entity.

No need to wonder why. The owners are major money center banks, and regional banks, with some foreign ownership. The banks own the Fed. Meaning, the banks are able to and do use the Fed in their best interest against the interest of U.S. citizens. It is said that the Fed is the *lender* of last resort for the banking system. While this statement is true, it does not go far enough. It must also be said that the taxpayer is always the *payer* of last resort to maintain the Fed. Always. Particularly when they've overstepped their mandate, or failed, as a regulator, to enforce their mandate.

Since 1913 (the creation of the Federal Reserve System) the bankers have been winning. But this time they may have shot themselves in both feet. *They* will be unable to "walk away" unscathed unless they receive a significant historically unprecedented taxpayer bailout. Are you ready to dig deeper into your pocket?

"Fed actions only effect the economy accidentally. Their total focus is on protecting banks." James Rickards, widely quoted World Class economics analyst, 12/19/2011.

The question is, will the people take back the money power this time? While *Use Foreclosure Law! Keep Your Home* has no intention, or ability to answer that question directly, what we are suggesting is that it's high time that you begin to think for yourself. You must no longer be swayed by media controlled public opinion. You must learn to understand that you must ultimately make a business decision for the benefit of your finances, moreover for your family.

Remember this current system is exclusively for the benefit of bankers, who live off your hard work. That is if you can keep or find a decent paying job with benefits. Good luck. Wall Street was instrumental in forcing manufacturing and white collar jobs off-shore. Arguably this is the single most cause in the destruction – the hollowing out – of the middle class, which has always been the engine of financial growth, prosperity and appropriate public infrastructure, including: schools, highways, bridges, a safety net, and so much more.

One more requirement was necessary. The U.S. had to be moved off the gold standard to enable the free issue of un-backed Federal Reserve notes so that they could print "money" at will. This is called "fiat" currency.

The Gold Standard Removed. Under great economic strife due to the Great Depression, President Franklin D. Roosevelt killed gold convertibility for citizens. He actually made it illegal for U.S. citizens to own and keep gold. Later, in 1965, our coins were debased because silver was removed from them.

Still later, in 1968, silver convertibility was eliminated. In 1971 the final blow to the remnants of the still existing world-wide gold standard was swung by President Richard Nixon who was operating under great financial dislocation. He eliminated the gold peg for foreign governments, who could no longer exchange dollars (they earned from exporting good to our shores) for gold. A stroke of the pen placed us completely in a new era of *total fiat currency*.

As long as we've enjoyed dollar hegemony – being the world's reserve currency – that has enriched our ruling elites at the expense of the middle class. However, in a nut shell, they've taken on too much national debt and the value of the dollar is diminishing dangerously, while wealth has been significantly redistributed to the already wealthy elites since 1980.

We believe it is important for you to understand these basics of finance to enable you to understand why it is now time to take control of your own life and protect your family. Even more importantly – in this book – you will discover that because they have gone too far – assumed too much debt – the American People have – right now – a rare opportunity to balance things out. Moreover, to once again be able to live in an *affordable* home that is not *underwater*. Don't worry about the Wall Street financiers – the ones that don't go to jail will survive – they always do.

With "Occupy Movements" in force, understand that the 99% are calling out the 1%. Ron Paul made nice comments regarding "Occupy." See our blog at UseForeclosureLaw.com.

"They got bailed out and we got sold out." A powerful and seemingly accurate concept. This has forced leaders to fast track authoritarian measures. Some are undaunted, and believe it's past time to stand up and Take Our Country Back. We're not charging you with that. We are suggesting that you stand up and take you home back using the law.

CHAPTER 1: OPENING STATEMENT

"The severity of the subprime debacle may be only a prologue to the main act, a tragedy on the grand stage in the corporate credit markets... Over the past decade, the exponential growth of credit derivatives has created unprecedented amounts of financial leverage on corporate credit. Similar to the growth of subprime mortgages, the rapid rise of credit products required ideal economic conditions and disconnected the assessors of risk from those bearing it." December 27, 2007, *International Herald Tribune.*

The "subprime mortgage debacle" was much more serious than let on by the press, including the financial press and financial TV. It is very clear that they had and continue to have a deep need to obfuscate and conceal the real depth of the problem. The facts are that the real overhang from this problem is a Systemic Threat to both the United States and World banking systems. Yet, the sun will set and rise again − even in 2010. It always does. Take action to defend yourself before the unknown occurs.

Current, Chairman of the Federal Reserve System, Dr. Ben Bernanke repeated over and over beginning in the 2nd Quarter in 2007, that the subprime matter was "...*contained.*" We argue that either he was not capable of actually understanding the real depth of the problem, or, he was and is carrying water for the major banks, and other lenders, until bailout schemes can be put in place to protect the banking system at the expense of homeowners and all U.S. taxpayers. They claimed financial system collapse in 2008. They fixed nothing. They reformed nothing. And, here it comes again, heralded by the excess money printing to save Europe. Ha. They only intend to save European TBTF banks, so they won't bring our TBTF banks down with them. Printing too much unpayable debt.

Treasury Formulated Plans. Beginning in the spring of 2008, there has been no end of various "Plans." "Government Tax Relief Stimulations." "Hope Now." "Jumbo Loan Relief through Fannie and Freddie." "Backed by FHA." Today, more than 80% of all loans are either FHA guaranteed, or, are "conforming" loans passed on by originators to Fannie and Freddie. The great cesspool.

In the spring of 2008, it seemed a new "Plan" was introduced nearly every two to three weeks. These "Plans" and other schemes floated in Congress and Washington D.C., were often and notably presented by former Secretary of the Treasury, Henry Paulson. In 2006, Secretary Paulson came directly from his position as the virtual titular Head of Wall Street from his seat as the Chairman of the venerable (now vulnerable?) Investment Bank, Goldman Sachs. Current Chairman, Lloyd Blankfein is famous for telling Congress, under oath, that "Goldman Sachs is doing God's work." No comment.

In other words we are suffering such dire economic dislocation that the Prince of Wall Street, himself, Henry Paulson had to leave his Goldman Sachs, Eagle's Aerie, which has been good for him to nearly $20 Million per year (some years well more than that, while he's amassed a $600 Million fortune). As they say in some retail stores. "You break it. You buy it." For Henry aka "Mr. Fix-it" Paulson that statement was amended to "We broke it. You *stay* in your home (underwater)." He offered dubious "Plans" – fixing as fast as he could.

He's gone, and Tim-Boy "Tax-Dodging" Geithner is the new public face, and lately the brunt of public disdain. Interestingly enough, both the far left and far right have him in their sights. Some reticent lefties – still all "hope and change" Obama acolytes – are flummoxed, and cannot summon the intellectual courage to denounce, or, perhaps fail to understand that Geithner merely represents the Banking Cartel that has captured the Young President. What's up *his* sleeve? Only time will tell.

Almost all of these "Plans" have the *stated* aim of *"keeping people in their homes."* In reality they only want to *"keep people in their homes"* to save the banking system. If people are fooled into staying – keeping on in their homes by accepting the new new fraudulent loan modifications – they will likely become long term indentured servants to the banking industry. They will make payments (for years and years and years, as in Japan) on mortgage loans that are higher in value than the now deflated value of the houses. Additionally, all taxpayers will ultimately pay a significant price to keep the mortgage lending and servicing industry, as we know it, from collapsing under the still defaulting debt they've assumed.

Worse, these new mods contain Indemnification and Warranty clauses whereby the borrower is signing away their rights to Confront Fraudulent Hosing Debt based on the illegal mortgage no in effect. Don't do it. And, don't strategically default. Confront Fraudulent Housing Debt.

One Plan Awry – Already. Here's an example of a taxpayer funded "Plan" being subverted. On June 25, 2008, Bloomberg presented an article titled, "Fannie, Freddie not helping jumbo market." They wrote:

"Agencies use new buying power to cut their losses. Three months after Fannie Mae and Freddie Mac won the freedom to step up home-loan purchases, the government-chartered mortgage-finance companies are doing what critics in the Federal Reserve and Congress had predicted. Instead of using powers granted by Congress to buy jumbo loans for the first time, Freddie Mac and Fannie Mae are <u>purchasing their own mortgage-backed securities,</u> helping reduce losses, company filings show. The large loans, above $417,000, made up almost a third of the U.S. market last year, according to the Mortgage Bankers Association. [Emphasis added.]

"'They were granted expanded opportunity to help recovery in a troubled housing market and yet have appeared <u>to focus on their own recovery,</u>" said former Rep. Richard Baker, a critic of the companies who left office earlier this year to run the Managed Funds Association in Washington.' The change places <u>taxpayers at greater risk,</u> without facilitating the policy goals I believe the Congress had in mind when they eased these portfolio limits,' said Baker, 60, a Louisiana Republican." [Emphasis added.]

"The slowness of Fannie Mae and Freddie Mac in injecting cash for new jumbo loans may have <u>exacerbated the housing slump in markets including California and Florida,</u> where prices have already fallen more than the national average,' said Jerry Howard, 53, president of the National Association of Home Builders. 'Had they been quicker into the marketplace, they could have <u>helped slow the downward spiral in housing prices,</u>' Howard said." [Emphasis added.]

Remember, this is a system created by lending and financing institutions to earn quick and large fees by inflating the value of all homes. They have been wildly successful. Now that things have changed and home values are rapidly deflating, they insist that taxpayers bail them out of the losses they are incurring. The Investment Bank's business (computer based) modeling was based on the continual appreciation of homes, and *did not consider* large amounts of defaults on loans that were pre-determined to fail. They drank their own Kool-Aid, and now the inevitable defaults are rising.

Why would any rational party stay in an over-valued home (unless they have a legitimate loan modification with principal reduction) because the bankers wrecked the economy? Shouldn't Investment Bankers pay for their own mistakes? Why should Congress bail them out, at the general taxpayer's expense? Frankly, in our opinion, they were smart enough to know exactly what they were doing and what would happen.

"As long as the music is playing, you've got to get up and dance.
We're still dancing."

They got up and danced all right. Today's crocodile tears may save most of them from prison sentences, but the model we might look to for historic comparison is the Nuremburg Trials. There, many Nazi's testified straight-faced that *they* had no idea of what was really going on in the prison camps. Please!

We believe that all homeowners who live in markets where house values appreciated exponentially (worldwide as well as in the U.S.) need to understand exactly what the situation is today in order to make plans. Ultimately to consider making a *seemingly* difficult business decision to defend and protect their families. By difficult business decision we mean that because most of us have been caught in a mania (more on that later) of heightened expectations ("real estate always goes up," "its a great *time to buy"*); compounded by our desire to operate both ethically and morally, we have a need to operate within the bounds, the framework of Social Responsibility. The Center Must Hold.

Stigma No More. Most of us were taught and informed (as we grew up), by important family values, socialized by a slanted education system and higher powers, that "bankruptcy" or "foreclosure" is akin to Social Stigma. In the Christian religious sense *"Stigmata"* are literally marks on the body, or painful sensations in body locations correlating to Jesus' Crucifixion wounds. The term in this sense came from Saint Paul's Letter to the Galatians in which he said, "I bear on my body the marks of Jesus." Yet, use of the word began well before that and was plural for the Greek word *stigma*. In the earlier Greek it meant a brand or a mark that was placed physically on the body, and used for the identification of an animal or a *slave*.

Our point is that we have been literally socialized over centuries to believe that we must act and operate to a higher ethical and legal standard than the business entities, corporations, with which we do business. We include the banking industry, which loans money, enabling us to "rent" a house from them, while we enjoy the dream of ownership, witnessed by a recorded Deed and Title.

Yet, the ingrained fear of social stigma (currently a virtual, a non-physical branding of the slave, alive in the unconscious) keeps us suspended in a superstitious state. We are appropriately socially processed so that we must try to do the right thing. That we act as honest and good members of our neighborhoods, our communities and greater society. Good and honest citizens. This is a very powerful and beneficial force. We mean, most people want to do the right thing and therefore be accepted and recognized as good and honest people within both local and larger communities.

Facing Reality. When individuals face the fact that their mortgage is resetting to a higher payment, which they discover they can't afford, they often become paralyzed, in denial, in fear, in anger, and sadly, all too often such pain is played out in the family, resulting in internal strife and worse. It has been recently well documented in press reports of psychological studies that people facing loss of their homes become victims, and subsequently exhibit aberrant behaviors. Children present in the home often suffer (silently) the most.

These dangers are a result of inappropriate or uninformed mindsets that *Use Foreclosure Law* ambitiously hopes to alleviate by bringing information to people in order for them to rationally deal with their situations through understanding the facts that lead us to this sorry pass. We intend to remove the fear of the unknown from underwater homeowners. We provide education – a step by step plan – to enable change. We suggest, that the finance side of the housing industry as a whole has been the perpetrator. It is now time that finance becomes responsible for their Machiavellian Schemes. That *they* pay the price for their practices. Not taxpayers, and/or homeowners who unwittingly believed – trusted – in them and are currently suffering the consequences of Predatory Lending and Fraudulent Securitization.

Many will and do argue that many homeowners are equally, or *more* at fault, for saying "OK / Yes" when a Mortgage Broker (the expert) told them what to say and do to qualify for the loan. We argue that the licensed professional, possessing superior information and often guilty of inducement to fraud, controlled the situation. That's our story and we're sticking to it.

Imagine dialogue between a Mortgage Broker and a potential homebuyer:

"You earn more than that. Don't you bring in money from other sources that you haven't mentioned? [softer voice now] You do want this house don't you?

"Yes – we do."

The homeowner answered the last question, *"You do want this house don't you?"* The Mortgage Broker *hears* the "yes" to mean *"... money from other sources...."* A slip between the lip and the tea cup? Predatory Lending? Inducement to Fraud? We think so. You need an attorney to make that decision, after you've obtained a Forensic Loan Audit and a Securitization Audit. And, time is a'wasting. A big mistake is to wait too long, fall into foreclosure status with a date set for an auction to sell your home. Then it's too late.

We won't go into actions taken by the notorious: Country Wide, Washington Mutual, Ocwen, and many others, where they used white-out and plain forgery to alter loan submission documents. It was an epidemic of blatant fraud.

You need to take action, obtain a Forensic Loan Audit and a Securitization Audit, retain an attorney, and go on the offense with the Lender. Even if you can afford your payments, perhaps, especially if you can afford your payments and are way way underwater, you must, through Audits, discover whether or not significant fraud is found in your loan documents. If so, you're on your way to a "legitimate" loan modification, which we call a Forced Debt Reorganization, with a significant principal reduction to just below current market value.

Further evidence for our position is the pile-on done by the media, pointing the finger at "irresponsible borrowers." Believe us, when you actually read and understand a Forensic Loan Audit and/or a Securitization Audit, you shake your head in disbelief regarding the amount of actionable fraud in the documents. The homeowner signed documents they did not understand because they were counseled to do so by someone they trusted. Someone, often an Independent Mortgage Broker that owed a legal fiduciary duty under the principal of Agency Law to the aspiring homeowner, which they violated, and it is actionable, but, likely not worth the trouble.

Homeowners who discover that their home is now worth less than what they owe on their mortgage are (in the vernacular) "underwater," or "upside-down." It has become all too clear to them that they made an unfortunate investment, particularly so for those who obtained "exploding" ARMs. The mortgage agreement they entered into was not financially sustainable once the mortgage rate reset higher, and they are unable to keep up with the increased payment and continue to put food on the table for their family.

As pointed out previously, while we believe that perhaps, 33%, are underwater in early 2012, we believe that at least 40% of all homeowners may become underwater over the next three years. Why? The value of nearly all homes was pushed up, promoted up, by a series of actors – stakeholders – who profited handsomely as their actions caused a dubious appreciation in the value of houses. Frankly, by knowingly, and as argued in many litigations currently going forward, fraudulently promoting a Housing Bubble, which became a National, actually a Global Housing Bubble Mania. We'll discuss the concept of this mania and historical manias in latter pages.

Politically Incorrect. Inquiring Minds are occasionally possessed by economists, professional financial analysts, and certified investment advisors that do not follow the party line. They are often called Bears or Contrarians. For these analysts, the events that are now occurring were foretold – baked in the cake. However, largely forced to ply their trade outside conventional financial media, on the fringe, on the margins (historically through subscription-based Newsletters and now as Internet Bloggers) they were not generally heard. Such contrarians are often not general or financial press "go-to" expert people. Fortunately the Web has changed that. We all now enjoy access to wiser voices that were not previously widely available.

Banking Armageddon? We are on the verge of, and likely about to witness one of the great banking disasters of modern time. But, it doesn't have to happen! If home owners who are underwater, who owe more than their house is worth, cooperate with the banks, and act as fully indentured servants and continue making their payments; and the powers that be (perhaps not for long) are able to convince Congress to create "bail-out" legislation, the "bigs" will survive as the "littles" will continue to pay them to maintain the charade. People will overpay to be allowed to stay in their overvalued homes. For these people – is this a good deal? A smart deal? A fair deal? We think not.

What happened? Under Chairman Alan Greenspan, The Federal Reserve System literally created the situation we are struggling under. In brief Greenspan failed at two of the major tasks in his job description. He choose not to regulate the banking institutions. And, he enabled, them to create too much debt money. And, years later, in 2012, it is blowing up Globally. Europe is only a metaphor, even a symptom, for the coming crash, caused by too many banks allowed to issue too much unpayable debt. Don't be in debt when the crash comes. Lose your debt or cram it down before the court systems are in complete chaos.

Following the dot.com bubble burst (2001-02), Greenspan forced down short term interest rates and lowered interest rates for overnight bank-to-bank loan borrowing. This enabled the banks to offer loans at very low rates.

Leverage and Liquidity. Massive Fed easing created liquidity (easily available debt money sloshing around the banking system). This liquidity enhanced leveraging where, for example, a Hedge Fund could raise $1 million from individual high-wealth investors and go to an Investment Bank (higher up the food chain with more capital available because they were higher up the food chain) who would lend the enterprising Hedge Fund an additional $5 – $10 million, if not more.

This allowed the Hedge Fund to leverage its original $1 million by at least five or more times. Some were able to leverage 20 to 30 times actual cash on hand. In other words Greenspan allowed (by refusing to use the Fed's regulatory powers) Wall Street, itself, to *create* more (debt) money, abdicating the historic role of the Fed on behalf of all Americans, to financial insiders who were knowledgeable, crafty, devious and swift. As we wrote above: "No state or nation can long endure if clever and ruthless people acting in concert − and, who possess and share unconscious aberrant sociopathic and/or psychopathic tendencies and urges − conspire in unison (with willing accomplices) to suborn, take and control a nation for their own purposes."

Carry Trade. Liquidity was enhanced by the *carry trade,* by which entities such as Investment Banks (broker/dealers) and other financial institutions, could take very low interest loans from, for example, Japanese banks, and use those loan proceeds to buy long-term assets such as bonds that paid higher interest rates. Therefore, make a profit on the spread, the difference between the low and high rates − aka − the carry trade.

Thank the central bank of Japan, known as the Bank of Japan (BOJ) for lowering its short-term rates to just above zero. Japanese national banks could borrow from the BOJ for nearly free (sometimes less than .05%), then re-loan those loan proceeds to U.S. Investment banks, or some large Hedge Funds at 1.2 to 2.1% with little perceived risk. That's what the Fed has now. A rate of less than .05%. Just like the Japanese. Their economy has barely emerged from its slump which began in 1990. Why so long? The protected *their* banks.

What are we doing? Protecting *our* banks. to the detriment of all Americans. It is not going well for the Financial Elites these days. The Global Economy hangs blowing in the wind, upside down, and about to fall − because of Greece? That's a joke son. Not a very good one, yet we enjoy a corny joke from time to time. Laughing on the outside − while crying on the inside.

This lasted from 1990 until nearly the middle of 2007, and even then, the Bank of Japan interest rate barely rose. In fact, it took until 2007, seventeen years, for home values to come back to the level where they were at the height of the Japanese Equity/Housing Bubble/Mania in 1990. Seventeen years? Could that happen here? Perhaps. It's certainly not impossible.

A Swindle? The result, where we are right now with housing, is seeing the largest bubble ever created in history − deflate. We think that the current situation may be considered in history as the Greatest Confidence Game ever created. That game was allowed to grow by a Fed who chose to abandon or ignore their oversight regulatory powers and even encouraged the process. It started at the top, virtual license by "accommodative" actions of the Federal Reserve System. (Loose, leveraged and easily available money, aka "liquidity.")

The action was buttressed by implied government backing for the Government Service Entitles (GSEs): both Fannie Mae and Freddy Mac; who bought "conforming" mortgage loans (under $477,000, which they've bumped up, and lowered again) from loan originators such as national and regional Mortgage Banks, local and regional depository banks and thrifts. They then sold the loans up the chain to Investment Banks who Securitize a large number of these loans into a single Mortgage Backed Security (MBS or bond). Fannie and Freddie also bought MBS. Nearly all loan originators sold new loans to Fannie and Freddie unless the loans were in excess of $477,000. Larger loans, called Jumbos were sold to the Investment Banks, or in rare cases actually kept in the loan originators portfolio.

Lender Fraud. This process may prove to be of enormous significance, particularly if fraud is found to have existed in the loan origination process. (Actually fraud is in, some say, 90% of all loans issued since 2000.) The point here is that while many parties colluded to create fraudulent loans, at some point, even if only for seconds, the Investment Banks bought and therefore *owned* those loans, nearly immediately after they were made, and therefore, the Investment Banks, actually owned the loans; and are thereby a party, a principle in the process.

Resulting from that the Investment Banks are vulnerable to being named as defendants to legal actions brought by homeowners alleging fraud. As you read this book, don't forget this fact. Homeowners that discover fraud, inducement to fraud or that Predatory Lending or Fraudulent Securitization was involved in the loan origination process are in an extraordinarily good position to utilize legal leverage to control the outcome. We will present much more information in this regard throughout the book, and breaking legal news on the blog. The point is that you must obtain a Forensic Loan Audit and a Securitization Audit to determine the degree of fraud in your loan. Then you Use Foreclosure Law to Keep Your Home.

Even Worse. *The Financial Times*, in a May 6, 2008 article entitled "Shrinking Investment Banks," wrote:

> "Forget what investment bankers say about profitability or shareholder returns – what they care most about is size. Managers constantly compare headcounts and obsess about "revenue gaps" to their nearest rivals. Now, after five years of gunning for growth, investment banks are going to have to get used to the idea of shrinkage. But in a deleveraged world, how much smaller do they have to get?"

> "Even excluding write downs, the shock to investment banking revenues has been severe. Dealogic data for the first quarter of 2008 shows global fee revenues down 45 per cent on last year. Sure, the opening few months were harsh, but that implies an annual run-rate of about $48bn – back to 2003 levels. The banks do not expect "normalized" revenues to fall by anything like that amount. For example, with additional cuts announced, UBS plans to reduce its investment banking headcount by only 18 per cent from the peak."

> "Part of banks' optimism is due to their confidence in the resilience of sales and trading activities, which often contribute more to revenues than fee businesses. Volumes (and volatility, which traders love) in equities, bonds and foreign exchange, in particular, remain high. Commodities desks are benefiting from the resources boom. But there are obvious risks in these areas too. Experience in Japan shows soggy equity markets eventually hurt volumes. Tighter credit conditions will hit fixed income trading and it is hard to see how the environment for commodities can get any better."

"Meanwhile, the outlook for mergers and acquisitions, which still made up 35 per cent of global fee revenues in the first quarter, is bleak. Equally worrying is the recent poor performance of some hedge funds. Credit Suisse estimates this client group is now the most important for investment banks, contributing a fifth of revenues. Should the few remaining bright spots in investment banking also begin to darken, revenues could easily remain at half of their peak levels for some time to come."

Structured Finance. This is a broad term used to describe a sector of finance that was created to help transfer risk using complex legal and corporate entities. Thanks to everyone's good friend Wikipedia and their open copyright position, below we're using their definitions with permission.

"Securitization. Securitization is the method which participants of structured finance utilize to create the pools of assets that are used in the creation of the end product financial instruments.

"Tranching. This is an important concept in structured finance because it is the system used to create different investment classes for the securities that are created in the structured finance world. *Tranching allows the cash flow from the underlying asset to be diverted to the various investor groups.* The Committee on the Global Financial System explained tranching succinctly: "A key goal of the tranching process is to create at least one class of securities whose rating is higher than the average rating of the underlying collateral pool or to create rated securities from a pool of unrated assets. This is accomplished through the use of credit support (enhancement), such as prioritization of payments to the different tranches."

"Credit enhancement. This is key in creating a security that has a higher rating than the issuing company.

"Credit ratings. Ratings play an important role in structured finance.

"Structure. There are numerous structures which may involve mezzanine risk participation, Options and Futures within structuring of financing as well as multiple stripping of interest rate strips. There is no laid-out fixed structure unlike in Securitization which is only a subset of the overall structured transactions. Esoteric transactions often have multiple lenders and borrowers distributed by distribution agents where the Structuring entity may not be involved in the transaction at all.

"Types. There are several main types of structured finance instruments:

"Asset-backed securities (ABS) are bonds or notes based on pools of assets, or collateralized by the cash flows from a specified pool of underlying assets.

"Mortgage-backed securities (MBS) are asset-backed securities whose cash flows are backed by the principal and interest payments of a set of mortgage loans.

"Collateralized debt obligations (CDOs) consolidate a group of fixed income assets such as high-yield debt or asset-backed securities into a pool, which is then divided into various tranches.

"Collateralized mortgage obligations (CMOs) are CDOs backed primarily by mortgages.

"Collateralized bond obligations (CBOs) are CDOs backed primarily by corporate bonds.

"Collateralized loan obligations (CLOs) are CDOs backed primarily by leveraged bank loans.

"Credit derivatives are contracts to transfer the risk of the total return on a credit asset falling below an agreed level, without transfer of the underlying asset.

Thank you again Wikipedia.

If you didn't get all that, remember, you're not supposed to, and trust us, you're not alone. Anyway, there it is – Structured Finance.

Like Greenspan. Allow us another modest corny joke, Structured Finance and its elements are like Alan Greenspan in that they are both *incomprehensible* – by design.

Remember, people in the industry who work with, create and trade these financial products – under the name, derivatives– don't often understand them. This is the real *esoteria.* This is what they don't want you to understand because use of these *largely unregulated financial products* has allowed them to leverage their bets to make more money. For example a Hedge Fund could raise $5 million from individual investors and an Investment Bank would loan the Hedge Fund 5 or 10 or 20 times that amount to invest in these and other products. The Investment Banks Bear Stearns and Lehman Brothers went down because of this. Some estimate they were leveraged *thirty to forty times* their actual capital. That is leverage. How did they get it?

In 2004, when Henry Paulson was still Chairman of Goldman Sachs, before taking a demotion to become the Secretary of the Treasury, he led a group that met with the SEC, the Fed and Treasury to obtain permission for Investment Banks to leverage up to 40 times. They received permission. We received a housing bubble.

Then, *"they got bailed out – we got sold out."*

The Good News is that you don't have to understand all of this dense stuff. One basic concept is that derivatives are basically like an insurance policy, one party will bet that something *will* happen, the other side takes the bet and bets it *won't* happen. Remember only one thing, Warren Buffet said: *"Derivative are financial weapons of mass destruction."*

While slightly more esoteric, in his book, *A Short History of Financial Euphoria*, back in the day, noted economist John Kenneth Galbraith said, "Financial operations do not lend themselves to innovation. What is recurrently so described and celebrated is, without exception, a small variation on an established design.... The world of finance hails the invention of the wheel over and over again, often in a slightly more unstable version."

According to the Bank for International Settlements (BIS) there were well in excess of $700 Trillion derivatives in June 2011. Significantly more in the last six months. What does that mean? Well frankly – so what – let them go down. Force-close, a cram-down elimination of this entire casino. Let the gamblers, the players on all this ruthless gambling take that hit. Incidentally, this is why the Fed and Treasury are moving on the taxpayers, they don't want their friends in High Finance to *"...take that hit."*

They want *you* to *"... take that hit"* on top of the debt your owe for an underwater house. Good morning! It's going to be a great day if you decide to Use Foreclosure Law to Keep Your Home, or walk away under *your* terms if that is your choice.

Credit Worries. Do you worry about your credit? Stop it. When you've restored your credit and saved for a down payment they will welcome you back with open arms. They'll have no choice. You will be – will have – the hammer. The banks will need your savings. Desperately need your savings on deposit with the surviving banks. Credit hit? That's only publicized in the press to keep you scared and indentured. To *"keep people in their homes."* Please, they need you in indentured servitude. However, if you do not force a cramdown, a Forced Debt Reorganization to keep your home, if you leave through a Strategic Default and come back to the housing market in two or three years with steady employment, bills paid on time, restored credit score, and a 10% down payment, they will lust after your business. Welcome Back. But, don't do it. Use the law to Confront Fraudulent Housing Debt.

Loan Securitization. Loaded with liquidity and capital, Wall Street's Structured Finance operations stepped into the money fest, and purchased loans from mortgage originators, including Jumbo loans (in excess of $477,000) and created Mortgage Backed Securities (MBS) (aka bonds), which had the physical property (the house) as underlying collateral for the Promissory Note issued to the borrower. And, they promoted Commercial Mortgage Backed Securities (CMBS). The market for this orgy of new and (then) profitable paper (which was sold to Institutional Investors) grew to include Asset Backed Securities (ABS), which were created from the purchase of almost any kind of standardized collateralized loans including home and auto loans; and non-collateralized debt from credit cards and student loans among other types.

Credit Card Reform? If you use credit cards you are aware of changes that have taken place in the last few years. Changes that impact you negatively. When you couple the new regulations with the Bankruptcy Act of 2005, an effort to keep people indentured as debt serfs for the rest of their lives even when the bankruptcy ends, you may begin to think that this debacle was planned in advance. We do. In February 2008, MSNBC reported on this issue and possible reform.

> "Could it be? Is Congress really ready to put an end to the credit card industry's most abusive practices? A bill introduced a few weeks ago by Rep. Carolyn Maloney (D-NY), would change the way most credit card companies do business and provide significant consumer protection for every cardholder. 'In recent years the playing field between credit card companies and credit cardholders has become very one-sided,' Maloney said. 'A credit card agreement is supposed to be a contract, but what good is a contract when only one party has the power to make decisions?'"

> "The Credit Cardholders' Bill of Rights Act of 2008, known as H.R. 5244, would protect cardholders from arbitrary interest rate increases and unfair fees. Maloney, who chairs the House Financial Institutions and Consumer Credit Subcommittee, is quick to point out that her bill does not have any price controls. It does not cap rates or fees. 'I firmly believe the free market works best when consumers are empowered to make their own choices,' she says. 'This bill helps foster fair competition and free market values.'"

Blogger Mish made astute comments regarding this legislation:

> "Some aspects of this legislation have little to do with the free market, but then again many of the abuses it is attempting to correct have nothing to do with the free market either. For example, the Bankruptcy Reform Act of 2005 attempted to make people debt serfs forever, even after bankruptcy. That legislation fueled a massive increase in predatory credit card lending that would not have occurred in a free market where lenders would have been more concerned about the credit risks they were lending to. Legislation on top of legislation is where we are today, each attempting to undo previous wrongs. The best thing to do would be to scrap everything and start over, but realistically that is not going to happen."

Student Loans. In October, 2011, USA Today, reported that unsecured student loans will hit nearly $1 Trillion this year. Far exceeding outstanding unsecured credit card debt. Problem for the college grads is they can't dump that debt through bankruptcy. Yet, their parents can dump their credit card debt with bankruptcy. Plus, the kid graduates can't find jobs. Plenty of time on their hands to Occupy Everything. To protest the "unfairness" of our current society.

Rating Agencies. While it is one thing to create a new financial instrument (a new loan product, or new asset class, a new bond), someone (an alleged disinterested third party) has to say it's OK. Has to say that these are good bonds, this is good paper. Very very very good paper would receive an AAA rating. Risk on loans/bonds could be rated all the way down to CCC for junk bonds. If such a process did not exist, there would-be no confidence or interest in investing by Institutional Investors such as insurance companies, pension funds, foreign central banks, hedge funds, high wealth investors, etc.

Complicating the matter slightly as we'll see below, pension funds and insurance companies are constrained by law to invest only in AAA rated paper. If a bond loses its AAA rating, these entities must sell the securities. So, the bond ratings are critical and pressure is placed by Institutional Investors on the Rating Agencies to give (accurate) ratings. This house of cards is in grave danger, and directly resulting therefrom are the pensions of millions of Americans. Be warned. And, remember, your friendly state foreclosure judge, has his pension tied up in investments of the MBS. Down go the banks, down goes his pension. Conflict of Interest? Direct.

Riding to the rescue, rather rationalization of AAA ratings were the so-called credit Rating Agencies: Moody's, Fitch, and Standard and Poor's. Without digging deeply into complexity here, the simple point is that the Investment Banks are facing grave solvency issues. The major Investment Banks left standing are: Credit Suisse, Goldman Sachs, Morgan Stanley and Merrill Lynch. Bear Stearns and Lehman Brothers imploded due to its exposure to Mortgage Backed Securities, and other issues, and has been removed from the list.

Entities such as Citigroup and Merrill Lynch and others have been forced to take money from Saudi Arabia and China and other "Sovereign Central Bank Funds" to remain solvent. The point here is that the Investment Banks hired and paid the Rating Agencies to rate the Securities/bonds as AAA. Of course they did. Yet, the Investment Banks also included questionable Adjustable Rate Mortgage (ARM) loans in the batches of loans they packaged together to form a Security, which, arguably the Rating Agencies *overlooked* in terms of their actual risk potential. A batch of loans in a Security would be further sliced and diced into a number of *tranches* (smaller groups of loans), which contained a mixture of different types of loans, including very risky ARMs. Miraculously the Securities and various *tranches*, were rated AAA. Please!

These Institutional Investors were clearly asleep at the wheel in terms of doing their own due diligence regarding the credit worthiness of these Mortgage Backed Securities (MBS). In ensuing litigation, now on the rise, Institutional Investors are claiming they were misled by the reputations of the Investment Banks, and moreover the AAA ratings by the Rating Agencies. Ponzi Finance, a scheme, threatening to bring down the Financial System.

We'll close out this bit on Rating Agencies with an excellent article that appeared in the *New York Times*, by Roger Lowenstein who wrote,

> "In 1996, Thomas Friedman, the New York Times columnist, remarked on 'The News Hour With Jim Lehrer' that there were two superpowers in the world – the United States and Moody's bond-rating service – and it was sometimes unclear which was more powerful. Moody's was then a private company that rated corporate bonds, but it was, already, spreading its wings into the exotic business of rating securities backed by pools of residential mortgages."

> "Obscure and dry-seeming as it was, this business offered a certain magic. The magic consisted of turning risky mortgages into investments that would be suitable for investors who would know nothing about the underlying

loans. To get why this is impressive, you have to think about all that determines whether a mortgage is safe. Who owns the property? What is his or her income? Bundle hundreds of mortgages into a single security and the questions multiply; no investor could begin to answer them. But suppose the security had a rating. If it were rated triple-A by a firm like Moody's, then the investor could forget about the underlying mortgages. He wouldn't need to know what properties were in the pool, only that the pool was triple-A – it was just as safe, in theory, as other triple-A securities."

"Over the last decade, Moody's and its two principal competitors, Standard & Poor's and Fitch, played this game to perfection — putting what amounted to gold seals on mortgage securities that investors swept up with increasing élan. For the Rating Agencies, this business was extremely lucrative. Their profits surged, Moody's in particular: it went public, saw its stock increase six fold and its earnings grow by 900 percent."

"By providing the mortgage industry with an entree to Wall Street, the agencies also transformed what had been among the sleepiest corners of finance. No longer did Mortgage Banks have to wait 10 or 20 or 30 years to get their money back from homeowners. Now they sold their loans into securitized pools and – their capital thus replenished – wrote new loans at a much quicker pace."

"Mortgage volume surged; in 2006, it topped $2.5 trillion. Also, many more mortgages were issued to risky subprime borrowers. Almost all of those subprime loans ended up in securitized pools; indeed, the reason banks were willing to issue so many risky loans is that they could fob them off on Wall Street." [Emphasis added.]

We find *"fob them off on Wall Street"* to be disingenuous at best. Wall Street Investment Banks actually created this market They actively and aggressively solicited business from the local lenders. Whereas previously, Fannie Mae and Freddie Mac would buy "conforming" (until early 2008, under $417,000) loans from mortgage lenders. Now the Investment Banks would also buy and securitize them. From jumbo loans to subprime, it did not matter. Get the (inflated fraudulent) appraisal, make the loan, and we'll buy all you can create. *"They got up and danced."*

Law Professor Christopher L. Peterson nailed the point is in his white paper entitled "Predatory Structured Finance," published in September 7, 2006. He wrote,

"Some have pointed out that lenders no longer 'lend' in the sense that they themselves expect repayment. Rather they manufacture a commercial product – borrowers – that are measured, sold, and at times discarded by a consuming capital market. Many of today's mortgage lenders are assignment production companies that create income streams for the nation's capital markets."

That's really it. *Borrowers* are now considered a commercial product. Homeowners are "measured, sold, and *at times discarded* by a consuming capital market." Please. Read on, it only gets worse. Rest assured there is light at the end of this tunnel. That's the part where you take back the power.

Ponzi Scheme. From Wikipedia: "A Ponzi scheme usually offers abnormally high short-term returns in order to entice new investors. The high returns that a Ponzi scheme advertises (and pays) require an ever-increasing flow of money from investors in order to keep the scheme going."

> "The system is doomed to collapse because there are little or no underlying earnings from the money received by the promoter. However, the scheme is often interrupted by legal authorities before it collapses, because a Ponzi scheme is suspected and/or because the promoter is selling unregistered securities. As more investors become involved, the likelihood of the scheme coming to the attention of authorities increases.

> "The scheme is named after Charles Ponzi, who became notorious for using the technique after emigrating from Italy to the United States in 1903. Ponzi was not the first to invent such a scheme, but his operation took in so much money that it was the first to become known throughout the United States. Today's schemes are often considerably more sophisticated than Ponzi's, although the underlying formula is quite similar and the principle behind every Ponzi scheme is to exploit investor naïveté."

Here it is simply that housing prices were continually bid up over five years. Then, some homeowners began to default on their mortgages because they could not make higher reset payments, and were unable to refinance out of harm's way because real estate had crested, reached its natural high-end limit in value based on supply and demand. And moreover resultant from a Credit Crunch, which put a "freeze" on bank lending, put a "freeze" on free-flowing "leveraged-liquidity." This in turn forced prices down. As banks attempt to sell foreclosed properties, it continues downward pressure on all homes.

It's still going down in 2012 and will likely continue downward for three more years. Hello! Good Morning! Wake up you sleepy heads <g>. Lenders have kept a large percentage of the houses they took back in foreclosure off of the market. Those empty houses are called Real Estate Owned (REO). They haven't been placed on the market because the market is over saturated with inventory. That's where we are. It will only get worse. Period. Ponzi schemes always fail. They run out of Greater Fools to continue pumping in from the bottom, which feeds the profit at the top.

Credit Crunch. But, wait – there's more – much more. The creation and sales of MBS continued into early 2007. Then in the summer of 2007, they didn't sell anymore. It just stopped. The Credit Crunch was on, leading to the panic in late 2008, in which the Banksters, AIG, and other corps were bailed out. We were sold out.

This is what happens with all Credit Bubbles. They grow and grow, then they rapidly deflate or crash. Housing values take longer to come down than equity (stock) markets, and down is where housing values are going. While we read about a Credit Crunch, which started in August, 2007, the much deeper crash is waiting to fully enter from stage right any minute now. This is what the major players are struggling to prevent because − like a Tsunami − it would sweep away many of those players, sweep some of them into bankruptcy. They simply want the taxpayers to bail them out. They simply want the taxpayers to make their debt whole. They simply demand that homeowners stay in homes that are underwater, or, the massive debt will collapse on these financial players.

The Treasury Department and the Federal Reserve System are scrambling in the backfield, but the full-on blitz of the market is bearing down on them. Time for the Hail Mary Pass, normally reserved for the end of the first half, or the end of the game, which as many know is a desperation long pass in the face of the defense knowing it's coming, making it highly unlikely for success. A catch in the end zone. As from its name, a prayer is said, asking that a receiver can catch the ball and carry the day. What's bearing down on the banking system is the end of the Credit Bubble. The deeper ramifications stagger the imagination, and are frankly not being reported in the press, nor by politicians who are seeking your vote.

We wrote the previous two paragraphs in August 2008 for the first iteration of this current book. How right we were. We did not attempt to call the politics as in the November election which gave us a Young President who offered Hope and Change. Many on the left now (December 2012) feel betrayed by their new President. It is beyond appearance that Obama has been capture by Wall Street.

Oh Joe, say it ain't so. We delve into this in more detail in other sections of the book, but, what is clear is that the banks are being bailed out, the people are being set up as indentured servants in their own homes with a new, arguably fraudulent loan modification − with a teaser rate and all. Most important is that without a principal reduction − cramdown − million will remain underwater indefinitely − while the banks get a pass.

The Past is Prologue. In other words history does occasionally repeat itself, and those who fail to remember or study history are doomed to think that if their investment is in early, they are participating in an ever growing boom. Either out of greed or ignorance, they stay too long at the party, or, as Mania Victims do a greed based re-fi, using *their home* as an ATM, and end up in the bust. Bust is upon us. Time to remember history. More on that later.

The Flippers. Here, flippers are people who buy [real estate] with the intention of holding for a short time and making a quick profit through a sale. Some bought houses and condos under construction. Some bought and remodeled. They shared the same goal. In and out as quickly as possible. Many are still holding properties they believe they should continue to hold until the market comes back. Living in yesterday's dream world. Yesterday's fantasy.

So, they'll rent their property, and because it does not cash-flow (rental income is less than their monthly payment and cost of insurance and repairs), will dig deeper into their pocket every month to make the payment. Going deeper in the hole. Losing on their investment and not protecting their families. They are waiting for – hoping for – against all evidence, a quick-turn-around, a bottom to the market. Unfortunately for them, the quick-turn-around has been their basic plan all along. Get Rich Quick – the mantra, if not dream of the speculator. The quick-turn-around is long gone, particularly if they are underwater today.

Credit Impairment. Many of these *speculators* – remember *investors* got out of the market from the end of 2005 to the very latest in mid 2006 (market top) – are considering walking away, Strategically Defaulting – because lending institutions are making a short sale very difficult.

A short sale is for less than the loan is worth with the lender forgiving the difference between the sale price and the amount owed on the loan. Speculators are beginning to realize that as more people are walking away – they are – the credit impairment is fixable. More importantly, they are avoiding deeper losses by getting out now – walking away. However, as we point out, walking away – *under your terms* is only possible – if you Use Foreclosure Law!

Regarding credit impairment resulting from foreclosure, FICO spokesman Craig Watts said, "the impact of a foreclosure on an individual's score depends heavily on the payment history, length and number of credit trade lines in a consumer's file."

Evidence based on historical trends and previous events clearly shows that the down market will likely last longer than speculator's cash reserves can hold out. Adding fuel to the fire, lenders have frozen home equity loans and home equity lines of credit (also called "seconds" or "junior liens") (these are just beginning to default in very very large numbers). There goes the rainy day reserves. You may have been jealous of flippers from 2002 – 2006 when they were raking in the money, please consider extending your charity, some grace, and feel sorry for them now. Or not.

"Losses on home-equity loans are soaring, even at some lenders that avoided big blunders on subprime loans. When times were good, banks raked in billions of dollars in profit from home-equity loans, which allow borrowers to tap the accumulated value in their property with either a loan for a specific amount or a line of credit. As long as home prices were rising, lenders had little to worry about. But falling home values are leaving banks with little or nothing to collect on many home-equity loans in case of default. Some stretched borrowers are keeping up with their mortgage and credit cards – but not their home-equity loan." *Wall Street Journal,* March 14, 2008.

To fill out the picture we turn to Peter Navarro, UC Irvine business professor who wrote March 25, 2008 at SFGate.com:

"Over the next five years, 'flippers' entered the market in ever-increasing numbers, often buying multiple houses to turn. Meanwhile, renter family dupes desperate to get into the market often were gulled into signing zero-down, highly risky adjustable rate "subprime mortgages" doomed to foreclosure. Unscrupulous real estate appraisers "helped" by appraising any property as high as necessary for a borrower to qualify.

"As a vital part of the bubble's creative financing, Wall Street began to slice and dice home mortgages into complex "mortgage-backed securities." Huge financial institutions and hedge funds jumped in to speculate in highly leveraged schemes that allowed them to hold $20 or more of the securities per $1 of collateral. Like a deadly virus, these mortgage-backed securities spread out to infect portfolios all over the world.

"In July 2006, as home prices stretched far beyond underlying valuations, prices crested and began to fall. Finding themselves with too many properties and too little cash flow, many speculators pulled the plug by foreclosing.

"As home prices continued to fall, many homeowners with low- or zero-equity loans woke up to mortgages worth more than their houses and began to simply hand back the keys. Meanwhile, "exploding adjustable-rate mortgages" began to do just that – explode. As adjustable rates ratcheted up, many homeowners couldn't meet their monthly payments and joined the foreclosure ranks. This further depressed home prices and pushed foreclosures to record highs.

"The downstream consequences for world credit markets have been severe. As foreclosures have risen, the value of mortgage-backed securities has fallen precipitously. This has forced highly leveraged financial institutions like Bear Stearns and hedge funds like Carlyle Capital [hedge fund subsidiary of the Carlyle Group] to sell their securities to meet their leveraging commitments. This forced selling has, in turn, caused security prices to fall further and triggered more forced selling. The result of this fire sale has been a massive de-leveraging of world financial markets that has all but dried up credit. This credit crunch has come at the worst possible time – just as the economy has probably slid into its deepest recession since that of 1990-91. [Since this writing Bear Stearns and Carlyle Capital are gone – no longer exist.]

The Resolution Trust Corporation. The Resolution Trust Corporation (RTC), operating from 1989-95, was a U.S. government-owned and operated asset management company formed to liquidate real estate-related assets, including mortgage loans that had been owned by various Savings and Loan entities (S&Ls) that had become insolvent and had shut down operations. More than 740 S&L lending institutions fell in what has been called "… the largest and costliest venture in public misfeasance, larceny and malfeasance of all time." It has been estimated that the cost of the crisis totaled around $160 Billion, paid for by U.S. taxpayer. Of course that number is mere chump change for what the American Taxpayer is going to be expected to bailout this time.

Reconstruction Finance Corporation. The RFC was not the first government agency to come to the aid of banks and other players in the economy. Here once again we'll rely on Wikipedia for a brief explanation.

"The Reconstruction Finance Corporation (RFC), was an independent agency of the United States government chartered during the administration of Herbert Hoover in 1932. It was modeled after the War Finance Corporation of World War I. The agency gave $2 billion in aid to state and local governments and made loans to banks, railroads, farm mortgage associations, and other businesses. The loans were nearly all repaid. It was continued by the New Deal and played a major role in handling the Great Depression in the United States and setting up the relief programs that were taken over by the New Deal in 1933. (Sprinkel, 1952)

"The RFC was bogged down in bureaucracy and failed to disperse many of its funds. It failed to reverse the growth of mass unemployment before 1933. Butkiewicz (1995) shows that the RFC initially succeeded in reducing bank failures, but the publication of the names of the recipients of loans beginning in August 1932 (at the demand of Congress) significantly reduced the effectiveness of its loans to banks because it appeared that political considerations had motivated certain loans. Partisan politics thwarted the RFC's efforts, though in 1932 monetary conditions improved because the RFC slowed the decline in the money supply.

"Starting 1933 Franklin Delano Roosevelt kept the agency, increased the funding, streamlined the bureaucracy, and used it to help restore business prosperity, especially in banking and railroads. He appointed Texas banker Jesse Jones as head, and Jones turned RFC into an empire with loans made in every state. (Olson 1988)

"The RFC also had a division that gave the states loans for emergency relief needs. In a case study of Mississippi, Vogt (1985) examined two areas of RFC funding: aid to banking, which helped many Mississippi banks survive the economic crisis, and work relief, which Roosevelt used to pump money into the state's relief program by extending loans to businesses and local government projects. Although charges of political influence and racial discrimination were levied against RFC activities, the agency made positive contributions and established a federal agency in local communities which provided a reservoir of experienced personnel to implement expanding New Deal programs."

We've included this brief snippet on the RFC to add historical perspective. We think that we'll be seeing a new version of RTC/RFC coming in 2012. While this will be lauded by many – the key – our point throughout *Use Foreclosure Law* is that government entities should not be formed to bail out Wall Street Investment Banks at the expense of taxpayers – American Citizens.

Bail Outs. Some have argued that because a moral hazard was created, saving many financial institutions, it encouraged today's lenders and the Securitizers to make high-risk loans enabling the current crisis because they knew they would be bailed out by the taxpayers (the bailout belief *is* the moral hazard). This does make sense, because both the Fed and Treasury are consciously placing the

American taxpayer in harm's way right now, through their various and recent Wall Street bailout operations.

Moral Hazard. In economics this means the lack of any incentive to guard against risk when you are *protected against the risk.* In the matter at hand, there was little incentive by loan originators or Securitizers to take steps to see to the creditworthiness of borrowers, if the lenders reasonably believed, based on the evidence of previous practice, that the government will bailout bad, or defaulting debts, through legislation or other practices that force taxpayers to pick up the bill.

Such bailouts require complicity by both the financial institutions at risk and elected representatives. In particular the Lincoln Savings and Loan debacle led to the highly publicized "Keating Five" political scandal. Five U.S. Senators were implicated in this influence-peddling scheme. They called it the Keating Five because Charles Keating, who ran Lincoln Savings and Loan contributed over $300,000 to five U.S. Senators: Alan Cranston, Don Riegle, and Dennis DeConcini who lost office immediately; and John Glenn and John McCain, who clearly survived politically. Yet, these two were rebuked by the Senate Ethics Committee because they executed "poor judgment" due to inappropriate intervention with Federal Banking Regulators. A guy's gotta do what a guy's gotta do.

Ultimately, the RTC was formed in 1989, to avoid a devastating shock to the U.S. banking system because the Savings & Loans had extended themselves too far, because federal regulation had gone by the wayside. The method enabled the Government (through the taxpayers) to "secretly" subsidize the banking system. This method was merely a smoke and mirrors operation so the public would not understand what was actually happening.

Congress allocated nearly half a trillion dollars for this bailout, run through the RTC. Some have argued that the S&L debacle was the first real time test of what we have called the mortgage carry trade. Indeed the system could not handle the load of non-performing, defaulting property loans.

Now, here we go again. The banks had learned their lesson from the S&L debacle. They correctly believed the government would bail them out, as was done before. The government would step in to save them. So they've done it again with residential mortgages. The process was initially funded with carry trade money, Greenspan's liquidity and no regulatory oversight where he had the authority, and the game was on.

Real Economic Dislocation. The problem today is much worse, much more pervasive. The exposure is exponentially higher, and worse yet, it's worldwide in scope. It is dooming global capital markets that had rarely been involved in mortgages in the past. Why, for instance, did certain regional banks in Germany purchase U.S. Investment Bank issued MBS based on American homes, particularly MBS that contained sub-prime loans? They seemed to be great high interest paying, yet low-risk fixed investments. Recently some German banks have been forced to close their doors due to large losses in this arena.

The huge and oncoming litigation problem for America's very largest depository banks (money center banks), Investment Banks, Rating Agencies, Mortgage Banks, Mortgage Brokers and appraisers is that these insiders knew the system was being gamed. Sophisticated banking insiders knew that first time buyers were being sold overpriced homes. There was no way these borrowers could continue making payments once the ARMs reset. Further adding to the risk was that many loans called for no down payment, no provable income or job, or, additional asset based collateral. Many financially unsophisticated first-time buyers actually believed that their initial "teaser rate" payment would not increase. Lack of full disclosure from unscrupulous Mortgage Brokers? This is playing out in the courts.

Today many borrowers have little incentive to keep paying, because with no down payment they have "no skin in the game." Their only damage would be a credit mark which they could fix in a couple of years by paying their bills on time and repairing their credit. The potential for "reputation" damage, the so-called, stigma has dissipated as more and more people understand what actually happened. With more first time buyers entering the market, current home owners had the opportunity to move up, buy a nicer home. They called it home "appreciation," and housing prices *always* went up. Until they didn't.

Inducement to Fraud. Anecdotal evidence (some of which is occasionally presented in the conventional press), has shown that local Mortgage Brokers working with local buyers, fudged the paperwork by stating on no-doc loan applications that the prospective borrower had more income than they actually did. Some borrowers likely did say, *"Well, Ok. If you say so – you're the professional I'm trusting."* In many – if not the majority of these instances – these borrowers were obviously never informed that the Mortgage Brokers bumped the income numbers up to qualify for the loan after the fact. Verification? That verification is below in the chapter *Smoking Guns.* Be sure to note JP Morgan's "Zippy" practice. You'll see.

These loan applications were then brought to conventional bank lenders, and, particularly Mortgage Banks such as Countrywide that looked the other way. They did not demand pay slips or tax statements, and went ahead and funded the loans.

Their *looking away* actually gives you the ethical and legal right to Use Foreclosure Law, and discover the Predatory Lending and Securities Law violations and issues in your loan. Your contract may be voidable, if not subject to rescission. We explain what rescission can mean for you in Chapter 9: *Predatory Lending.* However, your best case process is to obtain a Forensic Loan Audit and a Securitization Audit. retain an attorney to utilize legal leverage and cramdown the principal amount on your loan to today's market value minus 10% for further home price drops.

Read this book, you are, and ALL of the posts on our blog – educate yourself. If you do so, and tell us you have by filling out a form on the blog (keep checking back it will be on the top right hand side under the book cover). We'll be in touch and offer you "tools" to deal with your situation,

The lenders went further to make the deals happen. According to investigations by then New York State Attorney General (now Governor), Andrew Cuomo, lenders intimidated appraisers to hit the high numbers. When the loans closed (funded and Escrow closed), everyone in the chain, including the Investment Banks who purchased these loans, securitized and sold them, took significant fees off the top. And they want a bailout? For them? Paid by the U.S. taxpayer. Is it time to just say: No? You say no – by Using Foreclosure Law to Keep Your Home.

Since then Secretary of the Treasury, Henry Paulson didn't go to Treasury until 2006 it's not hard to imagine that as Chairman of Goldman Sachs, the most successful Investment Bank in this game, he had a direct hand in the creation of this wonderful business. Then he moved to Treasury to keep a lid on things and direct taxpayer money to his friends like AIG, which took TARP money and immediately handed $12.5 Billion (with a "B") right back to Goldman Sachs. Yet, the press and politicos all they way up to the Young President, screamed bloody murder in the press about $100 Million (with a "M") for AIG bonuses. Chump change relative to the TARP $150 Billion to AIG, which they spread out to favored banks (like Goldman Sachs) here and in Europe.

Don't ever doubt Wall Street's hegemony (power) over our government and politicians. He who pays the piper (campaign contributions), calls the tune. They will stop at nothing in order to protect the banking industry, and frankly, keep many of them from facing prison. Henry Paulson, former head of Goldman Sachs, meaning the former *virtual titular head* of Wall Street is unlikely to be indicted himself.

The former head of Goldman Sachs should not have to give back multi-millions of salary, stock option profits and bonus dollars in restitution; and face criminal indictment (that would only be if in fact his firm was selling ((under legal tenets and requirements of good faith and fair dealing)) MBS to investor's, and at the *same time,* were making private investment bets that the value of those same MBS would go down in value) (that is exactly what they did) and possibly face prison. Wouldn't you agree? No? You say No? We're shocked!

Remember that many first time buyers were assured (not in writing) by the expert, the professional, the one they trusted – their Mortgage Broker, and oftern their real estate agent – that they would be able to refinance their loans to fixed status before the ARMs reset to higher monthly payments, because the home would continue to appreciate in value. *("Real estate always goes up!"* Sound familiar?) Appreciation occurred until it stopped in mid 2006. Different markets had their own peaks. This is a grave systemic problem that has had widespread implications. We are facing them now. Yet, rise up: Tea Party and Occupy Movement. As the Who sang: ♪"The kids *are* alright." ♫

Continuing – Crash. Anyone who purchased a home, or did a cash out refinance, from say, 2004 forward, that stays in that home or investment property is likely underwater right now. Worse, they've become an indentured servant to arguably fraudulent perpetrators up the food chain. Why would anyone do this – stay in the house paying a mortgage balance higher than the value of the home? Reduced to being a tenant in your own home. Reduced to praying – hoping – dreaming for a nominal valuation of your home value to your loan value that will never come – unless hyperinflation destroys our way of life. Waiting for Godot. Who never arrives. Why do people do it?

Fear. That's the only reason we can think of. Frankly, it's largely the fear of the unknown. We remind you that *Use Foreclosure Law* was written to give you the facts and point towards a course of action. Enable you to possibly throw off an untenable debt burden by utilizing legal leverage. By taking action to protect your family you instantly – in taking action – move away from fear. Of course, the precursor is educating yourself.

Beyond fear of the unknown, what else could cause people to stay – underwater? The fear of Stigma? The fear that walking away from your home would be devastating to your pride and reputation. Nonsense. Many families will take the business decision to Use Foreclosure Law. When you understand all of the facts, and particularly when you discover the amount of Predatory Lending and Securities Law violation issues involved in your loan, you will have no reason to please *them*. Now you have the option to Use Foreclosure Law to Keep Your Home.

More Bailouts. While various Federal Bailout Plans were presented, initially by Mr. Paulson and his right hand man, Dr. Ben Bernanke (who do you think really runs the show?), now the charade continues with Tim-Boy "Tax Dodging" Geithner to "fix" the problem. Yes. But, fix it for Financial Elite, not for the American People.

What we're seeing is merely a tightening of the circled wagons. If these new (always new) "Plans" are successful for the Banking Cartel, the result will be to leave captured homeowners in a home that has less value then is owed. Underwater.

The most astute experts in tracking historical trends believe that values will continue to go down, that a bottom won't be reached until 2015. (Japan's housing did not return to 1990 values (the height of their real estate bubble) until 2007, seventeen years later.)

We repeat: an academic study has indicated that a large number of retiring Boomers will begin relocation and down-sizing in 2011-12, flooding the market with even more homes for sale. Causing values to remain down for a longer period of time due to increasing inventory. Downward pressure to market value.

Notwithstanding that factor, if the bottom of the market actually appears on the horizon in 2015, *that will merely be the bottom.* It will likely require at least another five years for values to return to today's values. That is possibly ten years from now. Stuck underwater for ten years? Your decision, of course. And, also, remember we are in for a severe increase in Inflation over the next three years due to the Fed pumping more money, creating more fiat money to save the banks that own the Fed.

One could argue that American wages and salaries will go up as Inflation takes hold. One could argue – not by much – because so many are unemployed now and more to come. Those who have salary increases will be paying off their mortgage at it's face value with dollars that have less value overall, less purchasing power, but, get a break because the home loan is locked. Of course this only works for those with a fixed rate loan.

The actual timeframe for housing prices to recover to values prior to the credit crunch is unknowable. However, it is certain that will be a long-time in the future. A June 27, 2008 article in the UK's *Telegraph*, "House prices won't recover until 2015", stated, "'Families must wait until 2015 for the property market to start booming again,' according to Stephen Nickell, who heads up the unit which advises the Prime Minister on housing planning. 'The housing market – in terms of the price of houses – will not look much the same as it did before the credit crunch until after six or seven years.'" That was written in 2008, very brave – even outrageous at the time. Yet, the comment holds.

Price Discovery. We'd like to briefly explain why Structured Finance is so frightened of Price Discovery.

Price Discovery is a term for when home values return to their price when the run up started. The economic term is Reversion to the Mean which we'll explain in more detail later in the book. Simply put, if you live in a home in middle America that you paid $500,000 for in mid-2006. Depending on where you live, that home may go back down to a value of $250,000. You might wait eight – ten years or more underwater for it to come back to the original $500,000. A lot of things can happen in eight or ten years. But, still you'll be stuck in the home.

If you paid $300,000 nine years ago, and it inflated to $500,000 you're probably OK. Unless, of course you did a cash out refinance – had a high old time – and now owe $450,000 for a home that may, once again, be worth $300,000 because its price was discovered, it *reverted to the mean.*

Reversion to the Mean refers to a return to the prevailing price level *before* a strong up-tick appreciation took place. In this case we argue for a 2001-02 starting point when Alan Greenspan began pumping liquidity into the markets and consciously created the Housing Bubble to pull us out of the recently crashed dot.com Bubble, which had put us into recession by 2001-02. Naturally this depends on numbers you trust for evaluation of recession. Don't even think of trusting U.S. Government numbers. And, yes, things are that bad.

If you are in the market in Arizona, California, Florida, Nevada and some other states, it will likely be worse as home values in many areas in those states doubled, then tripled since 1997.

The reason that the TBTF banks (loan originators) and Wall Street Investment Banks (MBS Securitizers) will do anything to avoid Price Discovery is that it takes down the value of the collateral (the house) underlying the Mortgage Backed Securities that they sold to Institutional Investors. Today, those Institutional Investors are crying foul and bringing law suits to force the Securitizers to take the loans back at face value. This is good for the goose, good for the gander stuff, because the Investment Banks have demanded that Mortgage Banks, loan originators, buy back loans they sold to the Investment Banks, as the sales contracts declared. Well some lenders did (buy them back) until they couldn't do it anymore.

To date, since December, 2006, approximately "… 342 major U.S. lending operations have imploded," – gone bankrupt because they did not have the funds to buy back the defaulting loans from the Investment Bank Securitizers. See, Mortgage Lender Implode.com.

Where the Money Came From. Where did the Mortgage Bank loan originators get the money in the first place to make so many loans? To simplify, it was a process using issuance of a "warehouse credit line." The Investment Banks provided money (short term carry trade money, see, you know this stuff) to Mortgage Bank originators (such as Countywide and Washington Mutual and hundreds of smaller entities) to fund the loans, then bought the loans from the originators, allowing the originators to pay off the wholesale lending from the Investment Banks. All parties pocketed large fees. And, where did the risk go on these loans, many of which were very risky? Directly to the Institutional Investors, who wanted to believe that these were sound high interest (profitable for them) fixed-rate Securities.

Large fees were paid to unscrupulous Mortgage Brokers, who induced fraud, in making loans to homeowners who really couldn't afford the house in the first place. Worse, many Mortgage Brokers put individuals into higher priced loans than they actually qualified for. This was done for a simple reason. The Mortgage Broker would receive a higher fee if the interest rate on the loan was higher.

The shoe is on the other foot, and the Institutional Investors want their money back and the Investment Banks don't have the inclination or capital to buy them back. They are in fact (secretly?) insolvent, and yet, they can keep the ball in the air a bit longer if they avoid Price Discovery and do not have to take the defaulting paper back (the Securities they created) on their own books. Then, the clear fact of their insolvency would be on their books, and Chinese and Middle East government Sovereign Wealth Funds would not loan them more money as they were doing as late as spring 2008.

What you rarely ever read about is what will happen if the Institutional Investors are able to force the IB Securitizers to buy back loans at face value. It would knock down many Investment Banks, and create havoc, destroy international banking as we know it. Therefore, it's not likely to happen. The game is fixed. We ask, why would an underwater homeowner want to stay in a dead-end game? That doesn't sound like, feel like or look like a prudent business decision. Oh, that's right, many good folks are concerned about what other people will think of them. They wouldn't want the stigma associated with a voluntary foreclosure?

Or, will they realize they can protect their family by Using Foreclosure Law to Keep Their Home, or, walk away under *their* terms by using legal leverage to remove themselves from a fixed − from a fraud-based game?

Everyone in the process holding alleged investment grade paper that is now being defaulted on, particularly Institutional Investors, would like to get out. Ironically, homeowners in-residence are in the cat bird's seat, in the enviable position of being able to Use Foreclosure Law! Getting on with their lives and building a new future.

What if everyone in the process (except most homebuyers) had understood enough of what was going on to have been aware that inducement to fraud − Predatory Lending and Securitization Fraud − was taking place? What would that mean?

If you were a potential homebuyer, and had understood what we've explained above *before* you bought in, would that have affected your decision to buy a home from 2004 to the present time? If so, then we hope you conclude that it's logical to Use Foreclosure Law − now! You need to do that before being underwater in what was/is an overpriced home begins to have an extremely negative effect on the *quality of your life*. On your ability to sleep at night. On relationships in the home − let alone on your finances. You might conclude that it really is time to protect your family. People who hear and understand this advice are going ahead and Using Foreclosure Law to Keep Their Homes.

You can choose to stop playing a game, withdraw the bet you placed in good faith, particularly, when your, ahem, adversary possessed more information than you did and acted fraudulently to deceive you. It's reminiscent of two concepts.

One. The action of the State is based on the will of the people through a Republic, operating as a representative electoral Democracy, utilizing Regulatory Powers to keep the game of life and commerce balanced and fair. In this construct, the money supply is *controlled by the government,* which issues and loans money, and does *not* charge interest for doing so. There would be no privately owned (by the banks) Federal Reserve System under such process.

Two. The action of the State is based on the power of Enterprise ("Economic Royalists" as FDR called them) to co-opt the State in its own self-interest. Others have called such process Corporate Fascism, or Corporatism, as envisioned and enacted by the Washington Consensus (beginning in the late 1970's in South America, subsequently taken up by both Margaret Thatcher and Ronald Reagan), by Milton Friedman's University of Chicago, School of Economics, some of whose brightest graduates are called Neo-Cons. They brought us a continuing war in Afghanistan; a war, then, occupation in Iraq (just ended − well sort of). The Milton Friedman "Chicago School of Economics" gang and their minions have done much more. However, that is a different book, written recently by the brilliant Naomi Klein, The Shock Doctrine.

Speaking of Iraq, Former Presidential candidate and "friend to all veterans," John McCain voted in May against a modern G.I. Bill that would allow Iraq and Afghanistan vets to automatically receive paid scholarships to obtain a college education after their service. Even worse for veterans and their families is that they are losing their homes in record numbers due to foreclosure. Reporting in *Bloomberg*, Kathleen Howley wrote:

> "In the midst of the worst surge in mortgage defaults in seven decades, foreclosures in U.S. towns where soldiers live are increasing at a pace almost four times the national average, according to data compiled by research firm RealtyTrac Inc. in Irvine, California. As military families signed up for the initial lower rates and easier terms of subprime mortgages, the number of people taking out Veterans Administration loans fell to the lowest in at least 12 years.

> "'We've never faced a situation like this, not in the Vietnam War, World War II, or the Korean War, where so many military are in danger of losing their homes,' said Paul Sullivan, executive director of Veterans for Common Sense, a Washington-based advocacy group started in 2002 by Iraq and Afghanistan War veterans. 'No one asked them for their credit score when we asked them to fight for us.'"

Whether you agree or disagree with this barely disguised stance on the "war," the "permanent war on terror," to treat our young men and woman − who put their lives on the line, who die for the flag − like this is beyond travesty. They treat American youth like feudal slaves and send them into combat while denying them an education after their service. Perhaps worse, they do not protect the homes of their families when the troops are not home to defend their families themselves. Why?

Senator McCain continues to arguably be called a "Traitor" against our Constitution. We repeat our words from above: "New law enables the President or the military to declare any American a "suspected" terrorist and be detained indefinitely without right to counsel, due process, or enabled to bring a Writ of Habeas Corpus, long a pillar of our Constitution. A prelude to Martial Law? Congress debated this issue for one hour, it took Jon Stewart to put the matter forward strongly."

On March 18, 2003, two days before her son George began the war in Iraq, Barbara Bush, the President's mother appeared on Good Morning America and asked Diane Sawyer,

"Why should we hear about body bags and death and how many? . . . Oh, I mean, it's not relevant. So why should I waste my beautiful mind on something like that."

It gets worse, much worse. At one point after the Vietnam War, Henry Kissinger was quoted in the book, *Final Days* by Woodward and Bernstein, saying,

"Military men are just dumb, stupid animals to be used as pawns in foreign policy...."

Initially we weren't sure these were "actual quotes," we couldn't believe they would have said these things, let alone believe them. Please, as we did, we urge you to Goggle both those quotes. They said them.

Clearly then many of the elite have little regard for the lower classes – for those who actually give their lives – for those who act as armed indentured servants overseas to maintain power for those elites. This is not the America conceived and fought for by our Founding Fathers. It's time we *Restore America.*

Madness Exemplified. Astonishing is the widely reported fact (December 2011) that *more* American military men have *committed suicide* during or after serving in Afghanistan or Iraq than died in combat in those two Theaters of War. How can this be? What did they learn that caused them to take their own lives in such astonishing numbers? What deep and dark secrets need to be pried open? We have no definitive answers. Could it be that the realization that they killed and murdered for a Despotic Empire – have proved too much for them to live with themselves.

Some have suggested that it is the amount of expended Depleted Uranium found on U.S. "modern" war battlefields that they were exposed to that has caused such widespread aberrant – deadly – behavior. We mention it, but, can not take this any further.

Could some have them taken their live because while they were abroad fighting a war to "protect the American People from Terrorism," their homes were illegally foreclosed on, in violation of the War Services Act?

Animal spirits. That is the name that noted Fabian School British Economist John Maynard Keynes gave to a concept that he considered to be one of the essential ingredients of economic prosperity: *confidence.* Yet, he also later hedged his bet, indicating that he was being ironic and claimed that animal spirits are a *kind* of confidence. Moreover, *naive optimism.*

He allegedly meant this in the sense of the word denial. People would ignore negative elements, focusing on the positive, giving them "confidence" to soldier on – albeit naively. Where these animal spirits come from is something of a mystery. Attempts by politicians and others to talk up confidence by making optimistic noises about economic prospects have rarely done much good in face of the facts, which they might ignore. Yet, one can find Larry Kudlow and Jim Kramer, and other sycophants, doing it consistently on CNBC. Got to keep that "confidence" going in spite of the actual fundamentals in the economy.

Animal Spirits are encouraged to run wild by and for the financial elite until they collapse on their own greed, and then, the taxpayers, the people, are allowed to bail them out through excess taxation. Capitalism (for Wall Street) when times are good, and Socialism (for Wall Street), when they've broken the bank. Bailout events and actions by the Fed since the beginning of March 2008, indicate how dire, how perilous our current conditions really are. That's what many say.

But, is it really true. Is it more likely that the concept of *Too Big Too Fail* is simply another scare tactic? That is what we strongly believe. They control us. They encourage all of us to live in a Debt Society, which they label an "Ownership Society" to con the masses. They take profits off the top. When they've taken too much, blown the debt they and we carry out of proportion and it begins to fall on them due to loan defaults, they Cry: Help! *"You must save us we're Too Big To Fail, and it will all fall down, if you take us into Receivership – Nationalization".* Nonsense. We can pick up the pieces quite professionally. It's been done before and the sun still rose. We brushed off, and went back to work.

The sun will rise. Those that did not run their businesses properly, who took on too much risk should not only be allowed to fail, but, those businesses should be taken over by the government. The assets sold off at real market value to Vulture Funds; and, the Big One, all shareholder and bond holder claims extinguished in bankruptcy. What these bank bailouts are designed to do, beyond saving the banks, is to protect the bondholders. To heck with them. They invested in a business model that history tells us will fail – is failing. They didn't get out in time. The money was too fat. *"And, really, the government will come to the rescue. We've bought and paid for the politicians, they'll back our play, they'll save us – or we'll scare the hell out of Congress like we did in late 2008."* Again, *moral hazard.* See, you're beginning to get this stuff.

Current Condition. Under our current condition the money supply is controlled by a Central Bank, which loans the government money, and the taxpayer (in the U.S.) pays the interest to the Central Bank through the government, which collects the taxes. The interest paid to the Central Bank is profit for the hard work of saying, "Roll the Presses." Print the free money, the fiat money, because we can. If there is any doubt to the authority of this point, please see the top of your currency, where it clearly states, "Federal Reserve Note."

By law, the Federal Reserve System has two primary mandates written into their Charter.

First is to maintain the value of money through "stable prices." They fail this by the very definition of their actual practice. They issue more and more (debt) money, which by definition creates Inflation, which itself is a tax on all unsuspecting taxpayers, by increasing the costs of good and services.

Second is to ensure maximum employment. The actual words from the Feb web, http://www.federalreserve.gov/pf/pdf/pf_1.pdf are:

- "Conducting the nation's monetary policy by influencing the <u>monetary and credit conditions in the economy in pursuit of</u> **maximum employment, stable prices,** and moderate long-term interest rates. [Emphasis added.]

- "Supervising and regulating banking institutions to ensure the safety and soundness of the nation's banking and financial system and to protect the credit rights of consumers.

- "Maintaining the stability of the financial system and containing systemic risk that may arise in financial markets.

- "Providing financial services to depository institutions, the U.S. government, and foreign official institutions, including playing a major role operating the nation's payments system."

They are not even close in most areas and it is easily argued that they have completely abandoned *"… the pursuit of maximum employment."* They may argue that <u>maximum</u> (their interpretation of that) is good enough, and <u>full</u> employment can take the hind most along with the Middle class. The proof of our inflammatory rhetoric is in the putting. They've *put* the middle class out of work. These days and nights – at the Fed – they are working overtime, working feverishly to protect a banking system that they choose not to regulate, that they choose to allow to run wild and debase the value of our currency, while not giving a thought to maximum employment. We've all heard of outsourcing. Most of us have stories of family and friends who have been involuntarily down-sized as the middle class has been hollowed out. Over 50 mllion families are now on food stamps.

This examples put our argument into prospective. By taking control, they have created a Finance Capitalism. What grew this country over centuries was Industrial Capitalism:

- where things are manufactured in the U.S.;

- where jobs are created in the U.S.;

- where all Americans stand with equal rights; universal health care: a fair distribution of wealth; and strength – negotiated through labor unions, and, a legitimate safety net to protect the poor and unfortunate.

- where real National Wealth is created.

This is the only way it is ever created.

Industrial Capitalism. We must return to Industrial Capitalism or our Middle Class will join the poor of our nation, relegated to a Third World Life. This would suit the Banking Cartel; to have the 99% as debt slaves, with few rights and all under debt-tenant obligation. We don't exaggerate by much!!! As it stands in January 2012, the Cartel is well down this path.

If your elected representative doesn't recognize that in 2012, vote them out. Replace them with someone who understands and promises to carry that message, and act on it in Washington D.C. Believe it, good Democrats can learn from former Presidential Candidate, Republican/Libertarian Representative Ron Paul of the great state of Texas. We don't go the way of all of his stringent Libertarian constructs, but, he understands money, and we need leaders who understand money and are not beholden to the Banking Cartel. We hope this assuages the wraith of fierce individualist Libertarians that sometimes forget that taxes keep our highways safe; and that we need teaching, policing and firefighting; and a legal system that stands for the protection of all Americans. We have a number of postings on our blog that go to these issues. Many by Dr. Paul.

We might go on here and list other values to be obtained from the virtue of *The Commons,* things we all pay for through taxes, which benefit the high, middle and low. But, we won't. You get it. We hope so.

We proudly admit to *extremist inflammatory rhetoric* in the pursuit of presenting fact based truths. And, ultimately we do admire Barry Goldwater. You must be of a certain age to get the joke. OK, we'll tell you. In his acceptance speech as Republican candidate for President in 1963, Barry Goldwater said,

> *"I would remind you that <u>extremism in the defense of liberty is no vice!</u> And let me remind you that <u>moderation in the pursuit of justice is no virtue.</u>"* [Emphasis added.]

Where is Barry Goldwater now that we need him? Senator Goldwater went to his greater reward. Yet, before he left us, he privately counseled President Richard Nixon to resign. Nixon waited two days and resigned. It wasn't smart to be on the wrong side of Barry Goldwater. He was a man of truth and real independence, who stood for principles that the Neo-Cons can't imagine even exist in their thirst for power. Neo-Cons? Those such as Bush Jr., Cheney, Rice, Rumsfeld; Wolfowitz, *ad nauseum,* who brought us War and more of it.

"Deficits don't matter?" That is what Vice President Cheney claimed that President Reagan "proved." What do you think? Do deficits − debts − your debts − matter?

While certainly not talked about in the media, their work is ultimately designed to keep the yoke tight on your neck. Throw it away. You'll feel much better when you're free. If *"...freedom's having nothing left to lose,"* <u>real freedom</u> is extracting your self from fraudulent and untenable debt, particularly when those who convinced you to play in *their* game had ulterior motives, possessed more information. So much more that in their arrogance they are crashing the Global Economy.

We call for an honest, therefore necessarily regulated (to keep *animal spirits* at bay) Industrial Capitalism. We are Capitalist. Proud to say it. The Fed has placed itself in a box and can only print their way out of it to protect their owners, the Banksters. Homeowners lose. For now, a Middle Way is impossible. Protect yourself.

To buttress our general argument, throughout we'll give you numbers from reputable reporters. In March, 2008, the Wall Street Journal reported: "This couldn't come at a worse time for U.S. homeowners. American household debt has more than doubled in a decade to *$13.8 trillion* at the end of 2007 from *$6.4 trillion* in 1999, the vast majority of it in mortgages and home equity lines, according to Fed data. But the value of U.S. householders' biggest asset – their homes – is now falling." Homeowner wealth has declined some $6 trillion since September, 2006. .

———————————

In order to show you, tell you and have you get, moreover, really feel the depth of this dire situation, the immediately following chapters will set the economic historical stage a bit deeper than we've done above. Below we've stripped out most of the economist jargon, written plain language. We believe it is critical that you really understand where we stand today against a historical background. This can enable you to have your feet firmly on the ground enabling you to act within the context of "knowing what you're doing." And we believe, more importantly, "doing what you're knowing."

Housing Numbers Update. But before we go there, we invite you to take a close look at the state of the housing market in a snapshot from May, 2008 as provided by the excellent economic analyst, Stephanie Pomboy of Macro-Mavens, via reportage from the wondrous and inevitable Alan Abelson of *Barron's*. While commentary at the time by former Secretary of the Treasury Henry Paulson indicated that the credit crunch was nearly over, we bring Ms. Pomboy's sobering numbers and thoughts. According to Abelson,

"Ms. Pomboy has indicated that 'just as in March 2001 when the NASDAQ was off 72% from its top, so the home builders today are down eerily the same percentage from their all-time high.' What mitigates largely against the projection that the worst is over, is in her view, is that the source of the problem – home-price deflation – is not only continuing but intensifying. Pomboy stated that, 'According to the latest Case-Shiller Index, home prices are now deflating at a 32% annual rate, versus 8% six months ago. And the deflation is sure to intensify as the 4.6 million new and existing homes still sitting on the market find a clearing price.'"

"Pomboy states, 'Think of it...that 4.6 million inventory is nearly double the 2.6 million average inventory in the 20 years leading up to the bubble. More disturbing still, a record 2.27 million of those homes are sitting empty!' ... Further she points out that the 'those astonishing numbers do not include the homes 'stuck in purgatory at banks, which are now collecting keys faster than they can list the properties.' She reports that The Federal Deposit Insurance Corp., estimates that 'other Real Estate Owned (REO)' property by banks is up more than double the year-ago total."

"It is quite obvious that while the largest assets on household, commercial and Investment Bank balance sheets continue to deflate in value, we are nowhere near the end of the Credit Crunch, which in itself prohibits many current potential home buyers from stepping back into the market."

Bottom line, the worst has not arrived by any means.

Remember they are in excess of 6 million vacant repossessed homes. The market cannot clear until prices come down, and, we return to *historical actual gross housing debt to actual gross income ratios.*

Even More Recent Numbers. In a special mid-month HCM Market Letter update by the prescient Michael E. Lewitt, we find:

Housing – From Bad to Worse to Worse than Worse

"The housing numbers continue to worsen in ways that are truly frightening. In May, bank repossessions more than doubled and foreclosure filings rose 48 percent from a year earlier, according to RealtyTrac Inc. May was the 29th consecutive month of year-over-year increases in these figures. Nevada, California and Arizona posted the highest repo and foreclosure rates, and New Jersey entered the list of the top ten states experiencing difficulties, suggesting that the virus is spreading. Lenders repossessed 73,794 houses in May, far more than twice the 28,548 homes they took over a year earlier. All of the top ten cities on RealtyTrac's list are located in Florida and California with the exception of Las Vegas. The sad truth is that there is pain enough to go around geographically and otherwise.

"The still-tumbling housing sector is one reason why *HCM* agrees with Christopher Wood that 'there is zero possibility that the Federal Reserve is going to raise interest rates this year unless there is a complete collapse in the US dollar.' The dollar appears to have hit at least a temporary bottom against the Euro, removing the biggest reason for an interest rate hike. In the meantime, the 10-year Treasury yield that exercises the greatest influence on mortgage rates has pierced the 4.0 percent level for the first time in a while, another body blow to the housing market. The financial sector is weakening again on the back of just horrific housing numbers, suggesting that banks and other financial institutions are not only continuing to suffer from mortgage-backed securities losses but are now encountering losses on underlying mortgage loans."

"Mr. Wood is not the first to warn of impending doom in home equity loans. He is particularly concerned about so-called 'piggyback loans,' which were made when buyers purchased their homes to allow them to effectively obtain 100 percent (or greater) financing. Since only 5 percent of home equity loans have been securitized, these losses will hit bank balance sheets directly rather than through their holdings in mortgage-backed securities. This market exceeds $1 trillion in size, so there is ample opportunity for major losses. Perhaps of most concern is recent Federal Reserve data showing that homeowners' equity as a percentage of house values declined to a 60-year low of 46 percent at the end of the first quarter of 2008. In view of how quickly home values are falling, this is an indication of just how danger-ously leveraged American homeowners still are." [Emphasis added.]

That report was from 2008. The numbers are much worse now. Up, up and up; while home values continue down.

The Basics. You need to understand the basics. Below we give you the pattern, the step by step process. How we reached the situation we live in today.

Classical economics claims that "market rationality," is at the heart – the root of economies. That is the idea that every participant acts as a rational hu-man being in their pursuit of advantage through investment decisions. Today, in retrospect it is obvious that many market participants made irrational decisions.

While the very riskiest subprime mortgages are good examples of irrational markets, you must realize that at the time the various stakeholders believed they were acting in their own rational interest:

1. *Consumers* with low incomes became convinced that they could handle "mortgages" that in reality they could not afford. Why? What they learned from the media and from the stories from other people, particu-larly avaricious Mortgage Brokers, and, (naive yet willing) Real Estate Agents who *may or may not* have been caught in the mania, was that house values prices would continue to rise. Rise enough to enable them to refinance to a fixed rate loan *before* their mortgages reset to higher payments. At the same time the speculative dream of profit appeared to be stronger than the potential loss from foreclosure.

2. *Mortgage Brokers* extensively marketed subprime mortgages because there was so much money in it for them, and they encouraged the buy-ers to say anything to get in on the game. Often their activities went be-yond ethical behavior, to forging signatures, adding false income, etc. Countless numbers of them pressured appraisers to inflate the value of the property. Many, not all, engaged in Predatory Lending to make more money. At the same they had no transactional risk. Pure profit, fraudulent fees paid, simultaneous with Closing of Escrow.

3. *Investment Banks* packaged loans into Mortgage Backed Securities (MBS) simply because they were able to earn record fees. "They got up and danced," passing the risk to Institutional Investors.

4. *Institutional Investors* such as pension funds and insurance companies were the recipients of the ultimate risk. But they claim in pending litiga-tions that they trusted the Rating Agencies.

5. *Rating Agencies* were hired by the Investment Banks (very fishy here) to give the MBS high ratings. Why? Simply because this was very prof-itable for them, a new way to make a lot more money. Through "risk modeling" they were able to show the Institutional Investors that the risk on defaults would be very low. But, the risk modeling did not in-clude the likelihood of subprime defaults in large numbers. They wore blinders to make more money. And they made a lot of it.

6. *Financial Players* from around the world opted in. This included: Institutional Investors, such as insurance companies and pension funds; hedge funds; wealthy private investors; sovereign wealth funds and foreign central banks. They all got up and danced. While naive consumers were clearly deluded by outside forces, it appears that the Financial Players drank their own Kool Aid. But, did they? We suggest that many knew much better, but, had to join in the game to show profitability. After all their competitors – were doing it. Got to go along to get along.

7. *Moral Hazard* was what covered their backs. They knew that Greenspan, now Bernanke, and the Federal Government would step in and save their bacon when it all went badly. This gave them virtual license to make money any way they could. They knew – believed – that when they'd gone too far – the Feds would tax the serfs – the indentured slave taxpayers.

8. *Regulators* are ultimately to blame for allowing this to happen. Clearly, they did know better. Who was in charge of the Regulators? Alan Greenspan was. He claimed he couldn't tell a Bubble until it Burst. Don't believe it. His historical knowledge of economies and markets was very very deep.

Each step of the process may have seemed logical – rational – for most stakeholders (notwithstanding Regulators who stood down). Ultimately, because of potential outrageous rewards (greed enters) the end game (based on fraudulent Predatory Lending) created an irrational (mania) market. A Ponzi Scheme in a Casino Economy.

At the bottom, was the fact that all of this fell under the construct of "Control Fraud." See Appendix xx, where Bill Black makes it clear.

Loans absolutely destined to fail were securitized and sold to those who wanted a high return on a low risk investment. A Ponzi Scheme, which we've defined in detail above. Simply put, conspirators at the top of the chain create a scheme that fools the Greater Fools at the bottom. We believe that those at the top of the chain are the ones that should pay for both Actual and Constructive Fraud. And, don't forget many unscrupulous Mortgage Brokers. They were the ones with boots-on-the-ground – the ones who convinced and through Predatory Lending based deception fooled many would-be home owners that trusted them because they clearly had more knowledge than the homebuyer.

A Beautiful Model For Fraud

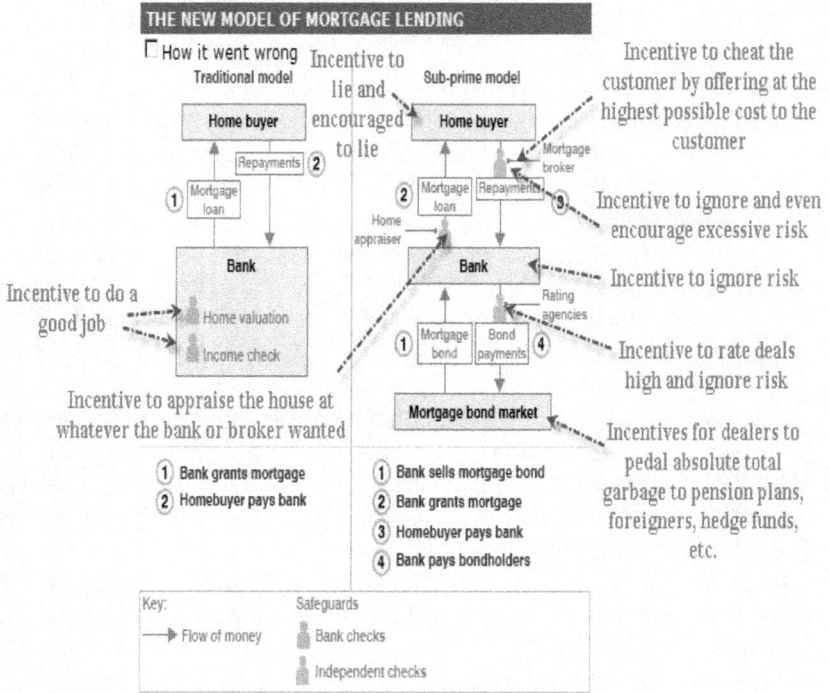

Courtesy of the Economist.com. // Exterior *"Incentive"* text by Mike "Mish" Shedlock.
http://www.economist.com/ // http://globaleconomicanalysis.blogspot.com/

CHAPTER 2: SMOKING GUNS

As you'll read below in Chapter 7, *Their Legal Issues,* Ohio Attorney General Marc Dann, has been building a case against credit-Rating Agencies like: Standard & Poor's, Fitch and Moody's for the role they played in rubberstamping many questionable securities that were issued by Investment Banks using mortgage loans as the underlying value for the securities. These are called Mortgage Backed Securities (MBS). We have much more to say about MBS throughout the book.

According to Attorney General Dann, "The ratings agencies cashed a check every time one of these subprime pools was created and an offering was made. The agencies continued to rate these things AAA. [So they are] among the people who aided and abetted this continuing fraud," adds Dann, as reported in *Fortune.*

Quoted in *Bloomberg,* Ohio's Dann said, "If someone was buying guns and giving them to people to go and take people's houses at gunpoint in Ohio, we'd be prosecuting them and throwing them in jail." Regarding current and pending litigation, Dann also said, "I want to see the e-mails, I want to see the documents…." If Dann finds those e-mails and documents and presents them in open court, those documents will become available to all homeowners who choose to aggressively stand up for themselves.

JP Morgan Chase. On March 27, 2008, *The Oregonian* staff writer Jeff Manning documented one of the first (of many many more to come) incriminating emails. This one was a JP Morgan Chase internal email that was circulated by a staffer to outside Mortgage Brokers. Manning wrote, "The memo's title says it all: *'Zippy Cheats & Tricks.'* It is a primer on how to get risky mortgage loans approved by Zippy, the name of Chase's in-house automated loan underwriting system. The secret to approval? <u>Inflate the borrower's income or otherwise falsify their loan application</u>." [Emphasis added.]

In the last chapter we mentioned Mortgage Brokers bumping income numbers up by tinkering with Zippy, JP Morgan Chase's automated loan processing technology. Here it is. They are *telling* – rather instructing – outside Mortgage Brokers to play with the numbers, "bump them" until the loan is accepted. Obviously, the Mortgage Broker isn't going to mention to the borrower that the numbers were bumped up – fudged. Will the borrower notice the fudging at the closing table when presented with over 100 pages of undecipherable language they are there to sign.

Obviously, JP Morgan Chase isn't going to challenge the numbers submitted by the Mortgage Broker when in fact they're telling the Mortgage Broker how to game the system. They wanted the loan. Then they wanted more and more of them. That's how we have great crimes, by starting with little ones.

Sure we're angry about this, and we invite you to join right in. It may cast enough hot white light on a gamed system to cause you to realize you have *no moral or ethical obligation* to these financial institutions. Not at all. For them, it's just another loan. For the nation it blew up the value(?) of all homes – to their benefit – to homeowner's ultimate detriment. Too good to be true? Clearly.

An "Ownership Society?" Hardly! A "Debtor's Society." Absolutely! Don't blame Bush the Younger. There is no possible way he had the intelligence to have understood this. Didn't he say: "I'm a war president. I make decisions here in the Oval Office in foreign policy matters with war on my mind." He said that, February 8, 2004 on Meet the Press,

---

Manning wrote, "Bank spokesman Tom Kelly confirmed that the 'Cheats & Tricks memo was e-mailed from Chase but added that it does not reflect Chase corporate policy.' ... The March e-mail was sent by Tammy Lish, a former Portland Chase account representative. Chase fired Lish days after discovering she sent it. Lish claimed that she did not write the email memo, saying 'I did not write it. It was sent to me by another (Chase) rep in another office along with some other documents that were more step-by-step customer training documents [for outside Mortgage Brokers].'"

Manning goes on to say, "During the boom, it was <u>common for lenders and brokers to get paid more for risky subprime loans than for 30-year fixed-rate loans</u> because the higher-interest loans fetched a higher price on Wall Street. Chase, the nation's second-largest bank, originates mortgage loans itself but also operates a wholesale arm that underwrites and funds loans brought to them by a network of Mortgage Brokers. The 'Cheats & Tricks' memo was instructing those brokers how to get difficult loans approved by Zippy. '<u>Never fear,</u>' the memo states. 'Zippy can be adjusted (just ever so slightly.)'" [Emphasis added.]

"The Chase memo deals specifically with so-called stated-income asset loans, one of the most dangerous of the mortgage industry's innovations of recent years. Known as 'liar loans' in some circles because lenders made little, generally no effort to verify information in the borrowers' loan application, they have defaulted in large number since the housing bust began in 2007."

This email suggests three 'handy steps' to loan approval:

- "Do not break out a borrower's compensation by income, commissions, bonus and tips, as is typically done in a loan application. Instead, <u>lump all compensation as the applicant's base income</u>." [Emphasis added.]

- "If your borrower is getting some or all of a down payment from someone else, don't disclose anything about it. <u>Remove any mention of gift funds</u>, even though most mortgage applications <u>specifically require borrowers to disclose such gifts</u>." [Emphasis added.]

- "If all else fails, <u>simply inflate the applicant's income</u>. <u>Inch it up</u> $500 to see if you can <u>get the findings you want, do the same for assets</u>." [Emphasis added.]

This is clearly fraud. Clear advice, actually instructions, by arguably the World's Leading Depository Bank, a mortgage loan originator, JP Morgan Chase, to independent Mortgage Brokers they work with. This goes beyond astonishing.

According to Manning, the email in question was of great joy to "local Mortgage Brokers [who] view the memo as vindication. Brokers have argued they've been unfairly blamed for the lax lending standards that led to a wave of defaults. The large national lenders drove the weakening standards, they argue."

Manning continued, "The Chase memo is 'a perfect example of one of the big five banks, out and out telling Mortgage Brokers to commit fraud,' said Todd Williams, a Mortgage Broker with Evergreen Ohana Group in Portland. 'And this has been going on for years.'"

Williams and several other Mortgage Brokers gave the memo to Oregon financial regulators. "It boggles my mind that any federally chartered organization would invite this kind of activity in such a flagrant way," said David Tatman of Oregon's Division of Finance and Corporate Securities.

Ironically, Tatman confirmed that state regulators, don't have "… jurisdiction over the federally chartered Chase." The actual federal authority, The U.S. Office of the Comptroller of the Currency has authority over Chase, yet their spokesman Dean DeBuck, refused to comment on the [email] document, according to Manning.

Kudos to the reporter for *The Oregonian*, Jeff Manning, for breaking this critical story, which further fuels outrage, further shows that the sub-prime debacle was a top-down driven con game, a Ponzi Scheme. Of course this is contrary to what Secretary of the Treasury Henry Paulson (who has authority over the U.S. Office of the Comptroller of the Currency) has been implying throughout this increasingly severe housing crash debacle, which literally poses a Def Con Five threat to the U.S. Economy and the U.S. Financial and World Banking Systems. Not trivial. Though the sun will likely rise tomorrow, it may set on a vastly changed and purged Financial System.

Some have intimated that the document itself may have been an internal joke between minions of J.P.Morgan. Something that was not real, only written as a joke for internal use. If so, then how did, rather why did the Mortgage Brokers quoted above receive a copy – part of the joke? We don't think so. They certainly didn't react that way. As above, they interpreted the memo as a vindication.

Finally noted here is that in March, 2008, JP Morgan Chase was given a "credit guarantee" (taxpayer bailout when push comes to shove) of $30 billion dollars by the Fed, in order to complete their buy-out of Bear Stearns. This would allegedly (and perhaps did) forestall a "meltdown" of the U.S. Financial

System. This is due to the fact of interrelationships between the Investment Banks, and the likelihood that if one of the Big Five went down hard, it might pull the rest of the Investment Banks down with it. How could this exist? No regulation! Alan Greenspan deferred.

After all, some wags have posited that (behind the scenes) JP Morgan and the Federal Reserve System are but a *single entity*. Well, they do have different "public" names. But still, if John Pierpont Morgan, himself was the U.S. power behind the formation of the Fed, it makes one wonder. If they really opened up their books and showed *all* of the holder's of the Federal Reserve's shares of stock (public and private), it might be revealing. Alternatively, such an act would finally discredit and debunk various Fed Conspiracy Theorists. Or would it?

Freddie Mac. A March 28, 2008, Cox News story was headlined, "Bleak Home Forecast Until 2010." Freddie Mac's Chief Economist, Frank Nothaft, said, "The homeowner foreclosure rate will rise for at least another year and residential real estate prices won't improve until 2010.... We're likely to have worse news and huge increases in the average amount of time it takes to sell a house." He predicted that prices will improve in about two years.

He said, "Since the housing market's peak in 2005, existing home sales are 29% lower nationwide, but even worse in some areas. California, Nevada and Florida home sale were down more than 40% in the fourth quarter of 2007, compared with the last three month of 2005."

Summary. *Smoking Guns* is included early in *Use Foreclosure Law* to give you a sense of what follows.

First. You need to understand that the Housing Bubble was driven by loose money, or *"accommodation"* by the Federal Reserve System. This was done by Alan Greenspan to pull the economy out of a 2002-03 recession that was one result of the dot.com bubble/mania and subsequent stock market crash. Rather than allow the economy to correct itself through market forces, Greenspan pumped in debt, or "fiat" money. Money created out of thin air, which created the Housing Bubble. In economic terms this is called an "accommodative" policy. By failing to regulate Structured Finance and allowing them to create "leverage" outside of regulation, he virtually licensed the Investment Banks and other major financial players to create a gorged, highly speculative system that is now choking on itself. We'll explain that last sentence in Chapter 4.

In a recent attempt to avoid responsibility for what he had done, on April 7, 2008, Greenspan wrote an op-ed piece in the *Financial Times*. His piece, was defensively titled: "The Fed Is Blameless On The Property Bubble." Here is Doug Noland from The Prudent Bear, to argue against Greenspan's case.

"Even today, Greenspan chooses to avoid a meaningful discussion about Credit. [Greenspan said,] 'I am puzzled why the remarkably similar housing bubbles that emerged in more than two dozen countries between 2001 and

2006 are not seen to have a common cause. The dramatic fall in real long-term interest rates statistically explains, and is the most likely major cause….' He [Greenspan] goes on refute those that place blame on the Fed for the housing Bubble, including arguing against the claim that the Fed's 1% funds rate triggered 'a massive Credit…expansion.' Greenspan wrote, 'Both the monetary base and the M2 indicator rose less than 5 per cent in the subsequent year, scarcely tinder for a massive Credit expansion.'"

"Tinder or no tinder, what transpired was indeed unprecedented Credit expansion. The Greenspan Fed cut rates aggressively in 2001, and Total Mortgage Debt (TMD) growth accelerated to what should have been an alarming rate of 10.4%. With rates dropping to as low as 1.25% in 2002, TMD expanded 12.1%. With rates dropping to 1.0% in 2003, TMD increased another 11.9%. Despite TMD increasing by a stunning 38% in three years, Fed funds remained at 1% through the first half of 2004. TMD growth surged to 13.5% in 2004, followed by 13.4% in 2005, and 11.6% in 2006. The Greenspan Fed sat idly as mortgage credit doubled in just six years."

Since Greenspan's earlier article he has admitted in Congress that his model was deficient, that in fact finance did not manage their risk appropriately. In the first quarter of 2009, he has written further articles in both the *Financial Times* and *Wall Street Journal* defending his actions, always deflecting blame from himself. Pathetic, not worth the space to reprint here. Google him.

What is a Bubble? The excellent blogger, Angry Bear provides a bubble definition we like:

"A bubble requires both overvaluation based on fundamentals and speculation. It is natural to focus on an asset's fundamental value, but the real key for detecting a bubble is speculation – the topic of this post. Speculation tends to chase appreciating assets, and then speculation begets more speculation, until finally, for some reason that will become obvious to all in hindsight, the 'bubble' bursts."

When this is coupled with the fact that starting in 2004, nearly 30% of all home purchases were made by non-resident investors, and to a lesser extent, by second or "vacation" home purchasers, clearly speculation also drove the market, ergo, the Housing Bubble.

Throughout history "accommodative" policies have always led to larger dislocation, disaster down the road. Simply put, it's impossible to set the economy straight – work out imbalances – by following the same policy that caused the problem in the first place. The practice of trying to jump start out of recession by merely papering over deeper systemic problems never works. Greenspan knew it very well. In his arrogance, he did it anyway. And, what the heck, his term at the Fed would be ending soon. He'd move on – write his book rationalizing his aberrant if not criminal behavior. He received $8.5 million, second only to President Bill "Smuggling the Blow Into Mena" Clinton.

He is still factually inconsistently and incorrectly defending himself in the Financial Times and Wall Street Journal. Why do they give him the space? His articles receive howls of derision in the Blog-O-Sphere.

Second. Above we included brief comments by Freddie Mac's Chief Economist because such comments are extremely rare. A major player in the national mortgage market is declaring that housing will continue down for *at least* two more years. Generally, government and other housing "experts" tend to put lipstick on the pig. They maintain, against all demonstrable facts that the picture is rosy, that the market will return soon. That the bottom will be in the next quarter or soon thereafter. They are saying, stay in your home, in fact, according to the National Association of Realtors (NAR) almost any market, any time, any place, is "a great (or good) time to buy."

We grant that Realtors need to make a living. Yet, it's *not* a – "good time to buy." In March 2009, sales went up. First time buyers came in. Why? Approximately 56% of these recent sales came from empty foreclosed houses. The tragedy for these newcomers to home ownership (and residential investors dipping their toe back in the market) is that recent statistics show that prices are likely to fall another 20% nationwide in the next three years.

As a former REALTOR® (we kept our California license but withdrew from NAR), over years we were appalled by announcements and pronouncements by David Lereah, the former cheerleading Chief Economist of the National Association of Realtors (NAR). He was subsequently kicked upstairs and out, because, we believe, the avalanche of press against his perennial sunny rosy pictures became overwhelming. But – he's back! Not really. Stepping into Lereah's shoes as NAR's new Chief Economist is one Lawrence Yun. This proves to us once again that the legend of the inscrutability of the Far East may be real.

One wag stated, "One could reasonably argue that Yun is committing consumer fraud by trying to entice people to buy into a market that is poised to fall farther." Hear Hear. We definitely agree as we make the case for Using Foreclosure Law to Keep Your Home. But, for now we'll move on.

- Well not right away. Recently discovered is the National Association of Realtors (NAR) has *"inadvertently"* been overstating the actual number of home sales for the last three years. Their numbers are widely used. Can you say: "It's a Great Time To Buy." Well don't. <g>

We'll provide evidence below that Freddie Mac's man is merely *whistling past the graveyard.* Putting on a brave face. Yet credit must be given to him because he is admitting to the fact that housing will continue down. We'll introduce evidence below that indicates such conjecture is too optimistic

In making the case for *Using Foreclosure Law to Keep Your Home* we will show beyond a reasonable doubt that due to current market forces, housing is likely, at a minimum, to continue down through 2011. Even worse, and due to the fact that in 2011-12, oncoming millions of Boomers will be retiring and downsizing their living accommodations during those later dates, putting their homes on the market, housing will continue down until 2015. We've been right about this since 2005. The only thing we've had to change, is that we've had to extend the bottom date outward because there has been no reform, only kicking the can down the road to protect the banks.

"Fed actions only effect the economy accidentally. Their total focus is on protecting banks." James Rickards, widely quoted World Class economics analyst, 12/19/2011

You must prepare yourself for this likelihood, unless you *choose* to "stay in a home" that is worth much less than what you owe on it. We wrote *Use Foreclosure Law* to show you options you might not have contemplated because the real facts of the situation are not widely disseminated.

What Really Happened. The business process at most lenders causes the *loan origination* team to bring in the deals – bring in the money. To motivate them many are partially compensated by commissions based on the number of loans that fund. Inside the lender the *loan processors* are also paid a commission based on the number of loans they process which fund. Sometimes their underwriters are paid bonuses on the sheer volume of loan reviews whether the loans go through or not. Consequently, loan officers and senior origination management, are in a regular struggle with underwriting staff.

Often a loan is denied by an underwriter, deeming it too risky, causing loan officers and Mortgage Officers to take the loan to senior origination people who *would approve the loan anyway.* This is because loan volume stepped ahead of sound underwriting. Over the last five years this increasingly became the case. Remember, they would be selling the loan into the Secondary Market (through Investment Banks) and none of the parties who appraised the property, created the loan or packaged it as a MBS would bear the risk. Seemingly home free. Pun intended.

Yet, on the other hand some homeowners who Confront Fraudulent Housing Debt, may receive very near "home free" opportunities. Or, with proper counsel a significant principal reduction through a Forced Debt Reorganization.

Because of Greenspan's low interest rates and accommodative policies, lenders increased their profits. Then the game became funny. As in *funny-money.* Rating agencies Fitch, Moody's and Standard & Poor's seemed to automatically give high ratings to Mortgage Backed Securities (MBS), which were created by Investment Banks buying loans from various types of loan originators and placing them into MBS, which Institutional Investors bought because they were high yielding fixed investment vehicles *carrying AAA ratings.* Where it was *funny* was due to the fact that they would include Subprime loans likely to fail (which failed) with higher rated loans, and the whole package would enjoy the AAA rating. Is this fraud on the Institutional Investors who bought the MBS? You'll have a better impression after your read, Chapter 7: *Their Legal Issues.* Hint: Investors are suing the Investment Banks who sold them the bonds.

More and more money was pumped into the system to create more loans, and home values skyrocketed from 2003 forward. It would never end. Not so. It ended. Worse for Moody's is that they are currently being investigated regarding awarding AAA ratings to now considered "toxic" Mortgage Backed Securities. That is one of the lynch pins. Pull that pin and down go the Rating Agencies, while the Investment Bankers tell the Institutional Investors, *"We're shocked. Shocked we tell you. We had no idea the paper wasn't AAA. Try to prove otherwise. Oh – you are?"*

Our deep thinking blogger Mike "Mish Shedlock writing from his blog, Global Economic Trend Analysis, threw another log on the fire on May 23, 2008, in an article called, "Fraud Probe at Moody's."

Mish wrote, "On May 20th the *Financial Times* reported Moody's error gave top ratings to debt products." He then quoted from the *Financial Times* article.

"Moody's awarded incorrect triple-A ratings to billions of dollars worth of a type of complex debt product due to a bug in its computer models, a *Financial Times* investigation has discovered. Internal Moody's documents seen by the FT show that some senior staff within the credit agency knew early in 2007 that products rated the previous year had received top-notch triple A ratings and that, after a computer coding error was corrected, their ratings should have been up to four notches lower.

"On discovering the error early in 2007, Moody's corrected the coding glitch and instituted methodology changes. One document seen by the FT says 'the impact of our code issue after those improvements in the model is then reduced.' The products remained triple A until January this year when, amid general market declines, they were downgraded several notches.

"The world's other major credit agency, Standard and Poor's, was the first to award triple A status to CPDOs but many investors require ratings from two agencies before they invest so the Moody's involvement supplied that crucial second rating.

"S&P stood by its ratings, saying: 'Our model for rating CPDOs was developed independently and, like our other ratings models, was made widely available to the market. We continue to closely monitor the performance of these securities in light of the extreme volatility in CDS prices and may make further adjustments to our assumptions and rating opinions if we think that is appropriate.'"

Mish continued, "Yves Smith at Naked Capitalism had this cynical comment, 'This begs the question that the so-called bug wasn't a bug at all but a feature, that the model was designed (or tweaked) to produce ratings that conformed with S&P. After all, if an issuer got an AAA from S&P and wanted a second rating from Moody's, it would kill Moody's chance of ever rating similar paper for it to issue a markedly lower score.'"

Mish closed out saying, "What Yves is referring to is the practice of 'shopping around' debt to whoever is willing to rate it the highest. Back in March, bond insurer MBIA even went so far as to ask Fitch to stop issuing credit ratings on its insurance units. See, Amazing Action In Ambac, MBIA."

Enter the Mortgage *Bankers*. These are non-depository banks focused on making mortgage loans. Some are public corporations, some are non-public firms (many were small). They made and sold loans to Wall Street Investment Banks. Such sales are called − selling into the Secondary Market − where Fannie Mae and Freddie Mac also live in part. Secondary Market participants package, or bundle individual mortgages into a large bundle and then create a new financial instrument, a Mortgage Backed Security (or bond), which they sell to Institutional Investors. The packagers are also called Securitizers, and they are generally the Investment Banks.

Many Mortgage Bankers (MBs) are approved by lenders and some established a line of credit with lenders. MBs would originate, underwrite, close and (seem to) fund loans and subsequently take the package to a larger lender who approved it and replenished the MBs line of credit and paid them an additional fee.

Backed By Mortgage *Brokers*. Independent Mortgage Brokers (firms as well as free-lancing independents) entered the scene by establishing relationships with various loan originators so they could utilize many different lending products offered by different loan originators. The intent was to match a borrower's situation to the best program.

You need to understand that Mortgage Broker compensation is basically all commission work. No loan approval − no funding of the loan − no compensation. So the Mortgage Broker would pressure the larger lenders with the real threat of taking their business to another lender. This caused lenders to accept loans they did not believe would be repaid. Literally. Why? They would sell the loans up the food chain and avoid risk and losses. They would receive their fees and be out of the deal. Is it beginning to sound and smell like Systemic Fraud? It certainly does and gives new meaning to the concept of Predatory Lending, which is the subject of Chapter 9.

Issues of Fraud. As in any profession there are legitimate players and those who are unscrupulous. Meaning many utilized various forms of fraud, falsified income documents, put borrowers into no documentation loans because the borrower would not have received any loan if income were verified. In other words many naïve borrowers were put into subprime loans simply for the benefit of the up-chain who received higher fees for funding loans. Truly disgusting is that borrowers (even those with good credit) would often be placed into higher interest rate loans with higher payments even though they actually qualified for better rates and lower payments. This occurred with regularity. This was particularly the practice of unscrupulous Mortgage Brokers who reaped the fees.

Mortgage Brokers qualified borrower ability to pay at the initial start rate (low rate), and not the full rate the loan would reset to in a few years. Many borrowers did not understand this, which is a clear example of Predatory Lending. Yes, and to be sure some borrowers went along with their Mortgage Broker and did participate in fraud.

However, remember that the industry set it up this way so that *borrowers* could be blamed and be potentially liable for fraud. *"Oh no. It wasn't us. It was lying borrowers. Bail us out – they the are bad people."* Unfortunately the media has perpetrated this myth. Why? They do it in deference to their banking advertisers; and to their deep need to regularly receive corporate bond based financing. The consolidation of media ownership has resulted in inter-locking Board of Director relationships. They call this *conspiracy* "The Establishment." If you're reading this book you aren't likely in that conspiracy. So start one of your own.

Such loans were commonly known as "liar loans" yet the very system that set it up certainly did not stop the practice. They encouraged it, and now come to taxpayers for bailouts. They knew what would happen. They set the borrowers up to fail, and now they want your help? They want you to blame unsophisticated people who did what their Mortgage Broker professional told them to do.

If it helps you to understand, remember, most of us trust someone who we perceive to have higher authority earned through superior knowledge. We want to, frankly, we must (due to our need to associate with like-minded people, our tribe, our community, our nation) believe that they are honest people – else we're lost. It's one reason we go to school. To learn. And, until we develop critical thinking, often through experience, we do what we're advised to do. Focus any ire you possess on the perpetrators – not the frankly naive victims. It's our point of view, and we're sticking to it.

According to Satyajit Das, who is highly regarded on Wall Street and who literally wrote the book on exotic derivatives, one thing you need to understand about MBS is that:

"Defaulting middle-class U.S. homeowners are blamed, but they are merely pawns in the game. Those loans were invented so that hedge funds (often spawned from and funded by Investment Banks) would have high-yield debt to buy."

Lenders continued to accept these loans that would certainly fail in time, and push them through the pipeline because they did not dare lose their up-link – Investment Bank purchasers of the loans. *"While the music was playing. We got up and danced."* Consequently borrowers were placed in loans sure to fail, or they were placed into stated income programs where the Mortgage Broker would falsely state actual income. Many who bought properties in 2006 when the market hit the top (arguably September 2006), and utilized ARM products with initial rate periods of 2-5 have defaulted – been foreclosed on. There are millions more foreclosures to come.

Bank Failures. The web site: Market Watch, recently published an article called, "Bank Failures To Surge In Coming Years." They said, "At least 150 banks will fail in the U.S. during the next two to three years." They reported that Joseph Mason, associate professor of finance at Drexel University said, "At this point in the crisis you can't stop bank failures." [Emphasis added.]

David Rubenstein Chairman of the Carlyle Group recently said, "US and European banks and financial institutions have enormous losses from bad loans they haven't yet recognized [on their books] and may have a harder times wooing sovereign fund rescuers. Based on information I see, it will take at least a year before all losses are realized, and some financial institutions fail. Many financial institutions aren't going to be able to survive as independents institutions."

Fraud Abounds. *Bloomberg* reported on June 20, 2008 in an article entitled, "Bear Stearns Fund Prosecutors Reveal 'Lot of Evidence' of Fraud."

"E-mails, witness statements and a money trail may help convict two former Bear Stearns Cos. managers accused of misleading investors and lenders about two hedge funds that imploded, legal analysts said. Ralph Cioffi, 52, and Matthew Tannin, 46, were charged yesterday with falsely saying the funds were thriving while knowing investments in subprime mortgages could cause their collapse. U.S. prosecutors claimed the men lied about liquidity, redemption requests, and their own investments before the funds shut down last June, costing investors $1 billion.

"'This one is a shotgun of all sorts of facts,' said former federal prosecutor William Mateja. 'They've got a lot of evidence to establish a securities fraud against hedge fund managers. Not having heard the other side of the story, it appears that they have a strong case.'

"'The subprime market is pretty damn ugly,' Tannin wrote in one e-mail to Cioffi. 'If we believe the [CDO report is] ANYWHERE CLOSE to accurate I think we should close the funds now. The reason for this is that if [the CDO report] is correct then the entire subprime market is toast.' [Emphasis added.]

"Tannin sent the e-mail from a personal account, not the Bear Stearns system, to the personal e-mail account of Cioffi's wife, according to the indictment. That e-mail and others cited in the indictment 'are really absolutely the key,' said Villanova University Law School Dean Mark Sargent, who read the indictment. 'They show that they knew the funds were cratering, that the bottom had cropped out of the subprime market, and their leverage was putting enormous pressure on the fund,' Sargent said.

"'The e-mails 'support the government's theory that the defendants are thinking one thing and saying another to investors or lenders or internal brokers,' said Paul Radvany, a Fordham University law professor and former federal prosecutor.' 'It's hard to imagine a compelling reason not to use Bear

Stearns's internal e-mail to talk about Bear Stearns hedge funds,' said Christopher Clark, a former federal prosecutor in New York."

Clearly these guys used private email accounts outside of their normal Bear Stearns accounts because they thought these private emails would not go on the record. They have gone on the record and provide another smoking gun to the practice of fraud at the highest levels of Wall Street finance. You can be sure that much more will surface over time.

We hope you're beginning to be outraged. The Fed paid J.P. Morgan to gobble up Bear Stearns, and the traders in question received a slap on the wrist. We hope you hear us and are beginning to have a sense, a feel for the fact that such practice was really a part of an overall trend based on Predatory Lending. You have the right, frankly the obligation to fight back in order to gain security for your family. Realize you must take action. Throughout the remainder of the book we'll document what has happened, and why it's time for you to assert your legal rights – by taking action. By Using Foreclosure Law to Keep Your Home. But first, you must obtain a Forensic Loan Audit and a Securitization Audit before you can take your matter to an attorney.

Head's Up. Here's a final near smoking gun for this chapter, though there are many many more. Intrepid blogger Calculated Risk wrote on July 2, 2008.

> "HousingWire has the story: 'FDIC Warns Banks on HELOC Freezes, REO Management.'

> "On the HELOC story: 'Banks are moving to freeze HELOCs globally, and then evaluating available credit later on a case-by-case, property-by-property basis ... The FDIC letter warned banks that such a shotgun-style approach to freezing HELOCs might violate Truth-in-Lending regulations; under Regulation Z, lenders can reduce an applicable credit limit only in the event of "significant decline" to the value of an individual property (a "material change" in the borrower's financial condition – such as the loss of a job – qualifies as well).'

> "On REOs: 'Our sources suggest that some banks are choosing not to pay taxes on low-value REO properties in hard-hit neighborhoods, in the hopes that local municipalities will take the property to a tax sale rather than force the lender to carry the property on its books. The FDIC reminded banks that doing so would violate existing bank safety and soundness guidelines ...'

> "Here is the FDIC Guideline on REOs. And some of the instructions:

> **'Maintenance.** ORE should be maintained in a manner that complies with local property and fire codes. Other requirements, such as homeowner association covenants, may also require careful attention. Efforts to ensure an ORE property is maintained in a marketable condition not only improve an institution's ability to obtain the best price for the property, but also minimize liability and reputation risk.

> **'Real Estate Taxes.** Taxes on ORE should be paid in a timely manner to avoid unnecessary penalties and interest.

'**Insurance.** A review of an institution's umbrella insurance policies should be performed to determine if adequate hazard and liability coverage for ORE exists. If not, management should consider obtaining policies on each parcel of ORE. If an institution decides to self-insure, this decision should be documented in the ORE file.

'**Other Expenses.** Management should implement reasonable procedures for managing any other miscellaneous expenses the institution may incur during the ORE holding period. These expenses could include, but are not limited to, sewer and water fees, utility charges, property management fees, and interest on prior liens.'"

Calculated Risk closed out saying: "In other words, pay the bills!"

We add, *"Pay the bills?"* Hey, these are banks, they're special, too special to have to pay the bills like they expect everyone else to do. In fact, if you think about it, if they won't pay *their* bills, why should we pay our bills to them? Why?

Think a little deeper, if the new Secretary of the Treasury, the man who is ultimately the boss of the IRS, Tim-Boy Geithner, won't pay his taxes until he's caught out, why should you pay your taxes?

We're not calling for a tax revolt, or a general revolt, *to the contrary*. What we are saying, rather asking is: what could have caused our Young President to have chosen such a compromised person to run Fiscal Policy? Is the answer you reach frightening? Count us in. We're with you.

CHAPTER 3: THE POLITICAL ECONOMY

"A branch of the social sciences that takes as its principal subject of study the interrelationships between political and economic institutions and processes. That is, political economists are interested in analyzing and explaining the ways in which various sorts of government affect the allocation of scarce resources in society through their laws and policies as well as the ways in which the nature of the economic system and the behavior of people acting on their economic interests affects the form of government and the kinds of laws and policies that get made." Defined by Dr. Paul M. Johnson of Auburn University.

Based on that definition, arguably all economies are Political Economies. While we often take fact-based contrary positions in this book, we have no intention to write with a point of view supporting or criticizing Republican or Democrat office holders. This Democrat, or, that Republican. These people are politicians. Throughout history, certainly from time to time, people have distrusted politicians. More often than not – for good reason.

This chapter is here to give you an overview of how and why Wall Street and Washington D.C. support each other *over* American Citizens. We intend to show – that while the game is fixed – they do not completely own it. In our Democratic Republic, which operates under the U.S. Constitution, your *willing and acquiescent participation* is required. If you choose to *withhold your participation,* they are forced to and will make adjustments to accommodate your position. But, you must do something that might be difficult for you. If not, they know you are beaten down –and like a good serf – you'll stay in line. Even though Congress only has an 11% approval rating right now, addicted to the campaign money, they continue to legislate against the American People. Remember, *"The banks own this place."*

Most members of the Administration and Congress either: don't understand both how and why, we've reached this sorry pass, or, those few who do understand are more than willing to pass the responsibility through finger pointing. Only after the fact of some devastation do they jump up and down. The deeper reality is that their hands are tied. If they do understand and reach conclusions similar to those presented in this book, regarding *Use Foreclosure Law! Keep Your Home,* they'd certainly not speak of it publicly due to the risk inherent in electability. No no no. That would require leadership, and likely cause major money investment in their opponents in the next election by the financial industry. So, as merely our elected representatives they will hurry-right-up both before and *after* the debacle, and propose "Plans and Solutions."

More To The Point. In early May of 2008, the *Wall Street Journal,* wrote a piece "Housing Bailout Backlash." They wrote:

"Democrats may be risking a backlash at the polls in November by pushing hard to use taxpayer money to rescue homeowners who can no longer afford their mortgages in the face of stiff resistance from current President George

Bush and many other Republicans. The Democrats in Congress and the party's presidential candidates frame the issue as doing at least as much for beleaguered homeowners as the government is doing for Wall Street. The White house and most House Republicans counter that this amounts to using taxpayer money to reward bad behavior.

"The Republican protests are striking a chord with some Americans who are paying their mortgages on time or who didn't buy more house than they can afford. President Bush is vowing to veto a bill the House passed last week – with the support of 39 Republicans, about a fifth of their ranks – that would, among other things, allow certain homeowners to refinance loans through a government agency if their lenders agree to take less than the full amount borrowed."

"Keith Hennessey, a top economic-policy adviser to President Bush, says 'gut-level public opinion' backs the White House. The reaction of people who are making mortgage payments on time, he says, is: 'Hey, wait a second, why are you helping him when I'm making hard choices every single month to stay current on my mortgage?' The line was drawn sharply in last week's House debate. Rep. Tom Feeney (R., Fla.) said less than 1% of homeowners would get help while the rest 'will pay the price of this bill.'"

"Rep. Barney Frank (D., Mass.), who wrote the legislation, and other Democratic lawmakers insisted the bill nicks both sides. Said Rep. Jim Marshall (D., Ga.), 'The deals that the borrowers get are not particularly good. The deals that the lenders get are not particularly good.... In my view, it's a bailout for the entire economy and all of these people that have been dragged into it.'"

"Austan Goolsbee, one of Sen. Obama's economic advisers, says the campaign weighed the downsides of rewarding bad behavior against the economic harm risked by inaction. 'That's not a political calculation, that's very much the economically valid thing to do,' he says. The issue, he added, is the threat that dropping home prices pose to the entire economy. Framed that way, Mr. Goolsbee said, voters are 'much more amenable' to government intervention to 'prevent something that's outside of people's control.'"

"Nearly all pending proposals purport to aid the deserving – usually defined as families who own their own homes and have a shot at paying a reduced mortgage – and shun speculators and those who lied on their loan applications. Sen. McCain made 'a very conscious decision not to throw money at Wall Street or people flipping second homes,' said his economic adviser Douglas Holtz-Eakin. 'You don't want to reward bad behavior.'"

These people all need to get a clue. Either they don't understand what you understand if you've read this far, or, they simply can't tell the truth and believe they'll still keep their jobs. They've been completely asleep on their own watch. Will you go running when they call "All Aboard." Or do you think it's smarter to hang back, in fact, if you're on it – get off the High Debt Train. Remember this, all taxpayers are going to contribute to the bailout, including you. Do you want an arguable taxation of paying for an underwater loan; and the *double taxation* inherent in being bound to a taxpayer bailout? Pay and pay – twice.

Why We Do This. Our overriding intent in this book and at this time is to support, inform and provide Service to American Citizens, particularly here, homeowners and individual residential investors. We bring forward news, information, analysis and opinion based on both domestic and GeoPolitical facts and economies, and in particular, historical trend lines.

We support residential property owners in their pursuit of the American Dream – homeownership. However, we all need to understand that the Dream has turned into an Epic Nightmare for millions. Only by waking up and stepping out of the nightmare can we literally take the power back to change the situation. Only then will we once again be able to exercise that dream. Now we must take action and put the dream on hold for the benefit, prosperity and happiness of our families. We believe, that action is to Use Foreclosure Law to Keep Your Home.

We also strongly believe that it is not enough to merely have the principles named on the loan and deed read and discuss this book. We believe that your teenagers must also read and discuss this book with you before you make a family decision. If not, if you're not all on the same page, that may create problems down the road. If their main reason for staying put is the fear of losing their friends by moving (a very real and profound issue for teenagers), you need to teach them, show them, that the upside is that they'll always have their *real friends.* Plus, and it's a big plus, they'll have new friends they never would have had. It's called growing up. Extending your vistas, your level of experience. Always valuable.

We believe (evidence abounds) that homeowners and residential investors receive short shrift by both politicians and economic policy makers who actually control our lives; moreover, the future for our families. We strongly believe that the average taxpayer, the middleclass American, has been set up – and is now taking a fall – for the financial institutions.

Witness: The 1990s Savings and Loan Debacle, arguably a witting fraud ultimately paid for by the American taxpayer.

Witness: The dot.com Mania in which highly regarded major Wall Street Investment Banks were recommending that the public buy newly issued stocks that some of their analysts making the "buy" recommendations were privately calling "dogs" in email. When will we ever learn that there aren't just a few rotten apples. The Wall Street barrel of apples is tainted by current systemic business practice, that has largely adopted an unethical "Who Cares – We're Making Big Money" attitude. And, worse, is aided and abetted, moreover, by their business models, which are arguably insured by moral hazard. Banking System Bailouts paid for by taxpayers.

Over here on the other hand, We Do Care and with intent and aforethought, we are bringing information to individuals so that they can make informed decisions. It really doesn't have to be scary to make your own investing (frankly, homeownership is not a right under the Constitution, it's a choice, and should not be a casual investment decision) decisions. That is if you possess accurate and up-to-date information. A cardinal rule of investing is to Buy Low and Sell High. Moreover, the wise investor goes against the grain, Warren Buffett comes to mind. He leaves a market when the public finally sees the opportunity and is just about "all in." Wise investors, not naive speculators, leave markets just before the market tops out, leaving unwitting speculators to take losses.

Consequently, the back story or deeper pervasive theme and direct message of this work is not a pleasant pill to swallow. Keep an open mind. We were Shocked and Awed as we dug deeper into the ways and wiles of Wall Street, Structured Finance, and moreover, the ethical (?) conduct of former Chairman of the Federal Reserve System, Alan Greenspan. If we were lied to about reasons for a war (nothing new there, this has been done throughout recorded history), is it a stretch, unthinkable, traitorous, to believe they would lie to us about the money. Hardly! As former President Nixon's campaign finance director, Maurice Stans said, regarding Watergate: "Follow the money."

Truth is the only path for a Patriot to pursue. Yet, it's not pleasant to bring information to people that goes against the grain – what they have in good faith believed. It's particularly difficult, if not impossible, to convince someone of something that goes against their appropriately paycheck-focused point of view. Presenting information, data, that defies "conventional wisdom" is a sure path to enmity. But, once you've learned the facts, taking action to bring them forward is a clear path to protecting, more importantly, defending your family.

We argue in this book that overall economic conditions (the numbers measuring percentage of debt to other aggregates such as GDP), are eerily similar to conditions that existed in 1928-29, just before the stock market crash and the subsequent Great Depression. We are talking for the most part about numbers that show an extremely unbalanced and distorted economy. In recent months an astonishing number of articles comparing current condition to the late twenties have been produced. For the most part these essays or articles are buttressed with charts and graphs, the statistics that prove the correlation.

The Federal Reserve System. The Bill Clinton Administration was hand-maiden to the Federal Reserve System (and vice-versa), as much as the current Administration, and we argue strongly that both (and previous) Administrations have and continue to consciously act in ways that do not benefit the American People, because they are not forthcoming with the truth. If they have a partner, nay more often a leader, in such behavior, its name is: Wall Street, whose profit intentions and strategies are obvious for all to see. This it good. It's their *tactics* that are hidden or obfuscated. This is bad.

Simply put, amass easy to raise capital (thank you Mr. Greenspan) to be used to make financial profits, and leave financially unsophisticated American people to take the hind most. Arguably, basic or rudimentary economics is taught at certain levels in our public school system, yet, how many Americans can say with any certainty who the "bank regulators" (banking system watchdogs) are, what they do, and more importantly who supervises them. This is an area lately in the news as a result of the Bear Stearns bailout. Secretary Paulson and now Tim-Boy Geithner make Great Noise regarding consolidation of banking regulation, to bring greater accountability and closer scrutiny.

But, peering between the lines, it appears that their beloved Investment Banks are not being tightly scrutinized; yet, they will and are receiving arguably illegal, if not very questionable, taxpayer bailouts in order that the corrupt system they've built will not be effectively monitored and regulated. This will enable them to continue to do it again and again for their exclusive benefit. For the continuing degradation of the middle class. Which class are you in? This class is called Homeowner's Economics 101. This book is the text book. Read it twice. Internalize the information.

THEY GO BAILED OUT – WE GOT SOLD OUT

Of even more significance, Dr. Bernanke has illegally (not within the legal charter of the Fed) broken historical precedent and allowed lightly regulated Investment Banks to borrower from the Fed discount window where previously only depository banks have had the "legal" right to borrow short term money.

The noted and vilified (sometimes by both sides) financier George Soros made comment in the *Financial Times* regarding this oncoming dangerous regulatory change. Soros said,

"The proposal from Hank Paulson, U.S. Treasury secretary, for reorganizing government regulation of financial institutions misses the point. We need new thinking, not a reshuffling of regulatory agencies. The Federal Reserve has long had *authority* to issue rules for the mortgage industry but *failed to exercise it.*

"For the past 25 years or so the financial authorities and institutions they regulate have been *guided by market fundamentalism: the belief that markets tend towards equilibrium and that deviations from it occur in a random manner.* All the innovations – risk management, trading techniques, the alphabet soup of derivatives and synthetic financial instruments – were based on that belief. *The innovations remained unregulated because authorities believe markets are self-correcting.*

"Regulators ought to have known better because it was their intervention that prevented the financial system from unraveling on several occasions. Their success has reinforced the misconception that markets are self-correcting. That in turn allowed a bubble of excessive credit to develop, which extended through the entire financial system. When the subprime mortgage crisis erupted it revealed all the weak points.

"Authorities, caught unawares, responded to each new disruption only after it occurred. They lacked the ability to foresee them because they were in the thrall of the market fundamentalist fallacy. They need a new paradigm. Market participants cannot base their decisions on knowledge, or what economists call rational expectations. There is a two-way, reflexive interaction between the participants' biased views and misconceptions and the real state of affairs. Instead of random deviations, reflexivity may give rise to initially self-reinforcing but eventually self-defeating boom-bust sequences or bubbles." [Emphasis added.]

Empowered and enriched, Structured Finance began making crazy (leveraged by more credit, more liquidity) bets (hedging, derivatives) on top of such products. This newly created debt, easy money, inflated and created a Credit Bubble, which, first, inflated the stock market (late nineties); and then the Mortgage Bubble, aka, Housing Bubble. The same easy leveraged money conditions that created the Crash of 1929 and the ensuing Great Depression. Bail them out?

The Inevitability of History. Our intent is to alert all Americans, and in particular, to warn homeowners and residential investors to consider getting out of harm's way. Use the law to Confront Fraudulent Housing Debt; and, either dump your debt, or, cause a Forced Debt Reorganization.

Wall Street financial institutions made nearly 40% of all profit in Corporate American last year. Over decades when their role was that of facilitating, making funds available for investment in productive U.S. enterprise, that ran closer to 20%. This is but further evidence of their control.

Over the last decade Investment Bankers led the movement for downsizing and outsourcing middle class jobs. Their method was simply to punish U.S. Corporations who didn't outsource by having their analysts put "sell" ratings on these corporations' stocks. That got the attention of CEOs' who ravish their own companies through lavish stock options, moreover excessive bonuses for themselves, even when their entity is having poor performance.

Over the shorter term of the last ten years, the finance sector has enjoyed a higher percentage of profit in all corporate earnings. Good for them. Clearly not good for the rest of us. Through essential political campaign contributions (and a recently suspect electoral process) they have arguably captured Congress. We have had little opportunity for recourse. (For the brilliant, well researched book on the challenged electoral process, read Greg Palast's, *Armed Madhouse.)*

Today, rather than performing a historic facilitating role, finance leads the way, politically as well as financially. The result: cheap, no-down, no-doc mortgages and appreciated home values may appear to be your friends. We don't think Wall Street considers you their friends. We think they consider all of the rest of us as fodder. Cash-flow fodder. If you stop flowing the cash to them through a conscious business decision to Use Foreclosure Law, their problem is that *they* become the fodder.

The taxpayer always pays when financial schemes blow up, as they always do, throughout the History of Civilization. Wall Street packaged up the housing loans, encouraged more of them, took their fees, paid for (arguably bribed) Rating Agency approval, then passed the junk, the risky loans to Institutional Investors, such as pension funds, which may default on American (and world wide) pensions when the losses on Mortgage Backed Securities are finally tolled, as they will be.

It isn't simply about current Administration Policies, prevalent over the last seven years, while this monster Housing Bubble grew. Under Clinton, certain definitions and changes were made to reporting criteria in the Department of Labor statistics that are far from reality regarding actual job reporting in our nation; and arguably much worse is the woefully inaccurate Consumer Price Index (CPI) measurement. By keeping the CPI artificially below actual prices on goods and services, the government does not have to give Social Security recipients payment increases they are entitled to by law.

These manipulated Bureau of Labor statistics are simply part of a systemic pattern that is designed to enable the game – the charade. Ultimately then, like the Energizer Bunny, the Fraud is perpetrated indefinitely. It just keeps on going and manipulates the American people whose currency is losing value significantly due to Systemic Inflation, the increase in (debt) money, liquidity, which forces the prices of everything higher. Until it doesn't.

Then prices plunge. They are doing exactly that in the housing market right now. It was always widely reported that the brilliant Mr. Greenspan's comments and pronouncements were impenetrable. Difficult to understand let alone interpret. That was by design, not accident. Some call it duplicitous behavior. Was it inducement to fraud?

> *Fraud in the inducement* n. the use of deceit or trick to cause someone to act to <u>his/her disadvantage</u>, such as signing an agreement or deeding away real property. The heart of this type of fraud is <u>misleading the other party</u> as to the facts upon which he/she will base his/her decision to act. [Emphasis added.]

By this definition Greenspan arguably did induce fraud when he encouraged all Americans (to act to their *disadvantage)* in February 2004, to take out Adjustable Rate Mortgages. Particularly when seen in the light of the fact that only three months later he began raising interest rates, his actions raise particular concern. Perhaps not criminal fraud. Greenspan is brilliant, but, therein lays his undoing, he is certainly guilty of Intellectual Fraud as we'll see below.

Banking Industry At Risk. If the American People really understood the dire condition of our Economy, would the People be so quiescent to these new bailout plans. The facts are that banks don't merely (as ballyhooed in the press) have a liquidity problem, the banks have a lethal *solvency* problem. Many people are self-righteously incensed that they must be taxed to help *foolish* homeowners who should not have taken out subprime loans. They are blaming the victims. They have the wrong target.

In late March of 2008, the Fed and Treasury used extreme pressure on the Office of Federal Housing Oversight (OFHEO) that effectively nationalized, publicly traded, Fannie Mae and Freddie Mac. This is what is done in communist countries. This is central planning by the state, and should never be allowed in a Republic operating through an electoral representative Democracy.

They offer an Ownership Society. Naturally this brings great pride. But, do you really even *actually own* your largest investment, your home. You have Title and Deed, but, really, if you're honest with yourself, you may conclude deep down that you're paying rent. Worse, paying rent in a fixed game. Fixed against the homeowner.

With some of our major banks facing actual insolvency, they have been forced to dilute their shareholders' value by taking equity capital from the Chinese and some Middle Eastern governments to stay in business. But that has not been enough money. The Fed is continuing to prop up the banks by loaning them more money based on the collateral of *full face* value Mortgage Backed Securities, which have in fact lost face – value. Are any prospective candidates for the Presidency speaking to these issues? It has gotten so bad that we heard that Yogi Berra said that Congressman Ron Paul talked about it so much that people *couldn't hear him anymore.*

We always like making up a corny joke. Yet never forget that their intent is to keep people in the dark, and confident that everything is sort of, well, OK. And, if its not? The Fed can fix it up right away. Well it isn't OK. What we have is a Ponzi Scheme in a Casino Economy. Don't be the Greater Fool. You might consider being early in the wave of people opting out of *their* game by Using Foreclosure Law to Keep Your Home.

Reconsidering the Clinton years shows that his claimed budget surplus was an accounting trick. At that time manufacturing and white collar jobs had not yet fled to foreign shores. Now they have. Globalization became the new thing: NAFTA and CAFTA, and other major trade initiatives were implemented, which did as Ross Perot successfully predicted, created a Great Sucking Sound as good paying jobs fled. Jobs with reasonable benefits were outsourced. The destruction of the Middle class by intent, and in earnest. All primed and pushed by Wall Street Investment Banks through their analysts who rewarded corporate outsourcers through stock analysis "buy" recommendations; or alternatively punished with "sell" reports if the corporation did not immediately begin significant foreign outsourcing. Corporate Officers who received significant stock options, as a major part of their compensation were quick to adopt the new trend.

All of this really got going over the last ten years in the name of Globalization. Wall Street has presented (with a straight face) that we've had a "Jobless Recovery." There is no such thing. A jobless recovery is an *oxymoron.* Meaning in this case that the two words have opposite meanings, and a false conclusion. One part is true. In so far as manufacturing jobs *go,* they do, they go! We've lost over ten million well paying, good benefit, manufacturing jobs in the last ten years. So relatively speaking we are: Jobless. However, the so-called: "Recovery" part has been created with smoke and mirrors and reportage of its success is not only cynical and inaccurate, it qualifies as a: Big Lie.

Globalization might be simply understood by the fact that the Federal Reserve System created and enabled creation of so much (debt) money. So much liquidity that U.S. economic forces (Wall Street) were empowered and enabled to invest abroad, and created new financial investment vehicles that are now collapsing. They were able to do this simply because there was so much (debt) money to invest. The Miracle of Structured Finance. Until it self-destructs.

The China [False] Miracle Syndrome. In other words multi-multi-billions of U.S. dollars were created, freshly minted with no backing, and invested in productive (off-shore) investment. Unfortunately for the American People, a principle beneficiary was the Chinese People and Government, which had been loaning dollars back to us to keep our government operating, through the purchase of U.S. Treasuries. Now, they're not buying them so much. So, the Fed filled the gap and is buying the Treasuries in order to monetize them − pay for Government out of fake money.

. The U.S. has been reduced to being the largest debtor nation in the World, and even more humiliatingly, our major banks must borrow money from a Communist Government to keep operating, to hide their insolvency from their own shareholders, bank regulators (who aren't looking that deeply, and doing little about what they do know), the investing public and depositors. We don't like it, we don't think you like it, and moreover we believe it is unsafe for the financial health of American families.

Worse is that China is clearly not our best friend, and keeps its currency artificially pegged low against the dollar to make their goods cheap for American purchasing. This historically unprecedented imbalance is now come to a head, resulting in current currency wars. The end result is a weakening dollar and even likely higher (oil driven) price increases ahead. At some point the overall imbalances will cause the Chinese to begin to shift loans they have made to us (in the form of their purchasing liquid short-term U.S. Treasuries they can easily dump, even at a loss if necessary) to other asset classes − abroad − not here.

Yet, beyond Treasuries, they are investing in (propping up) some U.S. major financial entities, with nary a squeak from a cowed Congress.

Further, the Chinese smart and unrelenting pursuit of oil and energy related opportunities in Africa, Canada, Iran, former Russian states (the 'Stans), and Venezuela, is clear writing on the wall. They intend to out-compete us for these future energy supplies. We cannot put the Genie back in the bottle. We cannot bomb our way to energy independence, or even cheap energy. What we've gained is a falsely called (*never-ending*) War on Terrorism against so-called Terrorists who wish us to leave their nations and stop taking their resources. Can you really blame them? They can never stop defending *their* Homeland. Sound Familiar. Sounds to us like George Orwell's seminal book: *1984*. The twist is the nearly unfathomable, to the Western mind, centuries mortal conflict between Shiites and Sunnis. Apparently, they can't ever just − get along.

China Sows Seeds of Destruction. Over the past several years, small Chinese entrepreneur/investors, rich with dollars gained by selling to the United States have ballooned their own stock market.

Reporting from Beijing news source, Xinhua:

"'China's smaller Shenzhen Bourse has warned investors of bubbles behind the soaring profits of its main board market.' They quoted a report from the Shenzen Bourse that stated, 'Although listed companies achieved rapid growth, investors should still beware of hidden bubbles behind the profit surge and invest in a prudent and rational manner,' said the report released on Sunday. According to the report, the interim profit figures relied too much on yield of investment in the securities market and the prospects of a continued profit increase is doubtful."

China is setting itself up for a drastic failure that will threaten it's own repressive corrupt "Communist" government. Their stock market is insanely over valued, and as the American consumer continues to slow down, their markets will shrink and bust. Many rivers in China are the most polluted in the world. Currently birth defects and disease is spreading because of rural dependence on these rivers for crop irrigation and for drinking water.

China's – On the Other Hand. Apparently China will not continue to suffer insults indefinitely from American politicians. In a *Financial Times* article from June 19, 2008, Stephen Schwarzman, Chairman and CEO of New York's Blackstone Group lays down the line, well encapsulated in the title. "Reject sovereign wealth funds at your peril."

"Gao Xiqing, the president of China Investment Corporation [CIC], China's sovereign wealth fund, spoke last week of his frustration that CIC's attempts at investing outside China sometimes run into political opposition. He went on to add, in words that should act as a chilling wake-up call to many politicians and bankers: 'Fortunately there are more than 200 countries in the world. And fortunately there are many countries who are happy with us.'"

"I have known <u>CIC since it bought a 9.4 per cent non-voting interest in Blackstone when we went public last year</u>. The fact that its president publicly suggests that CIC may invest only where it feels welcome – a view I know many other SWFs share – has serious implications for the economic well-being of the US and other western countries where political opposition to SWF investments has mounted. [Emphasis added.]

"From the point of view of a rational economist, this is frightening. It is difficult to think of how much worse off we would be in the current financial crisis without SWFs. Many of our commercial and investment banks have taken large hits to their balance sheets because of bad investments. The capital infusions from SWFs have enabled them to strengthen their balance sheets. Since the fourth quarter of last year, SWFs have poured about $55bn (€35bn, £28bn) into US and European financial institutions to the great benefit of their shareholders. That is a very good thing. Using SWFs to recycle the holdings of countries with large surpluses in the west, which needs the capital, rather than keeping that money at home, is a huge benefit to us.

"CIC is not alone in its <u>frustration with political grandstanding on SWF investments in the west</u>. When I talk to some of the SWFs (and I have been dealing with them for more than 20 years), they are <u>both amazed and annoyed that their actions, which are such a positive for the US economy, have been met with such hostility and anger</u> in some quarters. They have not done anything wrong; they are acting the same as any domestic pension plan or university endowment in a search for an acceptable return on investment. [Emphasis added.]

"This hostility is dangerous because we are reaching a stage in the global economy where, as CIC says, SWFs have other options. They could sell US equities or bonds, for example, and buy from other nations. This is not a threat but simply the SWFs following their own self-interest in search of the most hospitable investment environment.

"The US is the world's largest debtor nation and we are now in an uneasy relationship with our creditors. We cannot afford to get this wrong. The current account deficit is 7 per cent of gross domestic product – double that of the Reagan years. This makes a significant number of countries big holders of dollar reserves. They invest those reserves in part through financing a significant portion of the federal debt.

"Because foreigners are willing to buy Treasury debt in quantity, the Federal Reserve is able to keep interest rates low. If we were forced to rely mostly on domestic borrowing, we would have to pay very high interest rates. The consequences would be increased inflation, a dollar falling even faster and very slow (or negative) economic growth. If the investment climate for SWFs is poor in the US, the countries with large dollar reserves (which are the owners of most of the SWFs) could also look for alternatives. The euro already is proving increasingly attractive as a reserve currency instead of the dollar and that alone should be of deep concern.

"To alienate the managers of these SWFs could have severe consequences if they and their owners seek friendlier alternatives outside the US. Even the current talk of disclosure requirements is seen by some SWFs as problematical since it often fails to take into account the political realities in some of the countries managing SWFs, where their ties to the west are best left unstated lest they arouse domestic political opposition.

"When capital withdraws, it does so without notice or fanfare. Imagine a private meeting in a room far from the US; a decision is quietly made and billions of dollars that were invested here find a new and more hospitable home. Or billions of dollars that could have been invested here are reallocated to other more benign markets. Sixty years ago, we conducted a painful, expensive and accidental experiment called the Great Depression, with the Smoot Hawley tariffs to teach us the value of free trade. Let us not subject ourselves to another painful lesson in the value of direct investment and the free flow of capital by driving SWFs away."

Whew. Here we have Schwarzman at some length. He is one of the primary current Wall Street buccaneer/cowboys who heads a highly leveraged equity buyout firm, Blackstone, which has sold 9.4% of it's back side to the Chinese government. So he carries Chinese water in the *Financial Times*. Heck, why didn't China hire Rodney Dangerfield to just get up and say, "Hey give my pals, the Chinese Government, some darned respect, or, they may take their football and all their cash and go home."

At this writing in late 2011, by many many accounts China has foolishly created a huge bubble, building empty cities with empty officer towers, etc. Yes, they put their people to work, but, they fact is that their internal debt situation is stacked against their continuing success. Particularly because the West is increasingly unable to purchase their manufactured products. A day of reckoning looms. It will not be pretty.

Things are bad. Things are getting worse nearly daily, and we haven't figured out exactly how to definitively warn you that a *bystander* to the coming Tsunami – is something to be. A bystander does literally that. They remove themselves from further risk, and go to safety for their family. As bystanders, they watch a disaster high up on the sidelines, they are not caught in it. They withdraw from the game. But, they Use Foreclosure Law in order to understand their loan, and then use legal leverage, the rule of law, to gain their objective.

John Lennon said, *"A working class hero is something to be."* Well, that's fine. What we're saying is that you and your family would be much better off over the next several years if you didn't live in a house that you owned. And, if *you do* right now – live in an underwater house that you like to think that you *own* – think seriously about Confronting Fraudulent Housing Debt

Remember that is our personal position from a single man. Families who wish to keep their home must also Use Foreclosure Law.

Worse Daily? That's what we said above. Here's some more proof. "Things may start to get tricky from here ... " is the title of an article from the *Financial Times,* by Francesco Guerrera.

"Pity – if you can forget their monumental pay packages and jet-setting lifestyles – Wall Street's bosses, because this financial crisis is about to get tricky. Taking enormous write-downs and raising equally staggering amounts of capital looks relatively easy when compared with the task ahead: navigating still-treacherous markets while trying to kick-start their firms' moribund earnings.

"That is why, in recent weeks, the L-word of choice among banking types has shifted from 'liquidity' to 'leverage' – the financial equivalent of swapping glasses of water for shots of Eye-opener (for uncool readers, that is the vodka/Red Bull cocktail). Long-suffering investment banks are eager to bounce back from the current profit doldrums by putting capital to work in markets that are showing signs of defrosting.

"Unsurprisingly, Goldman Sachs, Morgan Stanley, Merrill Lynch and Lehman Brothers [now deceased] would love to power-charge a recovery in earnings by loading up their balance sheet with debt – or leverage. The snag is that, after witnessing Wall Street's recent risk-management failures, watchdogs and shareholders are not that keen on a hair-of-the-dog treatment for the brokerage houses' all-too-recent risk binge.

"Indeed, policymakers, including Hank Paulson, the US Treasury Secretary, and Tim Geithner, the president of the New York Federal Reserve, have been tirelessly urging banks to get rid of risky assets and raise capital to "de-lever" their balance sheets. To make matters even more complicated, the once-technical issue of leverage has become entangled in a morass of poli-tics and lobbying courtesy of outraged commercial banks.

"Well-connected executives at the likes of Citigroup and JPMorgan Chase express indignation at the fact that Lehman and others have been permitted to borrow from the Fed without having to comply with the strict leverage limits imposed on commercial banks. If it all sounds a bit nerdy, well, that is because it is: those who abhor financial jargon and technicalities should look away now. Everybody else, however, ought to pay close attention be-cause the fight over leverage will determine the winners and losers in the next financial cycle.

"The stakes are high: if borrowing constraints are set too low, already-battered investment banks could be condemned to years of middling to poor profits. *But if loose leverage hurdles allow a devil-may-care attitude to risk to flourish yet again, Wall Street is in danger of planting the seeds of its de-struction.*

"Regulators have so far taken the easy way out, arguing that final rules on how much debt investment banks can take on their books will not be final-ized for years, maybe decades. They are right: it will be up to politicians – scary, I know – to decide who regulates whom in the slow-burning legisla-tive feast that is certain to follow the credit crunch. But that does not mean that investment banks, hedge funds, private equity groups and other debt-hungry vehicles are not trying to exploit the legal vacuum. [Emphasis added.]

"It is an open secret on Wall Street that the less hurt among the investment banks – Goldman Sachs and, to a lesser extent, Morgan Stanley – would be prepared to forgo the Fed's borrowing 'window' in exchange for less draco-nian leverage limits. That view is, however, not shared by Lehman, whose ability to withstand bear raids relies on the fact that the Fed window ensures it will not end up like Bear Stearns. Meanwhile, large hedge funds and pri-vate equity groups are keeping a keen eye on the highly-leveraged areas – buy-out financing, securitizations, asset-backed securities and the like – va-cated by risk-shedding investment banks.

"Those are volatile and dangerous markets, but someone's got to do and it would not be a surprise to see large and professional operators such as Cita-del or Blackstone entering businesses once reserved for Wall Street firms. As a senior banker recently put it, this frantic jostling for position is giving rise to a series of "come to Jesus" moments for financial services groups. As they kiss goodbye to the easy debt and the gargantuan returns of the past few years, investment firms have to decide just what business model they want to pursue.

"They have two basic choices. Either they go it alone in the hope that their famed "earnings power" will not be crimped by over-zealous regulators – and frustrated commercial banks. Or they seek the comfort of strangers and merge with regional or foreign lenders in order to gain access to savers' deposits and other "safer" businesses. My hunch is that some form of consolidation in the brokerage sector is inevitable, but not imminent, especially if the liquidity squeeze persists.

"What kinds of deals will come about depends on how the crisis plays out. I said that the next phase of the crisis was going to be tricky. Take a good look at Wall Street today, because by the time the shake-up is over, it might look a whole lot different."

Granted, that was long. We want you to see that they will never stop unless and until they're responsibly regulated. As you read this book, and particularly if you're currently underwater – as at least 30% are in early 2012 – you'll come to realize that it is you and 14 – 17 million other homeowners stuck underwater like you – that are the only ones who can actually put these people where they belong. In the backseat, not driving the car. Some of them belong in the trunk for awhile to think it over.

Future Hope. Regarding oil and energy, we must simply use less petroleum based products, and, well, work to giving the planet a wee bit of a breather, by doing more with less. Some have argued that the planet does not "care" about the configuration of its molecules. While this may be true, our lungs cry out for clean air; and our circulatory systems must have clean water. Innovation and technology can only take us part way. Yet, it's China and India that are graduating unprecedented number of engineers, more in each country than we graduate here.

There is an old expression: "Don't bet against the Fed."

There are older expressions. "Don't bet against Mother Nature;"and, "Bet that all markets are ultimately corrected."

In order to have a legitimate and respected seat in the World Polity, if we must lead, we must do it by setting a good example. To do less is to perpetrate Empire. Empires are always resented. Are we not smarter than that now? Perhaps many are. However we have leaders and financial elites that believe that Control through Monetary, or Dollar Hegemony backed by bomb dropping F-18s, is in *their* best interest. No doubt it is. Yet, we wonder what families of 9-11; and, Iraqi and Afghanistan Occupation victims, think of such process. Do you think that they agree that loss of their loved ones is acceptable American Collateral Damage to maintain Empire?

What Can Be Done. Beyond such very unpleasant interpretation, even lofty (unrealistic?) ideals, the Bottom Line Point of this writing is that we resent any official or non-official U.S. Government Fiscal Policies and Federal Reserve Monetary Policies that hold (implicitly by their results) that full American employment is not important. In fact the Fed is charged in its mandate, its Charter, to work towards "maximum employment." They rarely mention that, and their practice has been to subvert it. We resent any policies which hurt the American People. Do you have seniors in your family, or that you know that were absolutely flummoxed by the new Medicare Prescription Drug laws?

Why were the new Medicare Prescription Drug laws so difficult to understand? Because they were designed to be so difficult to understand! Does this show respect to our seniors – to the Greatest Generation? No! Reminds us of a lack of body armor in War. How can they do this? Rather – why – why would "The Establishment" do this? It is beyond greed. We don't believe they deserve respect.

Regardless of political affiliation – of deep beliefs – you may vote *for* them by continuing to give them house payment dollars. Alternatively you can choose to vote *against* them by Confronting Fraudulent Housing Debt. You can Use Foreclosure Law to determine Predatory Lending and Securities Law violations and issues. If they are significant you may be able to obtain a Forced Debt Reorganization with a cramdown of principal owed, or, at your choice, possibly walk away with monetary damages in your pocket. Take another look at the cover illustration. Notice her purse is stuffed with cash.

Domestic Reinvestment in Infrastructure. We mentioned that U.S. productive investment funds are invested abroad. Frankly, we need money invested at home as productive investment. We need to re-industrialize our nation, and reduce our reliance on energy, and rebuild in order to create National Wealth shared by all of us.

Based on facts presented here, it is easy enough to be negative. Doom and Gloom. We believe it's our obligation (and our pleasure) to outline a positive outcome. Below is one idea in our arsenal that is practical, doable and very arguably holds merit.

The simplest way to immediately re-industrialize and rebuild the Middle class is to build a National High Speed Rail Transit System, to move the goods and people, immediately creating employment throughout the nation, while reducing our reliance on, and need, for massive amounts of expensive non-renewable energy consumption.

Adopting such a monumental program will enable us, on a cost productive basis, to extend the National Rail System by building tens of thousands of miles of short-run inter and inner-city and county light rail systems. To help fund the entire System, we will be able to export all of the above (for profit) to the Americas, both North and South. Build the world's state-of-the-art transportation system (an infrastructure investment) and encourage our closest neighbors to become our best trading partners. Nothing wrong with that, it's purely economic driven, not political, though it makes good sense politically. We can then invite the World to come, bring their money, buy an AmeraRail pass and tour the historic locales and magnificent vistas of our nation, and, the entire Continent of the Americas.

Bringing the Future Today. As we face the consequences of imprudent economic dislocation, we'll state belief that a politician, a President, that put the country back to work by implementing a high speed rail system would be considered by History as a Savior, as Franklin Delano Roosevelt was the by the people he led from the grinding poverty of a World Wide Great Depression. We'll cede a large point for those that argue that Hitler provided the actual reason for building up our industries, which certainly helped end the Great Depression. The overriding point that perhaps we can all agree on, is that we must reinvest monies for infrastructure and manufacturing here at home in order to rebuild National Treasure.

Domestic productive investment, with the goal of reaching full employment and real National Wealth, which will enable all boats to float again; and moreover, create the possibility of fair distribution of income. In a sincere attempt to avoid political judgments, we've not introduced the unbalanced distribution of wealth prior to this point. Now we have. Our country has been hollowed out economically because wealth is distributed disproportionably at the top. All politicians have aided and abetted in this process. Period.

Now comes Tea Party and Occupy Movements, which we believe will grow to become strong actors in hastening real change. After all, it is the awakening 99% that is confronting the 1%.

Clearly history has shown that a strong and prosperous middle class is the engine for growth. American consumers have lately provided 70% of Gross Domestic Product (GDP). Over the last eight years, the money came from consumers piling on debt enabled by inflated house values, not by increasing wages. To the contrary the hollowing of our economy, and our middle class, the destruction of our productive capacity leaves us all terribly vulnerable to the downturn created by Structured Finance. It will not be pleasant.

When we criticize current politicians and financial players (particularly their unethical, illegal and secret activities), we're simply demanding that the truth be told; and for Americans to be treated as adults, given the actual facts and information that will enable us to be legitimately informed regarding policy and actions that directly affect the security of our families. We've given our best in this context in a limited amount of space, yet, this not a book on politics. To see how we've been manipulated, we encourage you to read Thom Hartmann's brilliant book with a title that speaks to our national condition: *Screwed: The Undeclared War Against the Middle class-And What We Can Do about It.*

Remember, only in December, 2011, because of court activity did we discover that the Fed had also <u>secretly</u> (in 2008) granted an additional $7.7 Tril-

lion to Financial Elites, way way beyond the seemingly piddling $800 billion they passed out with TARP.

Summary: As you already know, based on the evidence presented here (you'll see more in the following chapter regarding the Federal Reserve System), we've discovered – we argue – that we are likely headed for Financial Armageddon. Because you won't read the whole truth in the popular press, in the financial journals, or see it on Tout-TV, we bring the facts forward here in order to enable you to make decisions for the safety of your family.

We wrote the preceding paragraph for the first book in July 2008. Some criticized us for being too dogmatic, to easy to see a conspiracy. We believe that events since 2008, have shown all of us, that we were "right on" then, and are "right on" now. If anything, because the Banking Cartel's hand has been forced, we now believe that more and more Americans "get it."

Public anger expressed over AIG bonuses (laughingly reinforced by our Young President who found a parade he could get in front of and lead) is merely the tip of the iceberg. As more and more people, in payment shock or underwater by the millions, begin to Use Foreclosure Law to Keep Their Homes, we will take back the power.

As the Tea Party rightfully says: "We want our country back." Trust us, they won't give it back. You must take action to Confront Fraudulent Housing Debt and take back your home for starters.

One more thing here. We believe that due to pressure from Occupy Wall Street, on at least two occasions in December 2012, the Young President stated on television (we paraphrase slightly), that "While Wall Street may have acted, unethically, they didn't break the law, didn't commit fraud." If he doesn't know better than that, then he really should be sent packing back to Chicago. If he lied, than all the more so.

CHAPTER 4: GREENSPAN'S BOOM – BERNANKE'S BUST

"In despair she then armed herself with the U.S Constitution, which prohibits central banking as drafted by the Framers." Anonymous

"Liquidate labor, liquidate stocks, liquidate the farmers, liquidate real estate. It will purge the rottenness out of the system. High costs of living and high living will come down. People will work harder, live a more moral life. Values will be adjusted, and enterprising people will pick up from less competent people." Andrew W. Mellon, Secretary of the Treasury, circa 1932.

[Note: In this chapter we are digging deeper. Taking you into the Belly of the Beast – our financial system. Why? In order to take action, to be empowered, you must possess a basic understanding of how we got here. We've stripped out the economic jargon. Dig in.]

We agree with the quotes above, and while we're not nearly as severely austere as the former Secretary of the Treasury, Andrew W. Mellon, he does make a powerful point. A planned debacle, an all hand's-on-board public winding down, would be less painful to homeowners, the investing public, and all Americans than if it comes out of nowhere. However, a well-thought-through program would be communist-like central planning that will never and should never fly in a Capitalist Society. Unless of course the Federal Reserve System does it in secret, like so much of what they actually do. Could they be planning it now?! Doing it (covertly) right now in, ahem, plain sight. Appears to be so.

Greenspan's Fraud. In a widely reported speech, on February 23, 2004, Alan Greenspan told the American People to use Adjustable Rate Mortgages (ARMs). Then just four months later he started raising interest rates. Nearly a year later he pulled the switcheroo, and said that people who had used ARMs could/would lose money. But, it was late, way too late, and worse, few were aware of his subsequent remarks.

According to data published by the Mortgage Broker's Association, over a third of all homes sold after his 2004 speech went to investors and speculator/flippers. He really pulled *them* in. It was good for a lot of them for a period of time. That is if they had flipped and were out by mid 2006 at the latest. Unfortunately, many Greater Fools were still caught in Mania and buying in. They are and will continue to pay a dear price. Many face foreclosure and we hope this book causes them to immediately obtain a Forensic Loan Audit and a Securitization Audit to determine if they can use the law to legally leverage a desirable outcome.

As house payment rates continue to reset through the summer of 2012, the ARM people will be severely affected. Many with underwater mortgages have simply walked away from homes and debt. That was a tremendous mistake. By Using Foreclosure Law many if not most of them could have Kept Their Homes.

Further indication of (unintended?) consequences of Greenspan's encouraging homeowners to use ARMs is a recent comment:

> "I also have a hunch with regard to Greenspan's now infamous prodding of households into adjustable-rate mortgages. I think he recognized clearly the degree to which the impaired GSEs [Fannie and Freddie] (and their scantily capitalized counterparties) had become acutely vulnerable to a rise in market yields. As the Maestro, his interest-rate policies (market manipulations) orchestrated a massive shift of interest-rate risk from the financial sector to the household sector. In the process, however, recklessly low interest rates spurred unprecedented mortgage lending and speculative excesses that today imperil borrower, lender, leveraged speculator and system stability alike." Doug Noland, <u>Prudent Bear</u>, March 21, 2008.

Doug was right on the money then, and continues to be right on the money today.

Dr. Bernanke. We believe that Dr. Ben Bernanke is ill-suited for the Chairmanship of the Federal Reserve System. Particularly for homeowners, investors in residential property, the general public, both domestic and international markets, and sadly, for his own historical legacy. By all accounts Dr. Bernanke is a "nice" guy, and some wonder why he would have placed himself in the position of coming on stage following Alan "Maestro" Greenspan. We believe that as events unravel, as the true history of the unprecedented Credit Bubble is exposed, Mr. Greenspan will be appropriately discredited.

Yet, we ask, why would Dr. Bernanke place himself in harm's way? *Hubris* comes to mind.

Hubris: 'hyü-bris, *noun*: exaggerated pride or self-confidence. *(Webster's Dictionary Online)*

Quotables:

> *"AG: 'Ben, Ben, you have so much to learn. That transparency stuff is fine for academic research. In the real world, never giving the market too much information means never having to say you're sorry. Or that you were wrong.' "* Caroline Baum, *Bloomberg*. November, 2005. Ms. Baum's reference to "AG" was likely to former Chairman Alan "AG" Greenspan.

> *"Bulls of 1929 – like their 1990s counterparts – had their eyes glued on improving profits and stock valuations. Not a thought was given to the fact that the rising tide of money deluging the stock [housing] market came from financial leverage and not from savings."* Dr. Kurt Richebächer. Circa, recent.

Continuity. By many accounts, *continuity* was near the first word Dr. Bernanke uttered when the announcement was made official, he would be the new Fed Head. This was what the equity market required and it heaved a sigh of relief. Meaning the stock market held very well, thank you very much. However, both the bond and dollar markets blinked. We'll explore why below and how this effects your home ownership.

Ultimate Responsibility. The Fed carries the ultimate responsibility for our current condition. In a pointed article in *Barron's*, highly respected Martin Meyer who is a guest scholar at the Brookings Institution and author of numerous books about banking and finance wrote,

> "Most commentators on the current credit crisis have argued that the banking regulators and supervisors played no role in its inception, because the bad mortgages were written and sold and packaged by unregulated mortgage brokers and Mortgage Bankers. But all the bank-holding companies had subsidiaries that were active in the mortgage market, *and virtually all the mortgages packaged for sale by private entities passed through some subsidiary of some bank-holding company or some bank-controlled investment vehicle at some time between the inking of the contract and its disappearance into a collateralized security."*

> "There was plenty of opportunity for bank examiners checking out the holding companies to notice that some of the paper in the vaults had inadequate or dishonest documentation, and to 'classify' it. When the examiner classifies an asset, he forces the bank to reduce its reported profits and discourages further investment in similar assets. Of course, Fed examiners don't look at individual loans any more; they just ask banks whether they are living up to their own standards of due diligence, and if it's OK with the bank it's OK with the Fed."

So, it was just OK OK OK all the way around as the Fed abandoned its responsibility to see to the integrity and soundness of money. Are these people incompetent? Ignorant? In a conspiracy? We can't say, but, for *some* reason they did not do their job.

Inflation – Inflationists – Inflationistas. Inflationists are unstated members of a Socialistic-Like Movement comprised of individuals, whose market credibility (moreover, livelihoods / professional careers), is based on an untenable belief system that everything will continue (lifestyles maintained / entities protected), through massively creating increasingly less valuable money (Fed accommodation, easy money for debt, fiat capital) to float their, *ahem,* bets on market movements. Inflationists are in the business of borrowing and loaning money.

Led by the Fed (the banking system), Wall Street, complicit academic economists and the MSM, operating though secrecy, and, by obfuscation, they confuse the public with disinformation. They operate under public banners such as Free Trade, Globalization and a New World Order. They have devalued the worth of the U.S. dollar 95% since 1933. Think of it. If you have more dollars (albeit they are worth less) because more dollars are around, when you pay off older debt with new (inflated, worth less) dollars, you are actually coming out ahead. That's the secret structure by which they profit.

The old debt is say, $40K. You pay it off with money that has been inflated in value, and so you're actually getting a break by paying off the $40K with money that is worth less than what you were able to borrow. Banks *love* this, when *they* are paying off debt they've taken on, and *hate* it when *you* are paying them off for loans they've made to you with inflated money. Believe us, at the bottom line, they love Inflation, are deeply committed Inflationistas, particularly when the Fed gives *them* more money before they give it to you. First users of new money always book the "big bucks." Simple, the way they make money is borrowing cheap, and loaning it dear to you. Which is fine, a little bit, except when they take too much. And, when they don't properly assess risk in making loans.

In other words [the Fed] continues to *enable,* actually *create* Bubbles (of which they deny exist, or cannot be named until they're ready to blow) that *Inflationistas* bet on (hedge, or not), while strongly encouraging (led by Treasury Secretary Paulson and now Geithner and through a complicit media) less sophisticated retail players (homeowners) to stay the course – keep paying them.

As they should be, Paulson and Greenspan, now Geithner and Bernanke, were frankly terrified by the phenomena of people choosing to walk away. Now that families are now increasingly Using Foreclosure Law to Keep Their Homes their panic is palpable. In a speech in Chicago on February 29, 2008 Paulson sounded like a dunning bill collector, saying,

> "Homeowners who can afford their mortgage should honor their obligations. And nearly all do. Homeowners who gambled in the housing market and viewed their purchase as a short-term investment may choose to walk away. Those who do this are nothing more than speculators, and they are not the focus of our efforts." [Emphasis added.]

Later, on March 8, 2008 in an interview with the San Francisco's Editorial Board he said,

> "My big focus here is to aggressively encourage any big financial institution that may need capital or think they many need capital to go out and raise it because it's available today. Because if they don't have enough capital, then they shrink their balance sheet and they restrain lending, which is vital to keeping our economy healthy and growing."

> "There's been a lot of discussion about homeowners who have zero or negative equity. The way I've looked at that is, if you are a homeowner and you can afford to make your mortgage payment, you should be honoring that mortgage payment. If you say, 'I don't want to honor that payment, and I'm going to leave unless someone else takes my losses,' I don't think the government should be taking those losses any more than the government should be bailing out any investor who has a loss. In many instances, people who are walking away are speculators who put little or no money down." [Emphasis added.]

This is an extraordinary statement and reveals a mind set of an individual who *had no business* being the Secretary of the Treasury. Repeating him, *"I don't think the government should be taking those losses...."* Astonishing. The government (taxpayers) *should not* be taking those losses. We say that the banks should take their *own* losses. His mind automatically, or unconsciously assumes, that *bank losses equal government losses.* That the government will bailout the banks by taking their losses and passing them onto taxpayers. Moral hazard baked into the cake – into their unconscious processes.

The privilege of the Lords To The Manor Born. As Queen Marie Antoinette said before she lost her head in the French Revolution regarding the common people. *"Let them eat cake."* French translation for "cake" in the sense she meant is: "feces."

It is more than outrageous, it is more than moral hazard. It is an assumption that the people *must pay* for banking incompetence, rather banking avaricious overreaching. The Rule of Law – the laws of business – including declaring bankruptcy, have been generally suspended for the banks, and you now understand why. The banks make profit when it's good for them, and the people (taxpayers) take the losses when the banks overreach. Sounds like Socialism to us. Well, actually it sounds like a system operated by and for Feudal Lords (now called banking corporations) enacting their will on defenseless serfs. The really good news is that we now have legal defenses we've haven't had before.

Always remember, a Securitization Audit is the key that unlocks the door to the true depths of the actual fraud perpetrated on borrowers.

Giving support to the concept, we have an, ahem, interesting representative in Alabama Senator Richard Shelby who was Chairman of Senate Committee on Banking, Housing and Urban Affairs from 2003 until 2007. As a U.S. Senator he switched from the Democratic party and became a Republican. Interesting! Ever mindful of being re-elected, it was reported on February 7, 2008, by the Dow Jones wire, that he said, "Once again, instead of thinking of ways to further protect the American taxpayer, we are actually considering ways to further expose them for the benefit of those making <u>healthy six-figure salaries</u>." [Emphasis added.]

We temporarily rest our case. But, before we do, we ask one question. In these economic times of (actual) ~~recession~~, OK Depression (we believe it and finally said it). and constant price increases (at the pump and grocery store), when homeownership is being attacked by increasing foreclosures, is it appropriate to say *"healthy six-figure salaries"*? What on earth is *healthy* about Feudal Lords, and Banking Princes (Citigroup's Chuck Prince comes to mind) continuing to earn "healthy" *seven and eight-figure salaries and bonuses* when their world is falling down on them. That kind of money even when their corporations are losing money? Paulson and now Geithner want to keep them going at our expense. Please! It is their mind-set: Elitism and Privilege. If we continue to allow it.

Inflation. While a contentious issue, we've come to believe (we are guided by the excellent Steve Saville of Speculative-Investor.com) that the word inflation is widely misunderstood by both the public and even some professional members of Structured Finance (Wall Street). As Mr. Saville instructs, inflation is the increase in liquidity, the money supply. If the money supply is increased as Mr.

Greenspan enabled for nearly eighteen years – prices rise. If the money supply is decreased, prices are apt to fall. Period.

Bowing to what we consider inappropriate convention, that which people have been convinced to believe against the facts, unless otherwise noted, we will accordingly use the term inflation to indicate growth of prices, asset appreciation. We have no intention to confuse you. We do intend to cause you to think below the surface. We believe you must begin to understand that Financial Players have a strong invested interest in confusing you. To *not* give you sufficient information to understand their business model – the game they are playing – to profit at your expense. They don't teach this stuff in school. Hopefully, now you understand why. You don't have to understand everything in this chapter in order to protect your family. You'll discover that if you read it twice, you'll get more of it the second time. Learning through repetition. Remember, repetition is the Mother of Memory.

Deflation – Deflationists – Deflationistas. While seemingly a great concern for then oncoming Chairman, Dr. Ben Bernanke, deflation is no more than a decrease in the supply of money, thus a contraction of debt, hopefully leading to savings, which might be invested for productive enterprise, rather than for the Inflationist's continuation and perpetration of Credit Bubbles. Clearly, as the Chairman of the Fed, deflation is anathema for an extreme Inflationista, such as Dr. Bernanke because it would be the beginning of the end of Financial Hegemony, control of all Americans (and beyond) by the Wall Street Elites.

Balance. A balance is important, and one of the Fed's two key mandates is to maintain the value of money. Within that context some maintain that a little (just a little) inflation is a good thing. In fact, after the Fed was created (1913), the money supply (inflation) has increased steadily since the mid-twenties. But, never so much as during Greenspan's long term. Moreover, Greenspan did this by enabling a monstrous Credit Bubble, which led directly to the late 1990s' dot.com Equity Bubble (popped to the destructive tune of nearly $7 Billion of Main Street shareholder values), to the current very dangerous, and now popped, yet still deflating Mortgage or Housing Bubble.

In its wake, people's savings are zero, and our unprecedented Current Account Deficit is a very real danger to domestic and international markets and economies. In fact the consumer has moved the income based personal savings rate into negative territory. It's not just that we have no household savings (which used to be deposited in banks enabling them to loan money), it is also the fact that too many Americans are getting through the month by growing their credit card debt. This cannot sustain. The last time we collectively had a negative savings rate was in 1933. By all accounts a very bad year. Depressing.

Under dollar hegemony (read dollar control), resultant from the historic Bretton Woods Agreement immediately following World War II in 1947, the U.S. dollar became the world's currency. And from there the Fed has become arguably the International Lender of Last Resort with lip service to the International Monetary Fund (IMF), the World Bank, and moreover, the Bank of International Settlements (BIS). Breath. Have a glass of punch. This is Homeowner's Economics 101, we'll not jump into the deep end.

The Punch Bowl Model. Without giving a detailed historical analysis of why, and without discussing the dollar as a store of value, we submit that Dr. Bernanke has a near impossible task ahead of him. History cannot judge him well over time, and that also, over time (and it might be a short time from now) he will likely be required to preside over a forced unwinding of the enormous Credit and Mortgage Bubbles. These were created and maintained by his predecessor Alan Greenspan. The process or dangerous game, was embraced and applauded by Wall Street's Structured Finance, who, having become intoxicated at Al Greenspan's party will turn very aggressive on anyone who threatens to, or actually takes the punch bowl away. Addiction demands supply.

The "punch bowl" model has been used widely over decades, particularly with regard to analysis of Fed practice. It was first named by legendary Fed Chairman, William McChesney Martin, Jr., who served as Chairman from April 2, 1951 to January 31, 1970 under five Presidents. Simply put, he used the *punch bowl* as analogy for the Fed increasing the money supply. They fill up the punch bowl, "animal spirits" prevail, and the party rocks on. When too much debt money (punch) has been supplied, participants become voluble, well frankly drunk, and fail to apply rigorous risk analysis.

When the economy is over-peaking, heating up, growing too fast to support itself, inflation and inflation expectations begin to rear up. Normally cautious and responsible risk analysis is thrown to the side of the road. Therefore, a wise Fed begins to close down the party by not supplying more punch (liquidity diminishes, less money available to loan for investment), and thus we reach the low side. After Boom comes the Bust. Every time. Bankruptcies occur, retrenchment, recession.

Then, the Fed comes back to the party and tenuously at first begins to fill the bowl. And, on we go. Boom and Bust. It's the nature of things. Some refer to it as the Business Cycle. Others look to longer term trend lines. The point here is that Greenspan and now Bernanke chose to keep the party going. They now want taxpayers to pay for rehabilitation of the drunken reeling monster – that they created. They want taxpayers to bailout banks who stayed too long at the party, who got up and danced all night. *"Hey. Knock it off. The Fed said it was OK. Can you help us out here? Moral Hazard? Sure we've got moral hazard. It's communicable? We don't know about that. We don't care about that. Hurry up – write the check – pour the punch – the wolves are howling and they are very very thirsty."*

Party in the Dark. We would add that there is one more thing that really puts the damper on an otherwise good party – too many lights. A good party likes dim lights. In fact Houston Chronicle, staff writer, Loren Steffy recently argued on May 8, 2008 in a piece called, "Wall Street Fears the Light," that, "Wall Street prefers the dark, where it can control the information meted out to investors. It's no coincidence, after all, that market participation exploded with the advent of the World Wide Web, which made stock prices readily available with minimal delay to average citizens.

Mr. Steffy also said, "Nor is it surprising that companies such as *Bloomberg* became multibillion-dollar businesses by taking **information once held exclusively in the dark hallways of Wall Street** and making it available to those with money at risk. In the 1970s, when the SEC forced Wall Street to disclose brokerage commissions, rates tumbled and Wall Street's profitability shifted to other businesses such as investment banking." [Emphasis Added.]

He concluded his piece by writing, "Who knows what other time bombs may be ticking on Wall Street's books? What other financial risks have investment banks understated in the name of fast profits? That's what Wall Street is worried about. When we turn on the lights, its party is over."

The lights are on, and they're running around trying to fill up the punch bowl (with taxpayer bailout money) and dimming the lights just as fast as then can. Rock on? We don't think so. It's more like, "Last Call – Last Dance – Get Out of Dodge"

There is a wide debate in academic and financial circles as to whether Dr. Bernanke is a dove or a hawk on the critical matter of inflation.

We argue that Dr. Bernanke is a Bull, not an inflation dove or hawk. The later are terms bantered about in the press, terms that merely obscure for the public his real role as Fed Head. He must be a bull. He must create a wide perception that in spite of contrary evidence – everywhere – that everything is just fine. Chief supplier of the punch becomes chief cheerleader for: *confidence* – Animal Spirits. The SubPrime Crisis is "contained" (well– he finally admitted it's worse than he had mentioned previously, just didn't want to be a party pooper, though no doubt pooping his own trousers) and that we do not stand on the brink of very very deep recession, if not, depression. He's no Alan Greenspan, but moreover, he's no Paul Volker – just when we need him.

Punch Bowl Removed. Need Paul Volker? Yes. In a nutshell as Chairman of the Fed from 1979 through 1987, Volker was brought in under Jimmy Carter in order to wring out extreme inflation. He began doing that in August of 1979, which didn't help out his benefactor President Carter who lost the 1980 election to Ronald Regan. Regan reappointed Volker in 1983, and he served four more years until 1987 when Greenspan came in. Volker significantly increased interest rates until inflation stopped. At the highest point in 1980-81, rates for a 30-year fixed mortgage were running from 17 to 20%. Ouch. Hard to believe today – but true.

But, have heart – Volker is back. Well, sort of. Well, kinda, but not really. During the campaign Obama reached out to him and Volker traveled with the President, gave him advice and taught him about Economics. Obama subsequently gave Mr. Former Chairman of the Federal Reserve System, Paul Volker an advisory job, heading a Commission that would be reporting to the White House. Unfortunately, nobody is listening or asking for input or reports. Volker has been sidelined without an active voice with the new Young President. He is fearless. Maybe that's why in the United States of ~~America~~, Goldman Sacked US they shunted him to the side. Volker is neither beholden to nor in thrall to Goldman Sachs. We don't hear much from Mr. Volker these days.

In order to maintain the confidence of foreign governments and their central banks who fund our Current Account Deficit, and our Government, and our War, rather our Occupations of Iraq and Afghanistan (where the opium grows freely and illicit narcotics cash money is created and laundered by our TBTFs), the Fed must tighten (raise interest rates) and be less accommodative (stop freely enabling the creation of massive amounts of dollars through liquidity growth for the banks) than has been the case. Not through Greenspan-like baby steps, but firmly and decisively in order to maintain the slightly diminishing flow of recycled dollars back to the U.S. that buy our Treasuries, Mortgage Backed Securities, Asset Backed Securities, and the like. As well reported for years in the financial press, we must have an in-flow of well over $2 Billion per business day, to keep us solvent. Well good luck for that. Another reason Financial Armageddon is swiftly approaching and will smash all the punch bowls, even the ones in the secret back room.

Bernanke must let the markets know that he is in charge. He must rein in banks and hedge funds that are allowed to create *unregulated* derivative markets, which are wildly esoteric investment vehicles that are not fully understood even by investors that invest in them. (Investment Bank trader to befuddled Institutional Investor's trader: *"Really? Are you kidding? Don't worry about it. You don't have to completely understand it. Only our geeks really get it. Everyone is doing it. It's OK."*) These are investments in financial instruments that may take down the banking system unless they are bailed out by taxpayers.

While this may sound overly aggressive, no less than Warren Buffet has called the unregulated derivative market, *"Financial weapons of mass destruction."* There are highly technical books written on this extremely complex market. We can't understand them. Yet, it's enough for you to understand that derivative markets exist, that they are largely misunderstood, and finally, they are instruments that connect, rather *interconnect* major market players.

Derivatives At Risk. These "interconnections" were cited by Bernanke when he illegally supplied the back up money for JPMorgan to acquire failing Investment Banking firm Bear Stearns in March, 2008. The fear was that if Bear Stearns fell into bankruptcy, or worse, was simply forced to close its doors because they didn't have money to pay their debts, their obligations on derivatives, one firm could bring down the other Investment Banks, and nobody knows how many other firms down with it. So, they did a controlled take down of Bear Stearns, with the Fed giving JP Morgan money to buy their assets for a song.

To summarize, regarding these exotic products, they are basically insurance policies that *this* or *that* <u>will</u> happen, or another party (interconnections) takes the other side of the trade/bet, that *this* or *that* <u>will not</u> happen. The take away here, all you really need to know is that this monstrous book of business, above

$540 Trillion in nominal value, is completely unregulated, and had been blessed by Greenspan as an appropriate method to mitigate risk.

The unregulated derivative market *is* arguably the greatest risk to our financial system. It needs to be unwound and shut down in an orderly fashion. They did it when forced with Bear Stearns and Lehman Brothers. But, the players we have in place, both Bernanke and Treasury Secretary Geithner have no intention whatsoever to do that. It's where the entities that they are loyal to play and are so heavily invested. As always, we pound the drum again. They want taxpayers to make the banks whole for their risky bets, which have turned into huge losses, as exhibited by both the Bear Stearns and Lehman Brothers meltdowns. Please.

So, the whole nation went berserk over the AIG bonuses. A drop in the bucket. Of the near $180 Billion handed to AIG, they paid Goldman Sachs over $12.5 Billion right out of the gate. Incidentally, the Chairman of Goldman Sachs was the only individual from the private sector who sat on the committee that green lighted the AIG payout under TARP. Game, Set and Match. They actually do some of this in the clear light of day. Does the media react with any sense of outrage. Are we sold out? Well … you know. Now you know.

The Man. By all accounts, Dr. Ben Bernanke is a nice guy, and that is good. However, can impeccable credentials and academic acumen confer (Wall) Street Smarts? Can, rather will, pressure from the markets and the Administration cause Dr. Bernanke to fold, to not be able to sustain his real (as we see them) duties, his deeper obligations to the American People and the U.S. and World Economies; or, will he continue enabling Structured Finance to make large bets with nearly free money, continuing a policy of Systemic Risk to the economy. Most new Fed Chairman do not have all the appropriate credentials when they come to the position, and consequentially must (and some do) learn on the job.

Widely reputed as one of our top academic economic theoreticians, disposed to econometrics, Dr. B. is also known as a top inflation fighter, based on econometric approaches, models and analysis of history. The reasoning and moreover, Wall Street sentiment goes that if he possesses such acumen, and he's down with *"Greenspan Continuity,"* it looks good, sounds better, and gives a fighting chance for the economy to stave off disaster by continuing to do what Greenspan always did.

Except this time they've finally gone too far. The increasing prices you pay for gasoline and food, for everything, are a direct result of their promiscuity. You'd be right to assume these increasing prices are additional taxation without representation. And, that is one of several critical reasons why our Founding Fathers said No More to Britain. Should we do less? Should we simply continue as indentured servants? We think not.

While a Harvard undergraduate Dr. Bernanke (like Greenspan) enjoyed Libertarian reasoning. As a professor and later Chairman of the Princeton Economics department, he was a casual dresser and widely noted as a rigorous thinker who did his homework. As a Federal Reserve Governor, he would chat informally in the cafeteria with staffers (unusual for normally austere, unapproachable Fed Governors). As the Chairman of Bush's Council of Economic Advisors, he became a fully buttoned-down careful member of the team. President Bush did chide him for wearing tan socks with a blue suit to a meeting, though Bernanke turned it into a joke the following day, showing his good humor and grace under fire. Grace over substance? Is that enough?

In some commentaries it has been suggested that Dr. Bernanke simply will not be able to continue to hold his own convincingly in the media spotlight, appearances on the Hill, etcetera. Remember, this entire house of cards is built on appearances – perception – appearances which show confidence. Television appearances show him to be the academician, not the cool-hand showman, not the obfuscating Maestro.

Yet, we'll give him some credit out of fairness. By April 2009, he was more than holding his own. That's what the media says, but, gosh, he's just handed your future taxpayer debt to the banks. And, what the banks like, the media likes. Why? The media in our nation has been taken over and consolidated by capital interests in the nation over the past twenty years. Only five companies control 90% of the MSM. Astonishing. This means interlinking Boards of Directors. Finance and media people on the same Boards. So, beyond the obvious advertising dollars, and essential debt financings done by Wall Street the MSM has not choice but to tow the Party Line (which party? the Money Party) they have a Prime Directive underlying their editorial content, and slant of articles they print or report on. Favor the banks.

That's why The Establishment is so rankled by the pesky Bloggers. Those pesky Bloggers are getting the truth out. Wave of the future. Wave of technology's disintermediation of the old tired, sold-out and controlled print vehicles. Viva the future. Actually the Blog-O-Sphere was an early leader of the Internet Renaissance – and a method for both the Tea Party and Occupy Movements to get out the word – rally the troops.

Alan Abelson of *Barron's* said, "The selection of Ben Bernanke has prompted a lot of mostly inane chatter by economists and press pundits…. All we really know about Dr. Bernanke is that he has degrees from Harvard and MIT was head of the economics department of Princeton, read Ayn Rand as a callow youth, … and is something of a monetarist." Ah ha. Like Greenspan, another callow youth, Ayn Rand reader. We were too at nineteen. Yet, thankfully we grew out of it and hope against all evidence to the contrary that Dr. Bernanke will as well.

All we'll say about author Ayn Rand and Alan Greenspan is that he did an apprenticeship with her long ago, and provided research for her opus, *Atlas Shrugged*. She was quoted by John Cassidy in The New Yorker, April 24, 2000 saying, "Alan might basically be a social climber," an "undertaker," and "an opportunist interested mainly in advancing his career." Amen.

Similar to Alan Greenspan comments over time, Dr. Bernanke has been quoted saying,

"I think it's extraordinarily difficult for the central bank to know in advance or *even after the fact* whether or not there's been a bubble in an asset price."

"Changes in asset prices should affect monetary policy only to the extent that they affect the central bank's forecast of inflation."

"A closer look reveals that the economic repercussions of a stock market [read: housing] crash depend less on the severity of the crash itself than on the response of economic policymakers, particularly central bankers."

He claimed to not be able to see an asset (stating there was no housing) bubble, but if one is there, he wishes it doesn't burst, but if it does (and they all do), the Fed can fix it right up by further inflating the money supply – eroding the value of purchasing power of the dollar so that Structured Finance can get out of Dodge OK. The taxpayers, won't even really know what hit them. They'll just pay and pay like they did in the late 1980s Savings and Loan debacle. This time not only we pay and pay, but so will our children and grandchildren. Burdon our grandchildren for a pay out to pernicious Banksters? There ought be a law. Whoops Congress is owned by the same Banksters. And, so is United States Department of Justice.

All we are saying is that you must do your own home loan cramdown by Using Foreclosure Law to Keep Your Home. None of the Powerz can or will come to your assistance. We try. Take us up on it.

Believes the Impossible. Dr. Bernanke has asserted over time that by merely pushing the interest rate up and down (he has espoused knowing when to take action based on modeling and strict formulas, as a good academic, a smart professor would likely assert), he can keep the ball in the air, the economy growing and prices stable. *Would it be so simple.* He's right there with Greenspan on that one, and many market participants and commentators marvel at their naiveté.

Or is it? Perhaps it's just a show tune (they are both saxophone players) they trot out to keep and manage expectations – propping up market and investor confidence. The well rehearsed rhetoric is only that, and some intelligent insiders know, really know, that it's all they can say publicly as they actually, in fact, continue to create inflation (increasing the money supply by enabling the growth of unregulated debt-based excessive liquidity), while claiming to control the price of things, through interest rate pushing. But, wait, interest rates are down, down, down – never pushed up. If they did that, they'd tank the stock market and the housing market.

A great charlatan such as Alan Greenspan, was able to control expectations in an extremely complex world, with more data sets to observe, study, analyze and make recommendations from. But, today with Globalization, we argue, there is too much input, too many changing, really changing international markets and political conditions that disallow projections based largely on historical precedent.

Economic Modeling. Dr. Bernanke, an academic economic modeler, may not be able to get his head out of the academic lab when they're banging on the door. In addition, never forget the impact of domestic and foreign political up-heavals, irrational political context and other factors jamming in (such as irresponsible MBS risk modelers failing to factor in, to anticipate, wide spread defaults on home mortgages) – breaking the model – chaos can rule. That is exactly what we're seeing today.

Can an academic who comes to understand that it can't be completely understood, stand up with a straight face, and say: "With a few exceptions – and occasional headwinds – we're on top of it, and, it's all good?" Ben does his best. The problem is exacerbated when the academic personality, and this one (claims he is) given to transparency, finds that the truth may hurt too much. It may cause the markets to attack the Fed Head (through a complicit press who receives advertising revenue directly and indirectly from market participants and their courtiers), attack the veracity of the bearer of bad news. Kill the Messenger. They don't have to. He's caved completely, and operates his illicit and illegal activities in secret. In October 2011, in a public meeting presented on the TV, Jamie Dimon of JP Morgan was verbally abusive to Mr. Bernanke, to Mr. B, who took it in a sense of humility and slight defensiveness.

The Evidence. A bit of the historical record is in order. In November of 2002, newly appointed Federal Reserve Governor, Ben Bernanke, gave a historic speech, which gave him the nickname, *Helicopter Ben.* The speech, entitled: *"Deflation: Making Sure 'It' Doesn't Happen Here"* was thought by some to be much more than Dr. Bernanke's personal opinions given to a major group of economists in Washington D.C. That, some have opined, he was speaking for and with (his boss) Mr. Greenspan's approval. But, of course!

> "As I have stressed already, prevention of deflation remains preferable to having to cure it. If we do fall into deflation, however, we can take comfort that the <u>logic of the printing press</u> example must assert itself, and sufficient injections of money will ultimately always reverse a deflation." [Emphasis added.]

> "Like gold, <u>U.S. dollars have value only</u> to the extent that they are <u>strictly limited in supply</u>. But the U.S. government has a technology called a printing press (or, today its electronic equivalent), that allows it to produce as many U.S. dollars as it wishes to at <u>essentially no cost</u>." [Emphasis added.]

At the bottom line, among other things, Bernanke said it would be appropriate to "shovel money from helicopters" if deflation were at hand. The currency and bond markets took him, and take him seriously, though they wonder if he will do it. If he doesn't do it (he *is* doing it), shovel money through the growth of the Credit Bubble, as Mr. Greenspan has done, then there is the distinct possibility that it will all unravel. (It is.) But just a minute, if he continues to increase the Credit Bubble, print more money, the dollar loses value, and there will be an international dollar sell-off, oil will continue to rise, and *all prices* at the pump and in the grocery stores will severely damage the American consumer. (They have.)

Some Housing Facts. Caught up in the mania from 2004 through 2006, many first time buyers (actually pressured by parents and friends) came to believe that if they didn't get in, they would *never be able to afford a home.* Taken to its logical conclusion this proves that there really was a mania mind set that prices could only go higher.

We wonder if qualified buyers (those with a good working history and credit, and able to raise a down payment) for the most part are already "all in." With the exception of newly forming families, we think so, and if correct, it destroys the "demand" argument. Will the next wave of buyers be high school seniors hoping to graduate in June, get a job and buy a home with an interest only loan? Ridiculous? Not so ridiculous in the summer of 2006, the height of market mania, when we used to tell that joke to other real estate agents. . Today the loan spigot has been shut down, even for many with solid credit histories. Consequently our little joke on high school seniors (sorry, it's just a joke) did not hold much past late 2006. But people did laugh when the boom was still on – because silly as it seemed – maybe they really could've received a loan – in 2006.

Real Debt. The U.S. government is now carrying gross public debt in excess of $13.9 Trillion. In 2002, the gross public debt was $6 Trillion. Meaning that the government increased debt 100% (a $$7.9 Trillion increase)in ten years through borrowing and spending. This astonishing figure does not include: business, personal, state, county or local government debts, which have also increased by trillions of dollars in this six year time frame.

The Federal Reserve System. What is the Fed? Simply put, the Fed is not a federal entity or agency. It is owned and operated (through a special U.S. Congressionally granted Charter) by a cartel of major national and large regional banks, who obviously see to their own best interests first. We don't know what the Fed owns, what they buy, or when they do it. In particular we don't know how much money they earn, nor the actual profit, which is distributed to the banks that own the stock issued by the Fed. Why not? The American people would not stand for it! So they don't tell us.

They won't even tell Congress, Literally, under oath, Bernanke told a U.S. Senator that he couldn't tell him who the Fed had just given over a trillion dollars to. That was a side handout, not the TARP ($800 Billion) funds being shoveled out by the Treasury department. The TARP was passed by Congress, but, the Fed keeps only it's own counsel. Mum is the word, and Congress let's the get away with it. Well. After all it is the Fed. Remember, it just came out they secretly gave away another $7.7 Trillion nearly simultaneously with the TARP funds. Does this become treasonous at any point? Well, we're not lawyers, so, we'll leave that one alone.

At its inception a function of the Fed was to maintain and control an "elastic money supply." This is not necessarily a bad idea, unless one is a gold fundamentalist such as Texas House of Representatives Libertarian Ron Paul, who we bragged on above, and that's enough. In good times shrink the money supply, and in bad times grow the money supply. What has happened is that Greenspan always grew the money supply through an "accommodative" policy which enabled easy creation of Liquidity – in other words – Debt.

The record shows that history does repeat itself occasionally, and nearly always does so when self-interested central bankers, who are controlled by the very banks they claim to regulate, call the shots. The consequences for the American Public are indeed frightening, and again we suggest preparing yourself in advance for the possibility of another Greater Depression, which is looming, and will also be world-wide in scope. If the American Consumer, arguably the engine for the world economy, is stopped, China, to take one example, will face widespread domestic unease when very low paying sweatshop factory jobs cease to exist.

The Wonder. Of it all. What many overlook (some call it denial), is that in this case it comes out of *moral hazard,* which is the financial markets' belief that the Fed will always save them through accommodation because they are *"Too Big To Fail."* This enables them, gives them belief – confidence. They are confident because the taxpayers will pick up their debts, and leave them in business to do more damage and continue to enrich themselves at the expense of all Americans.

President's Working Group. Actually the Fed could buy up all the General Motors shares available on the market through a private intermediary. Could they already be doing so to prop up the stock? It is well known that there is such a thing as the *Plunge Protection Team* (PPT), an irreverent nickname for the President's Working Group on Financial Markets. The Working Group was created by Ronald Reagan under Executive Order 12631, and signed March 18, 1988 to explicitly respond to financial markets events, in particular in response to the devastating October 19, 1987 "Black Monday." The Working Group makes recommendations regarding both legislative and private sector issues in order to "enhance the integrity, efficiency, orderliness, and competitiveness of [United States] financial markets and *maintaining investor confidence.*" [Emphasis added.]

Its members are: The Secretary of the Treasury (Geithner) (Chairman of the Working Group), the Chairman of the Board of Governors of the Federal Reserve System (Bernanke), the Chairman of the Securities and Exchange Commission (Shapiro), and The Chairman of the Commodity Futures Trading Commission (Gensler). Now there's a group that can fix anything. Let's see, Geithner and Gensler are Goldman Sachs related. Shapiro was a pal of Bernie Madoff. Bernanke is arguably Jamie Dimon's boy. Hello!

Theories abound regarding secret machinations. One prominent theory makes a claim that the Working Group, the PPT, is nothing more than a secret scheme, enabling the PPT to take actions in the equity markets. They allegedly secretly manipulate the U.S. stock market when a downturn appears that may go worse and create a market crash. They use government funds advanced by the Fed to directly and aggressively purchase stock index futures to raise confidence at critical times.

Others claim the PPT utilizes major broker-dealers, Investment Banks, through their off-shore entities that step into the market anonymously under the name of "private clients." They then follow the Fed's orders to buy (with "on our honor" repurchase agreements in place) stock market future indexes to show that investor confidence (coming from who knows where) is bouncing back. It's effective. But remember, their actual work is a secret so that the American People won't understand that markets are rigged. What a blow that would be. Is everything we know wrong? That would be ridiculous – but – still. Now we understand that they use it nearly every day, at certain critical time periods. Normally, 9:00 AM, and 3:00 PM.

Here's a source for construct above.

Writing Oct 30, 2006, in the Telegraph, Ambrose Evans-Pritchard, had the following to say regarding new Treasury Secretary Henry Paulson. "Hank Paulson, the market-wise Treasury Secretary who built a $700m fortune at Goldman Sachs, is re-activating the 'plunge protection team' (PPT), a shadowy body with powers to support stock index, currency, and credit futures in a crash."

"Otherwise known as the Working Group On Financial Markets, it was created by Ronald Reagan to prevent a repeat of the Wall Street meltdown in October 1987. Mr. Paulson says the group had been allowed to languish over the boom years. Henceforth, it will have a command centre at the US Treasury that will track global markets and serve as an operations base in the next crisis. The top brass will meet every six weeks, combining the heads of Treasury, Federal Reserve, Securities and Exchange Commission (SEC), and CFTC."

Take Down. Prescient we're not – we can't read the future. We know it's going to be a terrible fallout, but, we, or no one can say what day will be the worst. However, if history is a guide, we fear a terrible scenario likely to unfold. Even a modest glance at the facts presented above indicate we're in uncharted waters. It has never been done before? Maybe it has. This previous creditor nation, now a debtor nation, owes trillions of dollars. Might it be that we repudiate the debt by devaluing the dollar 40% as FDR did in 1933?

[We're Rome. Just kidding. Actually though, these debts are your tribute to us for keeping the world largely at peace, for enabling your economies to get up and roaring. Thank you very much.

[From time to time as the case may be, we go from nation to nation to show the rest of you the Mercy of our Terrible Swift Sword. Shock and Awe. You're not following the logic? Think of Iraq? Everyone now knows we lied to our own people to go to war. What do the frightened people do about it? Shake their heads? So listen carefully. Everything will go on as before.

[We continue to inflate the currency. We'll say it's worth less, devalue the dollar, which brings the real cost of paying these massive debts way down. And, then, of course we must continue inflating. You do want those jobs for

your people – don't you? We certainly want to keep some of our jobs, but well, manufacturing and service employees are on their own. In fact we sent their jobs to you at the cost of losing our Middle class. Enabling you to grow one. We think that's more than enough. Don't you?

[Our houses? Well, that's up to us, but since we're off the record here ... we may be forced to liquidate 25-30% of the so-called owners. Particularly, the ones with the sub-prime, no-money down, interest only loans. The ones who bought more house than they could afford, the ones who couldn't believe they could buy a house, or another residential house investment, the ones who really ought to have known better – that it really was <u>too good</u> to be true – the ones who bought into the mania.

[Frankly, we, well, we fooled them into it. Well, Greenspan did, and the money was so good for us, we kept it going as long as we could. What are they going to do about it? Walk away? Not likely, we've got them under control. For sure.

[They're what? Even people who are merely underwater are Using Foreclosure Law sounding in fraud to leverage their lenders? But, but, but....]

The Fed and Today's Climate For Homeowners. For some homeowners and residential investors the Fed's practices enabled a good ride – if they were out early enough. Out when it seemed to hurt. When greed says to a speculator (not a professional investor), a couple of more months, we'll do even better. Well they may not. In fact if they stayed, many are in trouble, owning properties that do not cash flow. Again we make it clear, the primary difference between a naïve speculator and a professional investor is that the professional understands when it's time to take profit and exit the market.

Clearly the market has changed. The smart ones, prudent investors, not just greedy amateur flippers, got out at or before the September 2006 top. Here we are in 2012 and houses are staying on the market much longer, and listing prices (dreaming of Summer 2006) are only very reluctantly lowered by seller's who for the most part don't understand what hit them.

Got the clue? The national inventory of property for sale is up to at least 12 months, or more, depending on which statistics you believe. Sales volumes have fallen through the floor. Lender's have not been making loans to even relatively well-qualified buyers. Lenders have been forced to get that old time Risk Adverse Religion back in their hearts and minds. Critically, the Investment Bankers are not buying the loans from the local lenders, because there are no buyers for the Securities, only would-be *seller*-Investors who cannot sell the securities without taking a loss. So, they continue to hold the securities. By not selling at a loss no one sees the loss on their balance sheets. Meanwhile, they're all praying and pounding various tables demanding that they be bailed out by the taxpayers. That dear reader is – you.

If interest rates increase, more ARMS will reset higher, resulting in more foreclosures, and home values will continue down – towards what some consider realistic pricing. Realistic pricing? Remember from this book's Forward, we will not have that until we have Price Discovery. Meaning, that home prices will reflect *historical actual gross housing debt to actual gross income ratios.* Because wages and salaries are not increasing, housing prices must, and will continue to go down.

The Fed is keeping interest rates low to minimize foreclosures, and prop the controlled stock market. That is the bottom line. The more foreclosures, the more derivatives will blow up in the face of those financial entities who invested in them. That is underneath the whole fiasco. But, because the Fed is dishing out so much "money" they cannot keep the interest rates low much longer. Or, there goes the dollar, and no one, except the Fed (with fake money), will purchase our U.S. Treasuries, which we've historically used to finance the government. With huge deficit's projected well into the future who would buy our Treasuries? So we buy them ourselves with fiat money that the taxpayers must pay back. Please.

A home is worth exactly what a ready, willing and able (and highest bidder) buyer can and will pay for it *today.* We are seeing home values rapidly plummeting. This trend is not likely to end anytime soon. Buyers have been sidelined because they believe they can get a better deal over time; and if not more importantly, credit markets have seized up, and therefore buyers are discovering that qualifying for a loan is more difficult, and lenders are now insisting on a significant down payment.

Yet, Washington D.C. and Wall Street are doing everything they can think of to *"keep people in their homes."* This is not a good place to be (unless you force a cramdown principal reduction) in the coming storm, particularly if your home is worth less than what you owe on it right now.

Don't be in denial, and don't be defeated! If dropping prices put you underwater, why, really why, would you choose to be an indentured servant for the next 8-10 years (or likely longer), making payments on a loan that is higher than the value of your home? Consider your *house* as an investment. *Home* is where the heart is. That is anywhere you live. A rational homeowner looks to the terms of the contract with the lender that are spelled out in the Promissory Note and Deed of Trust or Mortgage, and makes a rational business decision to Use Foreclosure Law.

Deed of Trust Mortgage. The intent for both is to secure property for the lender. When you borrowed money to buy a house, lenders demanded that you sign two documents: a Deed of Trust and a Promissory Note. A Promissory Note is basically an IOU, whereby you promise to pay the lender based on terms and conditions put forward in the IOU. It is also a negotiable instrument, like a check. And, is secured (backed) by the Deed of Trust or Mortgage.

Some lenders allow only one party to sign the Promissory Note. However, both husband and wife (all purchasing parties if they are not married) are required to sign the Deed of Trust. This is because when you sign it you are actually deeding the property – albeit in trust – to a third party trustee chosen by the lender. The Deed of Trust is recorded with the County Recorder. Once the loan is paid off the trustee is supposed to record a Release for the Deed of Trust. However, the dirty joke is on them. They sold and resold these loans, and failed to record who actually owned them in the appropriate County Recorder's office. Thus they've put a cloud on the chain of title. This you can use for legal leverage if you determine to Use Foreclosure Law to Keep Your Home.

The important part to understand here is that if you become delinquent on your payments, the trustee can sell the property at a foreclosure sale. That is a condition of the contract, of the deal. Consequently, if you do not make payments (for whatever reasons) they can, after going through the foreclosure process take back and sell the house. They are taking a lot of houses back, record numbers in foreclosure, but, having a heck of time selling them at the court house auctions, so the lenders end up being stuck with them. They are holding approximately six million vacant houses off the market because if they put them on the market, that would simply drive down values sooner. This they cannot stand. This we can stand. The sooner we achieve a balanced normal market, the sooner the economy will come back. Rome burns while ~~Nero~~, The Bankers, fiddle.

The whole construct was frankly a business deal, with terms dictated by the lender. It is just a business deal that you had little power to set up to your advantage. It was set up by lender's to secure their position. It's nothing personal. You are not bound by any conditions except the letter of the law. Repeat: it's just a business deal. So doesn't it make sense to Use Foreclosure Law to Keep Your Home?

A New Choice To Consider. Rather than pay high mortgage payments you cannot afford, or are payments on a debt higher than the actual value of the property, you can release that debt by Using Foreclosure Law to Keep Your Home. If you use the law to withdraw from the market, the smart thing to do is to rent a home. That's right. We believe it's smart to rent, particularly during these tumultuous times. The numbers prove that it's cheaper than home ownership. Then come back to real estate ownership when the market has been wrenchingly cleansed. Don't be in it when the ship is sinking, which is happening right now, and worse to come. You have the legal and ethical right to Get Out. But, as we've said above, easy for us to say. Not so easy if you do not *wish* to disrupt your families life. We understand, which is why we say, well, you know.

Ultimately, what will drive prices down, cause inevitable Price Discovery, will be lenders owning a large number of vacant houses which they can't sell on the MLS without a huge hit to their balance sheets. At some point a threshold will be crossed – a signal will be given – and like the safety in numbers of lemmings all the lenders will start getting rid of properties through auctions. But, these will be a different kind of auction than a foreclosure sheriff's sale, which has a definite, and today, a high minimum bid.

When the day finally arrives, unsold properties will be sold rapidly through what are called *Absolute Auctions* with no minimum bid. Professional residential investors are waiting for those days to arrive. And you now have the clue to be there with them. That is of course if you Use Foreclosure Law and make the decision to push the property back on the lender under your terms. Though we understand, that many families will choose to stay after using legal leverage to obtain a proper loan modification, with a reduction in principal amount owed. Obtain their own cramdown, principal reduction

Beneficiaries of Absolute Auctions will be former homeowners who courageously walked away. People who rented and waited. People who have paid down all their debt, such as credit cards, repaired their credit and saved for a down payment. The day is coming.

Fed Accounting Out of Control. We've presented information above to give you a sense that something is fundamentally wrong when the Federal Reserve System is owned by banks, yet alleges publicly that it "maintains the value of money" and "maximizes employment." Their recent bailout of Bear Stearns by backing JP Morgan's takeover was action taken outside the mandate of their Charter. Nobody sued them. In fact Secretary Paulson is pushing very hard to give the Fed more regulatory power. Please. Well actually, why? So they can engage in further schemes to save the Financial System, which has come to be operated in direct disregard for the American People. Yes, it is that bad. Let's take a look at how they operate, usually in secrecy, but, they've attracted so much attention of late that more information is coming out.

We're the beneficiary of excellent commentary by *Bloomberg* columnist, Jonathon Weil, writing on June 18, 2008. We've included this article in 2012, because the underlying points are well made and hold to this day. The excellent Mr. Weil wrote:

"The Federal Reserve is just days away from completing the financing for its bailout of Bear Stearns Cos., after which the central bank will have another big decision to make: how to account for it. Flip through the footnotes to the Fed's latest annual report, and you'll come across an open secret. The Fed doesn't follow normal accounting rules, as promulgated by any of the major standard-setting boards. Rather, the Fed writes its own, in a document called the Financial Accounting Manual for Federal Reserve Banks. [Emphasis added.]

"If you ever wanted to design an accounting regime to help a bank cook its books, the Fed's would be perfect. This doesn't exactly inspire faith in the U.S. financial system, at a time when a good example might help a lot. Imagine if there were no rules specifying when a bank must bring an Enron-style special-purpose entity onto its own balance sheet. The Fed's accounting manual has none. Now picture an accounting system where a bank never had to recognize losses on any securities it holds, as long as it continues holding them. That, too, is the Fed's policy.... [Emphasis added.]

"Now that the Fed is taking on the risk of Bear Stearns's assets, though, the game has changed. And the Fed's rules should, too, at least for these particular holdings. Indeed, the Fed's Board of Governors can change the rules anytime it wants. The reason is that the Fed will bear most of the risk of losses. Under the Fed's 161-page accounting manual, however, there's no such requirement. That's because the manual doesn't have any rules on the subject. The Fed hasn't said yet what it will do. [Emphasis added.]

"The worst thing the Fed could do now is resort to accounting trickery to avoid losses. If the Fed won't be marking all the Bear Stearns assets at fair value on its balance sheet, it at least should record write downs whenever generally accepted accounting principles would require them.

"The Fed also should eliminate the secrecy around its precious accounting manual. You won't find the manual on the Fed's Web site, even though it's cited by name in the Fed's financial statements. To get my copy, after the Fed's press office initially declined to provide one, I had to file a request under the Freedom of Information Act. The Fed sent me a lightly redacted version 18 days later. [Emphasis added.]

"While that's fine, it's not enough. Good disclosure is no cure for bad accounting. And talk about a confidence killer: The last thing our financial markets need now is the knowledge that the world's most powerful central bank is fudging its figures. If the Fed doesn't do the right thing here, we all could be in trouble." [Emphasis added.]

While the section above is lengthy, it's important that you get a sense that at the most fundamental level the Fed is in uncharted water. Today these guys, Geithner and Paulson (do you think he's really retired to, oh, say The Bahamas where he might keep his money hidden?) and Bernanke are trying very hard. They're trying to stay at the rudder, to guide the ship into safe waters – out of the storm. The problem is that they're avoiding the much larger picture as they're forced to spend so much of their time bailing and bailing and bailing to keep the ship from sinking. If they had the interest of the Good Ship America as their first priority, we'd give them our best wishes and a hearty Go With God's Speed.

Unfortunately, they're working so hard to stave off Greenspan's perfect storm – the Maestro's oncoming bust. Worse, they're caught in denial, and, as masters to the Banking System as they've known it, they're in over their heads, also, underwater. They're having to react so quickly to huge leaks in the dyke, this one, and that one, that they have no time to really think through the consequences of the seem-to-make-sense actions of the day. The problem is that of unintended consequences. And, they are getting them. Including an increasingly angry population who have for good reason *lost confidence* in the system. What do they do. They retrench. They save their money, and the economy continues to sputter and job losses increase foreclosures, and down the spiral goes with its velocity increasing nearly daily.

They've lost sense of ethical conduct, even ignore the Rule of Law as they struggle to defend a failed-system. A failed financial system that took too much for itself. The center is not holding. Frankly, the center of the Financial System should not hold if the cost to Americans is remaining as indentured slaves to a broken system. This sun will rise on a new day.

Background. In this chapter we've shown the background of how money has been manipulated at the Fed, first by Greenspan, now by Bernanke. And by the Treasury, the banking industry and ultimately politicians who looked away.

In Chapter 3, *The Political Economy,* we showed you the background that enabled the current fiascos. How U.S. economic history proved the value for:

- a strong middle class for a sound economy,
- a fair distribution of wealth for a sound economy; and,
- how the financial industry has hollowed out the middle class for their profit.

In other words how you've been duped and set up to fail. You entered home ownership in good faith. They kept the Real Rules of Economics behind closed doors – worse, in their arrogance they believed they could bend them to their will – by pumping more money. Due to the prevalence of Predatory Lending and Securities Fraud homeowners didn't have a chance. As you well know your allegiance, your loyalty belongs to your family, not a financial industry that ignores it's real mandate and changes the rules behind closed doors.

We've shown you that to survive, really to thrive, you may have no other viable decision to take other than to *Use Foreclosure Law*. It is not an easy decision to take. We know that. It is heart and gut wrenching.

If you have mortgage issues, and/or are underwater, initially they may have convinced you to believe it was your own failure. That's what they want you to think and believe. Our intention is to give you the information, which can give you the power to move on with your lives – to be the master of your own ship. By Using Foreclosure Law to Keep Your Home – now – you create the opportunity to repair the damage that has been done to you. It is our intention to remove the fear of the unknown. You're reading this book, which means that you are on the road to taking control of your life by Confronting Fraudulent Housing Debt

Authority Speaks. Near the end of this chapter on the Fed we offer an excerpt from an article by noted economic analyst Frank Shostak, writing at Mises.org. Mr. Shostak is an adjunct scholar of the Mises Institute and a frequent contributor to Mises.org.

"Most commentators have endlessly praised the innovative methods that Bernanke and his colleagues are introducing to counter the financial crisis. Bernanke, who has written a lot about the causes of the Great Depression, is regarded as the ultimate expert on how to counter the current economic crisis. In short, most commentators are of the view that the man knows what he is doing and he will be able to fix the current financial problems.

"Bernanke is of the view that by means of aggressive monetary policy the credit markets can be normalized. Once credit markets are brought back to normalcy, this will play an important role in preventing serious economic crisis. Remember Bernanke's financial accelerator model: a minor shock in the financial sector could result in large damage to the real economy.

"In short, Bernanke, by means of his so-called "innovative" policy of fixing the symptoms of the disease, believes he can cure the disease. What is the source of the disease and why are investment banks so heavily infected by it? The root of the problem is the Fed's very loose interest rate policy and strong monetary pumping from January 2001 to June 2004. The federal funds rate target was lowered from 6.5% to 1%. It is this that has given rise to various mal-investments, which we label here as bubble activities.

"We define a bubble as the outcome of activities that have emerged on the back of loose monetary policy of the central bank. In the absence of monetary pumping, these activities would not have emerged. Since bubble activities are not self-funded, their emergence must come at the expense of various self-funded or productive activities. This means that less real saving is left for real wealth-generators, which in turn undermines real wealth formation. (Monetary pumping gives rise to misallocation of resources, which as a rule manifests itself through a relative increase in nonproductive activities against productive activities.)

"When new money is created out of thin air, its effect is not felt instantaneously across all the market sectors. The effect moves from one individual to another individual and thus from one market to another market. Monetary pumping then generates bubble activities across all markets as time goes by.

"As with any other business, participants in financial markets like investment banks are trying to 'make money.' It is this that gives rise to the creation of various products like collateralized debt obligations (CDO) and mortgage-backed securities (MBS) in order to secure as big a slice as possible of the pool of newly created money. (Financial entrepreneurs are basically trying to exploit opportunities created by the Fed's loose monetary stance and get as much as possible out of the expanded pool of money.)

"As long as the Fed kept pushing money into the system to support the low interest rate target, various activities that sprang up on the back of the loose stance <u>appeared to be for real</u>. When money is plentiful and interest rates are extremely low, investment in various relatively high-yielding assets like CDO's and MBS's that masquerade as top-notch grade investment becomes very attractive. The prompt payment of interest and a very low rate of defaults further reinforce the attractiveness of financially engineered investment products. However, once the central bank tightens its monetary stance – i.e., reduces monetary pumping – this undermines various bubble activities. [Emphasis added.]

"The damage from the loose monetary policies of the Fed from January 2001 to June 2004 cannot be undone by trying to fix symptoms. Various activities or financial bubbles that sprang up on the back of loose monetary policies have weakened the bottom line of the economy. This fact cannot be undone by another dosage of policies that attempt to suppress the symptoms. If anything, such policies are likely only to weaken the bottom line further."

Clearly the breakdown has occurred and is continuing. It will become much worse.

To close out this chapter on the Fed, here are some brief comments from Anna Schwartz who co-authored, with Milton Friedman, *A Monetary History of the United States* (1963). Some argue that is the definitive account of how misguided monetary policy turned the stock-market crash of 1929 into the Great Depression.

Regarding Benanke, she recently said in the *Wall Street Journal,* "This was [Bernanke's] claim to be worthy of running the Fed. He was familiar with history. He knew what had been done. I don't see that they've achieved what they should have been trying to achieve. So my verdict on this present Fed leadership is that they have not really done their job."

Ms. Schwarz is a towering figure in modern economics. Hers is a stunning denouncement of Dr. Bernanke. You must understand that like the Young President he too has been captured by the Banking Cartel.

In 2002, when the word "deflation" began appearing in the business news, Bernanke gave a speech about deflation. In that speech, he mentioned that the government in a fiat money system owns the physical means of creating money. Control of the means of production for money implies that the government can always avoid deflation by simply issuing more money. (He referred to a statement made by Milton Friedman about using a "helicopter drop" of money into the economy to fight deflation.) Bernanke's critics have since referred to him as "Helicopter Ben" or to his "helicopter printing press." In a footnote to his speech, Bernanke noted that "people know that inflation erodes the real value of the government's debt and, therefore, that it is in the interest of the government to create some inflation."

Is it better to be in – all in participants in this surging debacle operated by those who may not know what they are doing? Knowingly living in an underwater house? The thing that you must consider doing to protect your family and your home is to Confront Fraudulent Housing Debt.

CHAPTER 5: A BRIEF ANALYSIS OF BUSINESS CYCLES

"That men do not learn from history is the most important lesson that history has to teach." Aldous Huxley

"There seems to a general conviction, cultivated not just by Mr. Alan Greenspan, that the U.S. economy has become virtually immune to recession. It is widely seen just as a bursting of strength due to ingrained 'flexibility' and 'dynamism'. In addition, of course there is unbound faith in the virtuosity of the Fed to avoid a serious recession." Dr. Kurt Richebächer, *The Daily Reckoning*. August 3, 2003.

"This disposition to admire, and almost to worship, the rich and the powerful, and to despise, or, at least, to neglect, persons of poor and mean condition, though <u>necessary</u> both to establish and to <u>maintain the distinction of ranks and the order of society</u>, is, at the same time, the great and most <u>universal cause of the corruption of our moral sentiments</u>." Adam Smith, *Theory of Moral Sentiments*. 1759. [Emphasis added.]

It is only normal, even natural, that people want to – and do – trust their leaders. Trust their leaders to protect them from famine, war and economic dislocation. Leaders themselves become imbued with intentions. Some elegant and sharing, others lean to a nefarious bent. Regardless, over time, leaders wish to maintain a status quo, which is fine – for them – as long as *they* possess the "status."

Unfortunately, history has shown that the more the people, and particularly, when the leaders believe in their power to keep the ship upright, the greater the danger becomes to those people who trusted them. We are speaking of, generalizing on, what has occurred over time. Some argue that the opposite occurs. We stay in the camp that believes that excess nearly always brings more excess. The Boom and the inevitable Bust. The so-called Business Cycles.

The Maestro. To be very specific, frankly, to name names again, Mr. Alan Greenspan has been called the "Maestro" of the economy, of the Federal Reserve System. He is certainly the singular person in economics, "the expert," in nearly all of the final quarter of the 20th Century. But, in reality, Greenspan is the Maestro of little more than "parlor tricks" which have as their natural result, unintended consequences (we are being generous).

Most notably, Greenspan has been adept at robbing the middle class through misappropriations of Social Security and Medicare funds, increased payroll taxes and worse he has created bubbles – which he claims cannot be recognized until it's too late. Nonsense. We saw it in 2005, while writing on our web site at the time, The Homeowner's Economist. How could *we* have seen the bubble in 2004 when we were just beginning to learn about the economy and how it pertains to real estate? How could we have been writing about the real estate bubble? Simply because the facts were on display in public.

We cared and did our economic studies as we were on the verge of obtaining a real estate sales license in California. New agents most often must rely on representing buyers, because the more experienced agents often have relationships with sellers and obtain the valued listing. As we began to understand what was really going on, it became impossible to represent home buyers, who would surely be slaughtered when the bubble burst. So, we began writing on the issue, and, naturally no one was listening then. Many are still living in their denial, buried underwater, and hoping for a real estate bottom. Likely in 2015.

Greenspan was claiming in 2007, when the bust arrived, that he couldn't have seen a bubble coming. And, he went so far as to indicate that maybe *we didn't have one anyway*. How could I know, and he not? Never happened. He lied and continues to lie.

Beyond overtaxing the middle class (but that is a different book, *Greenspan's Fraud,* written by the brilliant economist Dr. Ravi Batra), Greenspan's main contribution to Wall Street was manufacturing bubbles which provided cover regarding the fact that the actual economy was being hollowed out – the middle-class was being devastated. We argue that the highly publicized (in the financial press) Jobless Recovery was no recovery at all over the long term, particularly if no monies are invested for productive domestic investment, commercial and public infrastructure, which create wealth by growing the National Treasure. As each succeeding bubble burst he pumped more money into the system (the cause of bubbles in the first place), creating a new debt based bubble, and then he observed that bubble deflate.

He made a steady increase of money (liquidity) available providing the foundation for a near twenty year "bull" equities market; reflated following the S&L bubble; then again after the "dot.com" bubble; then the final touch, blowing up the housing market, creating the Housing Bubble. All underpinned with the Credit Bubble, floating many financial entity boats, and which enabled a mighty proliferation of inadequate risk analysis, ultimately backed by moral hazard. Then he claimed in 2008 to a Congressional committee that he was "shocked" that the big banks through caution to the winds and did not manage *their* risk. This is the same guy who told all Americans in February, 2004 that they should all take out and ARM and manage their own risk. Most Americans don't possess the financial acumen (not taught in schools) to understand what "manage their own risk" really means.

The Big Con won't work this time. In fact it's clearly not working. Things really are different – for America – for the World. Today America is the largest debtor nation in the world. Its citizens are squeezed and less and less able to make their debt payments. Lowering interests rates and injecting money into the banking system will not – does not – have the same impact as it had in the recent past as mentioned in the preceding paragraph. Banks must *want* to lend, and borrowers must *want* to borrow. However, because of current conditions, including the ability of financial entities to hide their toxic assets "off the balance sheet," the players cannot trust one another (who is solvent?), and do not know who they can safely lend money to.

The banks don't trust each other and they certainly don't trust "Average American" borrowers. Why not? Very simply, the price of homes has begun a historic downturn. House price appreciation was the last crutch propping up the consumer/borrower. The banks know it, and some home owners are catching on. Smart residential investors, particularly in new residential construction projects and in existing residential houses as well, who were purchasing nearly 30% of all sold homes from 2004-06, headed to the exit, only the speculators have been caught. The really smart ones left in the spring of 2006 just slightly before it peaked out. They received top dollar, from the lamented Greater Fools.

Sold by the media, relatively non-sophisticated individuals (those who are not insiders) mentally invested in the perpetual Perma-Bull euphoria of a "Goldilocks Economy" (not too hot, not too cool).

On June 26, 2008, the Dow closed at 11,453, its lowest finish since Sept. 11, 2006. That is a staggering 3,000 point drop from 14,446 just over a year before. Then, it lived in the mid-13s for a few months, then the mid-12s, then the mid-11s, then mid-10s. And so on and so forth. Currently, the market is having what is called a "dead cat bounce." Up from mid 6,000 to nearly, almost 12,000, on any given day. This is a direct result of pumping from the Plunge Protection Team, a rally that cannot last. Why? The economic fundamentals cannot sustain in the face of falling employment, tapped out (now saving) consumers, and a huge volume of foreclosures that are just beginning (all over again) in late 2011. The foreclosures will continue. The economy cannot continue in face of falling employment and rising foreclosures.

Yet, many naïve folks stay in the market hoping for a bounce back when in fact the fundamentals, the recession, and even investor confidence goes lower and lower. Yet, as the housing market continues lower, gas and food and medical care continue higher, the market will continue on down. Why do they stay in? Clearly denial. Blinded to reality, they simply can't – won't – hear. They refuse to listen to actual facts. It goes against their preconceived notions – their belief system. That everything will be OK if they go along to get along. We hope you are listening.

Manias. Great speculative manias rarely occur but once in a lifetime. Generally there are two per century. In other words they used to be rare, at least before they became "unofficial official policy." Alan Greenspan regularly pointed to the superiority of U.S. productivity to rationalize high stock and house prices. In fact "productivity" was his mantra. Few could argue with his knowledge, his grasp of raw facts and ability to talk over any objections – and seem brilliant at the same time. That's why they named him Maestro. Increased productivity seemed a good enough explanation to enable euphoria.

ARM City. We remind you that in February, 2004 he recommended that Americans, "…utilize Adjustable Rate Mortgages (ARMs) to manage their own risk." Those comments were widely reported from a speech he gave to the Chicago Builder's Association.

This spurious advice was picked by the media and played out to millions of Americans who may not have completely understood what "… manage their own risk…." really meant. In fact, he chided those with traditional 30-year fixed mortgages for missing out on the Next Great Big Deal!

As a result of his advice many people refinanced and turned their homes into ATM machines by taking out equity. It has turned out to be a disaster for the economy, the finance industry and for many millions of Americans. The mortgage and banking industries, and particularly Wall Street Structured Finance took this as a "green light" to push inappropriate and unsound loan products. And push them they did. Fog a mirror, get a loan to buy a house you could turn into a Home, for your family. The Great American Dream, now a Nightmare for millions.

Good News Society. The human psyche is susceptible to good news, particularly when the mind believes the good news affects the participant directly, and especially when others are already benefiting (or appear to be). Buy a house, no money down, because: "Real estate only goes up." "It's a great time to buy," and other such slogans from advertising campaigns by the National Association of Realtors, repeated endlessly in the media can literally "brainwash" susceptible "good news" people. There was more reinforcement, portrayed on such TV shows as: "Flip This House," "Flip That House," "Property Ladder," and "This Old House," etcetera. Many were "getting rich" flipping housing, or, simply staying home, doing cash out re-finances (re-fi's) then *flipping* their home equity into their wallets and spending it. How many times have we read of using one's home as an ATM?

There was more pabulum: "They're not making any more land." and the Mortgage Bankers/brokers advertising: "Mortgage interest rates may never be this low again." Yet what difference does it make if your interest rate is comparatively low, if your payments have reset higher than you can afford? Equally bad is if you have no equity and the home's value in today's market is less than the mortgage loan you took out. You're underwater. It becomes increasingly frustrating if not fundamentally irrational to keep paying down a debt where the asset you allegedly "own" is not worth what you owe.

Once again, *hubris* is a term from the ancient Greeks. It refers to a supreme arrogance that causes nations and individuals to defy accumulated wisdom. Even to be contemptuous of history. The punishment for *hubris* was to confuse the judgment of arrogant victims. Causing them to take actions that would ultimately be self-destructive, though they seemed rational – to make sense at the time. Everyone's doing it!

Timing the Real Estate Market. But everyone wasn't doing it. The smart ones, the investors, not naive speculating flippers, took their profits during the run up, then began removing themselves from the market in the middle of 2006, well before the mid-2006 peak. If you closely followed the advice of real estate expert and economist, Robert Campbell, who wrote the prescient book, *Timing the Real Estate Market*, you were out in time.

Campbell states (in part here) on his web site: Real Estate Timing:

"Imagine for a moment how you would feel if you could predict major turning points in the real estate market. Suppose somebody handed you a 21-year time-tested system that would tell you ahead of time when property values were going to hit a peak ... and then when prices were going to hit bottom years later. If you could anticipate these kinds of critical real estate events in advance ... then not only could you make spectacular profits, but you could protect your money as well. Sounds pretty amazing, doesn't it? Actually, it's not. The real estate market does signal its future intentions if you know where to look.

"Based on a major breakthrough in tracking and predicting real estate trends, the book reveals the real estate timing technique that I call The Campbell Method, which as far as I know is the only proven method in the world that shows how to accurately anticipate upcoming changes in your local real estate market. What this means is that when you read *Timing the Real Estate Market,* you are going to learn how to make – and protect – your fortune in real estate in the same way that J. Paul Getty, the Rockefellers, Warren Buffett, and other super-rich investors made their fortunes: by focusing on WHEN to buy and sell. It's true. When it comes to making money in real estate, nothing beats good timing.

"The reason that The Campbell Method is going to change the way you think about how to buy and sell real estate is that I share my truly remarkable discovery of five key real estate indicators. I call them 'Vital Signs,' and they're able to predict the peaks and valleys of real estate cycles with an almost uncanny accuracy. As 'leading indicators' to what's looming on the horizon for real estate prices, these Vital Sign indicators act like windows into the future, giving you advance notice of approaching trend changes from three to six months before they become obvious to the general public."

Campbell speaks with authority to residential investor groups around the country. What he told them in January 2007 (we know, we heard him), was not to their liking. He basically said: *Get Out Now.* As an economics metric statistician he puts up the charts and tables (the numbers, the historical trends) on overheads and proves his case. He's been right so far. His data shows and he calls for the market to not find a bottom until much further out than today. This is a very very big deal not only for investors – but for homeowners – who are underwater.

In a private conversation in late November 2011, he stated that he did not see a bottom until 2015. We concur.

There is a basic question to ask yourself. Why am I staying in a home which is underwater, and likely to become further underwater over the next two to three years? And then at least another four (or more) years after it's bottomed before it starts back up. A *best case* would be that it goes back to *today's* prices in seven years. Yet, you're still underwater and throwing money in the sewer, because you are not gaining any equity. We believe it will take longer because there is absolutely nothing on the horizon that will cause the U.S. economy to begin to accelerate unless we radically change current policies.

Caught in Mania. People still caught in mania often point with contempt to those who would warn them – "the Cassandra's" – arguing that they must be delusional. "You don't understand. Everyone's Doing It." So many people can't be wrong?" Poor Cassandra, she could see into the future, but could not convince people of what was coming. A lonely gift/curse.

According to Wikipedia: "In Greek mythology, Cassandra (Greek: *Κασσάνδρα* "she who entangles men") (also known as Alexandra) was a daughter of King Priam and Queen Hecuba of Troy. Her beauty caused Apollo to grant her the gift of prophecy (or, more correctly, prescience). However, when she did not return his love, Apollo placed a curse on her so that no one would ever believe her predictions."

Alas poor Cassandra, we think we know how she may have felt. When we were warning people in 2005-06 that home values would drop precipitously, they often shot arrows in the back of this messenger. We pulled out the arrows long ago, and hope you are taking the time to digest and really understand the message herein for the benefit of your family. Several friends came to us later, saying, "You were right. We didn't listen. How did you know?" The answer is always the same, *"... did the homework."* You're reading this book – *doing the homework.* Stay the course, and read all of the blog. Then, and not until then, we can begin a conversation.

The message, loud and clear: Use Foreclosure Law to Keep Your Home. Use legal leverage to force (cramdown on the lender) the outcome you intend based on the leverage afforded you by a Forensic Loan Audit and a Securitization Audit.

Business Cycles. In every business cycle we see shifts between times of rapid growth of output (recovery leading to prosperity), and reduction of output (recession, contraction, leading to decline). Many argue that such fluctuations in terms of economic growth and decline simply are not qualifiable by purely mechanical or predictable periodic pattern. Others beg to disagree, sometimes strongly.

Juglar Cycle. One cycle has been named for Clement Juglar, who was an early proponent of "the" business cycle. According to his theory, recovery and prosperity were associated with a positive correlation in growth of productivity, consumer confidence, demand and prices. In such cycles, acceleration or growth usually ends with the failure of speculative investments that were a result of confidence bubbles which ultimately collapsed. In such cycles, times of contraction and stagnation are witness to elimination (bankruptcy) of failed enterprises. Tide comes in – tide goes out.

Then, optimally, market forces re-allocate resources from less productive uses to more productive uses. But recent U.S. cycles between 1945 and the 1990s were restrained, and not allowed to work through the cleansing removal of debris. They've been were intentionally directed and highly influenced by those in control of the money. The influence was openly exerted via Monetary Policy (through the Fed) and Fiscal Policy (spending priorities of Congress and the President). The Treasury Department writes the checks to fund government spending and borrows the money from the Fed – thus creating our National Debt – and taxpayers pay the Fed back *plus interest* earned by the Fed, which goes to the Banksters that own the Fed. It's a sweet game for the Fed, and it's Financial Elite owners.

Arguably it is this interest – paid to Banksters for money created out of thin air – that is responsible for a huge portion of annual deficits and national debt. Yes, we're tax slaves to Banksters. That's the model – the secret story of our entrapment. What to do?

Confront Fraudulent Housing Debt
Occupy Your Home.

There are other business cycle modelers who attempt to explain economic fluctuations through political decisions. One administration will influence growth for the financial sector. A different administration enacts social legislation. Whichever is done, plenty of blame naturally abounds as the down cycle inevitably occurs.

Before and since the World Wide Great Depression (1930-33), Western nations have given overt lip service towards limiting wide disruptions. Unfortunately, as always, human nature intervenes, and financial and corporate sector greed transcends the fawning incompetence (even if well meaning) of political sector beneficiaries, i.e., Congress, and the cycle repeats.

Alternatively, through Fiscal policy accommodation, political leaders license, or look the other way, using the Fed to create ample liquidity in order to engage in foreign excursions designed to reinforce objectives of (today economic) dominance of other nations, to continue nation building and accumulation of raw power. Empire building. Ideally practiced with an arched eyebrow, rather than bombs. However, bombs are available and easily airborne if the recipient fails to gain the significance of the arched eyebrow.

On December 6, 2011, Iran picked up one of our highest tech brandie new drones on their Sovereign Soil. Uh-ho. Great gnashing of teeth. "Give us back out stuff." Will they sell it to China who can figure out the tech, and loan that back to Iran. If they get that tech and start over flying Kansas, what will we do?

Now (12/27/1) we've called for sanctions. They've responded that they'll close the Straits of Hormouth, shut down the shipping of oil.

Will we have WW III over this? Empire demands compliance. Dick Cheney would love it. We wouldn't.

Saddam Hussein is dead, replaced with a murderous Occupation that some call the War Against Terror. Rather a *never ending* War Against Terror, which we can no longer afford. (Our troops allegedly left in December 2011, except for the $200K a year private security folk – mercenaries – still on the ground, numbering 4-5,000.) Funding such a war has hollowed the Nation's Wealth, lowered the value of the dollar, which has forced the price of oil through the roof, and increased the cost of all consumer goods. Some argue successfully it is nothing more than a tax on all citizens that goes under a different name, so they can claim that they aren't raising taxes. Please.

Over time we have been witness to: failed Communism; failed Keynesian Theory; failed Monetarism; etcetera *ad nauseum.* And, of course, "Neoclassical Economics" negates "Keynesian Theory," or vice versa depending on your point of view. You do not need to understand the two previous sentences. This book is not about economic apples and oranges. We are simply touching on this material, saying the names, to enable a very general surface-only awareness of terms and concepts that have been used historically. You do not need a PhD in Economics to understand that you have been duped by the "System." However, please stay with us; we'll go just a bit further.

The Austrian School. There is another school of economic thought, which is unpopular, unloved, and long-abandoned by trendy powerful global financial elites. It does not fit their heavily debt-based over-leveraged model. This would be the Austrian School of Economics. Founded by the exceptional, Ludwig von Mises (1881-1973), the Austrian School completely rejects theories that suggest that the business cycle is a built-in feature of an economy free of heavy intervention.

Ludwig von Mises argued that booms and busts are entirely caused by intervention in the money supply, the banking system, and economic policy. Austrians recommend, nay demand, a return to the Gold Standard – hard money – in order to rein in excesses and prevent manipulations which cause great woe and gnashing of teeth for the powerless and non-understanding multitudes, but due to moral hazard, little pain for the Financial Elites.

The Austrians argue further that recessions and depressions are signs that the immediately preceding manipulations have failed, and are in fact evidence that markets are crying out to be permitted to correct themselves by flushing out the "rot." They haven't been allowed to do so freely since 1913. That year the Federal Reserve System entered stage right into the U.S. Economy. Remember, the Fed is a privately owned entity, chartered by the Federal Government, but is not directly accountable to the Government or to Congress which allowed it's creation.

Without massive economic intervention, the Austrians argue that recessions and depressions are replaced by periodic banking/investment "panics," and when unavoidable (due to human nature) speculative manias collapse. The result are "mini-depressions" where related businesses fail and labor and capital are re-allocated. Austrians observed that since our current financial regime was implemented with the founding of the Fed in 1913, we've had the dubious pleasure of the Great Depression, and the stagflationary depression of the 1970s and early 80s, both nearly eclipsing in severity anything experienced in the U.S. in the 19th century or earlier.

Not a very good track record for fiscal and monetary intervention! Observers are beginning to notice that manias such as the dot.com and Housing Bubble are actually fueled and made worse by the "credit forcing" policy of our current system, which creates the "need" for more intervention to "mop up" the mess.

Kondratieff Cycle. We'll look at a longer modeled cycle which gives an extended framework in which *we might see more clearly what has happened and what is likely to happen next.*

On March 4, 1892, Nikolai Dimitrievich Kondratieff was born near Moscow, into a peasant family. His early promise and brilliance enabled him to be educated at the University of St. Petersburg before the revolution. On October 5, 1917, at 25, he was appointed Minister of Supply of the final Alexander Kerensky government after the Czar was removed by the revolution.

Following the revolution, he focused on academic research and soon founded the Institute of Conjuncture in Moscow. In 1923-5, he focused primarily on an original five-year plan for the development of Soviet agriculture. This was the vehicle in which he brought forward his theory regarding major economic cycles. He did not find that capitalism intrinsically and inevitably reaches some "end point." As his reward for this discovery, he was arrested by Stalin on July 1930 on trumped up charges of being a member of an illegal, perhaps non-existent 'Peasant's Labour Party.'

He was able to continue his writing while imprisoned for nearly eight years, while his health deteriorated. Some of his works were completed and published in Russia. During Stalin's Great Purge, he was tried again, and sentenced to ten years. His communications with the outside world were stopped. Still in prison, Kondratieff was executed by firing squad at age 46. Fifty years later in 1987 he was officially "rehabilitated" by the Soviet Politburo. His theories defied Stalin's belief and practice (the vaunted Five Year Plans) for the oncoming Uber Supremacy of Russia as a World Economic Power.

Kondratieff Seasons. The cycle Kondratieff discovered (or modeled) is divided into four "seasons," after earth's own seasons, and each Kondratieff season is similar in key characteristics to our climatic seasons.

The Kondratieff cycles follow like this:

- *Spring* constitutes the re-birth or renewal of the economy.
- *Summer* the economy bears fruit.
- *Autumn* we have the season of harvest and satisfaction.
- *Winter,* the economy dies, becoming negatively impacted.

The overall cycle takes about fifty years. Each season lasts approximately one quarter of the cycle, some 15 years.

Over decades various writers, academics and economists have extolled, or at least thoroughly examined Kondratieff theory, and the tenets and specifics of the Kondratieff Wave Cycle. Many argue that the Kondratieff Cycle identifies only beginnings and endings of each season. These have been recognized at market tops and bottoms, bull and bear markets. Boom and the inevitable Bust. And then it repeats itself.

The Kondratieff Cycle is at its heart an economic cycle of boom and bust including the effects of intervention and large-scale collusion. Principal cycles (some overlapping) within the Kondratieff Cycle include: an investment cycle, an interest rate cycle, a credit/debt cycle, an inflation cycle and a confidence cycle.

Watch, now, how this cycle unfolds in our current economy: Real estate, precious metals and commodities are seemingly appropriate investments during inflationary periods – spring into summer. In the following autumn, massive speculation and (subsequent denial) begins to raise its ugly head. Real estate bonds, and stocks become the rage. Inflation is viewed as "mild." And massive profits are often made. This process continues because monetary inflation (the printing of more and more so-called money, which is really debt) does not actually stop when summer ends. It merely shifts to "higher" forms of debt, such as Wall Street's dangerous derivatives and their foul offspring.

During autumn, easy credit and large infusions of money are supplied to the banks through actions of the central bank and as a result of the willing failure to regulate rouge elements such as hedge funds and buy-out firms. Promoting speculation and ignoring risk factors due to high math based computer "modeling," which we see today have missed, or ignored, growing risk factors. With the brief exception of the dot.com mania/bust, we've seen a gargantuan and extremely lengthy 25 year bull market in equities, coinciding with the "Greenspan Era." As no other Fed Chairman since 1913, Greenspan also clearly enabled – if not created – the Housing Bubble. Near the end of this extended autumn cycle, the price of real estate doubled nationally, and tripled in some bubble markets like California, Arizona, Nevada and Florida.

Due to easy money and easy credit from 2004 until August of 2007 (when the inevitable Credit Crunch arrived, freezing even inter-bank lending), a feeding frenzy of mass speculation captured the imagination of the entire country, arguably the world, with Housing Bubbles in most nations, all due to huge liquidity pumping. In each of the four Kondratieff cycles of the last 200 years, autumn always followed a summer-ending recession, which has led to speculative booms based on the ultimate bubble, the Credit Bubble. Sir Greenspan, but one man, facilitated and promoted that bubble. While this may seem incredulous, one man with such power, the fact is that he dominated the Federal Reserve System, and in particular, the Federal Open Market Committee (FOMC).

The FOMC is a critical element in the decisions of the Fed. Under U.S. law it supervises open market operations and is the principal tool of U.S. Monetary Policy. A critical function of the FOMC is selling and buying U.S. Treasury Securities. In addition, they set Monetary Policy through orchestrating short-term goals through target levels for the federal funds rate. This is the interest rate that commercial banks charge each other for overnight loans to enable them to keep their accounting straight, reconcile their books daily so that they are holding adequate reserves against their loan portfolio.

At bottom you simply need to understand that the Federal Reserve System is the lender of last resort for banks. When banks do not want to loan (short-term overnight) money to other banks that may be in jeopardy, that are functioning in a state of insolvency (have more liabilities than assets), the Fed will step in and loan such banks money in order to not have disruptions (major or minor) in the banking system.

Yet it is these same banks who receive the largesse of Fed protection that are have been refusing to do work-out deals (including principal reductions) with homeowners facing foreclosure. By and large, at this point they still refuse *legitimate* loan modifications that call for a reduction in the principle amount owed on the loan, in order for the payment to be reduced to an affordable monthly payment. This occurs even though the press states that modifications are going forward under Hope Now, which claims to have done over one million loan modifications. Yet, they've never produced the data to the press. Why not?

Reporting in *Bloomberg* on Mary 30, 2008, Josh P. Hamilton and Bob Ivry wrote:

> "'Modifications are not occurring nearly at the numbers necessary to stem the foreclosure crisis,' Allen Fishbein, housing director for the Consumer Federation of America in Washington, said in a May 19 interview. 'People are still going into foreclosure when, with a write-down on existing principal, they could still stay in their homes. Part of the problem is that so many of the <u>loans were securitized</u>, making it difficult to determine who has the legal authority to modify them, or even who owns them,' Fishbein said. [Emphasis added.]

> "About <u>90 percent of subprime loans</u> have been bundled into securities, according to Inside Mortgage Finance, a Bethesda, Maryland-based industry newsletter. Borrowers with subprime mortgages, which were available to those with poor credit histories, <u>are behind in their payments at more than five times</u> the rate of prime mortgage borrowers, according to the Washington-based Mortgage Bankers Association. [Emphasis added.]

> "The median home price fell 8 percent compared with April 2007, a report last week from the National Association of Realtors said. Falling prices <u>increase the odds of homeowners walking away</u> from their property while decreasing lenders' chances of recouping their costs by seizing the property, ultimately leading to higher mortgage insurance claims. [Emphasis added.]

Short Sales. Further, regarding short sales (a lender approved sale of a home for less than the amount owed, wherein the lender takes a loss on the difference) the lenders are Monuments of Obstruction for homeowners behind in their payment and/or are underwater. The homeowner has found a ready, willing and able (qualified) buyer, usually through a real estate agent and the MLS system. Lender approval for the sale to go forward is requested and the lender holds back approval for 30, 60, 90 or more days. Consequently the buyer finally gives up in disgust and walks away.

Bank Help. As previously mentioned, banks have historically borrowed overnight from other banks when they need to show additional funds to maintain their required loan reserves and close out there balance sheet at the end of every business day. Consequently, other correspondent banks loan to them (at minimal interest rates set by the Fed, the Overnight Rate) when the other banks have ample resources. When a bank cannot borrow (is not trusted by) other banks, the Fed steps in as the *lender of last resort.* Remember, the American People are the *payers of last resort* – taxpayers.

The FOMC does more, such as coordinating with the Treasury Department regarding foreign currency exchange markets. It has been reported by many authors, other authorities and endlessly in the press that Greenspan dominated the Fed and the FOMC like no other figure in Federal Reserve System history. While a seemingly democratic by-vote system, rarely did any Board Governor or Market Committee member publicly dissent from the Greenspan Way. The Maestro's Way.

Greenspan Arrogance. As we've shown, the Fed in the name of (and with the veto over regulation) the Maestro, created the mess, and quite astonishingly – and as proof that Mania – if not personal arrogance – can extend to all parties – Greenspan allegedly came to believe that *he* could defeat the Kondratieff winter. The winter is when it all backfires, all goes up in smoke, and deep recessions and even depressions occur, as have occurred over recorded history. The Ultimate Unwanted Correction.

We are in winter as we enter into 2012. Several more years to observe the Fed play with intervention, attempt to beat winter. Quantitative Easing (QE) is the name of the game. We had QE I, then QE II, and now we have QE III, but, the Fed calls it something else. The equity market wants QE, and, more of it to prop up our moribund corporations. The more the better. These interventions are and will destroy the value of the dollar, which still looks good against the devastated Euro.

Value of the dollar? Equities don't care about long term considerations, they're talking: This Quarter – hang the rest. If the equities market finally breaks free from Monetary Manipulations, and appropriately drops on normal PE ratios, etc. , it will destroy confidence. That's all the Boyz really have left. Falsely engendered: *CONFIDENCE.*

It isn't necessarily just that our memories are short, which is true for many of us, it's that we are not taught about these things in public schools. Why not? Well, if we don't know what really happened throughout history – therefore what is likely to happen this time – we can't very well tell our leaders we're headed down the wrong path. Rather, we can't hold them accountable (at the vote) for leading us down the wrong path. Consequently, we are limited in making sound investment decisions. In essence, we're set up to fail. Wall Street chuckles and collectively, rather metaphorically, buys a new Fed-Funded round of Martinis and delivers them in Hookah-driven Maseratis to the *Playas. . "Set 'em up Joe, give us a round on the house. Oh Yeah– everyone here is all-in."* Think of wolves on the blood lust.

In his 1962 essay, *Gold and Economic Freedom,* Alan Greenspan wrote:

"Belatedly, Federal Reserve officials attempted to sop up the excess reserves and finally succeeded in braking the boom. But it was too late: by 1929 the speculative imbalances had become so overwhelming that the attempt precipitated a sharp retrenching and a consequent demoralizing of business confidence. As a result, the American economy collapsed. The excess credit which the Fed pumped into the economy spilled over into the stock market, triggering a fantastic speculative boom."

Alan Greenspan understood precisely what his direct interventions in the markets would create during the end of the Kondratieff autumn, and he did it anyway. He inflated the money supply and brought interest rates to 1%. Accounting for inflation, interest rates were actually below zero. In other words you could (if high enough in the food chain) essentially borrow money for free.

Regardless of affixing blame to an individual who worked hard to gain his intellectual growth and came of age as a close follower of Ayn Rand; over time, young Alan saw the folly of his ways, dropped his saxophone playing, and since he was born and raised in New York City, he did what many young men have done for more two centuries. He followed his father's example and went downtown to business.

By dint of hard work and his exceptional brilliance, he partnered with a wise and well connected older mentor and built-up a very successful independent corporate finance consulting firm. He rose to being a consultant to Investment Banking leader, Morgan Stanley, among other high profile positions, and ultimately landed at the Fed. We'll let him rest for a moment, and look further into what he has done, and what is likely to happen as a direct result.

Boom and Bust. Historically markets dance from Bull to Bear. Boom to Bust. The higher they go, more often the further they fall, generally to an equilibrium based on long-run performance. Each boom or bust always creates the foundation for the next change. The tide goes in, the tide goes out, every six hours.

The up and down nature of markets is a direct result of what John Maynard Keynes called "animal spirits." These are an essential ingredient for economic prosperity: (optimistic) confidence. Keynes did go further to elaborate that it really meant "naive optimism." Or, when nearly everyone believes in the *perpetuation of the present,* it is more likely that a strong turn is waiting in the wings. In economic terms "reversion to the mean" is likely.

Meaning, that house prices are likely to return to prices confluent with real long-term growth rates which prevailed before the run-up. Some have charted house prices from 1995 to 2006, and were astonished to see not merely a doubling, but a tripling in house prices in some bubble states. Others suggest that prices will fall 20% across the nation and 30% or more in California and Florida. In Nevada they've already fallen 50% from the late 2006 top. This is happening right now. Is it wise to stay in a home and keep paying on a debt that will likely be even more severely underwater before the year is out? Perhaps, but, only if you Use Foreclosure Law to Keep Your Home.

More Kondratieff. Returning to the concept of the Kondratieff winter – if it holds true again, this time – we are facing a potential repeat of the previous Kondratieff winter of the 1930s. That culminated in a World Wide Great Depression. The credit bubble has become unsustainable. Support is diminished by efforts of the Fed, with the exception of their support for the major banks (who issue Dr. Bernanke's paycheck), and for the Fed's beloved Investment Bank broker-dealers. Who, some well argue also act as secret agents for the Fed in secretive gross market manipulations. We brought your attention to the PPT, the Plunge Protection Team above.

A conspiracy? No. Not at all. Let's spin it – simply a private, secretive and heretofore very successful Business Plan. Depends on your point of view. If you're on the team – you go along to get along. If you're on the *other* team (this is America, we have competition), they consider you to be in the way unless you are paying them tribute. The rest of us may consider them to be in the way. After all they've had their day – now they want us to pay for their dancing. They want us to buy them new dancing shoes – they've worn out their old ones.

Both commercial and Investment Banks are in more than trouble – many are insolvent. Otherwise, why would they be taking "equity capital infusions" from China and Saudi Arabia and other Middle Eastern nations? To cut through the euphemisms, this means that some Investment Banks have been forced to sell pieces of themselves to the highest bidder.

Because that has not been enough, the Fed has now begun loaning money to (largely unregulated) Investment Banks in violation of the Fed's own charter. Frankly, in violation of the law. Because they are Too Big Too Fail? Depends specifically on your point of view.

For underwater homeowners , what difference does it make if these perpetrators go under or are forced to reorganize under Federal bankruptcy laws? Would it be better that they focus their considerable energies and brain power on survival rather than continuing to mislead the American Public? We think so. Let them be distracted by focus on their potential extinction. Let the smart young ones find careers in America that perform valuable service for their country – not merely their wallets. It is time for major change. It is coming.

We sometimes wonder .f Investment Banks, susceptible to being in denial, and, actually and actively protected through the practice of moral hazard, even fully understand what is occurring – how fragile their situation really is? Then we remember, *"When the music was playing, we got up and danced."*

Now, the concern is pitchforks from the 99%. Actually stronger metal purchases are taking place.

In a May, 25, 2011, cross-posting at the Huffington Post, an article from Bloomberg titled: "Goldman Sachs Staff Buying Guns 'To Defend Themselves Against Public Uprising,'" Alice Shroeder wrote: "I just wrote my first reference for a gun permit," said a friend, who told me of swearing to the good character of a Goldman Sachs Group Inc. banker who applied to the local police for a permit to buy a pistol. The banker had told this friend of mine *that senior Goldman people have loaded up on firearms and are now equipped to defend themselves* if there is a populist uprising against the bank."

What's up with this story? How can it be, after all Lloyd Blankfein, CEO of Goldman Sacks, told Congress under oath that Goldman, "… was doing God's work." No further comment.

In *Use Foreclosure Law* we are giving you information you require to make an informed decision to Confront Fraudulent Housing Debt. Frankly information to enable you to not only understand the larger picture, but information to allow you to explain what is really going on to your family, friends, neighbors, co-workers, frankly anyone you come into contact with that has a mind open enough to listen and learn.

Nearly everyone knows that something funny is going on, with this book and information on our blog, you will have the education and tools to – frankly give you the spine you need – to take action. You have every right to be morally, ethically and fiduciarily outraged. You have every right to follow the Rule of Law, contract law and choose to Confront Fraudulent Housing Debt.

Credit Contraction. Credit is contracting because of the deflating housing bubble. Many families, millions of them, can't make their payments. Or some seemingly smart ones are choosing not to make their payments when the financial stress of being underwater is too great. Or, because it doesn't make sense as a business decision, they plan to walk away or take action under their own terms as rational market participants under the terms of the contract formed by the Promissory Note. Our economy is already in recession, and in consideration of the ramifications of the huge numbers involved, our credit dislocations may result in a depression. Is that what Kondratieff winter demands? It did in the thirties, and in previous cycles.

Depressions are always deflationary. In depressions unemployment rises, demand for anything but life essentials dries up. Assets values, like real estate, crash. Banks fail. Credit becomes scarce even to the credit-worthy. Funds for loans are not there. We have that today.

So what can the Fed do at this time, right now, to stop, or hold back a vicious financial Tsunami? If they really engage the printing presses ("drop money from helicopters") the dollar will sink below the floor, and oil will continue up, dragging with it, the prices of consumer essentials. More taxation with arguably very little representation from lawmakers who allowed the current condition, and are only now (after it's too late) making great noise about helping homeowners. Stop those AIG bonuses, they shout in unison. It's altogether ridiculous and naive.

Door Number Two. The Fed's other option is to "ditch" the domestic economy, with no support, making no additional money available to insolvent banks. Some choice? But they built it, and now they must deconstruct it. Who will pay for that? As always, taxpayers. It is likely that millions of homeowners will see the value of their properties reduced well below what they owe, while simultaneously facing higher gasoline, food and medical care expenses – to bailout some Investment Banks? Please.

If they print the money and keep interests rate low (they are), they guarantee a massive sell off in U.S. debt, which will, ultimately *force* much higher interest rates and lock in a depression. If they raise interest rates right now to realistic levels in order to stamp out the inflation of prices, same depression – simply arrived via a different path. The Fed for now has said "Deal" – or was that – "No Deal?" Good-bye to the dollar!

The point for homeowners, whether holding ARMs, or underwater, is that rates will/are rising. As they do higher mortgage payment resets will force many more into foreclosure and when those foreclosed houses come back on the market as Real Estate Owned (REO) (many are), the lenders will be forced to sell at prices that further drive down the value of *all* homes. At the same time, as rates go higher (they will), buyers stay away, also forcing down prices. If you are not underwater, you may be sooner than you think. Consequently those who chose to walk away sooner are not, and will not, be the *cause* of lowering all home prices, it is the systemic actions (previous and current) of the Fed that created a Bubble, which always requires correction by market forces. However, guess who'll they'll blame in the press? Unscrupulous borrowers.

Some believe that this is occurring as part of a plan that certainly does not have the interest of American homeowners in mind. The usual suspects are of course banks in panic mode. They don't want the U.S. to fail economically, but their legal obligation to shareholders under their corporate charters, requires them to act in defense of their shareholders (and wink wink, their personal interest in CEO stock options and bonuses). The Fed is obligated by *their* charter issued by Congress to protect the value of money and seek "maximum" employment. Again, the banks own the Fed, so in reality – where the rubber meets the road – whose interest comes first? Whose charter will be violated? The Fed's Charter, the Fed's legal mandate – of course.

Nearly unprecedented recent rapid lowering of interest rates, some argue, was done ostensibly to save the stock market, and therefore not destroy investor confidence, which is the key to most markets – confidence – animal spirits. But, it's deeper than that. Bernanke must keep mortgage rates as low as he can, as long as he can. This both tempts first time buyers, falsely believing real estate is bottoming, and stops some ARMs from resetting much higher right now.

Moral hazard. The Investment Banks, the entire financial system, knows that this Fed is there for them, come what may, and damn the taxpayers. They got up and danced all night. They stayed too long at the Money Party. They created the sub-prime market crisis by issuing Securities that were bound to be defaulted on by new homeowners, many of whom never had a chance to make the reset payments.

Unprecedented in history, starting in mid-2006 and continuing through 2007, were the number of defaults from people who hadn't even been in their homes for 90 days, and then started missing payments. The flood of defaults increased exponentially when the first year was up on extremely low teaser rates. And, now nationally, the number of foreclosures continues to increase near double digits on a (year-to-year) monthly basis. Well beyond any previous percentage of defaults in history. This is a very big deal. Doesn't the sweet American Dream of homeownership look like an Epic Nightmare right now? You can wake up from that nightmare by taking action and Using Foreclosure Law to Keep Your Home.

Many unscrupulous Mortgage Brokers were well aware of what lay ahead, and induced fraud by making clear misrepresentations to unsophisticated first-time buyers who relied on – and trusted them. They were the professionals. They were supposed to know what they were doing. Owing a fiduciary obligation to these buyers, they violated their duty and served themselves to make more money. We explore this in depth in Chapter 9, *Predatory Lending*.

Pumping Hope. The Fed invented a "secret" (non-public, non-transparent, behind closed doors) auction process to pump money into ailing banks so that outsiders – taxpayers – wouldn't realize which banks are in trouble. This is all backed by taxpayer money. The Fed prints more money through the FOMC, the government issues Treasuries, but ultimately, it's the taxpayer that makes good on these paper instruments, paying the interest to the Fed, which are backed by the full faith of the U.S. Government.

Ben Bernanke was going to run a "transparent" Fed. Now he finds events pulling him in over his head. Now that he and his Fed are deeply underwater, out the window his claim for transparency went. If Greenspan was the Wizard of Oz, poor Ben Bernanke is the *little wizard*. The new man behind the curtain (enabled by the media) pulling levers.

Can we believe them anymore? Hope Now! Or is it Hope Not! One thing's for sure: Hope-Hope-Hope and Change-Change-Change, is on the rocks, under the bus, kicked to the curb. You name it!!!

They are not interested in maximum employment or in helping you. The Fed disregards and does not respond to one of its charter mandates, that being to maintain "maximum employment."

"Fed actions only effect the economy accidentally. Their total focus is on protecting banks." James Rickards, widely quoted World Class economics analyst, 12/19/2011.

Banking Trouble. All these recent plans, which they state will keep "keep people in their homes," are designed to avoid Price Discovery – for the banks. This will be when house prices drop dramatically. This is also known as "reversion to the mean," mentioned above. If your home goes into foreclosure the bank must sell it for whatever they can get. Then they must take the *loss on their books*.

They must show the loss. There goes the balance sheet, there go the value of the bank's stock. There go the jobs of decision making executives. Note that CEO Chuck Prince of Citigroup was put out the door. Of course he walked with multi-millions. Hush money? The CEO of Merrill Lynch was put out, and likely many more to come. They walk with multi-millions, assured of comfortable "retirement," having done their "duty" on the front lines. "Hey, it was great (for us) while it lasted. Heck, none of us saw it coming." Either a fraudulent comment, or proof of incompetence. If it's fraud, where are the indictments.

Rather than just be angry, as frankly we are from time to time, put your time into formulating your own exit strategy. Protect yourself. Obviously the Masters of the Wall Street Universe will not protect you by damaging themselves. They won't bring themselves to Justice. No, they'll take the money and run. They are running right now with the money that is left. *"Oh hold on, Bernanke just printed a bunch more, for Europe, as it passes through us, we'll stick around to grab some of that, then, it's on to the exit strategy. See ya, in Paraguay."*

Global Immolation. The problem for Wall Street right now is that still following Greenspan's lead, world wide global markets have become extremely intertwined with "interrelationships" in the last ten years. One sneezes, many get a cold. You need to understand that a great deal of Securitized housing debt paper (loan notes) is worth less than "as advertised" or "face value" because people are defaulting on house payments. This is very very serious.

Some argue that the back-room geniuses who promoted the Securitization process based their risk evaluations on computerized modeling, which failed to take into consideration the realities of the failed, moreover, fraudulent loan origination process. And failed, to take into consideration that there would be enormous amounts of defaults, particularly for those who really couldn't afford to buy a home.

They allegedly did not take into consideration that those lower on the food chain, particularly Mortgage Brokers, would do and say anything to shoehorn a marginal – well, unqualified buyer – into a loan. Others have a more sinister view and believe that the brilliant Investment Bankers knew all along what would eventually happen. They would do the business, collect incredible fees and fool the Institutional Investors into taking the risk. That of course is exactly what *did* happen.

In Chapter 7, *Their Legal Issues,* we paint a picture of what is going on with Investor law suits aimed at Investment Banks. It's very important for you to have a basic understanding of that information, because information and discovery that comes out in that arena may be very valuable in terms of your own possible recovery for damages based on a general theory of Predatory Lending and Securitization Fraud. We're not lawyers, and don't offer legal advice, so, we'll leave it at that for the moment.

All over the world, banks made (currently under or non-performing, defaulting) loans on the assumption that the expansion of credit based on debt would continue *ad infinitum.* Who told them so? Alan Greenspan for one. One thing he grew for sure – was moral hazard. Meaning that there was the hidden wink and grin, that when push came to shove, it would be the taxpayers squashed under the tires of the bus.

Moral Hazard. We remind you that moral hazard is based on the concept that if a party is insulated (protected) from risk, that party will likely behave differently than if they were fully exposed to loss from the risk. Because a financial institution does not fear the consequences of its actions, it will assume greater risk, take more chances in search of larger and larger profits than it otherwise would. Push up the bonuses for the financial elites.

Moral hazard at the theoretical level is prone to asymmetric information, where one party in a business deal (or in particular, contractually) possesses more information than other party. The party with superior information informing its actions and intentions has the advantage over the party who will ultimately pay the consequences when things go wrong as they ultimately (over time) do. Taxpayers, and increasingly, homeowners are the ones to pay, the ones to be hurt, the ones to lose their homes. The beef here is often based on Fraudulent Inducement. If this happened to you, that might the foundation for legal leverage if you determine to Confront Fraudulent Housing Debt. But, repeat after us *"... not attorneys – don't offer legal advice."*

As we've pointed out, most of us are really glorified renters – long-term lessees who have a Promissory Note, a Security Instrument such as a Mortgage or Deed of Trust. More to the bone, moral hazard occurs when the party with superior information acting on "animal spirits" has an incentive to behave inappropriately from the perspective of the party with less information. In street vernacular – a "rip-off."

Principal-Agent Conflict. Another type of moral hazard is called a *principal-agent conflict.* One party, the agent, acts on behalf of another, the principal. This is the relationship you had with your real estate agent. Even though a fiduciary relationship may exist by law and is based in general ethics, almost always the agent, the professional, has more information than the principal.

An unethical, if not fraud-inducing agent (Mortgage Broker or appraiser) is given an incentive by the lender to act in their and the lender's best interest – against the interest of the borrower. This leads directly to Predatory Lending. The deck was stacked against the would-be home owner, the borrower. Prices were inflated, appraisers (often under the pressure of the threat of no further business) went along, deals closed at higher prices than they should have, generating higher fees all the way up the food chain. All to the detriment of the homeowner.

More critical in this most recent bubble was the agent-principle conflict between Investment Bank *agent/securitizer/creator/sellers* of mortgage-backed securities, and the *principal/buyer* Institutional Investors. The later are pension funds, insurance companies, hedge funds, foreign central banks, and others controlling institutional funds.

Deceiving Institutional Investors, provided the funding to keep the game going until defaults began to tear apart their business model. The insurance companies and pension funds, who must react using the law, may prove to be the real undoing. These entities have the funds to litigate longer than the Investment Banks will ever be able to do without direct government and/or judicial intervention.

We're certain the outlier Investment Banks will never have the sympathy of the public as these matters surface (witness: Occupy Movement), perhaps forcing politicians to side with the Institutional Investors, and perhaps, maybe, defrauded homeowners. Nah. They take their money from Wall Street Financial Elites. When push does come to shove, for example just prior to the 2012 elections, we might see them move to protect homeowner and their own re-election. Nah. Well, maybe, if enough folks Confront Fraudulent Housing Debt. And, simultaneously make their voices heard through the Tea Party and Occupy Movements. We won't take that bet. OK. In an act of positive intent, we'll take the bet for five cents.

Mountain of Debt. Over the last twenty years the economy of the United States has grown on a mountain of debt. Low interest rates, growth of the money supply, and moreover, growth of liquidity or leveraged credit has made this possible. This trend massively advanced "animal spirits," not only in the financial sector and structured finance, but all stakeholders saw their potential prospects grow with the inevitable increase in asset prices.

Debt Accommodation. Excess debt due to central bank "accommodation" is a world-wide phenomena based on fiat currencies. You can print (or counterfeit, as some wags say) as much as you like; and so long as currency traders don't bet too heavily against the value of your currency going down because you created too much, you're OK.

But, if everyone's doing it (as most nations are, forced and allowed to keep up with the ringleader – the United States) well, then, all prices become overvalued, all currencies are inflated, and various economies heat up with the over-building of production facilities, and then bid up the price of material commodities. This results in economic distortions that have historically and necessarily corrected over time. Think of the Great Depression. With a Greater Depression likely to occur in 2012. If possible, they'll hold off a reckoning until after the Novembe 2012 election.

All that excess money (really debt) floating around is referred to as "liquidity." A tremendous amount of debt-based money and credit fills the punch bowl. But, when the punch bowl runs dry, the party is over. Greenspan's Fed always said, "Have another drink. I'll fill it right back up." Now the Fed has lost a great deal of their power to do so without completely devaluing the dollar. Yet, they soldier on. Now defending European Bonds, moreover, the TBTF banks that own them.

At the same time some of the hung-over Bankster imbibers are reluctant to have another drink. Even if the Fed makes money available to the banks to loan, it doesn't mean the banks will take and loan it. It doesn't mean entities and individuals will borrow, and do productive things if they believe the economy is under recession, or facing worse. That is today. The Banksters are not loaning money to the housing market. Why Not? They know for certain that all American homes will lose 20 – 40% in value over the next three years.

The Fed cannot force (sobered) entities and individuals to continue their previous binge drinking, cannot force them to borrow money, even though the Fed is reflating and has loaded the banks up with money to loan. This runs the great risk of inflation-certain, now baked into the cake. Perhaps, drastic hyperinflation arriving at a market check stand or gas pump near you by the middle or end of 2012.

von Mises Was Prophetic. Our Austrian economics guide, Ludwig von Mises said, "There comes a time when it becomes impossible to keep the expansion going through the issuance of more debt, because debt starts to go bad. When debt goes bad, banks refuse to lend and credit contracts. Debtors are cut off from extending their loans, which forces them into bankruptcy and creditors get hurt because the loans are not repaid."

Don't Choose Bankruptcy. In the case of homeowners with no ability to pay higher resetting house payments, and those with underwater mortgages, we might add, or rather strongly suggest, *bankruptcy is only a matter of last resort.* Whereas voluntarily Confronting Fraudulent Housing Debt and seeking a Forced Debt Reorganization may be a far better choice, unless also confronted by significant credit card debt. If that is the case, you work with sophisticated bankruptcy counsel that understands the value of your Securitization Audit.

In pandering to voters, nearly all politicians are recklessly suggesting "We want to help keep Americans in their homes." As Ronald Regan said, beware when they say, "We're from the Government and we're here to help."

They mean they really want to keep you in over-priced debt to support Wall Street and Institutional Investor gamblers who cover their campaign expenses. Shackled to your home may be the last place you want to be when your debt is larger than the actual value of the home. Estimates are that 29%, (Zillow.com) of all American homeowner are underwater right now. If one adds in an additional 7% transaction cost − to sell today − we believe 33% are actually underwater. Anywhere from 14 to 17 million out of a total of 56 million mortgages are under water. Astonishing numbers. This center cannot hold.

Kondratieff Redux. As long as asset values continue higher, debt is sustainable and can be a wonderful thing. However when the value, the price of stocks and real estate, begins to fall at the end of "autumn," the collateral no longer supports the debt. So, what do we see: The Credit Bubble − become a Debt Bubble − is unwinding because more and more people are unable − or unwilling − to make their house payments and are defaulting in record numbers. We have only begun to see the unwinding. The decline is gathering momentum as demonstrated in the drop in value, echoed in the plunging prices for houses listed on the market. This demonstrated decline then feeds back into the markets, negative feed-back loops, to accelerate the decline further. Bullish perception is shattered. This is the stuff of depressions, of Kondratieff winter.

We allege here that the Kondratieff winter is underway, has been brought into season by the onslaught of time, and exacerbated by the excess in creation of debt based money. It can't be stopped because (based on underlying actual events, over time, Centuries) it's arguably built into the nature of cycles. It may well lead to a socially horrible and destructive deflationary depression. While certainly depressing, people can choose to stay in denial, or choose to Confront Fraudulent Housing Debt, refute a so-far fixed game and protect their families.

At the outset we warned you we would use repetition, so, we will say it again, whether you wish to stay or go, we believe you must Use Foreclosure Law to Keep Your Home. Without a Forensic Loan Audit and a Securitization Audit there is no way to use the law − through legal leverage based on *their* fraud − to negotiate your objective from strength.

We end this chapter with some spice (congratulations, it's been a tough slog to here), a story told by the esteemed Canadian, Ian Gordon, from his November 7, 2007 newsletter, the *Long Wave Analyst*. Mr. Gordon wrote:

"My deceased friend, Teddy Butler-Henderson, met Alan Greenspan in the 1960's. They apparently discussed The Kondratieff Cycle. According to Teddy, Alan Greenspan confided that he hoped he could be Federal Reserve Chairman at the onset of a Kondratieff winter, because he felt he could defeat winter by substantially increasing the money supply and reducing interest rates to near zero. He had his wish and effected those actions following the 2000 stock market peak.

"This effectively *put winter on hold* but massively compounded already excessive credit to the extent that people who should never have had access to loans were willingly given them. Now the credit bubble that Alan Greenspan initiated is beginning to unwind. The process will be horrific and cannot be reversed.

"Incidentally, Mr. Greenspan told Teddy during that same conversation <u>that if he failed to thwart the Kondratieff winter, it would make what followed 1929 look like a 'Sunday school picnic.'</u> This is what we have to expect. The rapidly advancing monetary crisis centered on the dollar is reminiscent of the previous Kondratieff winter crisis, which was focused on the British Pound. Some argue that the Pound's collapse in 1931 brought down the world monetary system and caused the abandonment of gold as a backing for money." [Emphasis added.]

Astonishing. Another tip of the hat to Mr. Gordon who has provided anecdotal evidence that the Maestro may be one of the greatest criminals of all time in *terms of major disruption of the lives of millions of individuals all over the world.* We wouldn't call him a Hitler because murder was not his operational focus. However, there will likely be many deaths attributed to the disruption that is coming – just like there were in the Great Depression. The history books generally did not record the number of deaths due to starvation of many our seniors. Hopefully, the current social safety net will prevent that this time.

Mea Culpa? This came in from the UPI on March 20, 2008. "Former U.S. Federal Reserve Chairman Alan Greenspan defended his interest rate policy, but said he should have monitored banks more closely. 'I don't know a of a single example of when interest rate policy has been successful in suppressing gains in asset prices,' he said. Greenspan said low interest rates during his years as chairman were due to global economic forces. The current economic crisis came after a period of 'disinflationary forces' and a long period of 'under pricing of risk,' Greenspan told *The Washington Post…*" Yeah, sure Alan, however, it's what you don't say that's more interesting, more to the point.

It has been written that when Mr. Greenspan appears in public these days, he has an aide on either side of him to support him in an upright position. Frankly, we wonder how he sleeps? On medication? In blissful (senile?) denial? Well, you've got to go along to get along. Unless, of course, you've made a business decision to no longer be on the losing end of the "getting along." Protect your family.

Reach for Optimism. Where are you in the Cycle of Market Emotions below? The sooner you move up the last leg from Hope to Relief the sooner Optimism is in sight, in your life. Sound good? Sound like a smart idea? Hope and relief can be achieved when you choose to take action. Remove yourself from oppressive debt. When you take action with legal leverage you have immediate relief in your life and move into Optimism.

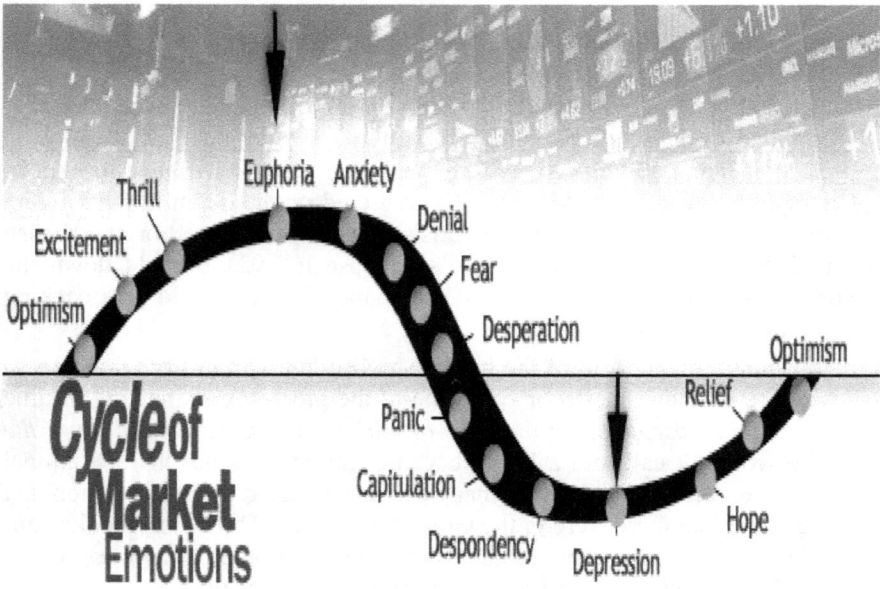

Cycle of Market Emotions

Optimism — Excitement — Thrill — Euphoria — Anxiety — Denial — Fear — Desperation — Panic — Capitulation — Despondency — Depression — Hope — Relief — Optimism

Courtesy of Mackensen & Company, Inc. Fee-Only Financial Planners.

CHAPTER 6: THEIR LEGAL ISSUES

"A sound banker, alas, is not one who foresees danger and avoids it, but one who, when he is ruined, is ruined in a conventional way along with his fellows, so that no one can really blame him." John Maynard Keynes, 1931.

If everyone is at fault, who's to blame? Moreover, who will be held accountable in a rampant, a veritable Tsunami, of court-based litigation taking place all over the country. This is not trivial.

As one might imagine, "It's not my (our) fault – it was the other guy!"

- Homeowners are suing originating Mortgage Lenders (local, regional banks and national Mortgage Banks).
- Homeowners are suing Mortgage Brokers.
- Homeowners are suing Appraisers.
- Appraisers are suing Mortgage Banks (local and national).
- Investment Banks are suing Mortgage Banks.
- Investors are suing Investment Banks.
- Investors are suing Rating Agencies who blessed with AAA ratings the new securities (bonds) (that used the home loans that serve as underlying collateral for the securities) that were created by the Investment Banks.
- Investment Banks are suing Investment Banks. (OK. OK. A corny joke, but they have been swallowing them whole: Bear Stearns and Lehman Brother eaten up real quick. Wait a minute, weren't they "Too Big To Fail?" They failed. Yet, the sun rose this morning. Have they been conning us all along? Well, yes.

Above is only a partial list of private party actions. The FBI and SEC are investigating Investment Banks for possible criminal violations. Various state Attorney Generals are planning and bringing litigations against Investment Banks and Mortgage Lenders. Various states and local cities and towns are suing Investment Banks for misrepresentation. Yet, the U.S. Justice Department is missing in action. Actually, no action. No indictments for obvious fraud.

Speaking of the FBI, an arm of the Justice Department, they used to have over 500 hundred agents investigating finance. The Bush Administration saw to it that 400 of them were assigned to different duties. To this day, they do not seriously investigate Wall Street fraud.

On May 5, 2011, the indefatigable Issac Gradman, writing from his, Sub-PrimeShakeout.com, offered an article titled: "Top Five Reasons that MBS Lawsuits Are Just Beginning." You can Google the article to read the whole thing. Below we offer only his major five points.

"5: Statistical Sampling Gains Widespread Acceptance in MBS Cases.

"4: Bank of America Settles Repurchase Claims with AGO for $1.6 billion.

"3: AIG Jumps into the Fray. The sleeping giant has finally awoken.

"2: Duetsche Bank and MortgageIT Sued by U.S. Department of Justice for Reckless Lending Practices.

"1: Levin Report Referred to the SEC and DOJ for Potential Criminal Charges."

We'll concede that naming the Big Five is inadequate for real comprehension, but, frankly, please take our word for it that this is the beginning of something big. Please read the entire article, if so inclined, here: http://www.subprimeshakeout.com/2011/05/top-five-reasons-we-havent-seen-the-last-of-the-mbs-lawsuits.html.

What Went Wrong? Many things went wrong. Throughout this book we've given you information that is not widely available. We've done this to enable you to intelligently understand that the entire system was gamed from the top down. Of course, many, fooled by the media, will blame unsophisticated home purchasers that ultimately trusted their mortgage professional (Mortgage Broker) but, that misses the point. It came from the top down.

On May 27, 2008 NPR reported,

"Now that millions of people are facing foreclosure because they got into loans that never should have been approved, everybody's looking for someone to blame. Borrowers, or their brokers, lied on loan applications. Others got high interest rates they couldn't afford. A big unanswered question is whether the Wall Street investment banks that were packaging these mortgages knew they were selling garbage loans to investors. A wave of litigation is starting against these firms.

"'This is a smoking gun,' says Christopher Peterson, a law professor at the University of Utah who has been studying the subprime mess and meeting with regulators. 'It suggests that auditors working for Wall Street investment bankers knew how preposterous these loans were, and that could mean Wall Street liability for aiding and abetting fraud.'" [Emphasis added.]

Flood of Litigation. According to one source, by December, 2007, thirty-two class-action suits were filled by investors against Investment Banks and various other suits by investors who bought shares of hedge funds, bond funds and securities containing exposure to subprime loans.

Many believe that this oncoming flood of litigation, combined with regulatory issues (let us not forget the injection of politicians in an election year), will make the issues following the dot.com bust and Enron and WorldCom debacles look like a walk in the park. It will make the late 80's into early 90's Savings and Loan debacle seem like grade school games. This is because the complexity and the gigantic size of today's modern mortgage market (in excess of $11 Trillion) will cause this mess to be nearly unsolvable. Some of the litigation mentioned above crosses continents.

"This particular species of litigation will be manifest in many different types of lawsuits in many different jurisdictions. It will be a multi-ring circus," said Joseph A. Grundfest, a professor of law and business and co-director of the Rock Center for Corporate Governance at Stanford University.

Underlying all of the real and potential litigation is fraud. Towards understanding fraud and how it may have affected your situation, the following chapter gives a lengthy legal definition of fraud to give you more information. Information which may have a serious and perhaps beneficial impact on your decisions. The good news is that it may be good news for you. There is more. In that various claims, as above, allege failure to disclose information regarding loan packages which were subsequently sold to third parties. There are breach of contract issues regarding due diligence on mortgages before they were packaged as CDOs (very complex securities ((risk betting vehicles)) based on securities that, believe it or not, many high level financial executives did not and still do not understand because of their mathematical complexity), are also involved.

Lawsuits have been filed against title companies, appraisers, realtors and Mortgage Bankers alleging numerous Predatory Lending practices, and Securitization Fraudulent violations based on misrepresentation in the very process of loan origination.

Many have charged that loans were granted without consideration of a borrower's actual ability to pay; that excessive fees and charges were actually financed into the loan principle amounts without the borrower being aware of the facts; and despicably, borrowers, even those with good credit, were issued loans with higher interest rates than they actually qualified for. Why? Higher fees were garnered for Mortgage Brokers and Mortgage Bank loan originators, who then promptly sold the loans off to Investment Bankers, eliminating their risk. The Investment banks then eliminated (so they thought, rather, so they hope) their risk by selling the resulting securities to Institutional Investors.

At the very heart of many litigations are two primary issues:

1. Did Investment Banks (Securitizers) and lenders (loan originators) *disclose* to and inform investors and home buyers regarding the risks involved with subprime loans and/or the securities that were backed by them?

2. What were they legally obligated to disclose?

Tamar Frankel, a law professor at Boston University, recently said "What strikes me here is that this is a tainted system from A to Z. Everybody blames everybody else. If you look at what is being said, there isn't one who doesn't blame another and there is half-truth in everything."

Below is a partial list of some litigations that are in the process of being resolved.

Countywide Indicted. James Temple, wrote in the San Francisco Chronicle, "State attorney general sues Countrywide, Executives." Mr. Temple said,

"California Attorney General Jerry Brown sued Countrywide Financial Corp. and two of its top executives, alleging they used <u>misleading advertising and unfair business practices to dupe consumers</u> into accepting risky home loans that would eventually force thousands of them into foreclosure. [Emphasis added.]

"'Buyers were led down the primrose path, fed extremely complicated and risky mortgage instruments and beguiled into signing up for what turned out to be a disaster,' Brown said. 'This lawsuit is important because <u>it exposes and seeks remedies for what became a cancer in our entire financial system.</u>' [Emphasis added.]

"The attorney general of Illinois also filed a lawsuit alleging deceptive practices, the governor of Washington said the state will seek to fine the company for predatory lending and Countrywide shareholders approved Bank of America's pending $3 billion acquisition by a wide margin. The deal is expected to close July 1.

"AG Brown claims Countrywide <u>pushed dicey mortgages on customers by emphasizing low initial interest rates while obfuscating the downsides, including prepayment penalties and the fact the rates would rise sharply</u>. In turn, the company sold those mortgages on the secondary market as securities or whole loans, often earning higher profit for riskier loans. Mozillo and Sambol <u>encouraged the loosening of lending standards</u>, allowing a surge in the number of issued loans, the attorney general's office claims. The company routinely sold mortgages without verifying the applicant's income, provided financial incentives for brokers landing loans with higher and adjusting interest rates, and handed out scripts to loan officers that downplayed rising mortgage costs, it alleges. [Emphasis added.]

"Many observers draw a direct line between <u>deceptive mortgage practices and the recent flood of foreclosures in communities across California and the United States</u>. Resetting subprime loans and falling home values sparked growing numbers of defaults last summer, eventually leading to the international liquidity crisis that would nearly topple Countrywide and take down hundreds of other mortgage companies. [Emphasis added.]

"'The bad practices that we've seen and hear about from Countrywide and from others ... represent the seeds of the foreclosure crisis,' said Kevin Stein, associate director of the California Reinvestment Coalition of San Francisco, which advocates equal access to financial services for low-income households.

"The lawsuit seeks '<u>restitution for thousands of victims who were ripped off by these deceptive practices</u>,' said Gareth Lacy, a spokesman for the attorney general's office. State statute allows for a $2,500 fine for every violation of the unfair competition statute, but the number of instances will have to be determined in court, Lacy said. 'If the court issues a sweeping restitution order, we could easily be talking <u>tens of millions and possibly significantly</u>

more,' said Kurt Eggert, professor of law at Chapman University School of Law in Orange." [Emphasis added.]

"Consumers who believe they were victimized by Countrywide can file a complaint by writing to: Attorney General's Office, California Department of Justice, Attn: Public Inquiry Unit, P.O. Box 944255, Sacramento, CA 94244-2550, or through an online complaint form, *links.sfgate.com/ZDXY"*

On our blog we have extensively documented current activity regarding a fiasco that has been going on over the past year. The joke loosely called the *"50 State Attorneys General Settlement With The Major Banks."* You can follow that on the blog. Suffice to say, that only five or six state Attorneys General have stood up to their peers, and are not inclined to settle this issue by allowing the Banksters to avoid criminal indictments. Serious business.

Lehman Brothers – R.I.P. But before they went down, they were facing suits from many different directions, as well as widely reported solvency issues. Lehman Brothers, the Investment Bank with arguably the largest mortgage business, was being sued by towns in Australia that have indicated that a division of the firm sold them risky mortgage-linked investments without informing them of the risks involved. Obviously the firm denied the charges claiming that everything was done appropriately. Members of a wealthy New Jersey family sued Lehman for $4.14 billion, indicating the firm inappropriately convinced them to purchase complex securities that are now difficult if not impossible to sell without taking a huge loss.

At the same time Lehman was suing several Mortgage Bankers and lenders claiming they sold Lehman "dubious" loans wherein appraisals were inflated, or the homes were in bad condition, and/or the incomes of borrowers were fraudulently overstated. In this type of case, lenders contest the basic allegations, moreover, they resist the demand from Lehman that the mortgage lenders buy back loans that have defaulted or are non-performing. The buy-back clause in many of these contracts has resulted in many major U.S. home lending operations going out of business. According to the Mortgage Lender Implode – O - Meter, "Since late 2006, 387 major U.S. lending operations have "imploded."

PMI Group. In a similar case, mortgage insurer, the PMI Group, sued WMC Mortgage and its corporate parent, General Electric. PMI is attempting to cause WMC and GE to buy back loans that the firm contracted to insure. PMI claims that the loans were issued fraudulently, or not in compliance with standards WMC claimed to be operating under. One consultant's review of many of these loans claims that WMC did not utilize "sound underwriting standards and practices."

David J. Grais, partner at New York law firm Grais & Ellsworth, an expert on the legal liabilities of credit rating companies said, "This is going to be much more complicated to prove, and it's going to be case by case as opposed to class-actions. This resembles the S&L crisis in the '80s much more than it does the tech bubble in the '90s."

Some argue that securities fraud cases will be more difficult to prove because of recent Supreme Court decisions favoring Wall Street Investment Banks and other professionals. Yet, other legal experts indicate that that those decisions, based on class action and individual law suits by shareholders, will not impinge on the complex issues that arise from mortgage securitization.

BoyO BoyO Boyko. Taking strong exception to the actions of plaintiff, Deutsche Bank, which consolidated and filed a dozen foreclosure cases in the Cleveland, Ohio court of Federal District Judge Christopher A. Boyko, the judge dismissed them all, with a stern admonition. The following is taken from footnote 3 of his Order, which dismissed the cases without prejudice, meaning the plaintiff can re-file the cases (perhaps in state court) when it gets its paperwork right.

Judge Boyko's, footnote 3:

"Plaintiff's, 'Judge, you just don't understand how things work,' argument reveals a condescending mindset and quasi-monopolistic system where financial institutions have traditionally controlled, and still control, the foreclosure process. Typically, the homeowner who finds himself/herself in financial straits, fails to make the required mortgage payments and faces a foreclosure suit, is not interested in testing state or federal jurisdictional requirements, either *pro se* or through counsel. Their focus is either, 'how do I save my home,' or 'if I have to give it up, I'll simply leave and find somewhere else to live.'"

"In the meantime, the financial institutions or successors/assignees rush to foreclose, obtain a default judgment and then sit on the deed, avoiding responsibility for maintaining the property while reaping the financial benefits of interest running on a judgment. The financial institutions know the law charges the one with title (still the homeowner) with maintaining the property. [Emphasis added.]

"There is no doubt every decision made by a financial institution in the foreclosure process is driven by money. And the legal work which flows from winning the financial institution's favor is highly lucrative. There is nothing improper or wrong with financial institutions or law firms making a profit – to the contrary, they should be rewarded for sound business and legal practices. However, unchallenged by underfinanced opponents, the institutions worry less about jurisdictional requirements and more about maximizing returns. Unlike the focus of financial institutions, the federal courts must act as gatekeepers, assuring that only those who meet diversity and standing requirements are allowed to pass through. [Emphasis added.]

"Counsel for the institutions are not without legal argument to support their position, but their arguments fall woefully short of justifying their premature filings, and utterly fail to satisfy their standing."

Clearly the Judge was angered by tactics of the Plaintiff, which could not prove to the satisfaction of the court that it had the legal standing to bring the cases in foreclosure. It either did not own, or did not physically possess the critical Promissory Note, the original, signed by the parties.

The deeper question is "Who Owns a Loan That Has Been Securitized?" Nobody knows because the securitization process has fundamentally altered former bedrock practice. Loans were placed in Securities that were then sliced and diced into smaller segments, and investors owned various slices, which were not necessarily tied to one particular loan. Worse, for the Investment Banks who purchased loans from lenders, often these Securities were traded several times. Some were sold illegally to *more than one party* − pure fraud. Double dealing.

At the same time the loan Servicers (institution who collects home payments and are responsible for borrower contact, often the Servicer is the original lender) do not hold the actual Promissory Note, the physical loan document signed by the lender and the borrower. While it may seem ridiculous, the box of documents that holds the Promissory Note and other documents from the Close of Escrow, may be in one of several places, such as a trust entity, which held the box. So, if the Security is traded/sold, the box must be sent to the new trust entity or the new Servicer. A mess. Where is the box? Where is the Promissory Note? In order to foreclose, the foreclosing must have the Promissory Note in their possession, and moreover, be able to prove that they are actual owner. Many of these were simply destroyed. Thus, began what has been called Robo-Signing, the fraudulent forging of signatures on likely hundreds of thousand of legal documents. This continues, even though the Banksters have said they don't do it anymore. Likely not. The farm the work out to feral law firms and other entities that enlist naive employees to do this signature forging, etc.

The bottom line to all of this, particularly in states that require Judicial Foreclosure (which requires a law suit in order to foreclose) is the fact that in order to have legal standing to bring a foreclosure action, the entity bringing the foreclosure must have possession and be able to bring the loan document into court to prove that they have the right, the legal standing, to foreclose. Because Ohio is a Judicial Foreclosure state Judge Boyko appropriately threw these cases out of his court.

Echoing Judge Boyko, two other Ohio Federal Judges followed suit and dismissed a number of other foreclosure cases. While the cases are likely to be filed again, in Ohio State courts, the fact is that the Securitizers and plaintiff attorneys are going to have to do some fairly expensive and complicated work to satisfy this Judge, and an increasing number of other judges across the nation. They have to find the file box where the actual signed loan document exists. The box may not have kept up physically, been shipped to the new loan owner (or its designated trust entity or Servicer), as the Security was traded between various Institutional Investors and new Servicers were brought on board.

Boyko's dismissal is being echoed across the country in Federal courts, as well as by Local and State Judges (some of whom are elected to their positions) and may possess a sympathetic view towards homeowner voters who are being displaced. All mind you, while following the letter of the law, but importantly, not simply bowing to the power and prestige and connections and money of large institutions and their high-powered legal firms who have over time built relationships with the Judicial Authorities.

You Better Own the Note. *Bloomberg* News reported in February 22, 2008, that,

> "Judges in at least five states have stopped foreclosure proceedings because the banks that pool mortgages into securities and the companies that collect monthly payments haven't been able to prove they own the mortgages. The confusion is another headache for U.S. Treasury Secretary Henry Paulson as he revises rules for packaging mortgages into securities.

> "'I think it's going to become pretty hairy,' said Josh Rosner, managing director at the New York-based investment research firm Graham Fisher & Co. 'Regulators appear to have ignored this, given the size and scope of the problem.'

> "More than $2.1 trillion, or *19 percent,* of outstanding mortgages have been bundled into securities by private banks, according to Inside Mortgage Finance, a Bethesda, Maryland-based industry newsletter. Those loans may be sold several times before they land in a security. Mortgage Servicers, who collect monthly payments and distribute them to securities investors, can buy and sell the home loans many times."

> "Joe Lents hasn't made a payment on his $1.5 million mortgage since 2002. That's when Washington Mutual Inc. first tried to foreclose on his home in Boca Raton, Florida. The Seattle-based lender failed to prove that it owned Lents's mortgage note and dropped attempts to take his house. Subsequent efforts to foreclose have stalled because no one has produced the paperwork. *'If you're going to take my house away from me, you better own the note,'* said Lents, 63, the former chief executive officer of a now-defunct voice recognition software company."

Emerging Trend. As these Ohio Judges are setting a pattern in Ohio of standing up for the little guy, a national pattern is emerging and becoming a Social Movement, the little gals and guy are standing up for their own selves. Not merely going quietly in the night. Lots of folks are standing up by Using Foreclosure Law to Keep Their Homes.

If Predatory Lending and Securitization Fraud was present in any way, who could rationally blame them if they stayed in their home, payment free, for as long as possible? Then exiting broom clean, with no damage to the property, after reaching settlement with any (fraudulent) participants to the loan origination process. In other words, if you do leave a property, be smart and make sure that you leave the property in good broom clean condition (take photographs that include the front page of the local newspaper to establish date) in order to be sure there is no backlash from doing the wrong thing. As you begin to understand that you are taking the high ground, fear of the unknown slips away.

Alternatively and highly recommended, when fraud is present with Predatory Lending, homeowners may end up extracting punitive damages, compensation, which is allowed under contract law, and under Federal and State laws and regulations, if they in fact are damaged. Trust us, these issues are now sounding large nationally for attorneys who practice homeowner-protection foreclosure law. You know the drill by now, but, once again: Confront Fraudulent Housing Debt using the law – legal leverage – to obtain a Forced Debt Reorganization.

State Level Litigation. Ohio Attorney General, Marc Dann, is building a case against credit-Rating Agencies like: Standard & Poor's, Fitch and Moody's for the role they played in rubberstamping many questionable securities.

According to Dann, "The ratings agencies cashed a check every time one of these subprime pools was created and an offering was made. The agencies continued to rate these things AAA. [So they are] among the people who aided and abetted this continuing fraud," adds Dann, as reported in *Fortune*.

Moody's alleges that Dann's allegations/accusations are ridiculous. "We perform a very significant but extremely limited role in the credit markets. We issue reasoned, forward-looking opinions about credit risk," said Fran Laserson, vice president of corporate communications at Moody's. "Our opinions are objective and not tied to any recommendations to buy and sell." [Emphasis added.]

According to Dann, he believes that the intimate relationships between ratings agencies and Investment Banks "heightens the appearance of impropriety." The astonishing factor here isn't simply that the Rating Agencies receive fees from the bond issuers, the Investment Banks, but that they don't perform *due diligence* on the data that the bond issuers give them. As stated in Moody's Code of Conduct, "Moody's has no obligation to perform, and does not perform, due diligence." Well, what are they good for? Who is watching out for the chickens while the foxes circle and invade the henhouse? [Emphasis added.]

While the agencies maintain that their ratings are just "opinions," in fact, investors have historically relied on such opinions, and may not at all be aware that the Rating Agencies are doing what the Investment Banks, the Security issuers, tell them to do and say. So they get paid, and when everything was rolling along, investor's were none the wiser. Now it's stopped rolling. Attorney General Dann contends that ratings are used "as benchmarks by Institutional Investors."

"The rating drives everything," adds Sylvain Raynes, a former Moody's analyst and currently a principal at R&R Consulting, a firm that examines these securities, as pointed out in *Fortune*.

As others have suggested, Wall Street brought many people into this process because of the tremendous profitability, now it appears they've brought a lot of trouble to themselves.

The Music Has Stopped. As Chuck Prince, former CEO of Citigroup (the bank is subject to various allegations in the financial press that it may be insolvent, and is being forced to dilute shareholder value by taking billions of dollars from

China's Central bank in exchange for equity; and are drastically cutting shareholder dividends) neatly put it, "When the dancing was going on. We got up and danced."

He was actually quoted in the *Financial Times* stating, "As long as the music is playing, you've got to get up and dance. We're still dancing." [Emphasis added.]

Mr. Prince did dance off Wall Street. Removed by the Citigroup Board of Directors his golden parachute enabled him to drop out of the sky and was measured in multi-millions. Some have wondered if that was "hush" money? If everyone is at fault? Then who is to blame? Hush hush. Perhaps, Mr. Prince is one. Congressman Henry Waxman using the venue of his Congressional Committee raked Mr. Prince over the coals under oath. Mr. Prince was reluctant to, and did not admit that he might have made "too much" money presiding over what has become a debacle for his former employer. These guys always get paid. Surely by his own reckoning, Mr. Prince had to do it. Another "fancy dancer" going along to get along.

Iowa Attorney General Tom Miller heads a multi-state task force that won $800 million in settlement from two subprime lenders, Household International (2002) and Ameriquest Mortgage (2006). According to *Bloomberg*, Miller is on record stating, that he's "... focused on prodding lenders and bond investors to help consumers avoid foreclosure and getting other states to do the same. We've got to do something to avenge those homeowners and to deter this type of conduct in the future, and hopefully create a pool of money to restore some of these folks to homeownership."

This sounds laudable. Yet, we ask, is it wise for an individual family to maintain homeownership at this time, when house values are plunging? Thiswill lead to more and more, perhaps millions of un-informed people, continuing to pay high mortgages on houses that are going to be worth $20 - 50\%$ less than the value of the loan. Make your own decision after you obtain a Forensic Loan Audit and a Securitization Audit. We can guide you through that process.

See, www.UseForeclosureLaw.com

Quoted in *Bloomberg*, Ohio's Dann said, "If someone was buying guns and giving them to people to go and take people's houses at gunpoint in Ohio, we'd be prosecuting them and throwing them in jail." Regarding current and pending litigation Dann also said, "I want to see the e-mails, I want to see the documents. I'm guessing somebody at some or all of these places was predicting the bottom was going to fall out."

If Dann had found those e-mails and documents and presented them in open court, those documents would have become available to all homeowners who choose to aggressively stand up for themselves. [Unfortunately, he lost his election and is now back in private practice.] Or, is it more than likely that out of court settlements and the legal moving papers contained in the suits, that show advantage to homeowners, will be Judicially Sealed as a result of settlements? Cynics that we are.

Investment Banks Under Attack. According to *Bloomberg*, "Goldman Sachs Group and Morgan Stanley, the two biggest securities firms, said they were responding to requests from regulators for information on subprime-mortgage securities. Morgan Stanley said the requests concerned 'the origination, purchase, securitization and servicing of subprime and non-subprime residential mortgages and related issues.' "

"Connecticut and New York are among states, along with the Securities and Exchange Commission, investigating the home-loan industry after surging defaults paralyzed the market for mortgage-backed bonds. The largest banks and securities firms have posted at least $133 billion in credit losses and write-downs related to subprime loans, typically given to borrowers with weak credit histories."

"Goldman said it was cooperating with the requests, which came from 'various governmental agencies and self-regulatory organizations.' Morgan Stanley said it received subpoenas and has been named as a defendant in civil lawsuits related to the mortgage market.'"

"Neil Power, chief of the FBI's economic crimes unit, wouldn't identify the companies, though he said the cases involve 'valuation-type stuff.' The probes include reviews of subprime lenders, housing developers and Wall Street banks that package loans as securities, he said. 'We're looking at the accounting fraud that goes through the securitization of these loans,' Power said at a briefing. 'We're dealing with the people who securitize them and then the people who hold them, such as the Investment Banks.'"

"Power said another area of criminal inquiry is insider trading – whether executives sold shares when they knew loan defaults were going to surge." [Emphasis added.]

Merrill Lynch. According to the *New York Times,* "The top securities regulator in Massachusetts accused Merrill Lynch of defrauding the city of Springfield with subprime-linked investments, casting light on how Wall Street banks sold complex mortgage securities that are now plummeting in value as the housing slump deepens."

"William Galvin, the Massachusetts Secretary of State, filed a civil fraud complaint against Merrill a day after the firm took the unusual step of agreeing to reimburse Springfield for losses on the investments. Merrill agreed to buy back the securities at their original value, $13.9 million, after determining that its brokers had not been authorized by Springfield to buy the securities on the city's behalf."

"'They are alleging fraud against a municipality, which carries with it much more *gravitas* than a simple lawsuit,' Mark A. Flessner, a partner at Sonnenschein Nath & Rosenthal in Chicago, said of the complaint. An official in Mr. Galvin's office said the Springfield case was part of a larger investigation into Merrill's sales of similar investments to other Massachusetts towns and cities."

"Asked about the Springfield case, Mark Herr, a spokesman for Merrill Lynch, said, 'We are puzzled by this suit.' He declined to comment on the broader investigation." [Emphasis added.]

"The case underscores how subprime investments keep turning up in unexpected places and raises new questions about Wall Street's sales practices and its role in the mortgage crisis. In recent years, as home prices soared and mortgage lending boomed, Investment Banks packaged hundreds of billions of dollars of home loans into securities for sale to investors around the world. Now, record defaults are resulting in huge losses for municipalities, states, banks, insurance companies and nonprofit organizations."

"Wall Street banks have lost billions of dollars of such investments themselves. Merrill has been one of the hardest hit, writing down almost $25 billion, the bulk of which came from mortgage-related securities."

According to *Bloomberg* reporter Jody Shenn, "Merrill Lynch & Co. sued XL Capital Assurance Inc. to force the bond insurer to honor $3.1 billion of guarantees on collateralized debt obligations as the securities firm attempts to avoid more write downs of mortgage-backed debt. 'We filed suit to make clear that XL Capital Assurance Inc. is required to meet its contractual obligations,' Mark Herr, a spokesman for...Merrill, said... 'Apparently in light of the current dramatic downturn and deterioration in the credit markets, defendants are having 'sellers' remorse,' Merrill said..." [Emphasis added.]

Appraisals. Of extreme significance to homeowners, both sellers and buyers, and to the entire housing industry is the issue of valid appraisals on homes that are on the market to sell. The Savings & Loan Debacle, which started in the late eighties and finally concluded with a massive taxpayer bailout in the early nineties was a cause for significant changes in Federal law relating to the appraisal industry, which had been subverted by mortgage lending entities.

History is once again repeating itself, and appraisers have and are being subjected to pressure and duress. In order to keep working in the industry many many appraisers were coerced into inflating the value of homes they contracted to appraise. An Appraisal is a Certified document performed by a licensed appraiser who is bound by law to provide an accurate Appraisal. In other words it goes beyond mere *opinion.*

Former New York State Attorney General, now Governor, Andrew Cuomo, of New York State brought an action against national thrift organization, Washington Mutual ("WaMu"), regarding appraisal issues. Specifically, AG Cuomo, sued an appraisal management company, First American eAppraiseIT, for succumbing to pressure from WaMu to inflate property values for loans that WaMu was deciding to grant, and thereby contributing to ongoing mortgage market losses.

Courageous Appraiser. Jennifer Wertz, a long-time certified appraiser in California filed suit in Superior Court in Sacramento, California in which she named WaMu and eAppraiseIT, and also LSI, a unit of Fidelity National Information Services, who are appraisal sub-contractors to WaMu. This suit is being closely followed by all industry stakeholders, particularly by appraisers.

Ms. Wertz has claimed that she was blacklisted because she refused to provide favorable appraisal values. Moreover, she had shown on appraisals that certain properties were in "declining" markets. (It amounts to checking a box if the property is in what is considered to be a declining market.) Wertz documented in her suit that she began performing appraisals for WaMu in 2001. She earned "in excess of $100,000 a year" from her work for the bank. Things changed last May. Language in her suit asserted that a WaMu manager criticized her for describing local property values as "declining." In order to approve the loan, the manager allegedly ' insisted that (Wertz) change her report to indicate 'stable' conditions in order for the loan to be approved."

This is really nothing new. Reports show that experienced real estate appraisers have complained over years regarding loan officer demands that they inflate the home values – "hit the number" – in order to allow deals to close at inflated values, resulting in higher fees for the players.

Wertz refused to change her opinion, maintaining the properties were in "declining" neighborhoods. She alleges she was told she would never receive any future business from WaMu if she refused to play ball. She declined to make the changes and cited "federal, state and professional rules requiring her to provide only objective and accurate reports free of outside influence." They did not give her any further business. According to the suit, Wertz was cut off from any additional WaMu business through the named appraisal sub-contracting companies.

The suit carries Causes of Action based on: breach of contract, unfair business practices, interference with her ability to earn a living, fraud, conspiracy and slander, among other alleged violations.

WaMu had no comment on the suit. But appraisers all over the county have gone online with a majority of them applauding Wertz for having the courage to blow the whistle. Gary T. Crabtree, the lead appraiser for Affiliated Appraisers in Bakersfield, California recently stated that pressure on appraisers to inflate values "has been endemic, industry-wide" and is a "significant contributing factor" in many mortgage fraud cases and foreclosures.

The deeper problem with inflated values, is that they create an ever widening upward spiral, as each inflated appraisal sets the bar higher, falsely forcing up values on all homes in the market.

So what will happen? Same ol' same ol'? Legislation pending in Congress may increase penalties for anyone who attempts to influence or otherwise interferes with an appraisal, whether by punishing appraisers who refuse to go along, or, perhaps worse, offer appraiser's inducements for favorable valuations.

Below we provide another recent example from the Appraiser Trenches. The following is a letter in which the identity and location of the appraiser has been removed. The letter was originally printed in the May 5, 2008, Newsletter from Appraisal Buzz.com, which is an excellent industry source.

"I am writing to you today to inform you of a serious matter that myself and my fellow colleagues; are aware of. Firstly I should explain that I am a Certified Residential Real Estate Appraiser with over 12 years experience and also the owner of my own Appraisal Firm.

"The Real Estate Settlement Procedures Act (RESPA) prohibits charging for services not actually performed. The Bank Owned/Affiliated and/or contracted Appraisal Management Companies, however, are deliberately charging and collecting from the consumer inflated appraisal fees of $500+ and abating a small portion of that fee (as little as $125 or lower) to the appraiser. As a result the appraisal fees paid by the consumer on the HUD-1 statement are not what is being billed, invoiced and collected by the appraiser.

"This is outright fraud to the consumer and the big banks are the reason.

"This practice is outright deception to the consumer and not a good reflection on our profession. I can only imagine the millions, if not billions, of dollars the consumers have been over charged for appraisal fees. The Bank Owned/Affiliated and/or contracted Management Companies are profiting from the appraisal business which is a clear conflict of interest and this has to be stopped immediately.

"I hope this letter is clear and precise to what is going on in our industry, and I hope as a member of the Board of Real Estate Appraisal something can be done. Please feel free to call me anytime with any questions and/or concerns as I would be more than happy to become involved and provide any additional information you would need."

Current mortgage market problems are not new news. Two decades ago the mortgage process generally took one month. An appraisal was ordered on the first day and usually completed by the tenth day. That was the foundation, the basis for a loan. Today one month has been shortened to five to seven days. Without the benefit of an appraisal the parties are already in agreement on how much they are going to lend or borrow. This has dramatically changed the role of the appraiser. Rather than being a licensed and certified guide, the appraiser has been placed in the position of making or breaking the deal. As you can imagine great pressure is brought to bear on the appraiser to make the deal happen. The threat is clear, unspoken or not. Hit the numbers or we won't be calling you in the future. Appraisers have families, they have to feed them, they have to make appraisals even if it means "hitting the numbers."

Someone should be prosecuted. Who? The appraiser who followed orders? Or, The Mortgage Broker, or lender who put the pressure on the appraiser? If this pressure could be proved (likely it could) we'd thank the appraiser for being forthcoming, and deal much more harshly with the other two parties. It should be up to a jury to determine who was telling the truth. We'll grant that this best-case scenario is woefully naïve in regards to how the world really work.

Worse ... Much Worse. We've barely scratched the surface regarding legal problems for many institutions. We've also indicated that many large institutions will not survive. Below we'll bring in some more specific facts through intrepid and highly respected reporter, Herb Greenberg, columnist for online MarketWatch, a wholly-owned subsidiary of Dow Jones & Company. Mr. Greenberg can often be found on Tout TV's CNBC. Quite the contrarian he generally takes a very bearish tone among a sea of cheerleaders. He wrote on the deeper issues in a column named, Straight Talk on the Mortgage Mess from an Insider. He wrote:

> "What we are experiencing should be called 'The Mortgage Meltdown' because many different exotic loan types are imploding currently belonging to what lenders considered 'qualified' or 'prime' borrowers. This will continue to worsen over the next few of years. When 'prime' loans begin to explode to a degree large enough to catch national attention, the ratings agencies will jump on board and we will have 'Round 2'. It is not that far away.

> "The 'second mortgage implosion', 'Pay-Option implosion' and 'Hybrid Intermediate-term ARM implosion' are all happening simultaneously and about to heat up drastically. Second mortgage liens were done by nearly every large bank in the nation and really heated up in 2005, as first mortgage rates started rising and nobody could benefit from refinancing. This was a way to keep the mortgage money flowing. Second mortgages to 100% of the homes value with no income or asset documentation were among the best sellers at CITI, Wells, WAMU, Chase, National City and Countrywide. We now know these are worthless especially since values have indeed dropped and those who maxed out their liens with a 100% purchase or refi of a second now owe much more than their property is worth.

> "How are the banks going to get this junk second mortgage paper off their books?

> "WaMu, Countrywide, Wachovia, IndyMac, Downey and Bear Stearns were/are among the largest Option ARM lenders. Option ARMs are literally worthless with no bids found for many months for these assets. These assets are almost guaranteed to blow up. 75% of Option ARM borrowers make the minimum monthly payment. Eighty percent-plus are stated income/asset. Average combined loan-to-value are at or above 90%. The majority done in the past few years have second mortgages behind them. Not considering every Option ARM a sub-prime loan is a mistake."

He wrote that some time ago and it continues to come on full force. Alt-A, second mortgages and pay option arms, have been imploding, and will continue through 2012 The downward death spiral cannot be stopped no matter what bailouts they attempt. What they will likely do is recreate the Government sponsored Resolution Trust Corporation.

This will enable the Too Big To Fail Banksters that are still standing to pick up all the defaulted mortgages for a song. More important those still standing large financial institutions will only be still-standing because they will be given taxpayer money to stay standing. They will be bailed out first. We will all pay for the privilege – for *their* privilege.

In fact they have a better plan with Tim-Boy Geithner's Public-Private Partnership Plan. Just as we indicated above, that is exactly what they are doing. Setting up dummy entities to purchase the toxic debt from themselves, to clean up their balance sheets at above market prices, and, allowing the taxpayers to take the loss, and then selling the assets back to themselves. Arguably fraud and no where near ethics. That's where we stand collectively. Only individuals can take back power for themselves. How? Use Foreclosure Law to Keep Your Home. Really homeowners must do their own cramdown. Using the law for a Forced Debt Reorganization which grants a legitimate loan modification with principal reduction.

Note how naive we were in August 2008, when we wrote the original book. How we sipped from the Kool-Aid of ...

"Unless of course, we have a new administration elected in 2008, that will choose to follow the will of the people and enact real change, by reforming the financial system; and simultaneously re-building our nation's infrastructure and putting the middle class (our economic engine) back to work. This is not only possible, but, as the real facts come more and more into evidence, into plain daylight, we believe the American People will rise up and declare their Independence once again.

Our Young President won the election by 9 million votes. A message was sent by the People. How little we understood. How foolish were we to believe that an avowed Hope and Change President would stand for the people. As we've said above, we hope he has an endgame in sight. Seems as though it will be too little too late for millions of families. That is why you must stand up for your own family, assistance will not come from official power.

CHAPTER 7: FRAUD

There are never wanting some persons of violent and undertaking naturees, who, so they may have power and business will take it at any cost. Francis Bacon

Below we present a rather lengthy definition (in its entirety and with permission to reprint) from the excellent legal source, The "Lectric Law Library." http://www.lectlaw.com. We urge you to visit the "Lectric Law library" for your own research. You'll find the site very friendly to the average person who seeks basic understanding of the law.

We've made it clear throughout this work that we are not attorneys, and are not offering investment, legal or tax advice. We strongly urge you to work with experienced counsel.

We offer the following definitions in order for you to begin to come to terms (and understand some legal terms) with regard to your personal decisions. This concept is further developed in detail in Chapter 10, *Your Legal Issues.*

While you might think to gloss over this chapter because it's legalese – don't. For your own good, please read it a couple of times before moving onto Chapter 9, *Predatory Lending.* There will be no quiz, however, you may run across something that pertains to your own situation, how you were treated and informed (rather misinformed) during the loan origination process.

Consequently, you'll be better prepared for Chapter 10, *Your Legal Issues,* where you may discover that Hope Doth Spring Eternal. Particularly if Predatory Lending or Securitization Fraud played any part of your loan origination process. This is important information for you to have, informing a basic understanding of fraud, especially for those who are contemplating a business decision to protect their family.

"FRAUD, TO DEFRAUD. The term 'fraud' is generally defined in the law as an intentional misrepresentation of material existing fact made by one person to another with knowledge of its falsity and for the purpose of inducing the other person to act, and upon which the other person relies with resulting injury or damage. [Fraud may also include an omission or intentional failure to state material facts, knowledge of which would be necessary to make other statements not misleading.]

"To make a 'misrepresentation' simply means to state as a fact something which is false or untrue. [To make a material 'omission' is to omit or withhold the statement of a fact, knowledge of which is necessary to make other statements not misleading.]

"Thus, to constitute fraud, a misrepresentation must be false [or an omission must make other statements misleading], and it must be 'material' in the sense that it relates to a matter of some importance or significance rather than a minor or trivial detail.

"To constitute fraud, a misrepresentation [or omission] must also relate to an 'existing fact.' Ordinarily, a promise to do something in the future does not relate to an existing fact and cannot be the basis of a claim for fraud unless the person who made the promise did so without any present intent to perform it or with a positive intent not to perform it. Similarly, a mere expression of opinion does not relate to an existing fact and cannot be the basis of a claim of fraud unless the person stating the opinion has exclusive or superior knowledge of existing facts which are inconsistent with such opinion.

"To constitute fraud the misrepresentation [or omission] must be made knowingly and intentionally, not as a result of mistake or accident, that is, that the person either knew or <u>should have known</u> of the falsity of the misrepresentation [or the false effect of the omission], or that he made the misrepresentation [or omission] in negligent disregard of its truth or falsity. [Emphasis added.]

"Finally to constitute fraud, the Plaintiff must prove that the Defendant intended for the Plaintiff to rely upon the misrepresentation [and/or omission]; that the Plaintiff did in fact rely upon the misrepresentation [and/or omission]; and that the Plaintiff suffered injury or damage as a result of the fraud.

"In some cases [depending on the specifics of the case and the law] when it is shown that a Defendant made a material misrepresentation [and/or omission] with the intention that the Plaintiff rely upon it, then, under the law, the Plaintiff may rely upon the truth of the representation, even though its falsity could have been discovered had he made an investigation, unless he knows the representation to be false or its falsity is obvious to him.

"In other cases, when it is shown that a Defendant made a material misrepresentation [and/or omission] with the intention that the Plaintiff rely upon it, the Plaintiff must prove that his reliance was justified. If, in the exercise of reasonable care for the protection of his own interests, the Plaintiff could have learned the truth of the matter by making a reasonable inquiry or investigation under the circumstances presented, but failed to do so, then it cannot be said that he 'justifiably' relied upon such misrepresentations [and/or omissions].

"For injury or damage to be the result of fraud, it must be shown that, except for the fraud, the injury or damage would not have occurred.

"The word 'material' means that the subject matter of the statement [or concealment] related to a fact or circumstance which would be important to the decision to be made as distinguished from an insignificant, trivial or unimportant detail. (e.g. re: insurance fraud – to be material, an assertion [or concealment] must relate to a fact or circumstance that would affect the liability of an **insurer** (if made during an investigation of the loss), or would affect the decision to issue the policy, or the amount of coverage or the premium (if made in the application for the policy).

"Torts. Unlawfully, designedly and knowingly, to appropriate the property of another without criminal intent. For example:

"1. Every appropriation of the right of property of another is not fraud. It must be unlawful; that is to say, such an appropriation as is not permitted by law. Property loaned may, during the time of the loan, be appropriated to the use of the borrower. This is not fraud, because it is permitted by law.

"2. The appropriation must be not only unlawful, but it must be made with a knowledge that the property belongs to another and with a design to deprive him of the same. It is unlawful to take the property of another; but if it be done with a design of preserving it for the owners or if it be taken by mistake, it is not done designedly or knowingly and therefore, does not come within the definition of fraud.

"3. Every species of unlawful appropriation, not made with a criminal intent, enters into this definition, when designedly made, with a knowledge that the property is another's; therefore, such an appropriation, intended either for the use of another or for the benefit of the offender himself, is comprehended by the term.

"4. Fraud, however immoral or illegal, is not in itself a crime or offence for want of a criminal intent. It only becomes such in the cases provided by law.

"Contracts, Torts. Any trick or artifice employed by one person to induce another to fall into an error or to detain him in it, so that he may make an agreement contrary to his interest. The fraud may consist either, first, in the misrepresentation or, secondly, in the concealment of a material fact. Fraud, force and vexation, are odious in law. Fraud gives no action however, without damage and in matters of contract it is merely a defense; it cannot in any case constitute a new contract.

"Fraud avoids a contract, *ab initio,* both at law and in equity, whether the object be to deceive the public, third persons or one party endeavor thereby to cheat the other.

"The following is an enumeration of frauds for which equity will grant relief:

"1. Fraud, *dolus malus,* may be actual, arising from facts and circumstances of imposition, which is the plainest case;

"2. It may be apparent from the intrinsic nature and subject of the bargain itself; such as no man in his senses and not under delusion, would make on the one hand and such as no honest and fair man would accept on the other, which are inequitable and unconscientious bargains;

"3. Fraud, which may be presumed from the circumstances and condition of the parties contracting;

"4. Fraud, which may be collected and inferred in the consideration of a court of equity, from the nature and circumstances of the transaction, as being an imposition and deceit on other persons, not parties to the fraudulent agreement;

"5. Fraud, in what are called catching bargains, with heirs, reversioners, or expectants on the life of the parents. This last seems to fall under one or more of the preceding divisions.

"Frauds may be also divided into actual or positive and constructive frauds.

"Actual or positive fraud. The intentional and successful employment of any cunning, deception or artifice used to circumvent, cheat or deceive another.

"Constructive fraud. Means such a contract or act, which, though not originating in any actual evil design or contrivance to perpetrate a positive fraud or injury upon other persons, yet by its tendency to deceive or mislead them or to violate private or public confidence or to impair or injure the public interests, is deemed equally reprehensible with positive fraud and therefore is prohibited by law, as within the same reason and mischief as contracts and acts done *malo animo*. Constructive frauds are such as are either against public policy, in violation of some special confidence or trust or operate substantially as a fraud upon private right's, interests, duties or intentions of third persons; or unconscientiously compromit or injuriously affect the private interests, rights or duties of the parties themselves.

"The civilians divide frauds into positive which consists in doing one's self or causing another to do such things as induce a belief of the truth of what does not exist, or negative, which consists in doing or dissimulating certain things in order to induce the opposite party into error or to retain him there. The intention to deceive, which is the characteristic of fraud, is here present.

"Fraud is also divided into that which has induced the contract and incidental or accidental fraud.

"Contract Inducement. Is that which has been the cause or determining motive of the contract, that without which the party defrauded would not have contracted, when the artifices practiced by one of the parties have been such that it is evident that without them the other would not have contracted.

"Incidental or accidental fraud. Is that by which a person, otherwise determined to contract, is deceived on some accessories or incidents of the contract; for example, as to the quality of the object of the contract or its price so that he has made a bad bargain. Accidental fraud does not, according to the civilians, avoid the contract but simply subjects the party to damages. It is otherwise where the fraud has been the determining cause of the contract; in that case the contract is void."

For granting permission to print this definition in complete form, we offer a double tip of the hat to the wise people at The "Lectric Law Library." http://www.lectlaw.com.

CHAPTER 8: PREDATORY LENDING

"You must have a willingness to do something when everyone else is petrified. You must learn the lesson of following logic over emotion."

Warren Buffett

"The credit system, which has its focal point in the allegedly <u>national banks and the big money-lenders and usurers that surround them</u>, is one enormous centralization and gives this class of parasites a fabulous power <u>not</u> only <u>to decimate the industrial capitalists periodically but also to interfere in actual production</u> in the most dangerous manner – and this crew know nothing of production and have nothing at all to do with it." Karl Marx, *Capital*, Volume 3, Chapter, 33. [Emphasis added.]

We are NOT communists, but, the fact that American jobs (blue and white collar) and industrial manufacturing have been outsourced, indicate that Marx had a point regarding, *"... lenders and usurers that surround them...."* Let's go back farther and reflect on why Jesus Christ threw the money-changers from the Temple.

These would be Investment Banks, and their wretched spawn: Hedge Funds. With the late June, 2008, Bear Stearns indictments, it really is a smoking gun. And these are merely small fry who were caught-out and indicted. The Wall Street bunch forced the *industrial capitalists* to close American factories and service providers, and switch production to the East – principally manufacturing to China, while outsourcing white collar service jobs to India. [By late 2011, the Bear Stearns Boyz got off with a slap on the wrist.]

Their method was to downgrade the stock of corporations that were reluctant to put American citizens out of work. Because a CEO's obligation under corporate charter is to increase shareholder value (and personally their own stock options and bonuses), Wall Street had the upper hand. They formed it into a fist, put on an iron glove – and they were obeyed. Maybe Marx is right and they are "parasites." We mean, what do they actually do that is a social good. They do not create National Wealth. They push money around. They do not make or create anything of value beyond endless new financial products, and collect fees from those products, ultimately they have failed on a worldwide scale. And, now they'll another bailout, and plenty more to follow. Please!

We suggest all Powerz will the charade until after the 2012 election. Then they'll attempt a well planned take down of the Global Economy, set up in such a way that they can maintain Hegemony. Continuing Political Control. Don't be in it at that point –unless – you have utilized legal leverage and executed a Forced Debt Reorganization, bringing your housing debt down to – oh, say – 10992 levels. Not joking. Don't love your home to much.

Before we explore and explain what Predatory Lending is, and how and why so many trusting homebuyers were duped, we'd like to share words from the legendary and now deceased Tanta, aka Doris Dungey. She was a brilliant and independent long-time mortgage professional who blogged at Calculated Risk. Himself, Calculated Risk (he's also a real person) is a retired long-time corporate financial professional. Both of these highly regarded individuals are widely quoted throughout the Blog-O-Sphere, and in the Wall Street Journal and in other financial media. See their work at: Calculated Risk.

Regarding walking away, Tanta has decidedly not been sympathetic for those who are, as she says, "ruthless walk aways." Let's listen in.

"I do not claim that 'just walking away' isn't increasing; I don't have enough facts one way or the other. I remain convinced, however, that it's pretty damned convenient for the mortgage industry to convince you that these folks *can afford their loans* and *are not even trying* to get caught up. Blaming it on borrower ruthlessness deflects attention from lender ruthlessness, like the ruthlessness of making loans to people who cannot display any particular evidence that they can afford the payments. I simply refuse to play into their hands here. [Emphasis added.]

"I certainly agree that the industry is *scared to death* that 'just walking away' will become fashionable. But that's a slightly different matter. We are having more than enough troubles with borrowers who simply cannot afford to keep making house payments and can't sell. It will surely be Armageddon if the better-heeled among us just walk off. On the other hand, these people with money are going to have to live somewhere, and if they're walking away in order to rent from struggling investors or buy REO, then while they're passing the losses onto the lenders, they're not so clearly contributing to further price drops. [Emphasis added.]

"It's possible to imagine – just as an exercise – that the whole thing stabilizes only *when* the moneyed walk-aways make it stabilize, at the expense of lenders and investors as bag-holders. My guess is that's the kind of ending the industry didn't have in mind. But you can easily imagine that the industry is sounding the alarm about 'walk-aways' because they're rather desperate to show their lawmakers and their regulators and their monetary policy-makers that they're the 'real' victims here." [Emphasis added.]

We admire Tanta's far reaching, if not prescient, supposition, *"...the whole thing stabilizes only when the moneyed walk aways make it stabilize."* They may do so. They may not. The important point is that they *can*. When enough people realize that they have been lied to and tricked, they may decide to act in their own self interest – in the long term financial interest of their families and Use Foreclosure Law to Keep Their Homes.

Ironically, the power of that self interest is what can set us free from the predatory lender's grasp. That is, if we can agree that returning to housing affordability is Freedom. We argue that re-enabling the American Dream in pride of ownership of an "affordable" home is definitely Freedom.

Below we're presenting data from a number of authoritative sources. At the conclusion of the chapter we'll sum it up and leave you with options to consider.

By the end of the chapter (parts of it are well worth reading twice) we'll give you some options.

Forensic Loan Audit and a Securitization Audit. This is the means and method of having all of your loan documents comprehensively and professionally examined.

There are Forensic Loan Audits and there are Securitization Audits. The former are initially run through a software program to determine if the numbers are correct and not inflated. Then the documents are gone over meticulously by hand by an experienced loan officer or underwriter. Many Forensic Loan Audits are simply run through the software, which can catch some TILA and RESPA violations. You need a Securitization Audit, which is more expensive, but, also determines whether or not you were a victim of Securities Law fraud violations. The computer software won't catch these, which can be extremely valuable leverage in obtaining your best and desired outcome. It comes down to the amount of fraud contained in your docs.

Yet, be wary, and remember this. A Securitization Audit introduced in court is merely a "report." It is not "evidence," which the court must well consider. The key is to have an Affidavit prepared by an experience Securitization Auditor who has also been granted status as an "expert witness." Now you have teeth. At the same time your attorney drafted "pleadings" must be expertly prepared. We can make referrals to folks that we believe in, whose work has been tested in the courts, and, moreover, have been able to achieve settlements. Do your homework – educate yourself – book and blog, and we can help you with referrals.

Rescission. "In contract law, rescission (to rescind or set aside a contract) has been defined as the unmaking of a contract between the parties. Rescission is the unwinding of a transaction. This is done to bring the parties, as far as possible, back to the position in which they were before they entered into a contract (the "status quo ante"). This is an equitable remedy and is discretionary." Definition from: Wikipedia.

What this can mean is that your contract may be voidable, or subject to rescission. You may – after litigation using an attorney – be able to receive all the monies you have paid so far (including interest payments, closing costs, and other fees as well as attorney fees), back to you in a settlement or at trial. It seems too good to be true. However, because Predatory Lending became so prevalent, a great many homeowners qualify for rescission but never realize it, and are subsequently subjected to foreclosure.

They never realize that options are available to not only save the situation, but, it is possible for some of them to be compensated in monetary damages for the wrong that was done to them. Immediately below is information that you need to understand. At the end of this chapter we will bring it all together and show you various options, rather courses of action you might follow to your advantage. You must receive legal advice in this regard. *Remember, we are not attorneys and are not offering legal, investment or tax advice.*

The section immediately below is from our old friend Wikipedia, the free encyclopedia on the internet.

"Predatory lending is a pejorative term used to describe practices of some lenders. There are no legal definitions in the United States of predatory lending, though there are laws against many of the specific practices commonly identified as predatory, and various federal agencies use the term as a catch-all term for many specific illegal activities in the loan industry.

"One less contentious definition of the term is "the practice of a <u>lender deceptively convincing borrowers to agree to unfair and abusive loan terms,</u> or systematically violating those terms in ways that make it difficult for the borrower to defend against. [Emphasis added.]

"Although predatory lenders are most likely to target the less educated, racial minorities and the elderly, victims of predatory lending are represented across all demographics. Predatory lending often occurs on loans backed by some kind of collateral, such as a car or house, so that if the borrower defaults on the loan, the lender can repossess or foreclose and profit by selling the repossessed or foreclosed property. There are many lending practices which have been called abusive and labeled with the term "predatory lending." There is a great deal of dispute between lenders and consumer groups as to what exactly constitutes "unfair" or "predatory" practices, but the following are sometimes cited.

"**Risk-based pricing**. This is the practice of charging more (in the form of higher interest rates and fees) for extending credit to borrowers identified by the lender as posing a greater credit risk. The lending industry argues that risk-based pricing is a legitimate practice; since a greater percentage of loans made to less creditworthy borrowers can be expected to go into default, higher prices are necessary to obtain the same yield on the portfolio as a whole. Some consumer groups argue that higher prices paid by more vulnerable consumers cannot always be justified by increased credit risk.

"**Single premium credit insurance**. This is the purchase of insurance which will pay off the loan in case the homebuyer dies. It is more expensive than other forms of insurance because it does not involve any medical checkups, but customers <u>almost always are not shown their choices,</u> because usually the lender is not licensed to sell other forms of insurance. In addition, this insurance is usually financed into the loan which causes the loan to be more expensive, but at the same time encourages people to buy the insurance because they do not have to pay up front. [Emphasis added.]

"**Failure to disclose loan price is negotiable.** Many lenders will negotiate the price structure of the loan with borrowers. In some situations, borrowers can even negotiate an outright reduction in the interest rate or other charges on the loan. Consumer advocates argue that borrowers, especially but not only unsophisticated borrowers, are not aware of their ability to negotiate, and might even be under the <u>mistaken impression that the lender is placing the borrower's interests above its own</u>. Thus, many borrowers do not take advantage of their ability to negotiate. [Emphasis added.]

"Failure to clearly and accurately disclose terms and conditions, particularly in cases where an unsophisticated borrower is involved. Mortgage loans are complex transactions involving multiple parties and dozens of pages of legal documents. In the most egregious of predatory cases, lenders or brokers have been known <u>to not only mislead borrowers, but actually alter documents after they have been signed</u>. [Emphasis added.]

"Servicing agent and securitization abuses. The servicing agent is the entity that receives the mortgage payment, keeps the payment records, provides borrowers with account statements, imposes late charges when the payment is late, and pursues delinquent borrowers. A securitization is a financial transaction in which assets, especially debt instruments, are pooled and securities representing interests in the pool are issued. Most loans are subject to being bundled and sold, and the rights to act as servicing agent sold, without the consent of the borrower.

"A federal statute requires notice to the borrower of a change in servicing agent, but <u>does not protect the borrower</u> from being held delinquent on the note <u>for payments made to the servicing agent who fails to forward the payments to the owner of the note</u>, especially if that servicing agent goes bankrupt, and borrowers who have made all payments on time can find themselves being foreclosed on and becoming unsecured creditors of the servicing agent. Foreclosures can sometimes be conducted without proper notice to the borrower. [Emphasis added.]

"When the debtor demands that the current claimed note owner <u>produce the original note with his signature on it</u>, the note owner <u>typically is unable or unwilling to do so</u>, and tries to establish his claim with an affidavit that it is the owner, <u>without proving it is the "holder in due course,"</u> the traditional standard for a debt claim, and the courts often allow them to do that. In the meantime, the note continues to be traded, its physical whereabouts difficult to discover. [Emphasis added.]

"Disputes over predatory lending. The organization ACORN claims that predatory loans are usually made in poor and minority neighborhoods where better loans are not readily available. Organizations such as AARP, Inner City Press, and ACORN have worked to stop what they describe as predatory lending. ACORN has targeted specific companies such as HSBC Finance and H&R Block, successfully forcing them to change their practices.

"Some subprime lending practices have raised concerns about mortgage discrimination on the basis of race. African Americans and other minorities are being disproportionately led to sub-prime mortgages with higher interest rates than their white counterparts. Even when median income levels were comparable, home buyers in minority neighborhoods were more likely to get a loan from a subprime lender, though not necessarily a sub-prime loan.

[A political hit was done on ACORN, and, effectively stopped it from coming to the aid of distressed homeowner. No surprise.]

"Underlying issues. There are many underlying issues in the predatory lending debate:

"Judicial practices: Some argue that much of the problem arises from a tendency of the courts to favor lenders, and to shift the burden of proof of compliance with the terms of the debt instrument to the debtor. According to this argument, it should not be the duty of the borrower to make sure his payments are getting to the current note-owner, but to make evidence that all payments were made to the last known agent for collection sufficient to block or reverse repossession or foreclosure, and eviction, and to cancel the debt if the current note owner cannot prove he is the "holder in due course" by producing the actual original debt instrument in court. [Emphasis added.]

"Risk-based pricing: The basic idea is that borrowers who are thought of as more likely to default on their loans should pay higher interest rates and finance charges to compensate lenders for the increased risk. In essence, high returns motivate lenders to lend to a group they might not otherwise lend to – 'subprime' or risky borrowers. Advocates of this system believe that it would be unfair – or a poor business strategy – to raise interest rates globally to accommodate risky borrowers, thus penalizing low-risk borrowers who are unlikely to default. Opponents argue that the practice tends to disproportionately create capital gains for the affluent while oppressing working-class borrowers with modest financial resources.

"Some people consider risk-based pricing to be unfair in principle. Lenders contend that interest rates are generally set fairly considering the risk that the lender assumes, and that competition between lenders will ensure availability of appropriately-priced loans to high-risk customers. Still others feel that while the rates themselves may be justifiable with respect to the risks, it is irresponsible for lenders to encourage or allow borrowers with credit problems to take out high-priced loans. For all of its pros and cons, risk-based pricing remains a universal practice in bond markets and the insurance industry, and it is implied in the stock market and in many other open-market venues; it is only controversial in the case of consumer loans. [Emphasis added.]

"Competition: Some believe that risk-based pricing is fair but feel that many loans charge prices far above the risk, using the risk as an excuse to overcharge. These criticisms are not levied on all products, but only on those specifically deemed predatory. Proponents counter that competition among lenders should prevent or reduce overcharging. [Emphasis added.]

"Financial Education: Many observers feel that competition in the markets served by what critics describe as "predatory lenders" is not affected by price because the targeted consumers are completely uneducated about the time value of money and the concept of Annual Percentage Rate (APR), a different measure of price than what many are used to. [Emphasis added.]

"Caveat Emptor: There is an underlying debate about whether a lender should be allowed to charge whatever it wants for a service, even if it seems to make no attempts at deceiving the consumer about the price. At issue here is the belief that lending is a commodity and that the lending community has an almost fiduciary duty to advise the borrower that funds can be obtained more cheaply. [Emphasis added.]

"Discrimination: Some organizations feel that many financial institutions continue to engage in racial discrimination. Most do not allege that the loan underwriters themselves discriminate, but rather that there is systemic discrimination. Situations in which a loan broker or other salesman may negotiate the interest rate are likely more ripe for discrimination. Discrimination may occur if, when dealing with racial minorities, loan brokers tend to claim that a person's credit score is lower than it is, justifying a higher interest rate charged, on the hope that the customer assumes the lender to be correct. This may be based on an internalized bias that a minority group has a lower economic profile. It is also possible that a broker or loan salesman with some control over the interest rate might attempt to charge a higher rate to persons of race which he personally dislikes. For this reason some call for laws requiring interest rates to be set entirely by objective measures. [Emphasis added.]

"It should be noted that mortgage applications are usually completed by mortgage brokers, rather than by borrowers themselves, making it difficult to pin down the source of any misrepresentations. [Emphasis added.]

"United States legislation combating predatory lending Many laws at both the Federal and state government level are aimed at preventing predatory lending. Although not specifically anti-predatory in nature, the Federal Truth in Lending Act requires certain disclosures of APR and loan terms. Also, in 1994 section 32 of the Truth in Lending Act, entitled the Home Ownership and Equity Protection Act of 1994, was created. This law is devoted to identifying certain high-cost, potentially predatory mortgage loans and reining in their terms. [Emphasis added.]

"Twenty-five states have passed anti-predatory lending laws. Arkansas, Georgia, Illinois, Maine, Massachusetts, North Carolina, New York, New Jersey, New Mexico and South Carolina are among those states considered to have the strongest laws. Other states with predatory lending laws include: California, Colorado, Connecticut, Florida, Kentucky, Maine, Maryland, Nevada, Ohio, Oklahoma, Oregon, Pennsylvania, Texas, Utah, Wisconsin, and West Virginia. These laws usually describe one or more classes of "high-cost" or "covered" loans, which are defined by the fees charged to the borrower at origination or the APR. While lenders are not prohibited from making "high-cost" or "covered" loans, a number of additional restrictions are placed on these loans, and the penalties for noncompliance can be substantial." [Thank you Wikipedia.]

Common Predatory Lending Tactics. While there any number of variation and methods that constitute Predatory Lending, below are many standard forms. The Center for Responsible Lending (from which we borrowed some of these tactics, and have added additional ones) is an excellent source to more thoroughly familiarize yourself.

Abusive prepayment penalties. Borrowers with higher-interest subprime loans have a strong incentive to refinance as soon as their credit improves. However, up to 80% of all subprime mortgages carry a prepayment penalty – a fee for paying off a loan early. An abusive prepayment penalty typically is effective more than three years and/or costs more than six months' interest. In the prime market, only about 2% of home loans carry prepayment penalties of any length. [Emphasis added.]

Excessive fees. Points and fees are costs not directly reflected in interest rates. Because these costs can be financed, they are easy to disguise or downplay. On competitive loans, fees below 1% of the loan amount are typical. On predatory loans, fees totaling more than 5% of the loan amount are common.

Bait and switch. This is when a higher rate at closing comes after a lender has initially promised a lower interest rate.

Failure to disclose terms of loan. Federal laws such as the Truth In Lending Act ("TILA") and the Real Estate Settlement Procedures Act ("RESPA"), demand that creditors disclose terms of loans to the borrower. Failure to disclose or when they are inaccurately disclosed, enable serious monetary penalties against the creditor to the benefit of the borrower.

Kickbacks to Mortgage Brokers. When brokers deliver a loan with an inflated prepayment penalty, or an inflated interest rate (i.e., higher than the rate acceptable to the lender), the lender gladly pays a Yield Spread Premium (YSP). This is a kickback to the Mortgage Broker for making the loan more costly to the borrower. [Emphasis added.]

Loan flipping. A lender "flips" a borrower by refinancing a loan to generate fee income without providing any net tangible benefit to the borrower. Flipping can quickly drain borrower equity and increase monthly payments – sometimes on homes that had previously been owned free of debt. This is also called Equity Skimming or Equity Theft.

Unnecessary products. Sometimes borrowers may pay more than necessary because lenders sell and finance unnecessary insurance or other products along with the loan. [Emphasis added.]

Elder Fraud and Abuse. Retirees are likely to have a large amounts of equity in their homes. Consequently they are targets for various Predatory Lending tactics and practice. Sometimes they are sold loans they do not understand, can not afford and do not need, but which benefit the loan purveyors with large fees.

Mandatory arbitration. Some loan contracts require "mandatory arbitration," meaning that the borrowers are <u>not allowed to seek legal remedies in a court</u> if they find that their home is threatened by loans with illegal or abusive terms. Mandatory arbitration makes it much less likely that borrowers will receive fair and appropriate remedies in cases of wrongdoing. [Emphasis added.]

Steering & Targeting. Precatory lenders <u>may steer borrowers into subprime mortgages</u>, even when <u>the borrowers could qualify for a mainstream loan</u>. Vulnerable borrowers may be <u>subjected to aggressive sales tactics and sometimes outright fraud</u>. Fannie Mae has estimated that up to <u>half of borrowers with subprime mortgages</u> could have qualified for loans with better terms. [Emphasis added.]

According to a government study, over half (51%) of refinance mortgages in predominantly African-American neighborhoods are subprime loans, compared to only 9% of refinances in predominantly white neighborhoods.

We thank the Center for Responsible Lending for this information, and you should as well.

Fraud Redux. We wish to remind you once again of the basics in fraud. We do this in order to equip you with a basic understanding and more importantly in order to have you be able to understand if fraud was present in your loan origination process. This in turn will put you in a much stronger position in terms of defending your family, enabling you to achieve justice if in fact Predatory Lending was involved when you bought your home. Frankly, it will enable you to become a Professional Client if you work with an attorney. The good ones appreciate it because they don't have to take so much time to bring you up to speed.

Civil Causes of Action: Fraud Law & Legal Definition

Fraud is generally defined in the law as an intentional misrepresentation of material existing fact made by one person to another with knowledge of its falsity and for the purpose of inducing the other person to act, and upon which the other person relies with resulting injury or damage. Fraud may also by made by an omission or purposeful failure to state material facts, which nondisclosure makes other statements misleading.

To constitute fraud, a misrepresentation or omission must also relate to an existing fact, not a promise to do something in the future, unless the person who made the promise did so without any present intent to perform it or with a positive intent not to perform it. The false statement or omission must be material, meaning that it was significant to the decision to be made. Also, an opinion does not constitute an existing fact and cannot be the basis of a claim of fraud unless the person stating the opinion has exclusive or superior knowledge of existing facts which are inconsistent with such opinion.

The misrepresentation or omission must be made knowingly and intentionally, not mistakenly or accidentally, so that the person either knew or should have known of the falsity or acted in negligent disregard of its truth or falsity. The person charged with fraud must have intended the Plaintiff to rely on the misrepresentation or omission and Plaintiff must have been injured by such reliance to prevail on the claim.

Sometimes, it must be shown that Plaintiff's reliance was justifiable, and that upon reasonable inquiry would not have discovered the truth of the matter. For injury or damage to be the result of fraud, it must be shown that, except for the fraud, the injury or damage would not have occurred. Fraud in the *factum* means fraud in the obtaining the execution of the agreement or delivery of a document. As opposed to fraud in inducing someone to sign a document, it is fraud regarding the contents of the document, so that the person defrauded is unaware of what they are signing.

As an example of what California has adopted in their civil code we present the following:

California Civil Code
Section 1565-1590

1565. The consent of the parties to a contract must be:
1. Free;
2. Mutual; and,
3. Communicated by each to the other.

1566. A consent which is not free is nevertheless not absolutely void, but may be rescinded by the parties, in the manner prescribed by the Chapter on Rescission.

1567. An apparent consent is not real or free when obtained through:
1. Duress;
2. Menace;
3. **Fraud**;
4. Undue influence; or,
5. Mistake.

1568. Consent is deemed to have been obtained through one of the causes mentioned in the last section only when it would not have been given had such cause not existed. ...

1571. Fraud is either actual or constructive.

1572. Actual fraud, within the meaning of this Chapter, consists in any of the following acts, committed by a party to the contract, or with his connivance, with intent to deceive another party thereto, or to induce him to enter into the contract:

1. The suggestion, as a fact, of that which is not true, by one who does not believe it to be true;
2. The positive assertion, in a manner not warranted by the information of the person making it, of that which is not true, though he believes it to be true;
3. The suppression of that which is true, by one having knowledge or belief of the fact;
4. A promise made without any intention of performing it; or,
5. Any other act fitted to deceive.

1573. Constructive fraud consists:

1. In any breach of duty which, without an actually fraudulent intent, gains an advantage to the person in fault, or any one claiming under him, by misleading another to his prejudice, or to the prejudice of any one claiming under him; or,
2. In any such act or omission as the law specially declares to be fraudulent, without respect to **actual fraud**.

1574. Actual fraud is always a question of fact.

1575. Undue influence consists:

1. In the use, by one in whom a confidence is reposed by another, or who holds a real or apparent authority over him, of such confidence or authority for the purpose of obtaining an unfair advantage over him;
2. In taking an unfair advantage of another's weakness of mind; or,
3. In taking a grossly oppressive and unfair advantage of another's necessities or distress.

1576. Mistake may be either of fact or law.

1577. Mistake of fact is a mistake, not caused by the neglect of a legal duty on the part of the person making the mistake, and consisting in:

1. An unconscious ignorance or forgetfulness of a fact past or present, material to the contract; or,
2. Belief in the present existence of a thing material to the contract, which does not exist, or in the past existence of such a thing, which has not existed.

By now, you're becoming familiar with fraud basics. You don't have to memorize them, there will be no quiz, but, this information can serve you well when working with your attorney. Ideally you will be a professional client, saving your attorney time in giving you the 101 basics. Cut to the chase.

Truth in Lending Act. From Wikipedia, the free encyclopedia

"The Truth in Lending Act (TILA) of 1968 is a United States federal law designed to protect consumers in credit transactions by requiring clear disclosure of key terms of the lending arrangement and all costs. The statute is contained in title I of the Consumer Credit Protection Act, as amended (15 USC 1601 et seq.). The regulations implementing the statute, which are known as "Regulation Z", are codified at 12 CFR Part 226. Most of the specific requirements imposed by TILA are found in Regulation Z, so a reference to the requirements of TILA usually refers to the requirements contained in Regulation Z as well as the statute itself.

"The purpose of TILA is to promote the informed use of consumer credit by requiring disclosures about its terms, cost to standardize the manner in which costs associated with borrowing are calculated and disclosed. TILA also gives consumers the right to cancel certain credit transactions that involve a lien on a consumer's principal dwelling, regulates certain credit card practices, and provides a means for fair and timely resolution of credit billing disputes. With the exception of certain high-cost mortgage loans, TILA does not regulate the charges that may be imposed for consumer credit. Rather, it requires uniform or standardized disclosure of costs and charges so that consumers can shop. It also imposes limitations on home equity plans that are subject to the requirements of Sec. 226.5b and certain higher-cost mortgages that are subject to the requirements of Sec. 226.32. The regulation prohibits certain acts or practices in connection with credit secured by a consumer's principal dwelling."

Don't Be A Victim of Loan Fraud. Below is data from the U.S. Department of Housing and Urban Development (HUD).

Protect Yourself from Predatory Lenders. "Buying or refinancing your home may be one of the most important and complex financial decisions you'll ever make. Many lenders, appraisers, and real estate professionals stand ready to help you get a nice home and a great loan. However, you need to understand the home buying process to be a smart consumer. Every year, <u>misinformed homebuyers, often first-time purchasers or seniors, become victims of predatory lending or loan fraud</u>. Don't let this happen to you!" [Emphasis added.]

10 Tips On Being A Smart Consumer:

1. Before you buy a home, attend a homeownership education course offered by the U.S. Department of Housing and Urban Development (HUD)-approved, non-profit <u>counseling agencies</u>.

2. Interview several real estate professionals (agents), and ask for and check references before you select one to help you buy or sell a home.

3. Get information about the prices of other homes in the neighborhood. Don't be fooled into paying too much.

4. Hire a properly qualified and licensed home inspector to carefully inspect the property before you are obligated to buy. Determine whether you or the seller is going to be responsible for paying for the repairs. If you have to pay for the repairs, determine whether or not you can afford to make them.

5. Shop for a lender and compare costs. Be suspicious if anyone tries to steer you to just one lender.

6. Do NOT let anyone persuade you to make a false statement on your loan application, such as overstating your income, the source of your down payment, failing to disclose the nature and amount of your debts, or even how long you have been employed. When you apply for a mortgage loan, every piece of information that you submit must be accurate and complete. Lying on a mortgage application is fraud and may result in criminal penalties.

7. Do NOT let anyone convince you to borrow more money than you know you can afford to repay. If you get behind on your payments, you risk losing your house and all of the money you put into your property.

8. Never sign a blank document or a document containing blanks. If information is inserted by someone else after you have signed, you may still be bound to the terms of the contract. Insert "N/A" (i.e., not applicable) or cross through any blanks.

9. Read everything carefully and ask questions. Do not sign anything that you don't understand. Before signing, have your contract and loan agreement reviewed by an attorney skilled in real estate law, consult with a trusted real estate professional or ask for help from a housing counselor with a HUD-approved agency. If you cannot afford an attorney, take your documents to the HUD-approved housing counseling agency near you to find out if they will review the documents or can refer you to an attorney who will help you for free or at low cost.

10. Be honest about your intention to occupy the house. Stating that you plan to live there when, in fact, you are not (because you intend to rent the house to someone else or fix it up and resell it) violates federal law and is a crime.

11. [We (not HUD) add. Many of the tactics above are the *art form* – the con – of unscrupulous Mortgage Brokers. While many are very ethical, and decry tactics of their unsavory competitors, make certain that *at least* you obtain references from a Mortgage Broker you are considering using in the future. Even better, obtain a referral from a personal friend who refers a Mortgage Broker who is a personal friend of *your* personal friend. This can assist in terms of *personal accountability,* which should never be underestimated.

What is Predatory Lending?

In communities across America, people are losing their homes and their investments because of predatory lenders, appraisers, mortgage brokers and home improvement contractors who:

- Sell properties for much more than they are worth using false appraisals.

- Encourage borrowers to lie about their income, expenses, or cash available for down payments in order to get a loan.

- Knowingly lend more money than a borrower can afford to repay.

- Charge high interest rates to borrowers based on their race or national origin and not on their credit history.

- Charge fees for unnecessary or nonexistent products and services.

- Pressure borrowers to accept higher-risk loans such as balloon loans, interest only payments, and steep pre-payment penalties.

- Target vulnerable borrowers for cash-out refinance offers when they know borrowers are in need of cash due to medical, unemployment or debt problems.

- "Strip" homeowners' equity from their homes by convincing them to refinance again and again when there is no benefit to the borrower.

- Use high pressure sales tactics to sell home improvements and then finance them at high interest rates.

What Tactics Do Predators Use?

- A lender or investor tells you that they are your only chance of getting a loan or owning a home. You should be able to take your time to shop around and compare prices and houses.

- The house you are buying costs a lot more than other homes in the neighborhood, but isn't any bigger or better.

- You are asked to sign a sales contract or loan documents that are blank or that contain information which is not true.

- You are told that the Federal Housing Administration insurance protects you against property defects or loan fraud – it does not.

- The cost or loan terms at closing are not what you agreed to.

- You are told that refinancing can solve your credit or money problems.

- You are told that you can only get a good deal on a home improvement if you finance it with a particular lender.

Always Remember: If a deal to buy, repair or refinance a house sounds too good to be true, it usually is [not true]! Housing counselors working at HUD-approved agencies can help you be a smart consumer. To find a counselor near you, call (800) 569-4287 or go to HUD's housing counselors list online.

Buying or refinancing your home may be one of the most important and complex financial decisions you'll ever make. Many lenders, appraisers, and real estate professionals stand ready to help you get a nice home and a great loan. However, you need to understand the home buying process to be a smart consumer. Every year, misinformed homebuyers, often first-time purchasers or seniors, become victims of predatory lending or loan fraud. Don't let this happen to you!

Victimized by Predatory Lending? It's very difficult – if not impossible – for a layman who is not an attorney to determine whether or not they've been victimized. Below we'll offer some suggestions to help you to make an early determination in order to enable you to understand whether or not you may have been a victim. With some knowledge you can then intelligently take your information to an attorney who is skilled in this area. Believe us, many attorneys may claim to understand these issues, but, they don't. Some may attempt to learn this specialty in the law on your time – on your case. That is *not* always bad if they are a skilled litigator, and particularly, if you have personal accountability with the lawyer. Be warned.

We remind you of the section above regarding the absolute necessity of obtaining a Securitization Audit. At the theatre they say, "You can't tell the players without a program." We say, "You can't know about fraud in your loan documents without a Securitization Audit." All the information below will be a part of a good Securitization Audit, but, it's smart to understand the basics before you begin to read your Audit.

Begin your process by determining if the loan you actually received and signed at the Close of Escrow (COE) is the same loan you thought (at the beginning of the process) you were getting. Does a prepayment penalty exist that you had not been told about? Is the Annual Percentage Rate (APR) the same as you were initially quoted? Are monthly payments exactly the same as you had been told? If any of this happened during your process, consider it a red flag issue, which may be to your advantage.

At the point of COE the documents you are presented with can be overwhelming, perhaps 100 pages of overwhelming. You may be pressed to just sign and be quiet in the interest of time. Don't do it. Don't rely on the Mortgage Broker (who had better be at the closing or you should leave) who may be responsible for issues in your final loan documents. Because they stand to make more money, they may not be telling you the truth during closing, and may attempt to hurry you through the signing. Ask questions if anything is different than what you were originally told. This is a red flag issue.

If you are told that the loan has already funded, that does not mean you *need* to sign right then, though the Mortgage Broker and even the Escrow Officer may indicate that you need to sign immediately. Remind them that you have a three day right of cancellation and are going to take the papers to your attorney because you did not receive answers to your questions *that you understood*. If you did follow their advice and signed anyway, you may find that you have alternatives to remedy the situation. When in doubt, walk away, and say you'll be back in two days after consulting with your attorney. They will wait for you to come back. All the parties want the deal to close. They want to get paid. They've likely already spent the money in their heads. This is a red flag issue.

Then immediately call an experienced mortgage law attorney in your state with any questions you may have. You should already have arranged for such an attorney to be "standing by." If it's too late and you're facing foreclosure or are underwater and are considering walking away, an experienced homeowner mortgage attorney can easily and quickly review your documents and make an early determination as to whether Predatory Lending was in there, the severity of any violations and recommend a course of action based on your ultimate intentions.

Three Day Right of Rescission. This is often called the Notice of Right to Cancel. A borrower usually has, and has by law, three days after signing loan documents to cancel the loan by changing their minds. Proper notice must be given and signed by the borrower at COE. Often mistakes or oversights are made in this process, which can be extremely valuable to you. If such mistakes are made you may have three more years from COE to exercise your right to cancel and seek contract rescission. Each signer on the loan must be given two copies of this document. This is a very very big deal.

Press Release

For Immediate Release: June 19, 2008 Washington D.C.

FBI National Press Office (202) 324-3691

More Than 400 Defendants Charged for Roles in Mortgage Fraud Schemes as Part of *'Operation Malicious Mortgage.'* Two Senior Managers of Failed Bear Stearns Hedge Funds Indicted Today in Separate Mortgage-Related Securities Fraud Case

"WASHINGTON – The Department of Justice and Federal Bureau of Investigation (FBI) announced today a national takedown of mortgage fraud schemes, the culmination of substantial coordinated efforts during the last three and a half months to identify, arrest and prosecute mortgage fraud violators through the United States. Operation Malicious Mortgage highlights the strong enforcement response undertaken by the Department of Justice and its law enforcement partners to combat the threat mortgage fraud poses to the U.S. housing industry and worldwide credit markets.

"From March 1 to June 18, 2008, Operation Malicious Mortgage resulted in 144 mortgage fraud cases in which 406 defendants were charged. Yesterday, 60 arrests were made in mortgage fraud-related cases in 15 districts. Charges in Operation Malicious Mortgage cases were brought in every region of the United States and in more than 50 judicial districts by U.S. Attorneys' Offices based upon the law enforcement and investigative efforts of participating law enforcement agencies. The FBI estimates that approximately $1 billion in losses were inflicted by the mortgage fraud schemes employed in these cases.

"In addition to fraud directly related to individual mortgages, the Department is committed to investigating and prosecuting cases of mortgage-related securities fraud. Today, the U.S. Attorney's Office for the Eastern District of

New York announced an indictment against two senior managers of failed Bear Stearns hedge funds, charging Ralph Cioffi and Mathew Tannin with conspiracy, securities fraud and wire fraud. Cioffi was also charged with insider trading. The indictment alleges that the managers marketed the two funds as a low risk strategy, backed by a pool of debt securities such as mortgages. The indictment alleges that by March 2007, the managers believed the funds were in grave condition and at risk of collapse, but made misrepresentations to stave off investor withdrawal. The funds subsequently collapsed in the summer of 2007 resulting in approximately $1.4 billion in losses to investors.

"Mortgage fraud and related securities fraud pose a significant threat to our economy, to the stability of our nation's housing market and to the peace of mind of millions of American homeowners," said Deputy Attorney General Mark R. Filip. "Operation Malicious Mortgage and our other mortgage-related enforcement actions demonstrate the Justice Department's commitment and determination to combat these criminal schemes, hold their perpetrators accountable and help restore stability and confidence in our housing and credit markets."

"Operation Malicious Mortgage is a concerted, joint law enforcement and prosecutorial effort aimed at disrupting individuals and groups engaged in mortgage fraud," said FBI Director Robert S. Mueller, III. "This operation is an example of our unified commitment to address this significant crime problem. The FBI will continue to direct investigative and analytic resources towards mortgage fraud and corporate securities fraud that threaten our nation's economy."

"Operation Malicious Mortgage represents the joint collaborative efforts of the FBI, U.S. Postal Inspection Service, Internal Revenue Service-Criminal Investigation Division, U.S. Immigration and Customs Enforcement, U.S. Secret Service, U.S. Trustee Program, Department of Housing and Urban Development Office of the Inspector General, Department of Veterans Affairs Office of the Inspector General, and Federal Deposit Insurance Corporation Office of the Inspector General. Operation Malicious Mortgage is the most recent coordinated sweep in an ongoing law enforcement effort to combat mortgage fraud, which also included Operation Continued Action in 2004 and Operation Quick Flip in 2005.

"Mortgage frauds employ a variety of tactics including misrepresentations, deceit and other criminal abuses to fund, purchase or insure mortgage loans. Operation Malicious Mortgage addresses primarily three types of mortgage fraud schemes: lending fraud, foreclosure rescue scams and mortgage-related bankruptcy schemes. Lending fraud frequently involves multiple loan transactions in which industry professionals construct mortgage transactions based on gross fraudulent misrepresentations about the borrower's financial status, such as overstating the borrower's income or assets, using false or fictitious employment records or inflating property values. Foreclosure rescue scams involve criminals who target legitimate homeowners in dire financial circumstances and fraudulently collect fees for foreclosure prevention services or obtain ownership interests in residential properties. Both of these fraudulent mortgage schemes may be furthered by filing bankruptcy petitions that automatically stay foreclosure.

"The President's Corporate Fraud Task Force, chaired by Deputy Attorney General Filip, is also responding to issues raised by mortgage fraud in the corporate sector. Created in 2002 to investigate and prosecute significant financial crimes, the Task Force includes representatives from ten federal departments, commissions and agencies, in addition to seven U.S. Attorney's Offices and two Divisions within the Department of Justice, combining the experience of thousands of investigators, attorneys, accountants and regulatory experts. Since July 2002, the Department of Justice has obtained nearly 1,300 corporate fraud convictions, including the convictions of more than 200 chief executive officers and corporate presidents, more than 120 corporate vice presidents and more than 50 chief financial officers.

"An indictment is not evidence of guilt. All persons charged with a crime are presumed innocent until proven guilty beyond a reasonable doubt."

And then, we had a new Young President elected who took office in January, 2009. And, it all stopped. The FBI apparently went elsewhere. Maybe it went where the U.S. Justice Department went. Which was clearly *nowhere* − in regard to helping American Homeowners. We don't know where they are − seems like *nowhere*. We haven't heard from them lately.

CHAPTER 9: YOUR LEGAL ISSUES

"Economic history is a never-ending series of episodes based on falsehoods and lies, not truths. It represents the path to big money. The object is to recognize the trend whose premise is false, ride that trend, and step off before it is discredited." George Soros

In 1992, an attorney for a very prominent Investment Bank said to us, *"In litigation – winning – is not losing."*

We replied. *"Yeah – as long as you have the deep pockets to keep a lawsuit going regardless of the facts – regardless of whether you're right or wrong."* That attorney smiled – then chuckled, and walked away.

Another Law Story. In civil litigation, when an attorney has the law on their side – they pound the table with the law.

When they have the facts on their side – they pound the table with the facts.

When an attorney has neither the law or the facts on their side – they pound the table.

Actually attorneys like this story, it shows they are tenacious bull dawgs.

If need for a decision regarding foreclosure issues arises, the first thing you must understand is whether your state calls for a Judicial or Non-Judicial foreclosure process. In other words you must understand the basic legal process in your state, and then, you need to obtain a Forensic Loan Audit and a Securitization Audit, and then, *talk to an attorney who is knowledgeable regarding foreclosure law in your state.* We are <u>not</u> attorneys, investment or tax advisors and are not offering any professional advice. We strongly recommend that you obtain proper legal, investment and tax advice before pursuing any course of action. For much more information follow our blog, and you will discover that if you read this book, read our blog, and do your homework, educate yourself, and let us know through the blog; we can offer "tools" to assist you to Confront Fraudulent Housing Debt

Regarding attorney stories, way back in the day, another very successful attorney once said to us, *"If you're involved, or going to be involved in a legal procedure or litigation you need to understand what you want your attorney to do and how you want them to do it."* We gave a long pause on hearing that and said, *"It sounds almost like your telling me to go to law school? Do I have to be an attorney if I'm involved in a foreclosure matter that may need to be litigated – may need to go to trial?"*

That attorney's point was that you don't need to be an attorney to hire one, however, you'd better be knowledgeable and prepared and self-educated if you want to *control* the outcome. Not law school, but some research is required, and it's readily available on the Internet. Goggle is your friend. Yet, your immediate new best friend may the complete State-by-State chart at end of the Appendix Sections, which provides a link to your state laws. Gives you a Head's Up.

Remember this book combined with our blog may actually be your new new best friend. But, after the book – it is essential that you also study the blog. This is your education.

This chapter will provide you with basic legal information that you need to understand before you make a business decision to protect your family. Below, are some terms you need to understand. But, even before that, we remind you again that we are not attorneys, *are not offering, legal, investment, or tax advice,* and strongly suggest you consult with at least a local foreclosure attorney. Then, when you understand the terms and context outlined below, within the context of the preceding chapters, you'll be much better situated to understand whether or not you agree with *your* attorney's outlined plan. Empowered. You Bet.

Judicial Foreclosure. Because they have such a high rate of foreclosure we'll look first at Florida, where foreclosures must go through court proceedings, thus a *Judicial Foreclosure.* Generally in Florida the process takes nearly five months.

The process starts in Florida when a lender files a court action for foreclosure and usually records a notice of a pending lawsuit *(Lis Pendis)* against the borrower. The lender notifies the borrower (and other affected parties) through personal service, someone knocks on your door and Serves you with papers. Or, in many cases through publication and by mail. If the borrower fails to respond within a specified amount of time, the county clerk can determine that the borrower is in default, giving the lender the right to move the court for a final ruling. If the court agrees, it makes a ruling against the borrower. Importantly, the ruling will also include the total amount owed to the lender as of that date, and the date for the foreclosure sale. You and your attorney need to be wary of additional (but not necessarily legal) "fees" that some unscrupulous lenders add to the process.

Generally under Florida state law the lender is not required to notify the borrower prior to initiating the foreclosure process. However, individual mortgages or deeds of trust might call for prior notification. *The borrower can stop the foreclosure from proceeding right up until the date of sale if they pay the lender the total amount owed.*

Notice of Sale / Auction. The date of the sale is generally 20-35 days after the court's initial ruling, but this is subject to the intentions of the individual court. When cleared by the court, the clerk issues the Notice of Sale, which must contain: the location, date, and time of the sale. This notice must be published weekly for two weeks, and the second notice must appear at least five days before the final sale.

The clerk of the court often supervises the sale (Judicial Foreclosures really are held on the Court House steps), generally at 11:00 a.m. on the published day of the sale. A winning bidder is required to provide a 5% deposit at the conclusion of bidding, paying the remaining balance by the end of that day. If that does not happen a new sale is scheduled at a minimum of 20 days later. After receipt of all funds, the clerk gives a Certificate of Sale to the winning bidder. Normally within 10 days of the sale, the clerk will transfer ownership to the successful bidder if the sale is not disputed.

Generally, a borrower has no right of redemption (cannot make it good by paying all past due payments and costs and fees) after the certificate of sale is issued. In other words, they cannot make up the difference and invalidate the sale held at auction. However, we repeat, you must become familiar with the specific laws in your state. The State by State table in the Appendix section contains a web link for every state to give you basic information on the specifics of your state.

Recourse Loan. This refers to the explicit right stated in the loan agreement for the lender (generally in a Judicial Foreclosure state, which must be brought forward in a court proceeding) to demand payment from the person who has taken on the obligation, here, the borrower, after foreclosure. A *Full Recourse Loan* enables the lender to take, after a Deficiency Judgment granted by Judicial Order, *any assets* of the borrower if repayment of the difference between the loan amount and the lender's recovery has not been made. Importantly, a *Limited Recourse Loan* only allows the lender to take the asset stated in the loan agreement – almost always the real property (the house) and not personal property of the borrower.

Another factor here is the significance of a mortgage refinance. In some Non-Recourse states when a mortgage is refinanced, the new instrument becomes a Recourse Loan. Again, we urge homeowners to seek skilled mortgage foreclosure counsel to analyze the laws in their state. Also, be certain to determine the terms of Home Equity Loans to determine whether they are Recourse or Non-Recourse Loans. Often, even in Non-Recourse states, Home Equity Loans are Recourse. It must be spelled out in your loan documents. Get them altogether and read them.

Deficiency Judgment. These are only allowed in various states, usually states that require a Juridical Foreclosure and have Recourse Loans. This type of judgment is effectively a lien against a debtor, a borrower or a defendant, where the foreclosure and subsequent sale of the property does not create sufficient funds to pay off the mortgage note in full.

The attorney for the lender, the plaintiff's attorney, must make a motion for a Judge to Issue an Order granting a Deficiency Judgment. *Otherwise, the amount gained from the sale shall be deemed the full amount owed, and the plaintiff (lender) has no right to collect the additional debt.* Yet, if the parties, lender and borrower, are in a Non-Recourse state some consider it unlikely the lender could prevail by bringing action to collect on the difference between the loan amount and the actual amount recovered by the lender.

A debtor who has a Deficiency Judgment awarded against them should immediately see an attorney (it might not be too late, but this should have been done at the outset of the matter) for possible remedies; including bankruptcy (which we <u>highly recommend against</u> unless all else is lost); an exemption from creditors; an appeal; or, a motion to reinstate the matter. But, all this depends on the laws of your state. Again, we recommend strongly that you speak to a knowlegible local foreclosure attorney before you do anything. Some argue that in the future the impact of bankruptcy will be diminished.

At the same time it is becoming clear that the 2005 Bankruptcy Act may be modified. Some politicians are recommending that a judge should be allowed to make major loan modifications. If this becomes law, it may avoid mass foreclosures because lenders would be highly motivated to make deep loan modifications. Some have argued that judges be allowed to lower the amount owed. The legal theory under which contract law would be thrown out the window has yet to be formulated, let alone tested Constitutionally. The lenders are vehemently against this. This remains to be seen, to be played out through the Political Process in an Election Year. Lots of lip service will be solemnly extended, veto proof bills may pass, and after the election the process may be reversed in the Supreme Court. Could be. Odds are not good for a positive outcome for underwater homeowners – as we say – that's why you must Confront Fraudulent Housing Debt on you own, assisted by professionals.

We've written extensively about this in at least two other chapters. The point being is that it is not likely that the Banking Cartel are going to allow their Senators to pass the bill (the House did pass it, but that was before the Tea Party took control of the House) allowing Bankruptcy Judges to cramdown the loan. In other words order a significant principal amount reduction to current value of the home. You must do your own cramdown Using Foreclosure Law to Keep Your Home.

Non-Judicial Foreclosure. To explain this type of foreclosure process we'll use California as an example. Judicial foreclosures are not common in California, they are nearly all Non-Judicial.

Court foreclosures in California generally happen if a lender seeks a deficiency judgment, which is rare because California is a Non-Recourse state. (See below.) If this does occur (repeat: very very rarely) this process gives a borrower up to one year to redeem the property even after the foreclosure sale. Naturally this is a huge disincentive for individuals or investors to pursue properties at foreclosure auctions.

Consequently, almost all foreclosure cases are handled out of court. After a lender has not received payments for 90 days or more, the lender may begin the process by filing a Notice of Default ("NOD") with the county recorder that identifies the default amount (total owed as of that date) and the date by which the borrower must pay off the default. A copy of the NOD is publicly recorded with the County Recorder and mailed to the borrower and other interested parties.

Caveat. This data at the Recorder's office is regularly swept by various entities and sold to investors. The phone begins ringing, and mailings and people begin showing up on your doorstep. Often they are "foreclosure consultants," as defined by Cal. Civ. §2495. (See *Appendix L.)* Do not <u>ever</u> pay anyone a fee in advance for "helping you out with your lender." Never sign documents by those attempting to "help you," until you've told them you'll consider the offer and consult your attorney. Then show them the door. If they don't come back, it's likely they know your attorney would not approve. You're much better off. While under severe duress – the fear of losing their home – many well intentioned and honest people have lost their home and equity to unscrupulous "foreclosure consultants." You are warned. Over the last couple of years, much of this has been curtailed through state law. You must still be wary.

Three months (90 days) after the NOD is filed, if unopposed, the lender can schedule a Trustee's Sale of the property. For up to five business days before the trustee sale, the borrower may pay off the default plus any applicable costs of foreclosure to stop the sale.

Notice Of Trustee's Sale / Auction. At least 20 days prior to the Trustee's Sale, the Notice of Sale must be posted on the property, and in at least one local public location. The notice is also published once a week for three weeks in a local newspaper. This must start at least 20 days before the sale date. In addition, the notice is mailed to the borrower at least 20 days before the sale and to anyone else who requests the notice. Obviously, the notice must contain all pertinent information such as: date, time, and location of the sale, property address, and the trustee's contact information. In addition, the Notice of Sale must be recorded with the county recorder at least 14 days before the sale. It is very important that the lender, their appointed Trustee and any attorney's involved follow this procedure to the letter. *Any failure can give grounds for the borrower to seek remedies in court, such as blocking the Trustee's Sale at that time.*

The Trustee's Sale is held as a public auction with the property being sold to the winning bidder. Generally these are "as is" sales and the winning bidder may not have had the opportunity to view the interior of the home, nor determine its actual condition (risky for bidders at auction). In addition, the trustee may demand that bidders pay the full bid amount in cash or cashier's check at the conclusion of the sale on that particular property. The bidding is open to anyone, including the lender and any junior lien holders. Also, a Trustee's Sale may be postponed (at the lender's request) at the last minute by announcement at the sale. If a sale is postponed more than three times, a new Notice of Sale must be issued.

After the sale is complete, the trustee transfers ownership to the winning bidder. The borrower *does not* have the right to redeem the property after the sale. The new owner will generally and immediately begin eviction proceedings, likely through a legal process by filing an Unlawful Detainer, if anyone – tenant or borrower – is still in possession.

Non-Recourse Loan. This is basically a secured loan that has collateral (the house and property) pledged against the loan. Generally in Non-Judicial foreclosure states a "Deed of Trust" is the instrument of indebtedness, rather than a "Mortgage." In this type of loan the borrower, is *not personally liable* if the home is foreclosed and sold by the lender after recovering the property, usually at a Trustee's Sale Auction, and subsequently selling it as Real Estate Owned (REO) by the lender to a third party either through a real estate agent and the MLS; or, if that fails, discounted to an investor, or a subsequent public auction.

If the borrower does not make the payments, the lender/issuer seizes the collateral (the house) through foreclosure and a Trustee's Sale Auction. The only recovery the lender can make from the borrower is limited to the collateral, which is the particular asset being financed (the house). This approach is common in home mortgages and other real estate loans. See the chart below to better understand your particular situation.

If the property has dropped in value below the amount of the loan, the proceeds the lender receives from selling the property – after foreclosure – will be insufficient to cover the outstanding loan balance. The lender is simply out the difference. Historically, Non-Recourse debt was typically limited to 80% or 90% of loan to value ratios, which would have called for a 20 to 10% down payment. And remember, this historical perspective also assumes that loans were traditional (standard) 30 year fixed-rate interest loans.

History of Non-Recourse Loans. Non-Recourse Loans were placed in the law specifically to force lenders to very carefully determine the credit worthiness of borrowers – their willingness, and moreover, their ability to make payments – it's called underwriting. As we've seen above, determining credit worthiness became irrelevant to lenders who knew full well they would be immediately selling the loan up the food chain to an Investment Bank, that also disregarded credit worthiness because they would be selling the loan packaged into a Security to an Institutional Investor.

Consequently the historical checks and balances were thrown out the window, and we are now seeing the result. We absolutely see no reason what-so-ever to see these lenders and Investment Banks bailed out at the taxpayers expense. In fact, your elected officials should be made aware that they had best not support such bailouts if they wish to be returned to office from your state.

Once upon a time lenders were very careful to obtain accurate appraisals of property and to thoroughly evaluate whether the borrower could repay the loan in order to mitigate the lender's risk. In the last few years, they were actually induced by higher loan origination fees to get the appraised value to come in at the highest possible number – a systemic pattern that falsely increased values.

In other words, they "looked away" and were not motivated to actually evaluate the risk involved. Many appraisers have argued that lenders unduly coerced appraisers to "hit the high number." And, as we saw previously some very serious litigation is pending and being prepared by various state Attorney Generals, notably in New York State by AG Andrew Cuomo, regarding appraisal fraud, which may well have induced buyers to believe the house was worth more than it *really was* worth. Naturally, this pattern has resulted in large numbers of homeowners being underwater today.

Alternatives. In Non-Judicial Non-Recourse states there are a number of actions (tactical and strategic) borrowers can use to slow or halt the foreclosure process while attempting to work out a Settlement with a lender. Anecdotal evidence (far from and even contrary to what is being reported in the press) indicates that lenders have been very difficult, in many cases impossible, to work with for borrowers who are attempting to work the situation out with a loan modification, a short sale or a Deed in Lieu, which simply means to give back the home and walk away without foreclosure, and reduction in cost for both the lender and borrower.

Not so long ago then Secretary of the Treasury, Henry Paulson, stated that he "… was shocked to discover that 50% of the time borrowers never contacted their lender before the foreclosure began." He may be shocked, though that may be doubted. Yet others have been shocked that lenders have not been interested in talking to borrowers who are experiencing difficulty with payments and reach out to lenders to no avail. Shocking all the way around!

Whether you've been in touch with your lender or not, there are legal actions (buying time) borrowers can undertake to considerably slow, if not stop, the process while seeking a reasonable settlement with the lender, prior to walking away, if that is the ultimate strategy. This is especially the case in Non-Judicial states that do not begin with the lender bringing a foreclosure action in court. But, we repeat, the key to having a position to negotiate from, with strength and real leverage begins with a Forensic Loan Audit and a Securitization Audit.

Temporary Restraining Order. In a Non-Judicial state, after receiving a NOD, the borrower may file a motion for a Temporary Restraining Order (TRO), which may be granted by a judge of the Superior Court (California). A TRO temporarily prohibits the trustee from proceeding with any further action with a specific foreclosure file until a trial is held or settlement reached. Generally a TRO is effective for a 21-day time period until a hearing is held, often the subject will be whether the judge will decide whether to grant or deny a Preliminary Injunction.

Preliminary Injunction. This is a judicial order issued by a judge of the Superior Court which prohibits the trustee from proceeding with the foreclosure, until a trial or further hearing is held, or, a settlement is reached. This can occur when there is a "dispute" between the property owner in foreclosure and the lender, otherwise known as the Beneficiary in the Deed of Trust.

A dispute may take many forms. In Ohio, as we saw in a previous chapter, many foreclosures were thrown out of Federal Court by three Federal Judges, because the Plaintiff, Deutsche Bank, who brought multiple foreclosure actions did not, or could not, prove that they were entitled to bring the action. By Federal law only the entity that actually *owns and physically possesses* the Promissory Note has the legal "standing," the right, to bring a foreclosure action in court, not a third party such as the loan Servicer.

In some cases, the Servicer may have been the originating lender, and they have often sold the note and mortgage to a Wall Street Investment Bank, which created a Security (Mortgage Backed Security, MBS), which may have been sold or traded many times. Therefore in most cases neither the Securitizer, or the original lender *owns or physically possesses* the original "wet ink" note. Generally, a "wet ink" original note is signed with a blue pen. If this is the case, this can become your new new new best friend. Seriously.

Some have recently argued that the fact that buyers were not informed during the loan origination process that the note would be sold, gives rise to a charge of withholding material information. This theory may support a claim of general Inducement to Fraud action brought by borrowers against those in the chain of events regarding the loan. Again, this remains to be played out. And, we urge you not to try this at home.

For the lending and Securitizing industry, it's not merely an issue of taking a small loss here and there. The real concern for them is that as this plays out in various courts, it may (will) lead to (some) Price Discovery. That will occur when the value of all homes *revert-to-the-mean* – dropping 25 to 50% (in extreme bubble markets) of values that we saw in 2005 to early 2007, and, ultimately reverting to 1998 values. A real disaster, which is possible could cause them to return to 1992 values, if they were to reach historic income to debt ratios. This of course would spell disaster for the banking industry. Of course as we see the politicians are bailing them out at taxpayers expense. But, how far can they go without collapsing the value of the dollar. We're all under extreme pressure. But, you can take steps to relive the pressure on you and your family – if you educate yourself. Hey. You are, you're reading this book.

Additionally, upon advice from counsel, a borrower in a Non-Judicial state might choose to formally protest an ongoing foreclosure action with pro-active litigation, such as a legal process or actually filling a Complaint against parties known and unknown, who participated in the entire loan and securitization process, including:

- the Mortgage Broker,
- the appraiser,
- the original lender or Mortgage Bank,
- the current loan Servicer, and even, (if not most importantly),
- the Investment Bank that bought and securitized the loan and subsequently sold the newly created bond to an Institutional Investor.

This is extremely ambitious as pertaining to the Investment Banks. Consumer Rights attorneys rightly point out that filing against Investment Banks is not likely at this point in time. A Summary Judgment Motion prepared by a major law firm can result in damages against the borrower if it is successful. Only over time, when we consolidate resources in a legal battle that will go on for several years will the borrower's side be able to mount such aggressive complaints. However our commentary there of is restricted to the Investment Banks, while the first four on the list are the obvious targets of borrower litigation. As you'll discover by reading our blog, we are beginning to win on the legal front. Some have opined that we may have reached a tipping point to the advantage of underwater homeowners.

It is likely that it will be argued that in a comprehensive search on the chain of title (whether they recorded the title or deed or not); or, more importantly, if in fact, at any point in time (even if only minutes until the Investment Bank assigned or sold the loan elsewhere) they were arguably the putative owner of the note. They were then a principal, and therefore a direct party to the matter. It will take more time to determine how this will play out. And, remember they put in place a legal "Trustee" for separation, yet, if is being discovered that many if not most of these Trustee's have broken the law, and the so-called "legal separation and bankruptcy remoteness" may not stand.

All such theorizing aside, today, in real time in early 2012, it is becoming clear that the path to successful litigation on behalf of underwater homeowners begins with establishing the facts through a Securitization Audit.

Who Wants the House. Regardless of ongoing issues and a changing legal landscape one thing is always true, the lender, someone, wants the house back as soon as possible to put it on the market. Yet lenders do not really want a house back. They must secure and insure the property, do some rehab, perform evictions, and moreover, they want the house in sellable condition without having to be involved in the expense and uncertainty in making minor and/or, major repairs resulting from neglect, vandalism or even damage by disgruntled borrowers who have lost their homes.

In legal terms it's called *bad faith wasting.* Don't <u>ever</u> take anger out on the property. Always vacate broom clean and take photographs, with the front page of that day's newspaper in the photos to prove the point. This is very important. Early settlement of the issue may be in the lender's best interest. Alternatively, this must be weighed against the best interest of the borrower still in possession.

This could lead to a private settlement involving all defendant parties, or negotiated with the lead defendant, the entity pressing for the foreclosure. In a Non-Judicial state such a matter would have to be brought by the homeowner's attorney through a litigation practice utilizing Motions mentioned above, starting with a Temporary Restraining Order leading to a Preliminary Injunction while the matter is sorted out. Possibly leading to a Complaint being filed on behalf of the homeowner We repeat, this is *not* investment, legal or tax advice.

These are issues to be raised with your attorney after you obtain a Forensic Loan Audit and a Securitization Audit.

One example of such process in a Non-Judicial state, is that the borrower, through local counsel, prepares and files a Complaint; or in a Judicial state, a Cross-Complaint could be based on various tort allegations relating to Predatory Lending and/or inducement to fraud, and other tort issues, which raises issues of malfeasance in the loan origination process. Moreover, if a *pattern* of fraud is discovered this could lead to filing under state (Federal, as the case may be) civil RICO statutes.

RICO. The Racketeer Influenced and Corrupt Organizations Act (RICO) is United States federal law providing for extended penalties for criminal acts performed as part of an ongoing criminal conspiracy. While it was originally intended to prosecute individuals in organized crime, it has been applied in many other cases as well including civil cases rather than strictly criminal prosecutions.

Under RICO, those who commit any two of thirty-five crimes – twenty-seven federal crimes and eight state crimes – in a 10-year period and in the opin-ion of the U.S. Attorney (or a private attorney for civil RICO) bringing the case, committed those crimes with similar purpose or results can be charged with racketeering. Individuals and entities can be found guilty of racketeering brought by Federal or State Attorney Generals and can be fined up to $25,000 and/or sentenced to 20 years in prison for each count. Moreover, the "racketeer" forfeits all ill-gotten gains and any interest in business gained through a pattern of "racketeering activity."

Importantly, there is provision for private parties to sue who have been a "person damaged in his business or property" and can sue one or more "racket-eers." A strong burden is that the plaintiff must prove existence of a "criminal enterprise." Though defendant(s) are not the enterprise; meaning, the defen-dant(s) and the enterprise are not one and the same. Further, one of four specific relationships taking place between the defendant(s) and the enterprise must be proved. Like many Federal civil lawsuits, such a suit can be brought in either Federal or State court.

To put real teeth in RICO matters, both the federal and civil components al-low for the recovery of triple damages, which would triple the amount of actual and compensatory damages awarded by a court or at a jury trial.

Why RICO? From its inception Congress did not intend RICO to only be appli-cable to organized crime. The sponsor of the Legislation was quoted as saying, "We don't want one set of rules for people whose collars are blue or whose names end in vowels, and another set for those whose collars are white and have Ivy League diplomas."

Under the law, racketeering activity means, among other things, any viola-tion of state statutes against any act of fraud, racketeering or securities fraud. While many Institutional Investor's are contemplating and in fact bringing suits and criminal actions against Investment Banks based on securities fraud and other issues, it is not impossible that such a remedy will be available to home owning borrowers after such matters work themselves out in various courts. This will especially be the case if successful investor suits, which settle, are *not* sealed as a part of settlement agreements. Nonetheless, the very Complaints which they file will be a treasure trove of information in terms of Causes of Action, which smart local attorneys may use in aggressively litigating on behalf of borrowers facing foreclosure.

Settlement. A settlement (allowing all parties to be done with this matter and move on with their lives) might be that the *borrower* agrees to:

- leave premises in "broom clean" good condition, xx months from the date of settlement;
- simultaneously return the keys (called in the industry) "cash for keys;"
- simultaneously receive a cashier's check equivalent to several months of payments; or,
- a significant settlement if fraud is found, which would be paid by the defendants;
- simultaneously have reasonable attorney fees paid to homeowner's attorney;
- withdraw their Complaint, with prejudice; against all named parties; and
- will not further protest the foreclosure action, which will go forward;
- unless contract rescission is agreed to in a Settlement.

To conclude a settlement the *lender* might agree as above and stipulate to:

- not seek further action beyond completing the foreclosure action unopposed;
- not seek a Deficiency Judgment;
- report to all credit agencies that the matter was completely settled, with no amounts owing by the borrower.

All of the above relates to a family that wants out. If a family successfully Uses Foreclosure Law to Keep Their Home, the ideal settlement includes a cramdown of the principal amount owed, a newly issued loan with no closing costs, a reasonable fixed interest rate in a 30 year loan.

As all of this plays out we might see some foreclosure attorneys instead of normally *practicing* law, actually *making* law. Forgive us, but that's been our little joke with attorneys over years. Feel free to use it.

Legal Disclaimer: We are not attorneys. We are not offering legal, investment or tax advice, or specific action. You need an attorney after obtaining a Forensic Loan Audit and a Securitization Audit. Don't look back and say, "Why did I try to do this on my own?" We are saying, do not do this on your own.

For assistance, see our web site: *www.UseForeclosureLaw.com*.

CHAPTER 10: CHOOSE – ACTION

"The Only Thing We Have to Fear Is Fear Itself."
President Franklin D. Roosevelt

From his first inaugural address in 1933, President Franklin D. Roosevelt was telling the American People to lose their fear. This charge by Roosevelt was a direct response to the fact that the U.S. had entered the Great Depression. Positive thinking and intention is the first step to securing the outcome you desire. Simultaneously, action can provide security for your family. Taking action is the opposite of rocking in a rocking chair, where there is plenty going on, but you're not going anywhere.

If you actually *Believe* that you'll be safe and happy because you've taken action to protect your family over the long term, your *Belief* can literally create a positive outcome. The concept is to frame or create a reference to a visualization of an outcome that you desire Rather than reacting from fear, which empowers paralysis and inaction (and high blood pressue), the idea is to consciously decide to pursue happiness. Then take action to move towards your goal. You do that by choosing to live in the Present. The past is past. While the future is unknowable it can be influenced by positive action and intention coming from the Present. We control our lives when we live and act in the present.

In your life, it's what you *Believe* that more often works out. To repeat, what you *Believe* more often works out. Confidence is King. While quantitative proof of this has been nearly impossible to show, particularly on a mass scale, to guide us we do have well known written works such as *The Power of Positive Thinking*. More recently we have scientific breakthroughs in Quantum Mechanics, in which monitored clinical experiments have shown that individuals and groups acting in – thinking in – concert have altered conditions. But this is not that book. That book *The Field*, and a second one, *Using Your Thoughts to Change Your Life and The World,* were written by Lynn McTaggert. Google Lynn. Smart.

While self-empowerment books are valuable, happiness is definitely achieved by providing security – by protecting your family – through removing potentially damaging uncertainty. Particularly regarding your home. Remember: home is where the heart is. Don't confuse your house, the place where your family lives, with your *home*. Your home moves with you. Your former house stays where it is. You can move on. If you *Believe,* positive intention can motivate you to action.

By becoming pro-active and acting as a self-reinforcing team, your family can control it's own destiny, rather than being controlled by avaricious outside forces. Also, if the violations of fraud law discovered through a Forensic Loan Audit and a Securitization Audit are significant, and they almost always are, you will have the legal leverage to determine the outcome of your situation. ♫*Should we go, ♪ or should we stay.* ♪

A Business Decision. Put simply, we've suggested throughout this book that you make a business decision. The lender offered a contract that said they would take the house back if you didn't make the payments! Fine.

If you can't make the payments, or moreover, if the actual value of the house (prices dropping radically all over the United States, and the Western world) is less than you owe – you can choose to walk away and let the *house* go to foreclosure, back to the lender. You move on and make a new *home*. Moreover, as we *always* say, you can choose to Use Foreclosure Law to Keep Your Home. However, the point of this book is to educate you and enable you to see that your best outcome can be achieved by Confronting Fraudulent Housing Debt, leading to Forced Debt Reorganization. A new loan you can easily handle achieved through litigation.

A Bright Future. If you use legal leverage as above to leave under your terms, will you be able to buy another house in the near-term future? Likely. Yet, it depends on your actions and timing. You must first make current all your other debts: credit cards, car payments and other unsecured debts.

History's Largest Scam. The overall scheme, or current "scam," is arguably the largest financial scam in history, much larger than Dutch Tulip mania, 1637; the South Sea Company, 1720; the Mississippi Company, 1720; English Channel Bubble; Railroad Bubble; the Victorian land boom of the 1880s; the Florida speculative building bubble; the stock market crash of 1929; or the dot.com bubble, 1997–2001. [This is not a complete listing.]

Do you feel sorry for – have empathy for individuals in the financial industry who earned huge salaries and obscene bonuses and profits by taking part in the Housing Bubble scam? The fact is that the scam – The Ponzi Scheme – has been stopped for several reasons. Notably the Credit Crunch has ensued, in part because home buyers were "all in;" and moreover, defaults began growing because of ARMs. As we say, it's not a Credit Crunch, it's an Unsustainable Debt Crunch.

At the same time, because so many of the loans extended were not sound (not based on historical, timeless lending standards, such as Loan to Value and Income to Debt); when the resets came, many people couldn't afford to make the increased payments. That is when the entire house of cards began to tumble. Initially, a couple of years ago they called it the Sub-Prime Debacle, and Dr. Bernanke made it clear this would not spread, that "contagion" would not put the financial system at risk. He said the problem was limited to Sub-Prime. He was wrong. If he actually believed what he said, he is incompetent as the Chairman of The Federal Reserve System. If he lied, obfuscated and did not tell the truth, he has broken his fiduciary obligation to the American People. Either way, he should be replaced.

They might replace him with former Goldman Sachs Chairman and former Secretary of the Treasury Henry Paulson, and allow Goldman Sachs protégé Geithner to stay on at Treasury. After all, there is no longer any doubt that these two are protecting Goldman Sachs? What's one more conflict of interest when *their* Financial System is at risk directly resulting in Paulson's case, from his previous work at Goldman Sachs regarding Mortgage Backed Securities. One of his nicknames is "The Fixer."

Your job, your assignment if you decide to take action and Use Foreclosure Law to protect your family, could leave him holding the remnants of the balloon he blew up until it burst. Let him fix that!!! Trust us – behind the secenes – he's a fixin' – as fast as he can Along that line, if it's true that Robert Rubin also former Goldman Sachs Chairman and former Secretary of the Treasury, still has the Young President's ear, and the Young President goes along, it might be best to be on the sidelines. Just sayin.'

So Many Plans. For several years now we have had a new bail-out "Plan" announced every six months or so – all designed to *"keep people in their homes."* What a terrible joke! All the bail-outs are designed to do is to *keep the financial interests from going bankrupt* as defaults swell and become foreclosures. They can only survive if homeowners decide themselves (*volunteer,* we'd say) to continue as indentured debt serfs and continue to pay on a loan that is worth more than the true value of the home. Unable to sell, stuck for years to come. Need to sell and move to take a job in another state. Sorry Out of Luck.

Take Control. That banking system, led by the Fed and Treasury, is now attempting to face down millions of underwater mortgage borrowers, many of whom are currently, and many more who *will be* underwater by perhaps trillions of dollars. The question is: will you, the borrower, take control over your life, as is your natural and legal right in such a fraudulent mass debacle *brought on by the very banks now demanding you keep paying?*

We ask again: Do you feel sorry for individuals throughout the financial industry who earned huge salaries and bonuses from their firms who earned obscene profits by taking part in the scam?

Well if you don't pity them, you can do your part to put a stop to that scam by refusing to play their rigged game. By refusing to be a debt slave, and thereby (literally) cause the values of reasonably priced, good middle-class homes to return to affordable levels. That is how you can position yourself to be able to purchase another home that will be affordable in the near term future. Or, litigate the fraud in the loan to obtain the outcome you desire, which for millions will be to Keep Their Home.

Wall Street drove the prices up. We've argued that Wall Street is the sub-culprit right after their chief enabler, Alan Greenspan, with a supporting cast right down to individuals in our communities who literally "took the money" to sell us out. We know of ethnic lending specialist entities, run by members of their own ethnic community, who nonetheless exhibited some of the most despicable predatory tactics.

Under California Civil Code §1632, the law is very specific, if a loan was negotiated in Spanish (or any other language) then the contract must be written in the language in which it was negotiated. Often this was not done, enabling homeowners to have a very very strong defense against this type of Predatory Lending. The problem for them may be that they can't read this book. A good neighbor will share this news and information. Be one.

Wall Street – supposed bastion of financial geniuses – provided the fuel for all of this activity, then instigated, if not aided and abetted Predatory Lending by demanding more and more loans to Securitize. The quality of the loans – the real risk factor – was completely ignored while rating agencies (were paid to) and regulators looked the other way.

If Wall Street (and the Fed and Treasury) believes the homes are worth so much money, let them have them back. Rather than driving up (promoting) the price of stocks as they did up until 1928-29 and again in 1998-2000, this time they drove up (promoted) the price of houses. Give them back the houses. Or force them to give you a *legitimate* loan modification based on principal reduction to just below today's current market price, in anticipation that values will go down lower until 2015.

Affirmation: On June 26, 2008, the Center for Responsible Lending issued a NewsBrief, "New York Tackles Reckless Subprime Lending...Will California Be Next?"

"Recent headlines have been gloomy: housing prices continue to sink, Wall Street executives knowingly pushed bad subprime investments, and mortgages keep failing in droves. As Congress debates how to put the economy back on track, the good news is that the states are moving ahead to prevent another subprime crisis in the future and strengthen communities now.

"New York is the latest to pass a tough law with stronger protections to put an end to many of the abuses that led to today's foreclosure crisis. This action came on the heels of new laws in Connecticut and Maryland, and Michigan is actively considering a robust bill, too. Approximately a dozen states, including Ohio, Minnesota, and North Carolina last year, have taken the lead in passing common-sense protections consumers should have had all along. The New York law, which the Governor will sign in the next few days, cracks down on some of the abusive practices that led to today's massive foreclosures. Among the key new protections are these:

- Puts the brakes on reckless lending–lenders must consider a borrower's ability to repay a subprime home loan.

- Stops trapping families in bad loans–prohibits prepayment penalties on subprime loans.

- Discourages destructive refinances–bans flipping of any loans into subprime loans without a reasonable and tangible net benefit to the borrower.

- Makes mortgage payments reflect true costs–requires escrows of taxes and insurance for all subprime loans.

- Gives homeowners a fighting chance–allows violations to be offered as a defense to foreclosure to help keep people in their homes.

- Provides more notice before foreclosure–requires a 90-day notice for delinquent borrowers who received a risky loan in the last 5 years, prior to beginning any foreclosure proceeding.

- Encourages better communication and options for homeowners–requires settlement conferences between the foreclosing lender and homeowner before foreclosure.

"California—the country's largest and most-expensive market—can especially benefit from adopting these critical protections. Despite being the epicenter of reckless subprime lending, the California Senate Banking Committee recently gutted an already-limited package of common-sense mortgage protections in favor of toothless legislation merely directing state regulators to enforce weak federal laws. California has the opportunity to be a leader in protecting home owners—and cleaning up the rampant abuses in subprime and nontraditional mortgages is the place to start.

"California and other states that have yet to act on the foreclosure crisis would do well to take a page out of the playbooks of states like New York. Our country's communities and economies can't wait."

Manage Your Own Risk. The financial cabal was led, aided and abetted by Alan Greenspan, who said on February 23, 2004, "All Americans should take out ARMs and *manage their own risk.*" Many Americans simply did not understand what he meant by "manage their own risk." He understood, and he understood more than perhaps any others, that the risk would be huge. It just didn't show at the time. The lending industry understood that this was *carte blanche* to go wild with risky, deceptive Predatory Lending, which also led them to add more fraud to the loans through Securities Law violations. After all, they were getting nearly free money to loan out, why not take a lot!!!

So whether it was fraud for Greenspan to make those kind of statements, or whether he simply didn't foresee the consequences is perhaps for a jury to decide. The Jury of Public Opinion, has come in with a decision: Guilty as charged.

The causality is unmistakable. Such behavior is much worse than unbecoming for a man who was the most powerful financial regulator in the world's largest and most important economy. Frankly, you are the jury. If you believe he set the American People up to fail, you can vote with your feet or stay in your home after you secure your interest in your home using legal leverage.

Economist Dr. Ravi Batra in his 2005, book titled: *Greenspan's Fraud,* provided a compelling argument that at the very least Alan Greenspan was guilty of Intellectual Fraud.

"Intellectual fraud involves the <u>misuse of intellect to fool others</u> or <u>offer baseless theses for personal gain</u>. The perpetrators of [intellectual] fraud generally contradict themselves, often changing their views with changing circumstances. It is <u>their intelligence that helps them con others</u>. They have no core convictions; they profit by cooking up theories or insisting on some-thing that is false. The main point is that <u>Intellectual Fraud involves the abuse of one's superior intellect to generate contradictory ideas or theories mainly for personal benefit</u>." [Emphasis Added.]

What we hope you clearly understand is that you're not under a moral, ethi-cal or legal obligation. You're not required to be bound for life (unable to sell your home if you wish) as an indentured servant to a contract, to a systemic process that was wittingly and fraudulently designed to rob so many of their life's wealth – for the gain of a small minority. Most people are not economists, therefore had little sense that we were in an *investment bubble* as housing prices ballooned 3 to 4 orders of standard deviation above their historical norms (in terms of income and the rate of inflation). But housing industry professionals, Wall Street, and the banking regulators (with Greenspan as their kingpin) knew better. They simply didn't care. Like Citigroup CEO Chuck Prince, they "… got up and danced."

You have no obligation to honor a trick. Clearly influenced by the media, most people became convinced by news article, opinion, advertising and mar-keting that *"real estate always goes up."* It doesn't. Honest assessment of the historical data shows that clearly. But they sold that aphorism to create a Social Mania. With Predatory Lending and Securities Fraud they induced millions of people into fraudulent transactions. Abetted by Congress – they caused unwit-ting millions of taxpayers to pay for it, instead of themselves, the ringleaders!

We have spoken to attorneys who are bringing these issues forward to ju-ries, to seek damages on a basis of fraud. Just because a majority in the industry did it, doesn't mean *no one* is responsible. There were certain specific points as it began to unravel where it was clear that certain Wall Street firms wanted to keep and eat their cake (and did). Many were taking positions (bets) *against* subprime and other types of MBS at the same time they were selling them to their clients – Institutional Investors and representing them as "prime," bullet-proof investments! The Rating Agencies, said, "OK. Oh yeah. Heck yes: AAA." This was a systemic scheme that pervaded the entire system. It's not OK.

Reporting by *Barron's* Jacqueline Doherty said, "Brace yourselves, home-owners. The current weakness in U.S. home prices could persist for years, espe-cially if you count the toll exacted by inflation. For all the wishful thinking in the housing industry, home prices can be remarkably stubborn. Just look at what happened in the '80s and '90s. The inflation-adjusted average price of an exist-ing home peaked in 1979, didn't bottom out until 1984 and didn't return to the 1979 level until 1995. In other words, <u>real home prices went nowhere for 16 years</u>." [Emphasis added.]

We add, that's just about exactly what happened in Japan from 1990-2007. In other words, house prices remained underwater for seventeen years. It is always a matter of: "How low can it go?" However, the prudent family taking the longer view must factor in: "How long will we wait?"

This is beginning to play out in courts around the world, as Institutional Investors have begun law suits against various Wall Street Investment Banks who bought loans from eager originating lenders, then Securitized them by placing them into Mortgage Backed Securities (fixed-income bonds) which they sold as 'AAA' rated investments. The latest reports say that lawsuits in the mortgage debacle, are now rolling out at twice the rate of the Savings & Loan crisis!

They want to *keep you in the house*. Believe it. You may not want to stay, or you may choose to litigate with legal leverage derived from a Forensic Loan Audit and a Securitization Audit. Don't be stuck. Stuck for a decade or more as an indentured debt slave of Wall Street. Can you say: Enough!!!

Moral Turpitude. We've done our best to give you the best case, best reasons for Using Foreclosure Law! To Keep Your Home by demonstrating just how craven our economic masters really are. But, it gets worse for them. It seems even their deity's, their wise men, their own ethics teachers have sold out in the race to the bottom line – self enrichment. We believe the following clearly shows the systemic rot within the financial system.

Reporting in the *New York Times*, Louise Story wrote:

"John F. Marshall spent decades teaching at business schools and watching his students parlay his lessons into fortunes on Wall Street. But when he and another professor reached for some of those riches themselves, events took a startling turn, the authorities say. Dr. Marshall, a retired professor at St. John's University and a fixture on the Wall Street lecture circuit, was accused by the Securities and Exchange Commission in March of passing inside information about a multibillion-dollar corporate takeover to a professor at Pace University.

"The developments have stunned Dr. Marshall's former colleagues and students, who describe him as a meticulous scholar and a generous, unassuming teacher. The accusations have jolted Wall Street, where Dr. Marshall is considered one of the wise men of financial engineering.

"At universities and on Wall Street, people who know Dr. Marshall are dumbfounded. Manuchehr Shahrokhi, a finance professor at California State University at Fresno, said he was so surprised to hear about the allegations that he looked up the S.E.C. complaint to double-check. He could not reconcile the accusations with the man he knew – someone he once heard speak on ethics in the derivatives markets. 'You know, sometimes greed takes over your knowledge and your skills and everything else,' Dr. Shahrokhi said." [Emphasis added.]

CHAPTER 11: CLOSING STATEMENT

"We hold these truths to be self-evident, that all men are created equal, that they are endowed by their Creator with certain unalienable Rights, that among these are Life, Liberty and the pursuit of Happiness." Thomas Jefferson from *The Declaration of Independence.*

Let it be noted that he struggled mightily against the fledging nation having a Central Bank.

At this point we focus generally on the Housing Market as we know it, as it is today, moreover as it will be over the next few years. We've given you valuable information to guide you in forming a business decision regarding your family situation, frankly, the preservation of your family. *"Life, Liberty and the Pursuit of Happiness,"* as Thomas Jefferson put it so well. We hope to remove the fear of the unknown for underwater homeowners through education.

At the bottom line is that in addition to valuable information it has been our strong intention to bring you Hope. Real Hope. Then by taking action you can force lenders to the negotiating table for a real cramdown – a *legitimate* loan modification – with a reduction in principal owed. What do we call that? You know by now: a Forced Debt Reorganization.

While the American Dream of pride of home ownership is a wonderful ideal, that ideal has been subverted by a tainted game that is not operating transparently, that is not operating in your interest whatsoever. The American People have been forced to play on an uneven playing field against a team that possessed information that was not made public, and worse, allowed and encouraged loan originations to be grounded in fraud. We've seen enough Forensic Loan Audits, and, moreover, Securitization Audits to believe and know that for certain.

Our closing remarks might also be taken as a Requiem for: the banking industry. You know the drill from the Preface. There names are:

- Rothschild's Centuries Old War Based Central Banking Process;
- Deep Generational Wealth;
- Entrenched Capital
- The Cabal;
- The Powerz That Be (TPTB);
- Financial Elites;
- Federal Reserve System (Fed);
- Wall Street Investment Banks (IBs);
- Too Big to Fail (TBTF);
- Financial Engineers;
- Structured Finance
- Banksters.

Not that these major institutions mentioned above will generally go out of business or close their doors, though some, perhaps many, will. The most reckless of them should be broken up, some allowed to fail, and the survivors be thoroughly regulated going forward. We would argue that the national TBTF banks be broken up and their assets sold to regionally, locally and state owned and operated banks and — local credit unions and savings & loans. Alternatively, they might be shut down in an orderly fashion using existing bankruptcy law.; or nationalize them and put them into Federal Receivership. Replace the highest officers, downsize them, and, over time — after being repaired — let some of them come back into public ownership.

Price Discovery, is the sub-theme for this book, *Use Foreclosure Law,* and must come from the ground up. Enacted by people saying: No More. People understanding that the game was stacked against them and they're simply "Mad as Hell and Not Going to Take It Anymore." They're not going to play by "rules and regulations and laws" designed to keep them indentured to a system which does not have their interest, let alone best interest, in mind. One could easily argue that our very Democratic Republic is under siege, that we stand on the brink of losing our Freedoms to a Corporatacracy that is nothing more than a modern-day Feudal System. Their system requires that citizens, now regarded as indentured "debt" serfs, remain on the land, remain where they are. They call it *"enabling people to stay in their homes."*

At bottom, they've engineered a coup. Time to take our Nation Back.

The rottenness permeates to the core of the system. Once again, Finance is asking (demanding) that bought and paid for politicians save them in order to keep the essential campaign contributions flowing. Naturally that's not played out in public. Now — in 2012 — there is a great deal of accumulating evidence that people are really angry. Occupy Tea Parties — share the love, join for the struggle.

A Tiny Bit of Politics. For us Nirvana begins as both the left and right find common ground. That ground is in the land where all those homes sit. This is not a matter of politics, of sophomoric ideological battles for folks with too much time on their hands. Yeah, sure, we want to make the reader a bit angry, but focus your anger into action against those who have done you wrong. Not at us who are basically kidding regarding the fervent politicization the political slant, but, not kidding at all in wishing to bring the left and right together in common cause to defend their families.

As we've pointed out previously, Henry Paulson, former Secretary of the Treasury and former head of Goldman Sachs, the Investment Banking world's dominant and most successful player, worked nearly non-stop to come up with solutions to *"keep people in their homes,"* and therefore (without mentioning it) stop Price Discovery, which really means making houses affordable once again.

Here we believe it's important to repeat the section on Price Discovery from the Forward. Remember what we told you about repetition – grows new brain cells.

In its simplest definition, Price Discovery is a method of determining the price for a specific commodity or security or product through basic supply and demand factors related to the market. In addition, Price Discovery is the general process used in determining prices. Prices are dependent upon market conditions, which affect demand. For example, if the demand for a house is higher than the supply, the price will typically increase, and vice versa. Yet, if the money available to purchase houses is greatly increased and loan standards are loosened – risk is ignored, rather passed on to a Greater Fool (Institutional Investors) – the result will always be a Housing Bubble.

Price Discovery *for the Federal Reserve and the U.S. Treasury* is discovering various "Plans" to *"keep people in their homes"* (to bailout Investment Banks) have failed. [They have.]

Price Discovery *for Investment Banks* is discovering that Mortgage Backed Securities are marketable at 30 cents on the dollar; and Institutional Investors are suing you to buy them back at face value. [They are.]

Price Discovery *for local, regional and national home lending institutions* is discovering that 50% of your privately held "portfolio" properties have been vacated (foreclosed by you or walked away from by the borrower); and you further discover that you can only sell them at 50-70% of the note value because there are so many similarly distressed properties on the market that prices have dropped dramatically.

Price Discovery *for Realtors and other housing and mortgage professionals* is discovering that the real estate market has returned to a normal and balanced market. You can once again do business assisting sellers to sell and buyers to buy homes that now have *affordable* prices based on historical loan to value ratios and income to debt ratios.

Price Discovery *for residential investors* who've been priced out of the market is discovering at the of summer 2009 that lenders have given up and are selling Real Estate Owned (REO) properties at absolute auctions (no minimum bid). Once again you can purchase properties at auction for "buy and hold," meaning that rentals will enable the deals to cash flow.

Price Discovery *for homeowners living in underwater homes* is waking up every morning for the next 3-4 years (if lucky) to discover that your home continues to decrease in value, yet your house payment increases, or remains the same.

Price Discovery *for homeowners who walked away from underwater homes* is discovering that a home similar to the one you bought 2-3 years ago at $400,000 (and walked away from at $325,000), can be purchased *by you* with the down payment you saved (over the last three years) for $250,000 – and you do it.

Price Discovery brings you *back* to an affordable home – the *Restored American Dream.*

Price Discovery then may ultimately be evidenced by house values returning to their pre-bubble prices from 6-10 years ago. Thus, *reversion to the mean,* which occurs in nearly every bubble throughout history. Thus, ultimately, homes become affordable once again.

If you think *HAMP, HARP, Hope for Homeowners.* will save you, you'll have to think again. If you think the Administration's "Stimulus Plans," will save you, you'll have to think again. If you think increasing the loan limits of Fannie Mae and Freddie Mac, well save you, you'll have to think again. All these "Plans," and no doubt more to come, have one thing in common beyond *"keeping people in their homes."* You'll have to read between the lines to discern what that is. Yet with reasonable certainty, we believe it's to halt Price Discovery. Yet, Price Discovery, like the sun, will rise on its day. To wit:

"The average American is getting slammed by rapid inflation in the prices for fuel, food, healthcare, education and other basis necessities. He was duped into various dangerous mortgage products to purchase homes with, in many cases, grossly inflated market values.

"Millions are in the process of losing virtually everything. He was also duped into various risky investment products, while the bursting of Bubble markets will leave him dreadfully unprepared for retirement. Now, he is seeing the returns from his savings crushed by the melee to bailout Wall Street "money changers" and speculators. Over the coming months, millions will lose their jobs with the inevitable adjustment and realignment to cope with post-Bubble realities. And now, apparently, the American taxpayer is to sit back and watch his contingent liabilities balloon (grow even larger) with the Nationalization of the U.S. mortgage market." Doug Noland, The Prudent Bear, March 21, 2008

House values will likely return to previous values (after a major dislocation). Yet during the oncoming disruption, millions may be gone from their previous homes. Not able to stay. Many will (and are) refusing to be indentured slaves – underwater. Ultimately this will force Finance to take the Securities and the loans backing the Mortgages and Deeds of Trust back on their books, and worse for them, they'll be forced (through litigation) to make restitution to Institutional investors who believed them and the Rating Agencies that the paper was relatively low risk. That it was safe. It wasn't. Of course there will be a banking bailout (it's on right now), and it will "virtually" bankrupt the nation, cause unpredictable chaos.

Yet the bankers have a plan. Actually several "Plans" have played out in the press since January, 2008. More often than not, these "Plans" seem to be one failure directly following the previous failure. Yet, they knew this day would come. Ultimately, they believed (remember moral hazard?) for good reason that the Fed and the Government would bail them out, allow them to survive. There will likely be more failures and consolidations.

Yet, at the bottom line, moral hazard – Rules the Day – the Taxpayer will Pay.

While that game plays out, putting the world's financial system at risk, underwater home owners would be foolish to stay involved. Foolish to live in a world of pain and deep anxiety when they can take action and Use Foreclosure Law to Keep Their Homes.

If a corporation can make a business decision to cut its losses, which they often do, shouldn't a homeowner caught up in a home that is rapidly losing value, while payments may be increasing, have the right to make a similar decision? They do have that right. Legally. See the Appendix section below where even the *Wall Street Journal* concludes that it is a rational business decision to walk away. All homeowners should carefully study all of their options. We strongly urge you to seek legal, investment and tax advice before acting, or not acting, as the case may be. But that comes after obtaining a Forensic Loan Audit and a Securitization Audit.

Historical Connotation. In the sense of historical context we've attempted to bring deeper economic information and interpretation to people who have a need to understand the actual ramifications of financial manipulations. One could well argue that the New Age of Structured Finance began with the Reagan Revolution, which was bolstered by Milton Friedman's, Washington Consensus, and then Structured Finance emerged. This opened the door to Globalization aka The New World Order. In other words, Finance Orders, People Obey.

All of this led to and directly caused a disintermediation and detriment to the Middle class in America, and, most all of the other in the Developed Nations as well. Debt was piled high on the back's of the Middle class through Greenspan's Housing Bubble, which was created literally to save Structured Finance and the equities and bond markets from the ramifications of the dot.com bubble, also created by Greenspan's consistent Accommodative Policies. Cheap debt money.

The Greenspan Method. He is a fierce ideologue and staunch adherent to a conscious or unconscious belief that His Crowd (in two words Wall Street) should not only lead the way, but, should control everyone's lives to the benefit of His Crowd.

Because they are smarter? Because they deserve the best? Because they can? All in service to Natural Selection? The survival of the fittest?

That's what many Conservative Libertarians seem to believe and Greenspan proudly states he is one of them. More often Greenspan's policies over years were frankly political reactions directly against his so-called principles. These were designed to cause the then current President to re-appoint him to his Chairmanship of the Fed. It worked. Perhaps, Ayn Rand, his former mentor, was right all along when she said, "Alan might basically be a social climber," an "undertaker," and "an opportunist interested mainly in advancing his career."

Such chiding aside, the bottom line is that the only means Americans have to take back our economy is to enable the focus of the People of our Once Great nation to assert themselves and act in their own best interest. We agree with Libertarians on that one. We see that average Americans have more power today to affect change than perhaps ever before in the history of our Republic. The method for millions will be to Use Foreclosure Law to Keep Your Home. If this is done in sufficient numbers this can cause Structured Finance to be *re-structured* and *regulated* as a result of being forced to take defaulted loans back on their balance sheets.

Lest the reader think we go too far – play the fool. We recommend to you Doctor of Economics, Ravi Batra, who wrote (among others) the brilliant book, *Greenspan's Fraud.* Dr. Batra wrote,

> .".. we are now more overvalued than Japan was in 1990. So certainly most American financiers know we are in a bubble economy but they hate to admit it because they think that they are one way or another responsible for it.... That could lead to a political revolution, but I do not believe it will lead to a dictatorship. I think we will see the rule of money end and that we (the majority of Americans and citizens around the world) will benefit by a tremendous revolution.... Well first there will be a lot of destruction of money." [Emphasis added.]

Return of Tariffs. Will such change once again call for tariffs on imported goods. Not impossible in a severe retrenchment or Greater Recession. The Chinese people have been lifted and assisted on their way to modernity by receiving our manufacturing base on orders from Wall Street to our former great manufacturers. Yet, the problem is that they will and are polluting the earth beyond sustainability. Today, 10% of the mercury in the Columbia river is from Chinese factories. This is unsustainable. As of 1/12/12, their bubble economy stands on the brink of failure – with all the rest of Sovereign Government economies.

The U.S. Government was initially financed by tariffs without a national income tax for well over *100 years.* This ended with the creation of the Federal Reserve System in 1913. Also later that year, the first national income tax was legislated to literally pay the interest (as profit to the Fed) on fiat money they created out of thin air to finance bank lending, evidenced by U.S. Treasury Bonds, creations of the Treasury Department. The point here is that America must begin to invest in *wealth creation* at home.

That begins with American savings with good ol' honest-bank savings accounts paying 5% interest. Such savings as bank deposit can fund loans for manufacturing, which will be successful – if cheap foreign goods are subject to tariffs, causing Americans to Buy America. This ain't no New World Order for the benefit of the Fascists and Plutocrats.

It will keep profits at home, and, moreover, re-building our national infrastructure, the Commons, will create long-term sustainable wealth – National Treasure. A Treasure that is beyond the grasping claw of Exploitive Wall Street.

In other words we must stop building the Chinese middle class with our dollars, and tend to our own nearly lost middle class, which has always been the engine of our growth.

In essence we are calling for a return to Industrial Capitalism and a complete rejection of Finance Capitalism. The latter is actually Socialism, complete with Central Planning, and no risk for the Financiers, who are bailed out when their exploitive business models bust.

We are hesitant to call for a return to a universal gold standard. While some do exactly that, we simply have not been able to understand how that could be feasible today, without gold rising to $6,000 to 10,000 per ounce. Yet, folks much more learned than we are in this area make a case for it happening, particularly if the rest of the world rejects the U.S. Dollar continuing as the Global Reserve Currency, as was enacted at the Breton Woods Conference in 1946 after WW II.

It's Begun. No sooner do we make these comments, an hour later we came across an *astonishing story* from today, 12/30/11. This does more than set a tone, it will enable many other nations to thumb their noses at us. It's one thing to be an Empire – and F-18s and drones are real good – but, when you've run out of money, and no one wants to trade with you – do deals with you – be your friend, you can only do so much in terms of making threats and carrying them out. Look out Iran.

It's like the Fed recently giving Banksters money to lend. They didn't want to lend it, and didn't. At the same time folks and some businesses did not want to borrower it. The reason they didn't want to lend it is quite simple – they know they can't trust anyone, any entity, any home borrower to repay it because we are on the verge of collapse. End of the Road.

"China, Japan Agree to Reduce Reliance on U.S. Dollar "

"The government of Japan and the communist dictatorship ruling mainland China announced a landmark agreement this week to facilitate trade between the two powers without using the U.S. dollar, relying instead on the Japanese yen and the Chinese yuan."

"According to the terms of the deal, the two governments agreed to encourage trade directly in yen and yuan without having to use American dollars as an intermediary — the current practice. Companies in Japan and China will soon be able to convert the currencies directly. And the Japanese government also agreed to hold Chinese yuan in its foreign-reserves portfolio."

"It remains unclear exactly how and when the agreement will be implemented. But according to news reports, both governments have already set up a working group to iron out the details. Officials said the move was aimed at reducing risk and transaction costs."

"The new currency deal comes as the communist Chinese dictatorship has been taking increasingly bold steps to expand the international role of the yuan. The regime's officials have also become ever-more vocal in <u>attacking</u> the dollar's global reserve status, calling instead for a more international system <u>managed</u> by a world entity such as the International Monetary Fund (IMF). "

"Of course, China and Japan are the second and third largest economies on Earth. And their governments are the two largest foreign holders of U.S. government debt. So the deal has huge implications — at least in the long term."

"The run on the dollar that could sink its value and bring surprise hyperinflation to the U.S. has just become a lot more likely," <u>observed</u> Alfidi Capital CEO Anthony Alfidi, who said the bilateral move would eventually mean higher U.S. interest rates."

....

The article was written by Alex Newman, came from TheNewAmerican.com, and it continues, you can read it here:

http://www.thenewamerican.com/world-mainmenu-26/asia-mainmenu-33/10359-china-japan-agree-to-reduce-reliance-on-us-dollar

---

What we see is disintermediation of the Federal Reserve System. The main job of creating money should be taken back into government. And, the US Treasury should issue the money at NO interest. Abe Lincoln and Jack Kennedy both did that, and, we know what happened to the two of them − in public − so that the message would be clear.

The Bank of England is not owned by banks. The Bank of Japan is not owned by banks. Granted every government will treat money issues differently. However, while we still *may have some* opportunities at the ballot box, we should be free to throw out the scoundrels, and replace them with our very own scoundrels − which ever side we are individually on. Looked at from the last day of December 2011, it looks like we have done exactly that. This is not a book on politics − so − we stop with this thought: it's really up to individual families to create their own safety zone. You know how. Ok, one more time, Confront Fraudulent Housing Debt through a Forced Debt Reorganization.

Human Toll. The dirty little secret the one area we haven't addressed in depth so far is *what happens* to families who are under mortgage stress. A riveting article in *USA TODAY,* by Stephanie Armour brought us to ground. Ms Armour wrote:

"Their suicides were a tragic extreme, but the Donacas' case symbolizes how the housing crisis is wrenching the emotional lives of legions of homeowners. The escalating pace of foreclosures and rising fears among some homeowners about keeping up with their mortgages are creating a range of emotional problems, mental-health specialists say. Those include anxiety disorders, depression and addictive behaviors such as alcoholism and gambling. And, in a few cases, suicide.

"Crisis hotlines are reporting a surge in calls from frantic homeowners. The American Psychological Association (APA) and other mental-health groups are publishing tips on how to handle the emotional stress triggered by the real estate meltdown. Psychologists say they're seeing more drinking, domestic violence and marital problems linked to mortgage concerns — as well as children trying to cope with extreme anxiety when their families are forced to move.

"'They're depressed, anxious. It's affected marriages, relationships,' says Richard Chaifetz, CEO of ComPsych, a Chicago-based employee-assistance firm that is counseling homeowners over mortgage fears. 'People tend to catastrophize, and that leads to depression. Suicide rates go up. We see an increase in drinking, outbursts at work, violence toward kids. Before, their houses were like ATMs, as they rose in value. Now, they feel trapped like a rat in a corner.'

"Foreclosure filings surged 65% in April compared with the same month last year, according to a report Wednesday by RealtyTrac. One in every 519 households received a foreclosure filing last month, and the number of homes with foreclosure activity in April was the highest monthly total since RealtyTrac began issuing the report in January 2005.'"

We are not qualified to comment on the far reaching mental damage that this current situation has created and will continue to create. We do feel we are qualified to ask: if your family is suffering, does it make sense to stay in an untenable situation that potentially – if not likely – holds severe unintended consequences that may be damaging to your children and family and partnerships?

Looking Inside. Often investors (homeowners are investors) make mistakes or fail. Courtesy of <u>John Mauldin</u> (we bring a report from Gavin McQuill of the Financial Research Center). John Maudlin said, "The thing that struck me as I read this report is that all the data was from periods prior to March 2000. I would expect more churning after the bear market crash in the NASDAQ, but this study shows that investors were becoming increasingly short-term as the bull market went to new heights. McQuill focused on six emotions that causes investors to make mistakes." We think the point that the penetrating analyst John Maudlin may have been making is that things have somehow speeded up. People feel pushed to take action.

1. **"Fear of Regret.** An inability to accept that you've made a wrong decision, which leads to holding onto losers too long or selling winners too soon.

"This is part of a whole cycle of denial, anxiety and depression. Like any difficult situation, we first deny there is a problem, and then get anxious as the problem does not go away or gets worse. Then we go into depression because we didn't take action earlier, and hope that something will come along and rescue us from the situation.

2. **"Myopic loss aversion** (a.k.a. as "short-sightedness"). A fear of losing money and the subsequent inability to withstand short-term events and maintain a long-term perspective.

"Basically, this means we attach too much importance to day-to day events, rather than looking at the big picture. Behavioral psychologists have determined that the fear of loss is the most important emotional factor in investor behavior.

3. **"Cognitive dissonance.** The inability to change your opinion after new evidence contradicts your baseline assumption.

"Dissonance, whether musical or emotional, is uncomfortable. It is often easier to ignore the event or fact producing the dissonance rather than deal with it. We tell ourselves it is not meaningful, and go on our way. This is especially easy if our view is the accepted view. 'Herd mentality' is a big force in the market.

4. **"Overconfidence**. People's tendency to overestimate their abilities relative to individuals possessing greater expertise.

"Professionals beat amateurs 99% of the time. Commodity brokers know that the best customers are those who strike it rich in their first few trades. They are now convinced they possess the gift or the "Holy Grail" of trading systems. These are the people who will spend all their money trying to duplicate their initial success, in an effort to validate their obvious abilities.

5. **"Anchoring.** People's tendency to give too much credence to their most recent experience and to show reluctance to adjust their current beliefs.

"We expect the current trend to continue forever, and forget that all trends eventually regress to the mean. They think long term is 2 years. They do not understand that it will take years – maybe a decade – for the process of reversion to the mean to complete its work.

6. **"Representativeness.** The tendency of people to see patterns within random events." Thanks again to John Maudlin.

Credit Hit? Many people are appropriately concerned regarding damage to their credit if they are foreclosed on. How long does it stay on your record? It depends. In reality it's not so bad at all considering the alternative. If you simply can't pay higher mortgage resets, you can rest assured that the bank is not going to *voluntarily* lower the value of your loan to the amount that you owe.

Ironically, in April 2008, Chairman of the Fed, Ben Bernanke suggested that lenders should do that. They were not amused. Why would he ask? Because he didn't want to have to create more money (that lowers the value of the dollar) and, charge taxpayers to bailout the banks. The banks, while decidedly not amused, realize that Bernanke *will* bail them out when push comes to shove. It did and he blinked. Big Time.

We ask? Will you push back, or, continue to be shoved around? Many folks already see the wisdom in hanging in – staying in the home without making payments – as long as possible until the house is foreclosed and auctioned and then leaving right after that. If that is your choice, we caution you, do not damage the house on the way out, it's not worth it, and may well cause you much more trouble than some temporary, ahem "satisfaction." It's a ploy of an angry teenager, and we're suggesting that you always place the security of your family first. People are doing it. We don't advocate that.

Ironically, as a (now former) REALTOR. on April 28, 2009 we heard a presentation from a high ranking member of Wells Fargo's national Loss Mitigation department, which is based in Indianapolis. She spoke to an angry mob of REALTORS in Marin County, California. They were angry, because just as it says in the press, people attempting to obtain Short Sales or Loan Modifications are unable to communicate with their lender in any meaningful way. Instead they are on the phone for weeks or longer, and can't find the "appropriate" party who can make a decision. This very nice and well mannered woman made it abundantly clear – she was firm – that you should <u>not</u> bring an attorney to these negotiations. Ridiculous.

She said that the bank could only do "… what we can do, and an attorney can't change that." Astonishing. She's upfront and playing Blind Man's Bluff. Because she was a guest, we did not advise her that anyone that attempted to deal with the Loss Mitigation department of a lender was simply naive. If you want to be taken seriously. you obtain a Forensic Loan Audit. a Securitization Audit and retain an attorney to use legal leverage and the talking is only done with the lender's Legal Department.

If you're underwater, and learn to realize in this book that housing values will continue down for years past what you're reading in most media reports, then you need to understand what will happen to your credit if you walk away.

Les Christie wrote in <u>CNNMoney.com</u>:

"Homeowners are abandoning their homes and, more importantly, their mortgages, rather than trying to keep up with rising payments on deteriorating assets. So many people are handing their keys back to lenders that a new term has been coined for it: jingle mail. Current lending practices have created an environment where a measure as extreme as abandoning a home actually makes sense to some people. The most serious consequence is a tremendous hit to credit scores. For some, that's better than throwing away money they'll never recover by selling their home.

"'And while a mortgage default can savage a person's credit record, <u>trying to pay off a loan they can't afford could be worse for borrowers if it leads to bankruptcy</u>,' said Craig Watts, a spokesman for the credit reporting firm Fair Isaac [FICO scores]. 'Credit scores are hurt much more by missing multiple payments – on credit cards, cars and so on – than by a single foreclosure. <u>The time it takes to regain your credit score [after foreclosure] can be shorter than after bankruptcy</u>,' said Watts. [Emphasis added.]

"Watts also said, 'It typically takes three years of a spotless payment record after a bankruptcy before credit scores recover enough for someone to think about buying a home again. <u>After abandoning a mortgage, a person may be able to buy a new house in two years or less</u>.' The trend of walking away is most pronounced among real estate investors, according to Jay Brinkman, an economist with the Mortgage Bankers Association (MBA). But families are doing it too. 'If they have to stretch to make mortgage payments for a home that will not recover its value, then yes, they may walk away,' he said. [Emphasis added.]

"Some statistics indicate that hard-pressed owners are deliberately courting foreclosure. An analysis by the consumer credit rating agency Experian last spring found that many borrowers were choosing to pay off credit card and other consumer debt before making mortgage payments. They were electing to put their mortgage at risk rather than their credit cards or auto loans. Similarly, Richard DeKaser, chief economist for National City Corp., (NCC, Fortune 500) notes that while all credit metrics are deteriorating, mortgage delinquencies are rising disproportionately. 'That makes sense if people are choosing to walk away,' he said.

"And now reports are emerging of homeowners skipping out on mortgages even though they can still afford to pay them. Wachovia (WB, Fortune 500) CEO Ken Thompson described these people on an earnings call last month. '[These are] people that have otherwise had the capacity to pay, but have basically just decided not to, because they feel like they've lost equity, value in their properties.'

"Lenders are afraid that borrowers may find it's worth the hit to their credit scores, if they can drastically reduce their housing expenses. Someone with good credit and a $600,000 home in a town with cratering real estate prices could buy a similar house nearby for $450,000, and then let the other $600,000 mortgage go into foreclosure. And for many homeowners, the prospect of becoming debt-free is growing increasingly alluring."

Writing in the *San Francisco Chronicle,* Kathleen Pender reported on September 11, 2007, that,

"According to the credit bureaus, any negative item – whether it's a past-due payment, charge-off, short sale, deed in lieu of foreclosure or outright foreclosure – stays on your credit report for seven years. The only exceptions are tax liens, which stay on your report until the taxes are paid, and bankruptcies, which generally stay on for 10 years. In some cases, a Chapter

13 bankruptcy can come off after seven years. How these negative items affect your credit score – and for how long – is another matter.

"Companies like Fair Isaac [FICO] take the data from your credit report and plug it into a formula that spits out your credit score. Your score depends on all the information – positive and negative – in your report. The problem is, there is no category on credit reports for short sales or deeds in lieu of foreclosure, which until recently were rare, says Craig Watts, a spokesman for Fair Isaac. He also said, 'a short sale, a deed in lieu or even a foreclosure will not hurt your credit score as much as a bankruptcy because generally they only involve one trade line. A bankruptcy involves multiple accounts going belly-up,' he says."

"Rick Harper, director of housing with the Consumer Credit Counseling Service of San Francisco, points out that just because a negative item stays on your credit report for seven years doesn't mean it will affect your credit score for seven years. 'Everything is time sensitive,' he says. 'The time period that is monitored most closely is the 24 months from the time the report is pulled. A negative item will initially cause your score to drop. But if you immediately start taking steps to improve your credit, in a few short months, you're going to see that score is going to begin coming back,' Harper says. [Emphasis added.]

"The first thing consumers should do is pay down all existing balances on their credit cards and make sure they make all payments on time. If they can't get a regular credit card, Harper suggests getting a secured credit card and charging one small item a month – $15 or $20. When the bill comes, pay it off within the grace period. 'Payment history is one of the highest rated factors' in your credit score, he says. [Emphasis added.]

"Harper says he has seen people file for bankruptcy and get their score back into the 600s within 24 months and into the 700s within three to five years. Watts says that's entirely possible. If you fall off the credit horse, 'get back on the horse as soon as you can in a measured way. Demonstrate once again that you will pay your obligations on time as agreed.'

"The most serious consequence is a tremendous hit to credit scores. For some, that's better than throwing away money they'll never recover by selling their home. 'And while a mortgage default can savage a person's credit record, trying to pay off a loan they can't afford could be worse for borrowers if it leads to bankruptcy,' said Craig Watts, a spokesman for the credit reporting firm Fair Isaac. [Emphasis added.]

"Credit scores are hurt much more by missing multiple payments – on credit cards, cars and so on – than by a single foreclosure. 'The time it takes to regain your credit score [after foreclosure] can be shorter than after bankruptcy,' said Watts. It typically takes three years of a spotless payment record after a bankruptcy before credit scores recover enough for someone to think about buying a home again. <u>After abandoning a mortgage, a person may be able to buy a new house in two years or less.</u>'" [Emphasis added.]

"And now skipping out on a home is easier, thanks to the Mortgage Debt Relief Act of 2007. Previously, if a bank sold a foreclosed home for less than the mortgage balance and it forgave the difference, the borrower had to pay tax on that difference as if it were income. Now the IRS will ignore it. 'That's going to help a lot of people,' said Mike Gray, a San Jose accountant who runs the web site Realestatetaxletter.com."

A Future Home. How will you buy a home in the future? Requires down payment. Where from? Americans have little to no savings. (Though that has ramped up a bit in the last two years. Good for you!!!)

Major changes in lifestyles must come forward. In other words, the U.S. must create gainful employment. Jobs – coupled with less extravagant consumption – can lead to savings, which, frankly will also be very good for surviving, albeit recovering banks, as it increases their deposits, their reserves and enable them to do what they must be able to do – loan money to practical home buyers.

Our Mantra. First the rot must be flushed out, which will include a continuance of decreases in all home values. This is occurring, in some part due to Option ARM resets, which continue until summer 2012 – and cannot be stopped. We must return to sustainable, historical context regarding debt.

Infrastructure Investment. A high speed national railway is one example that would create jobs all over the country, reduce our dependence on imported oil and create national wealth – national treasure. Investment in industrial capacity for practical use by all Americans. We call it the AmeraRail system. All abooaarrd!

It would be similar to FDR's CCC and WPA programs, which put the country back to work in the mid-thirties by creation of jobs. This began to pull us out of the Great Depression. Facing reality, the truth is that Hitler came along, and forced us to build massive industrial capacity, which enabled enormous domestic manufacturing capacity after the war ended. With the advent of the Breton Woods Pact in 1946, the dollar became the world's reserve currency. To the Victor goes the Spoils. It's also called dollar hegemony – dollar control. It's fading away. We had the spoils, and now they're spoiling, like milk sitting on a counter for two days in summer.

That is due to Greenspan's practice over nearly two decades. It felt good, now the price must be paid. They are so far out on the (debt) limb that it's begun to crack, ready to snap off. All their bandages and Quantitative Easing cannot repair the systemic crack. Yet, they'll fight tooth and nail to maintain *their* U.S. financial system. Who could blame them?

However, as they will discover, they are living in the past and history has not ended. Consequently, they will insist on another taxpayer bailout. That is inevitable. Don't pay twice. The first payment would be servicing enormous debt on an underwater property. The second payment will be born by all of us taxpayers to bail out failed banks. Lower the first payment significantly by Using Foreclosure Law to Keep Your Home.

Below the (double) bottom line, the fact remains – they've gone too far. Major corrections are coming.

In Conclusion. Often we are controlled by forces and "silent voices in our heads" that are seemingly outside of our ability to really understand them. Arguably such voices are the voices of our ego. Our ego chains us to our fears. Our ego demands attention, and if it can gain attention by creating anxiety – creating fear of the unknown – controlling our thoughts that way – that is just fine with the ego. For the ego it's really – *whatever* – as long as it's in control. But, this is not a book about that. *A New Earth*, which was so brilliantly written by Eckhart Tolle, is about that.

We believe it's important to address the deep issues of concern and frankly fear that people will have regarding a significant decision. Remember, we're not suggesting walking into the wilderness and leaving your cares behind you. We are suggesting, as President Franklin Roosevelt said to all Americans: "The only thing we have to fear, is fear itself." That fear is fear that you can easily give up. Think in the now. Be Present. The past is past, the future is unknowable, so what we have is the moment. Be with that. We consider our options and take actions in the Present. You cannot know the future, but you can influence the future by positive action taken in the Present. Our intent is to remove the fear of the unknown through education.

We've indicated that it's your choice to not be a debt slave, not to be indentured to an arguably fraudulent system. Which is better for you and your family? Do you attempt to retreat from pain through denial? Or, do you embrace change, act accordingly and choose to be happy?

Take Action. If enough people act, we will actually create our own Change Always remember, often the best defense, is a smarter offense. Take offensive action to defend your family – Confront Fraudulent Housing Debt.

Ironically, in the matter of a home underwater, the affirmative action was seen by many to really to do nothing. Many have chosen not to seek legal counsel and simply stopped making further house payments, then walked away.

But these people had no idea, no concept of Predatory Lending and Securitization Fraud. They simply walked away. While that may have seemed good for them – and it may have been – they did not realize that an opportunity existed for them under the law.

Various Processes. We've presented information we've assembled from many many sources to give you a solid course in Homeowner's Economics 101. Yet, we've not given you a plan – an action plan – you could begin following today. There are any number of different ways, or methods to approach a decision you may wish to take. Here are a few examples.

Loan Modification. This entails working with the lender to change the terms of the loan. Ultimately the current market has clearly shown that lenders are very slow to work with homeowners. We have much more on this section in the following Chapter. The bottom line, is that lenders are not reducing the amount you owe in a time when all U.S. home values are sinking and will continue to do so. Often they'll consolidate past due payments, penalties and additional fees and add them to the total balance owed. These plans are great for lenders. The are not great for homeowners in a sinking market. Such modifications guarantee many years of indentured servitude.

Worse, the new mods being offered demand that the borrower warranty that they will never take legal action even if they later discover they've been defrauded. Seems outside the Constitution, outside the statue-of-limitation laws regarding fraud, but, we're not attorneys. And, thank our lucky stars for that.

Deed In Lieu of Foreclosure. This involves giving the property directly back to the lender. The lender gains the property back without the expense of foreclosure, and with a small "cash for keys" payment to the borrower, conditioned on the property being left in good condition. Never do this without experienced professional legal and tax advice. Your credit will take a hit.

Chapter 13 Bankruptcy. This is called a "reorganization." All debts are consolidated into one monthly payment, unsecured debts are generally be discharged (cancelled), and the payment is tailored to your budget. This plan consolidates all missed mortgage payments and related charges and fees (some illegal, watch for them) into one payment which is spread over 3-5 years. Your mortgage is legally reinstated and you continue to make normal mortgage payments. So what!!!

One advantage is that you do maintain all your rights under Predatory Lending context: TILA, RESPA, HOEPA, FDCPA, FCRA, etc. Yet, you are continuing to bear the onerous cost of paying a loan where the value of the house is less, and will continue to be less and less – likely for the entire length of time you are in the plan. The bankruptcy will be reported on your credit report for at least seven years, and in some cases, longer.

Short Sale, You find a buyer, and the bank agrees to the sale with the bank assuming the loss for the difference between the sales price and the amount owed by you. If it's your principal home and not a refinance or Home Equity loan, due to recent national legislation you will likely have no tax obligation. Lenders are stringing people on after the short sale is proposed and not providing timely response. Why? They hope that Obama/Geithner will come to their aid, and they won't have to take the loss on their balance sheets. Well, now, they're shifting the debt over to Fannie and Freddie, the taxpayers, and trying to get out of Dodge before that defaulting debt slaps them down – hard.

After a short sale offer is made the bank sits tight, not accepting and not saying no. In countless cases the "new buyer" walks away because they don't know if the lender will ever approve. Also, because prices are dropping rapidly the potential buyer for your house finds a comparable house at a better price.

Your credit exposure is based on what the lender decides to put on their statement to the reporting bureaus. Watch out. Some legal firms advocate using a short sale with a bankruptcy, which does give you more leverage with the lender. But, then you've filed bankruptcy. Plan of last resort.

CHAPTER 12: USE FORECLOSURE LAW

"Those who do not learn from history are doomed to repeat it. "
George Santayana

The Rule of Law is at the center of all economies. Application of the Rule of Law allows families who are severely underwater, to use legal leverage when dealing with lenders. All around the nation average American families are obtaining justice if their real estate contracts are based in fraud. It seems astonishing, yet, most loan documents contain elements of fraud. In particular, if an Independent Mortgage Broker or Mortgage Bank was used for loan origination, Audits are consistently showing fraud is often present.

To be sure and fair, there are clearly some good and honest Mortgage Brokers. However, when the market went bananas from 2004 forward many shady characters, by the thousands entered the field for a fast buck.

Conventional Loan Modifications Do Not Work. The proof is in the data. The Office of the Controller of the Currency (totally compromised Govt. entity that unequivocally supports Banksters, not homeowners) released data showing that 58% of borrowers entering into these newer conventional loan modifications are re-defaulting after eight months. Thirty two per cent are behind one payment after three months. Recently Sean Dobson, chief executive officer of Amherst Securities Group LP, an Austin, Texas, firm that focuses on home debt said, "Most modifications are a sham done in the servicers' self-interest, and they do nothing to benefit the homeowner."

Yet, the powers that be soldier on. They kick the can down the road, instead of taking actions to fix the economy sooner, by letting actual market forces drive values down to true and historical Income to Debt ratios. Laws of economics dictate that this market will continue to reset lower, a reversion to the mean, regardless of temporary band aids.

Legitimate Loan Modification. For homeowners, the best hope for a *"legitimate"* loan modification, making the loan affordable, is a "cramdown" reduction in principal. This reduces the total amount actually owed to current market value, minus 10% (allowance for oncoming reductions in market value). These are generally only possible using legal leverage to obtain a Forced Debt Reorganization

Cramdown – Gone – Down! The Obama/Geithner loan modifications allowing for cramdown in bankruptcy failed because the Banking Cartel controlled Senate Finance Committee blocked the cramdown provision for principal reduction on April 30, 2009. Even worse is that fact that if the Senate had allowed the cramdown provision, homeowners would only qualify if they file for bankruptcy.

The path to "cramdown" Principal Reduction, better called "Forced Debt Reorganization" is through legal leverage utilizing Predatory Lending and Securities Law violations and issues, only discoverable

through a Forensic Loan Audit. Combined with a Securitization Audit. The latter is the key.

You Must Do Your Own Cramdown. The bottom line is that you must do your own cramdown using legal leverage obtained through a Forensic Loan Audit and a Securitization audit, and then, work with an attorney to Use Foreclosure Law to Keep Your Home.

Obligation To Family. People have the right, moreover the *obligation to family,* to utilize existing law to Confront Fraudulent Housing Debt that is based on Predatory Lending and Securitization Fraud

Debt Default. From Wikipedia.

"In finance, <u>default</u> occurs when a debtor has not properly met his or her legal obligations according to the debt contract, e.g. has not made a scheduled payment, or has violated a loan covenant (condition) of the debt contract. A default is the failure to pay back a loan."

Debt Repudiation. From Merriam-Webster: re·pu·di·ate:

a. to reject … as having no binding force <repudiate a contract>

b. to reject … as untrue or unjust <repudiate a charge>

c. to refuse … to pay <repudiate a debt>"

Don't Walk Away in Defeat. Our point is that generally, regarding housing debt − to default − is to walk away in defeat after foreclosure.

Here, by utilizing the Rule of Law to repudiate fraud-based debt, family objectives can be achieved by confronting a lender, utilizing an experienced attorney after obtaining a Forensic Loan Audit and a Securitization Audit. The family objective may be either to Use Foreclosure Law to Keep Their Home, or, if fraud is significant, to walk away with monetary damages in hand under the family's terms of settlement.

The "Long Con." A long con is often complicated and deep in its implications, and requires building trust (here, by bankers) from those who will ultimately be swindled (here, home purchasers in need of a mortgage). The facts are now emerging that most mortgages since 2000, were illegally originated.

A housing bubble came to exist because unregulated Investment Banks were able to "leverage" (borrow and "create" money), which they in turn "invested" by making money available to mortgage lenders such as Countrywide, who stood up, using ethical challenged mortgage brokers to enable almost anyone "who could fog a mirror" to buy a home. The "lenders" knew all the way to the top (Investment Banks) that millions of homeowners would not be able to keep their home once payments reset on subprime and Option ARM. They literally created a historic "Mania." "Housing always goes up." Until it doesn't.

On the brighter side, understand that judges throughout the nation are granting relief to borrowers under "quiet title" actions brought by their attorneys. The homeowner may receive the title to the home, free and clear, if the violations, the fraud, is manifest and shows in the loan origination documents. This is obviously the home run. Literally.

The (Current) "Short Con" – New Loan Modifications A short con is done swiftly and deceives by making promises and assertions that are simply too good to be true, even though they may seem too good not to take advantage of. They usually proceed quickly in order that the victim will not have time to analyze the situation, nor have time to gain proper legal advice. Often the victims may have some inkling that it doesn't quiet add up, but, in desperation – evidenced by denial and cognitive dissonance – over the fear of losing their home, they believe it is in their best interest to go along. Even though they will unwittingly be Warranting that they will not legally pursue loan originators for fraud.

Mod-in-a-box is a term used in the industry to describe Loan Modifications offered since December, 2008, by Fannie/Freddie, Sheila Barr's FDIC, and several major banks. We argue that such modifications are based on fraudulent intent. These modifications merely offer a reduced interest rate for 4-5 years, and stack the interest not paid during that time on the top of the amount owed, increasing the total amount owed. The problems are clear:

No Principal Reduction to current market value leaves the borrower underwater for years to come. Unable to sell without taking a significant loss, they become indentured servants. They are trapped for years as renters, or lessees in *their own home*. In Japan it took 16 years, from the 1990 top of their real estate market to 2006 for home values to return to 1990 values. Our downturn may not last that long, but we see no bottom for housing until 2015.

Indemnification clauses are included in these new modifications. This means that in order to get a lower rate for a couple of years, the borrower is unwittingly giving up the legal right to sue the lender when Predatory Lending and Securities Law violations are contained in their existing loan documents In our opinion there lays additional fraud in that the lender possess superior information. However, we are not attorneys and do not offer legal advice – only legal information and opinion.

Most borrowers are not aware of such violations, which is why we wrote this. Clearly if this new type of Loan Modification becomes Public Policy, we need to legally challenge such policy. We are not attorneys and suggest you consult with an attorney after obtaining a Forensic Loan Audit and a Securitization Audit.

What Is A Forensic Loan Audit? A comprehensive Forensic Loan Audit reveals Predatory Lending issues which can be the basis of legal claims under which lenders must negotiate loan terms (reach a settlement). A legitimate appropriate loan modification settlement should include principal reduction (amount owed) to market value, less 10% to account for future national declines in housing values.

Unfortunately, utilization of a Forensic Loan Audit without a Securitization Audit is weak gruel. While certain violations can be ascertained and brought forward, they simply do not have the impact with the judicial system that a Securitization Audit brings.

When the law and the facts are on your side and well pled by an experienced and knowlegible attorney, lenders will participate in settlements in order to avoid extensive, thus expensive (for them) litigation. If the violations are significant lenders will settle because they do not wish to be found out publicly in a trial of the facts. At the same time, by settling they avoid creating – legal precedent – regarding acts of fraud. A short list of issues shows that a Forensic Loan Audit and a Securitization Audit can discover:

- Tort and Statutory Law violations
- Attorney Fees collectible <u>against</u> lenders and their lawyers who file illegal foreclosure proceedings.
- UCC Holders in Due Course.
- UCC Accommodation Holders
- Property Law violations
- Securities Law violations
- Constitutional Law violations
- Civil Procedure Law violations
- Banking & Lending Law, where the <u>actual lender</u> was not licensed to make loans in the borrower's state and illegally "rented" the license of the so-called local lender, and,
- Much More.

These issues are both extensive and complex to determine. In that regard they are similar to indecipherable loan documents you were presented at the closing table. Most loan "packages" consist of 100 or more pages that are completely undecipherable by an average person. They are designed to be difficult to understand.

Yet, there was often no time (or money) to consult with an attorney before the closing table. Always implicit was the fact that the borrower really wanted the home. Borrowers trusted their Mortgage Broker.

What Is A Securitization Audit? While this has been discussed throughout the book, in short: it documents the entire trail the loan documents took on their way to be included in a Mortgage Backed Securities.

Are You In Foreclosure Or Underwater?

- Do you have an Adjustable Rate Mortgage whereby payments have increased or is about to spiral out of sight?
- Were you promised one thing when you began the loan process then delivered something different at the closing table?
- Did you know the difference?

- Are you experiencing the wrenching feeling of seeing your home plummet in value while the amount you owe remains the same, or actually increases?

Back to Modifications. The aforementioned modifications-in-a-box take missed payments including lender late fees, pack those up and stack them on top of the total debt (increasing total owed). They also reduce the actual monthly payment to approximately 4.5% for 3 or 5 years, and they may extend the term from 30 to 40 years. However, at the end of the 3 or 5 years, the payment shoots way up. Simply – another "teaser" rate.

Yet, you still owe more than the house is actually worth – increasingly – a lot more. You're stuck in the house and the bankers are very happy (for now – for a couple of years) because you did not walk away in default, even though you're locked into unsustainable debt, which is proven out when the payments increase.

Further, you're not reducing debt (loan is increasingly higher than declining market value) because the payment is mostly going to debt service – interest. If you sign one of these new loan modifications without *Principal Reduction* to actual market value you've signed yourself into indentured servitude. Because you will be unable to sell at a price near what you owe, you become a renter in your own home – for life. Many have followed this path to cling to their homes, falsely believing it would magically increase in value over the near term. This is not likely to be true.

You Are Not Alone. Tragically, homeowners are losing their homes every day (2 million in 2007-08) to foreclosures across the country. Originally, those unfortunate homeowners had the now infamous "subprime" adjustable-rate financing that exploded beyond ability to pay. Monthly payments increased to unsustainable amounts.

Understand that "lenders" knew full well that they were putting people into loans that they knew they would not be able to afford over time. *"When the music was playing, we got up and danced."* They did it anyway to gain fees and then passed the risk up to the next player in a chain that extended through Appraisers, Rating Agencies to Wall Street Investment Banks who packaged together and sold borrower's loans as Mortgage Backed Securities to Institutional Investors such as Pension Funds and Insurance companies, such as AIG.

One other factor is that the Powerz believed that when the loans defaulted, they could quickly recover the houses in foreclosure and still make a profit on the deal. That has changed. Now, if you act in your family's best interest by Confronting Fraudulent Housing Debt and achieving a Forced Debt Reorganization you very well may come out ahead.

Beyond the "subprime debacle" (and as employment continues to crash around the nation), homeowners with every type of mortgage:

- ALT-A,

- Pay Option ARMs,

- Prime, and,

- Jumbo loans …

… are more and more in danger of losing their homes. Tragic is the fact that a million or more families might not have lost their homes to foreclosure had they known that their lenders violated state and federal laws when the loan was originated.

Some Critical Data. Some readers accused us of being rather heavy handed in the initial book *(Choose Foreclosure: The Case For Walking Away)*, regarding our finger pointing at the culprits. Since that book went into print on Amazon in August 2008, much has happened since then that shows the we were prescient in describing what was sure to happen based on the facts – on the data. Now it is happening and increasingly becoming worse for homeowners.

The point is the subprime debacle is largely behind us. Some argue that brought down the economy, or froze the banks in August of 2008. In part, it did. But, there is much more to it, and much worse to come.

During the time of the housing bubble expansion, mortgage originations became different, and at the top of the bubble the growth of new originations were in ALT-A loans (good credit rating, but low or no requirement to *document* income). Also, and more significant, were Option-ARMs (initial very low teaser rates, with no required payments on principal. (Negative Amortization).

No Market Correction Until 2015. Many, particularly those in the real estate market, make hollow arguments that we are near or at the bottom. Significantly higher resets will occur on ALT-A, Prime and Jumbo paper through the end of 2012. Forcing more inventory on the market and forcing pricing to continue to drop through that time frame. One other factor is that most of these were originated at the top of the bubble, with the highest prices, and will therefore likely have the largest Debt to Value ratios.

The Federal Reserve, FDIC, and the Office of Thrift Supervision were well aware of what was likely to occur. In 2006 they published a booklet. "Interest-Only Mortgage Payments and Payment-Option ARMs: Are They For You?"

"Owning a home is part of the American dream. But high home prices may make the dream seem out of reach. To make monthly mortgage payments more affordable, many lenders offer home loans that allow you to (1) pay only the interest on the loan during the first few years of the loan term or (2) make only a specified minimum payment that could be less than the monthly interest on the loan."

"Whether you are buying a house or refinancing your mortgage, this information can help you decide if an interest-only mortgage payment (an I-O mortgage)--or an adjustable-rate mortgage (ARM) with the option to make a minimum payment (a payment-option ARM)--is right for you. Lenders have a variety of names for these loans, but keep in mind that with I-O mortgages and payment-option ARMs, you could face:

* *"payment shock.* Your payments may go up a lot--as much as double or triple--after the interest-only period or when the payments adjust."

"In addition, with payment-option ARMs you could face:"

* *"negative amortization.* Your payments may not cover all of the interest owed. The unpaid interest is added to your mortgage balance so that you owe more on your mortgage than you originally borrowed."

"Payment-option ARMs have a built-in recalculation period, usually every 5 years. At this point, your payment will be recalculated (lenders use the term *recast*) based on the remaining term of the loan. If you have a 30-year loan and you are at the end of year 5, your payment will be recalculated for the remaining 25 years. The payment cap does not apply to this adjustment."

"Lenders end the option payments if the amount of principal you owe grows beyond a set limit, say 110% or 125% of your original mortgage amount. For example, suppose you made minimum payments on your $180,000 mortgage and had negative amortization. If the balance grew to $225,000 (125% of $180,000), the option payments would end. Your loan would be recalculated and you would pay back principal and interest based on the re- maining term of your loan. It is likely that your payments would go up sig- nificantly."

"Be sure you understand the loan terms and the risks you face. And be real- istic about whether you can handle future payment increases. If you're not comfortable with these risks, ask about another loan product."

Well after the fact, well after the die was already cast, they published this self-serving document. Did you hear about it? Did you read about it? Not likely. They could say. *"We warned you."* They set the trap, and after the people were trapped, they can say. *"We warned you."* This would be the beginning of Alan Greenspan's irrelevant, disingenuous, ultimately false public *mea culpa,* to Congress in late 2008 after he was out of office at the Fed. He now regularly opines in the *Financial Times* and *Wall Street Journal* – to the effect, – *"It wasn't my fault."* He was the Regulator *who did not* regulate the financial enti- ties.

Negative Equity. It is a well known fact that borrowers with significant nega- tive equity are more likely to simply walk away. *That is a tremendous mistake.*

Indemnification Clauses Again. The crux of the matter is that embedded in fine print in new, new loan modification is a small "indemnification clause," which was written to not make any real sense to a borrower – desperate for help – who will likely sign anything to stay in their home. That indemnification states that the borrower is giving up any rights to contest any part of the original loan documents.

In other words if there are actionable <u>Predatory Lending</u> or <u>Securities Law</u> violations in the original loan docs, they are swept under the rug and the bor- rower is agreeing to never use said violations to litigate in the future against the lender or any party to the original documents, including the Securitizers, the Investment Banks who bought the illegal notes and created securities from them.

This blanket indemnification protects: assignees (Investment Banks), successors, servicers, lenders, appraisers, and you may have guessed it – Mortgage Brokers. At the heart of Predatory Lending is the fact that generally borrowers paid more for their loan than what they actually qualified for. Excess fees (called Yield Service Premiums) were tacked on by the MB which benefited the lender, who kicked back the Yield Service Premiums to the Mortgage Broker as a bonus for charging the borrower excessive fees. In short that's at the basis – the bottom – of the dirty game.

It's deeper of course, but that was the shake-down at the closing table. Borrowers did not know better and their Mortgage Broker who had a fiduciary obligation (based in Agency law) to them – sold them down the river. Now the MBs are back for another taste. It makes one angry just to write this out. Particularly one who also holds a real estate license, and highly honors ethical practice grounded in legal "fiduciary obligation" to clients.

Beyond Predatory Lending. Securities Law issues contained in the loan documents are the newest weapon in the legal arsenal for homeowner. While Predatory Lending legal actions against lenders have been pursued in growing numbers for the last two years, it is only recently that Securities Law implication have been raised. This is in regard to loans that were sold as Securities. Some estimate 90% of all loans since 2000 were Securitized. These issues revolve around the Securitization process itself wherein the loan and the Title were separated and taken up by different parties. This was done through unexecuted and unrecorded (illegally breaking the chain-of-title) receiver and assignment document transfers to different parties.

This in turn creates chain-of-title issues (often called a *clouded title)* and Federal & State Uniform Commercial Code (UCC) violations, some sounding in fraud due to: inadequate disclosures; unconscionability, lack of good faith and fair dealing, etc. These violations have only been recently asserted, on behalf of borrowers. Usury law and a host of other issues are now being aggressively pursued. Including what entity has the legal right to bring a foreclosure action.

Many borrowers have successfully challenged lenders and loan servicers on the grounds that because they do not possess the note, the physical loan document, they have no right under State and Federal law to commence foreclosure.

The actual owner of the note, the loan, is often not the party that starts the foreclosure process. Tragically, most of these illegal foreclosures proceeded through the courts, resulting in foreclosure because borrowers did not, do not know they can bring a simple action to stop such illegal foreclosures. These were uncharted waters. People did not know. Now we know.

With smart attorneys educating judges to these facts, the judge often quite willingly dismisses the foreclosure action. They lender or servicer may attempt again, but, this gives borrowers and their attorneys the necessary time to challenge the loan origination process itself, and when fraud is found through a Forensic Loan Audit and a Securitization Audit, the borrower is able to obtain a settlement, often resulting in a *legitimate* loan modification.

One of the top national litigators against foreclosure fraud is April Charney, a consumer lawyer with Jacksonville, Florida Area Legal Aid since 2004. She conducts attorney workshops around the country to teach other attorneys how to defend borrowers. Charney recently said, "It is common to prove that transfers and endorsements of notes were not properly made, and the real note holders are impossible to identify. The securitization process has failed, and the lenders cannot live up to the claims and contracts outlined in their 10 and 8K Securities and Exchange Commission filings."

You've been foreclosed on ... Is it too late? Is it possible to file fraud suits after the fact of foreclosure ... after the borrower has already given up possession? Many attorneys believe these cases are too expensive to bring, and take too long to litigate. As the deeper securities law implications are brought forward, these attorneys will understand that they can take actions against deep pocketed malefactors.

Generally the Statute of Limitations extends for one year after an individual discovers that they have been a victim of fraud. The clock starts ticking at the moment you have your Forensic Loan Audit and a Securitization Audit in your hands. When we are able to offer solutions to those already dispossessed we'll make certain that information is prominently displayed on our web site.

Below is a sampling of fraud issues that can be brought forward:

- Fraud in bundling and selling of Mortgage Backed Securities.
- Fraud in the conduct of rating agencies.
- Fraud in the illegal modifications of securitized documents.
- Fraud in the foreclosure process itself.

What To Do? – If you're Still In Your Home. Critically, you must take action by first obtaining a Forensic Loan Audit and a Securitization Audit in order to determine the actual leverage you have to bring a successful resolution to your situation.

Are You A Victim of Predatory Lending or Securities Law Issues? The only professional way we know of to determine if you have been the victim of Predatory Lending or Securities Law issues is through a Forensic Loan Audit and a Securitization Audit. This is a complex process that involves "dissecting" your loan documents, page by page. Each page is reviewed for violations that may be found, and summarized in an Audit Report given to you in a format for use by an attorney.

Some auditors claim (and they have done a sufficient number of audits to prove such claims) that "approximately 95% of all examined documents have some form of Predatory Lending, Securities Law issues, misleading disclosures, or other violations of Federal, State and Local law and regulations.

There are literally hundreds of checkpoints involved in the forensic examination of loan documents. Issues are identified that can lead to either legal actions against the lender or a Demand Letter from an attorney ordering that the loan be modified into something you can actually afford, if not outright loan rescission (canceling the loan) if this is your intention. This becomes a legal issue and you <u>require an attorney</u> both knowlegible and experienced in these matters.

Cost of an Extensive Forensic Loan Audit and a Securitization Audit. You might think that an extensive Audit may be too costly. We urge you to think again.

Research has shown that the fees charged by some <u>Loan</u> <u>Modification</u> companies (whether made up of former Mortgage Brokers or "attorney backed" entities), found on the internet, typically range from $2,500 to $7,000. Typically, they <u>do</u> <u>not</u> examine your documents in depth. Similar to their behavior in the original loan transaction they actually violate the law by acting in an *agency-capacity* with the Lender in violation of their *legal-agency* obligation to the borrower. Frankly, the list goes on and on.

Even worse many of these companies utilize a software program for loan analysis. Software programs are designed for mass utilization. As a consequence, they miss many violations. The key to a comprehensive Forensic Loan Audit and a Securitization Audit worth it's name is that it must be <u>done by hand</u>, page by page, by a knowledgeable and experienced <u>loan officer</u>, or <u>underwriter</u>. Not by entrepreneurial driven Mortgage Brokers, or, attorneys who simply miss the boat because they are not trained and seasoned loan underwriters. Often enough they solemnly declare they are seeking out TILA and RESPA violations. Inadequate today – Old School. That is the point.

On the other hand, many are simply not informed and believe in good faith that a simple Predatory Lending audit will do the job. It may do <u>some</u> good. But, the point of writing this is to show that most auditors and attorneys are <u>not</u> <u>aware</u> of the Securities Law issues.

Why not? Well, we're trying to break this news – this story – just as fast as we can. Generally, the MSM, dependent to some extent on advertising dollars, and, interlocking Boards of Directors, and, moreover corporate debt financings from the financial elites, don't really want to know about it. If millions of people were to heed the advice and opinions contained herein and on our web site, follow our program, we believe housing prices would rapidly drop to historic Income to Debt ratios, and the major ("too big too fail") banks would be severely diminished. Even Congress is slowly realizing that banks will have to be "Oh My Gosh" Nationalized – because they are insolvent. Then, amazingly, various key Congressional leaders discover a recent campaign contribution from the world of finance, and go quiet. If you've read our book, we believe we've earned your trust regarding our intent to bring you this information. You know where we stand.

Most attorneys, unless trained specifically in this new area of the law, the Securities implications, literally do not understand they are missing the depth of violations. Yet they are more than willing to collect a fee to do a sub-standard "loan audit" and conduct a "loan modification." They will find some violations, but, <u>not the total amount</u> of violations and actionable issues that are in nearly all loan documents created since 2000. Yes, it is that bad.

APPENDICES

Above are our arguments for:

Using Foreclosure Law to Keep Your Home.

In the following Appendix Sections we present exhibits which are third-party articles and data pertinent to the foreclosure crisis. These documents bear witness to the decision to Use Foreclosure Law! In fact we call these authors our "expert witnesses" in re the ultimate fact that herein we are indicting and prosecuting the Banksters in the Court of Public Opinion.

As with the text above, the following text is provided for informational purposes only. The authors presented below have not endorsed any material presented in this book. They are not responsible for any errors in this book, which are solely the responsibility of this author.

They have been kind enough to give permission to reprint their articles and content with attribution. We thank them very much for their generosity. Nearly all documents have a link back to the original article.

In real fact they are our mentors. We have learned and continue to learn from these authors, commentators, analysts. We highly encourage you to go to their web sites and read them regularly. We'll see you there. Great Good Luck!

CAVEAT

We are not attorneys or financial or tax advisors and strongly suggest that you confer with professionals before taking any action which may have legal or financial ramifications.

APPENDIX A: SAMPLE NOTICE OF DEFAULT ("NOD")

NOTICE OF DEFAULT
(Sample)

Date:

To:

Re:

Please be advised that the undersigned is the holder of a certain promissory note made by you dated _____, in the original principal amount of $_____.

You are hereby notified that you have defaulted under said note because you have failed to pay the installment due _____, 20__, in the amount of $_____.

Therefore, demand is hereby made upon you for full payment of the entire balance due on said note in the amount of $_____, including interest accrued to date.

If the entire amount due is not received on or before _____, I shall instruct legal counsel to commence legal proceedings against you.

Attention to the note, which obligates you to pay in addition to the principal balance and interest, costs of collection, including attorney's fees.

Your prompt attention to the foregoing is anticipated.

Very truly yours,

This SAMPLE is generic and your lender and/or state may utilize different language.

APPENDIX B: SAMPLE NOTICE OF TRUSTEE'S SALE

Notice of Trustee's Sale
(Sample)

The following legally described trust property will be sold, pursuant to the power of sale under that certain trust deed recorded in docket or book _____ at page _____ records of _____ county, [State], at public auction to the highest bidder at (specific place of sale as permitted by law) _____, in _____ county, in or near _____, [State], on _____, ____, at _____ o'clock ____m. of said day:

(street address, if any, or identifiable location of trust property)

(legal description of trust property)

Tax parcel number _____

Original principal balance $_____

Name and address of beneficiary _____

_____

_____

Name and address of original trustor _____

_____

_____

Name, address and telephone number of trustee _____

_____

_____

Signature of trustee _____

Manner of trustee qualification _____

Name of trustee's regulator _____

Dated this _____ day of _____, ____.

(Acknowledgement)

This SAMPLE is generic and your lender and/or state may utilize different language and process. This is based on a "Deed of Trust." The form for a "Mortgage" would be different, however, both go to the same point. This is Notice that the subject property will be sold at auction.

APPENDIX C: SAMPLE QUIT CLAIM DEED

Quit Claim Deed
(Sample)

THIS QUITCLAIM DEED, Executed this _____ day of _____, 20____, by first party _____ whose post office address   is_____   to   second   party, _____ whose post office address is_____.

WITNESSETH, That the said first party, for good consideration and for the sum of $_____ paid by the said second party, the receipt whereof is hereby acknowledged, does hereby remise, release and quitclaim unto the said second party forever, all the right, title, interest and claim which the said first party has in and to the following described parcel of land, and improvements and appurtenances thereto in the County of_____, State of_____, to wit:

IN WITNESS WHEREOF, The said first party has signed and sealed these presents the day and year first above written.

Signed, sealed and delivered in presence of:

_____   _____

Witness   First Party

_____   _____

Witness   Second Party

STATE   OF   }
COUNTY OF   }

On_____ before me, _____, personally appeared _____, personally known to me (or proved to me on the basis of satisfactory evidence) to be the person(s) whose name(s) is/are subscribed to the within instrument and acknowledged to me that he/she/they executed the same in his/her/their authorized capacity(ies), and that by his/her/their signature(s) on the instrument the person(s), or the entity upon behalf of which the person(s) acted, executed the instrument.

WITNESS my hand and official seal.

_____

Signature

Affiant: _____Known _____Unknown
ID Produced: _____

[Seal]

This SAMPLE is generic. Your state may utilize different language.

APPENDIX D: QUESTIONS TO ASK AN ATTORNEY

Before you retain counsel, it is essential to understand their practice areas of expertise; and understand how they operate; and, moreover, how they will communicate with you going forward. You cannot expect them to call you up all the time, that time costs money. Yet, you must let them know that you need to be informed as progress is reached.

Unfortunately, we cannot find the source for the following questions. Yet, we worked on Wall Street for law firms for 15 years as a document production expert, and believe these to be good questions to ask.

1. How long has the attorney been practicing foreclosure defense?
2. What are his/her strategies and tactics in that defense?
3. How many foreclosure cases has the attorney defended?
4. How many foreclosure cases has the attorney gotten dismissed?
5. How many foreclosure cases has the attorney appealed?
6. What are the names, case #s, court docket #s of those cases?
7. Is the attorney a litigator? ("litigation" is filing motions, taking depositions, subpoenas and appearing in court for hearings and trial)
8. What will the attorney do to prosecute or defend the case?
9. Is the attorney willing to fight it all the way and not settle for a standard loan mod unless it includes significant principal reduction to current market value?
10. Is the attorney familiar with all the topics of MERS, assignment fraud, signature fraud, HIDC (ownership to foreclose), securitization issues, etc.?
11. Does the attorney commonly work with a Securitization Audit as a deep element of their tactical and strategic efforts. (Extremely important.)
12. Has the attorney ever been disciplined or suspended from the bar?
13. Does the attorney offer bankruptcy as an integrated service?
14. How do they charge? Hourly? One big retainer, pay as they bill? Small retainer, pay as they bill? Small retainer and set monthly payments? If paying initial retainer and a set monthly payment, how does that monthly payment transfer into actual billable hours? If billable hours do not use up monthly retainer, will there be a credit to future billing? (e.g.$1000 payment but that month billable was only $500, will the $500 carry over?
15. Based on how they bill, will they charge for any copying, emails, phone conversations, etc. This is standard but with those that do a monthly set payment, they often will not charge for the incidentals.
16. Will they provide you a copy of all pleadings, complaints, actions, filings, responses, etc. regarding your case?

APPENDIX E: BILL BLACK: ENDEMIC CONTROL FRAUD

Reader's of our blog are well aware of William K. Black, Esq. Mr. Black, former Director of the Institute for Fraud Prevention now teaches Economics and Law at the University of Missouri, Kansas City.

During the Savings and Loan (S&L) crisis, it was Black, as Chief Regulator for the Federal Resolution Trust Company (who oversaw the S&L workout process), who made over 10,000 criminal referrals of S&L executives, of which 1,000 were indicted and sent to prison. Mr. Black also accused then-house speaker Jim Wright and five US Senators, including John Glenn and John McCain, of doing favors for the S&L's in exchange for contributions and other perks. So enraged was one of those bankers, Charles Keating — after whom the senate's so-called "Keating Five" were named — that he sent a memo that read, in part, "get Black — kill him dead." Metaphorically, of course. Of course.

"Now Black is focused on an even greater scandal, and he spares no one — not even the President he worked hard to elect, Barack Obama. But his main targets are the Wall Street barons, heirs of an earlier generation whose scandalous rip-offs of wealth back in the 1930s earned them comparison to Al Capone and the mob, and the nickname 'banksters'" Bill Moyers.

See, *Bill Moyers Interview with Bill Black. http://www.pbs.org/moyers /journal/04032009/transcript1.html*

At first glance, you may deem this tough stuff to read. Trust us – read it twice – and you will understand exactly how the they have done what they've done to all of us – the we – aka 99%. Critical to your education. Remember, this comes from a deeply experienced Master.

By Bill Black

When Fragile becomes Friable: Endemic Control Fraud as a Cause of Economic Stagnation and Collapse

Abstract. Individual "control frauds" cause greater losses than all other forms of property crime combined. They are financial super-predators. Control frauds are crimes led by the head of state or CEO that use the nation or company as a fraud vehicle. Waves of "control fraud" can cause economic collapses, damage and discredit key institutions vital to good political governance, and erode trust. The defining element of fraud is deceit – the criminal creates and then betrays trust. Fraud, therefore, is the strongest acid to eat away at trust. Endemic control fraud causes institutions and trust to become friable – to crumble – and produce economic stagnation.

White-collar criminology emphasizes incentive structures. A criminogenic environment is one that has strong positive incentives to engage in crime. While economists stress incentive structures, economics ignores criminogenic environments. The weakness comes from three sources. Economic theory about fraud is underdeveloped, core neo-classical theories imply that major frauds are trivial, economists are not taught about fraud and fraud mechanisms, and neo-classical economists minimize the incidence and importance of fraud for reasons of self-interest, class and ideology.

Neo-classical economics' understanding of fraud is so weak that its policy prescriptions, if adopted wholly, produce strongly criminogenic environments that cause waves of control fraud. Neo-classical policies simultaneously make control fraud easier and more lucrative, dramatically reduce the risk of detection and prosecution by maximizing "systems capacity" problems, and encourage crime by making it easier for fraudsters to "neutralize" the social and psychological constraints against deceit and fraud. Thus the paradox: neo-classical economic triumphs produce tragedy. Perverse policies led to four recent crises: the deregulation and desupervsion of the savings & loan (S&L) industry produced the 1980s crisis, "shock therapy" caused the collapse of the Russian economy, the "Washington consensus" produced a wave of control fraud in Latin America, and the desupervision of the U.S. economy in the 1980s and 1990s led to an epic wave of control fraud that contributed materially to the $9 trillion loss in U.S. stock market capitalization.'' With globalization, these crises can transmit to other nations through "contagion" or by causing key international investors to fail.

These recurrent disasters have discredited neo-classical policy nostrums through most of the world. In Latin America, for example, the perverse policies have led to the election of a series of explicitly anti-U.S. and anti-free market leaders. In Russia, the perverse policies discredited neo-classical economics and nascent democratic institutions. Yet, neo-classical economists learn nothing and proceed from failure to failure.

It is vital that criminological findings and theories about fraud become part of the economics canon. If it is bad criminology it is bad economics. If neo-classical economics predicts something (e.g., that control frauds cannot fool creditors and shareholders) that criminologists have shown to be false, then the economic theory is incorrect. Criminologists have found is that neo-classical economic policies, taken to the extreme, erode the institutions that constrain control fraud and make markets more efficient. Neo-classical policies damage markets and aid the financial super-predators whose predations discredit markets and democracy and bring Hugo Sanchez to power.

The intriguing issue is whether these results are unintended consequences or deliberate.

Introduction. White-collar criminology has a set of empirical findings and theories that are useful to understanding when markets will act perversely. This paper addresses three, interrelated theories economists should know about. "Control fraud" theory explains why the most damaging forms of fraud are situations in which those that control the company or the nation use it as a fraud vehicle. The CEO, or the head of state, poses the greatest fraud risk. A single large control fraud can cause greater financial losses than all other forms of property crime combined – they are the "super-predators" of the financial world. Control frauds can also occur in waves that can cause systemic economic injury and discredit other institutions essential to good government and society. Control frauds are commonly able to defeat for several years market mechanisms that neo-classical economists predict will prevent such frauds.

"Systems capacity" theory examines why under deterrence is so common. It shows that, particularly with respect to elite crimes, anti-fraud resources and willpower are commonly so limited that "crime pays." When systems capacity limitations are severe a "criminogenic environment" arises and crime increases. When a criminogenic environment for control fraud occurs it can produce a wave of control fraud.

"Neutralization" theory explores how criminals neutralize moral and social barriers that reduce crime by constraining our decision-making to honest enterprises. The easier individuals are able to neutralize such social restraints, the greater the incidence of crime.

Unfortunately, white-collar criminology has had no influence on neo-classical economics. This is largely due to mutual mono-disciplinary blinders – neither field read the other field's work. Some white-collar criminologists do now read the relevant economic literature. We have found that our core theories and recommended praxis are contradictory. White-collar criminologists (unlike many of our blue-collar counterparts) emphasize incentive structures and generally proceed from the starting assumption of rational, self-interested behavior and stress that the key attribute of a good model is predictive power – not descriptiveness. This is consistent with neo-classical economics, so the question becomes why our disciplines produce contradictory results.

White-collar criminologists believe that their empirical work established over 60 years ago that elite U.S. corporations frequently acted unlawfully. Sutherland's (who coined the term "white-collar crime") classic work reached this conclusion by relying on a study of adjudicated findings of violations of the law. There are inherent empirical limitations in studying such elite crimes that cause the findings to be substantially understated. Unlike typical blue-collar crimes, the victim of an elite white-collar crime generally does not know that they have been victimized. Most such crimes are secret and create indirect, generalized injuries, e.g., a cartel. Frauds, by definition, are hidden and elite frauds, e.g., the CEO that loots a firm by using abusive accounting to create fictional profits that make his stock options valuable, may never be discovered. Governments such as the U.S. keep detailed records of non-elite property crimes – but not elite property crimes. Even if a regulator or prosecutor believes that an elite fraud caused he injury no case may be brought. When regulators bring enforcement actions they typically settle through a consent decree that has no adjudication of guilt. Sutherland's findings are more powerful given these limitations.

Several neo-classical economic and finance theories, however, predict that control frauds will be trivial. These theories are logical extensions of the core theories underlying modern neo-classical economic and finance theory. These extensions rest on predictions about the behavior of other economic actors, e.g., external auditors, which assert that these actors will virtually never act abusively. White-collar criminologists' theories predict the opposite and have demonstrated superior predictive power. Top audit firms routinely provide "clean" opinions to deeply insolvent, pervasively fraudulent companies.

I argue that if it is bad criminology, it is bad economics and if it is good criminology it is good economics. Where economics, on the basis of an economic theory, makes a prediction about crime that criminologists prove to be empirically false the economic theory is false. Where criminology accurately predicts and explains perverse market behavior it should be become part of the economics canon.

White-collar criminology findings falsify several neo-classical economic theories. This paper discusses the predictive failures of the efficient markets hypothesis, the efficient contracts hypothesis and the law & economics theory of corporate law. The paper argues that neo-classical economists' reliance on these flawed models leads them to recommend policies that optimize a criminogenic environment for control fraud. Fortunately, these policies are not routinely adopted in full. When they are, they produce recurrent crises because they eviscerate the institutions and mores vital to make markets and governments more efficient in preventing waves of control fraud. Criminological theories have demonstrated superior predictive and explanatory behavior with regard to perverse economic behavior. This paper discusses two realms of perverse behavior – the role of waves of control fraud in producing economic crises and the role that endemic control fraud plays in producing economic stagnation.

Typologies of private sector control frauds. Control fraud theory explains why these frauds cause such disproportionate losses. In the private sector, the individual that controls the company (in practice) is typically the CEO. When the nation is used as a fraud vehicle ("kleptocracy") the head of state typically controls the nation. One can classify private sector control frauds by the nature of the primary intended victim of the fraud. In "looting" control frauds the CEO loots the company's creditors (which include the workers) and shareholders. Accounting fraud is the looter's "weapon of choice." The CEO uses it to overstate the company's profits and net worth in order to convert company assets to his personal use through seemingly normal and legitimate corporate mechanisms (e.g., salary, bonuses and stock options).

In anti-customer control frauds the CEO can use the company as a weapon in three distinct manners. He can join with other firms in a cartel. Not all cartels are unlawful – the ultimate success in control fraud is for the government to make one's action lawful. Most cartels, however, are unlawful and have to be kept hidden through deceit – fraud.

Another way to use the company as a weapon against consumers is the "scam." The seller defrauds the consumer about the quality, existence, or delivery of the good or service These are classic "lemons" market frauds. Scams against suppliers typically involve not paying the supplier for the goods. The other means of defrauding the consumer is procurement fraud. Such frauds rely on bribery the customer's agent in order to defraud. Procurement fraud can be used against both buyers and sellers.

A common anti-public control fraud harms the public by increasing pollution. A firm hired to dispose properly of toxic waste can decrease its expenses substantially by dumping the waste in a river and a company that pays an effluent tax can reduce the tax by fraudulently underreporting its emissions. Another common variety of anti-public control fraud is corporate tax evasion.

These forms of control fraud are all similar in several respects. Each is predatory. Each creates and betrays trust (though that is more tenuous in the toxic disposal case). Widespread control fraud operates like a strong acid that erodes trust. In each form of control fraud the gain to the CEO is far smaller than the loss to the victims. Each form of control fraud materially increases economic inefficiency. In each case the losses are far greater because the CEO rather than a more junior official runs the fraud. The CEO has unique ability to optimize the company for control fraud, unique capacity to shape the external environment to aid the fraud, unique apparent legitimacy, and can secure a larger gain in status from the fraud than any junior officer.

The three forms of private sector control fraud do not operate in the same manner. "Looting" control frauds create fictional income and real losses. Indeed, one the reasons they produce extraordinary losses is that they create perverse incentives to enter into the worst transactions because they produce the best accounting "profit." One optimizes a looting control fraud by rapid growth, e.g., by operating as a "Ponzi" scheme that uses a portion of the new funds brought in through growth to pay off old creditors. The Ponzi scheme extends the life of the fraud, increasing the "take" and the losses. If a wave of looting control frauds occurs it means that the companies will continue to invest in the asset categories optimal for accounting fraud, e.g., commercial real estate. This causes, and extends, a bubble. The bubble causes further economic inefficiency and the collapse of the bubble can cause systemic economic injury (e.g., the collapse of Japan's twin bubbles in 1990). Looting control frauds will eventually collapse unless they are protected by public sector control frauds. This is a variety of "crony capitalism."

The other two forms of private control fraud produce real economic profits, indeed, they are undertaken in order to reap supra normal profits. Anti-consumer and anti-public control frauds frequently endanger public safety. Inferior products are frequently unsafe products because it is more expensive to design and produce a safe product. The process of producing unsafe goods may also be unsafe, so workers may also be victims of lemons markets. The risk to public safety of improper waste disposal or the deceptive emission of additional pollutants is obvious.

Whenever fraud creates real cost savings an additional problem arises. Analogous to Gresham's law (hyperinflations causes "bad money to drive good money out of circulation"), frauds that produce a competitive advantage must be vigorously prevented by public authorities or they will create an incentive for rivals to emulate the fraud. KPMG (1998), for example, adopted a scheme of selling illegal tax shelters to rich clients on the explicit bases that (1) all of its competitors did so already and that acting unlawfully would put them at a competitive disadvantage, (2) the IRS was overwhelmed and was unlikely to spot the crime, and (3) the penalties for acting unlawfully were far smaller than the fees the firm would earn. The first point is a classic Gresham's law dynamic that made tax fraud endemic at top tier firms (according to KPMG) and the second two points are classic examples of severe "systems capacity" limitations that criminological theory predicts will lead to criminogenic environments and increased crime.

Cartels operate very differently from looting control frauds. Instead of expanding production and growing rapidly, a cartel optimizes by restraining production.

Looting control frauds and procurement fraud inherently cause damage to other critical institutions because they can only succeed by suborning agents, e.g., outside auditors and law firms or purchasing officers, who are supposed to protect the company and the public. This corrupts these institutions and harms the economy directly and by creating a Gresham's law-style dynamic in which bad accounting can drive out good accounting (NCFIRRE 1993; Black 2005).

The optimization of looting control frauds. The primary manner in which criminological and neo-classical economic theory contradict arises from looting control frauds.1 This paper will explain briefly how looting control frauds optimize as an exemplar. Control frauds are the optimal form of looting because the CEO has four unique advantages.

First, the CEO can suborn internal and external controls and pervert them into allies. The principal external control against accounting fraud is supposed to the outside auditor. CEOs control the hiring and firing of internal employees and non-governmental external controls. They, therefore, have the unique ability to "shop" for an auditor that will aid their looting. This does not require any explicit conspiracy. The CEO simply looks for an audit partner that stresses his aggressiveness and sophistication. Control frauds have consistently, world wide, shown the ability to get "clean" opinions for financial statements that purport to show that the company is highly profitable and solvent when the company is in fact deeply insolvent and unprofitable and pervasively corrupt. Moreover, the CEOs that engage in looting control frauds do not merely "defeat" the internal and external controls – they almost invariably choose top tier audit firms and use their reputation and "blessing" of their financial statements as their primary means of deceiving creditors and shareholders.

Second, only the CEO can optimize the company for fraud. He optimizes the company by having it invest primarily in assets that have no readily ascertainable market value. Professionals must value such assets – this allows the CEO to hire an appraiser or accountant that will provide a grossly inflated asset value. Because the asset has no obvious market value it makes it extremely difficult for the regulator (much less prosecutor) to contest the valuation. Such assets are also optimal for extending the life of the fraud. I have explained that rapid growth extends the life of the fraud, and increases the "take", by allowing a Ponzi scheme. The CEO has the unique ability to cause the firm to follow such a scheme. The CEO can also extend the fraud by arranging false "sales" of the troubled assets to "straws" or related parties – at grossly inflated prices that produce additional profits.

The combination of the first two factors means that the only real check on control frauds is often limited audacity. Audacious control frauds invariably get clean opinions for financial statements purporting to show record profitability. Indeed, the false profits claimed by audacious looters are far greater than the real profits produced by control frauds that target consumers or the public.

Third, CEOs have the unique ability to convert company assets into personal funds through seemingly legitimate corporate mechanisms. Accounting fraud is the key to this conversion. The record, albeit fictional, profits blessed by the top tier audit firm cause the stock to appreciate. The (U.S.) CEO will typically have a large percentage of his wealth invested in "his" company's stock. The CEO can then a large block of shares and profit. The CEO will also be rewarded with a raise (very large in the U.S.), a bonus, additional perks and new stock options. The CEO will also gain in status and reputation.

The theories also contradict with respect to cartels. Modern neo-classical economists argue that cartels are inherently unstable because they create an incentive for participants to defect. This destroys cartel discipline. Criminology has documented how illegal cartels can be extremely stable and cause severe injury (Black 2004).

Fourth, the CEO has the unique ability to influence the external environment to aid his fraud. Thus, Enron boasted of creating the "regulatory black hole" that left energy derivatives unregulated. Enron exploited this systems capacity limitation to form a cartel and produce the California energy crisis by taking production plants off line. During the S&L debacle the most audacious control frauds used their political contributions to fend off the regulators by influencing key members of the Reagan/Bush administration and Congress (Black 2005; NCFIRRE 1993; Calavita, Pontell & Tillman 1997). CEOs use the company's assets to burnish its apparent legitimacy by making charitable contributions. The political and charitable contributions also enhance the CEO's status and reputation.

....

Endemic control fraud can cause the key anti-fraud institutions and mores to crumble and produce economic stagnation and tyranny

Endemic control fraud occurs when corruption becomes pervasive. Corruption is a form of public sector control fraud. The means by which corruption becomes pervasive and the relationship between the public and private sector frauds varies by nation. Mixed systems of cooperating public and private control fraud are common. While the link between corruption and slower growth and a wide range of bad social factors is now well established, there has been little discussion of the role of fraud in corrupt systems. Endemic corruption invariably produces endemic fraud in both the public and private sector. Pervasive corruption simultaneously increases the take from fraud, maximizes system capacity problems, and leads to the most extreme form and breadth of neutralization. In deeply corrupt nations (non) taxpayers do not simply neutralize their guilt – they perceive themselves as heroes that have risked prosecution to deny the corrupt state additional funds they would steal. Fraud, at least among non-family members, becomes common and desirable. Again, fraud's defining element is deceit. This goes beyond corruption and causes not only economic stagnation, but also a culture that reinforces the deepest skepticism of government and leads to factional tyranny.

The article continues, and can be found here. http://www.peri.umass.edu/fileadmin/pdf/conference_papers/SAFER/Black_Fragile_Friable.pdf

APPENDIX F: ELLEN BROWN: WALL STREET LIKES YOUR AMNESIA

Ellen Brown is an attorney and president of the Public Banking Institute In *Web of Debt,* her latest of 11 books, she shows how a private cartel has usurped the power to create money from the people themselves, and how we the people can get it back. Her websites are WebofDebt.com and EllenBrown.com.

By Ellen Brown, Esq.

On November 27, Bloomberg News reported the results of its successful case to force the Federal Reserve to reveal the lending details of its 2008-09 bank bailout. [1] Bloomberg reported that by March 2009, the Fed had committed US$7.77 trillion in below-market loans and guarantees to rescuing the financial system; and that these nearly interest-free loans came without strings attached.

The Fed insisted that the loans were repaid and there have been no losses, but the Bloomberg report said the banks reaped a $13 billion windfall in profits; and "details suggest taxpayers paid a price beyond dollars as the secret funding helped preserve a broken status quo and enabled the biggest banks to grow even bigger."

The revelations provoked shock and outrage among commentators. But in a letter to the leaders of the House and Senate Committees focused on the financial services industry, Fed chairman Ben Bernanke responded on December 6 that the figures were greatly exaggerated. He said the loans were being double-counted: short-term loans rolled over from day to day were counted as separate cumulative loans rather than as a single extended loan.

Bloomberg was quick to rebut, denying any exaggerated claims. [2] But either way, the banks were clearly getting perks not available to the rest of us. As former congressman Alan Grayson observed in a December 5 editorial:

> The main, if not the sole, qualification for getting help from the Fed was to have lost huge amounts of money. The Fed bailouts rewarded failure, and penalized success. ...

> During all the time that the Fed was stuffing money into the pockets of failed banks, many Americans couldn't borrow a dime for a home, a car, or anything else. If the Fed had extended $26 trillion in credit to the American people instead of Wall Street, would there be 24 million Americans today who can't find a full-time job? [3]

All in the name of liquidity. It was all explained, said Grayson, with "the Fed's all-time favorite rationale for everything it does, 'increasing liquidity'." In 2008, bank liquidity dried up after Lehman Brothers collapsed, and the banks could not get the cheap, ready credit on which their lending scheme depends.

The Fed then stepped in as "lender of last resort", doing what it had to do to keep the banking scheme going.

Left unexplained is why the banks' need for "liquidity" justifies such extraordinary measures. Why do banks need cheap and ready access to funds? Aren't they the lenders rather than the borrowers of funds? Don't they simply take in deposits and lend them out?

The answer is no. Today when banks make loans, they extend credit *first*, then fund the loans by borrowing from the cheapest available source. [4] If deposits are not available, they borrow from another bank, the money market, or the Federal Reserve.

Rather than loans being created from deposits, loans actually *create* deposits. They create deposits when checks are drawn on the borrower's account and deposited in another bank. The originating bank can then borrow these funds (or others created by the same process at another bank) at the Fed funds rate - currently a very low 0.25%. In effect, a bank can create money in the form of "bank credit", lend it to a customer at high interest, and borrow it back at very low interest, pocketing the difference as its profit.

If all this looks like sleight of hand, it is. The process has been compared to "check kiting," defined in Barron's Business Dictionary as:

[An] illegal scheme that establishes a false line of credit by the exchange of worthless checks between two banks. For instance, a check kiter might have empty checking accounts at two different banks, A and B. The kiter writes a check for $50,000 on the bank A account and deposits it in the bank B account. If the kiter has good credit at bank B, he will be able to draw funds against the deposited check before it clears, that is, is forwarded to bank A for payment and paid by bank A. Since the clearing process usually takes a few days, the kiter can use the $50,000 for a few days and then deposit it in the bank A account before the $50,000 check drawn on that account clears.

Setting things right. As suspicious as all this appears, the economy actually needs an expandable credit system, and an expandable credit system needs a lender of last resort. What is wrong with the current scheme is that it discriminates against Main Street in favor of Wall Street. Banks can borrow very cheaply, while individuals, corporations and governments pay "whatever the market will bear". The banker middlemen take their cut in a scheme in which money is actually manufactured in the process of lending it. The profits are siphoned off to the 1% at the expense of the 99%.

To fix the system, the profits need to be returned to the 99%. How that could be done was suggested by radio host and political commentator Thom Hartmann in a recent editorial:

Have the central bank owned by the US government and run by the Treasury Department, so all the profits ... go directly into the Treasury and you and I pay less in taxes... [6]

For a model on the local level, he pointed to the Bank of North Dakota:

The good people of North Dakota ... established something very much like this - the Bank of North Dakota - and it's kept the state in the black, and kept its farmers, manufacturers and students protected from the predations of New York banksters for nearly a century. It's time for every state to charter their own state bank, just like North Dakota did, and for the Treasury Department to either buy the Fed from the for-profit banks that own it, or simply nationalize it.

We have been distracted here and in Europe by a sudden panic over our "sovereign debt" crises, when the real crisis is that our debt is *not* sovereign. We are indentured to a Wall Street money machine that creates our money and lends it back to us at interest, money our sovereign government could be creating itself, with full democratic oversight and accountability to the people.

We have forgotten our roots, when the American colonists thrived on a system of money created by the people themselves, debt-free and interest-free. The continued dominance of the Wall Street money machine depends on that collective amnesia. The fact that this memory is surfacing again may be the machine's greatest threat - and our greatest hope as a nation.

1. *Notes*
   Secret Fed Loans Gave Banks $13 Billion Undisclosed to Congress, Bloomberg News, November 28, 2011.

2. Bloomberg News Responds to Bernanke Criticism of U.S. Bank-Rescue Coverage, Bloomberg News, December 8, 2011.

3. The Fed Bailouts: Money for Nothing, Huffington Post, December 5, 2011.

4. Bank Management & Financial Services, McGraw-Hill/Irwin, 2009.

5. Loans Create Deposits -- how banks actually work, Winterspeak.com.

6. $7.7 Trillion to Wall Street - Anything to Keep the Banksters Happy!, Truthout.org, December 3, 2011.

This article appeared originally at Asia Times. The original can be accessed here.

http://www.atimes.com/atimes/Global_Economy/ML10Dj03.html

APPENDIX G: JAMES KUNSTLER: 2012 FORECAST

James Kunstler, is truly one of our great essayists. Why we've even used the words/names James Kunstler and Mark Twain in the same sentence, and told him we did. He was appropriately modest.

2012 Forecast: Bang and Whimper

By James Kunstler.

There's a lot to be nervous about, even if you don't subscribe to the under-cooked Mayan apocalypse lore moving through the gut of the Internet like a Staphylococcus-infected tamale. The casual observer might say that nothing seemed to give on the world scene in 2011 despite the Fukushima meltdown, the Arab Spring uproars, the train wreck of European finance, the disappearing act at MF Global, and the assorted injuries done to the Kardashian brand by the giant walking dildo Kris Humphries.

I demur. On close examination, the industrial world underwent complete zombification in 2011. Its member states and their institutions are now lurching across the stage of history like so many walking dead. Whole European nations are dead, their citizens squirming around the ruined bones of failed speculative condo projects, housing estates, and luxury hotels like botfly larvae. The USA lies in complete moral ruin despite the exertions of ten thousand evangelical preachers in dusty back-road tilt-up chapels from Texas to Carolina, several new museums of Creation Science, and the shining example of former Senator Rick Santorum. Just look at how we behave, from the cloakrooms of Congress to the piercing parlors of West Hollywood to the 7-Elevens of suburban Maryland: a nation of thieves, racketeers, reality TV sluts, wannabe road warriors, light-fingered gangsta-boyz, and crybabies living in an anomie-drenched decrepitat-ing demolition derby landscape of failure. When everybody is a zombie, whose brains are left to eat? Echo answers.... On to the predictions for 2012 then.

The biggest political shock awaiting us is the massive disruption of the ma-jor party nominating conventions next summer, when thousands of angry citi-zens descend on Tampa and Charlotte demanding a reality test. The parties will attempt to go about their ritual business, ignoring the mischief outside the con-vention centers, and both parties will make the mistake of siccing the cops on the protestors. The result will be a much bigger mess than the one I personally witnessed on the streets of Chicago, 1968, when the party hacks anointed the grinning sell-out Hubert Humphrey to run against Ole Debbil Nixie. Just before getting tear-gassed on Michigan Avenue that night, I saw some kid hoisting a sign that depicted the nominee with a Hitler mustache over the epithet: Mein Humph! It made my night, despite the subsequent retching in the gutter.

The two major parties are completely bankrupt zombie organizations and this election may be their last stand - if they even survive the conventions. Nei-ther of them can come to grips with the reality-based issues of the day: epochal financial and economic contraction, peak energy (and many other resources), climate change, the absence of the rule of law in banking, and generational grievance - or, perhaps more to the point, the manifestations of these giant trends as presented in unemployment, debt slavery, foreclosure, bankruptcy, homelessness, hunger, and X-million family tragedies. Both parties can only promise the return to a bygone status quo that is largely mythical.

President Obama, the putative "progressive" - spokesman of the Ivy League, Silicon Valley, Lower Manhattan, and all the other precincts where "folks" imagine themselves to be advanced thinkers - can't even wrap his mind around the simple fact that we will never be "energy independent" if we think that means running 260 million cars and trucks, no matter how many algae farms we pretend to invest in. Here is man who ought to know better and either doesn't, or is lying about it. He has other failures to answer for, too. Why, following the *Citizens United* decision in the Supreme Court, did Mr. Obama not prompt his party to sponsor federal legislation (or a constitutional amendment) that would redefine a corporation as not identical in "personhood" to a human being? Why does he still employ an Attorney General who has not started one prosecution for financial misconduct amid a panorama of arrant swindling and fraud? (Ditto: heads of the SEC, CFTC, etc.) And why did he not object loudly to the provision in the latest defense appropriations bill that allows for the capricious arrests and indefinite detention of anyone in the USA on suspicion of "terrorism?" Does this graduate of Harvard Law remember what *habeas corpus* means?

A lot of voters projected on Mr. Obama some notion of supernatural brilliance - our Hollywood fantasies are rife with wishes to be saved, and therefore redeemed, by our former victims - but he turned out to have a pedestrian mind. Could he possibly believe we have "a hundred years of natural gas" in the ground? Or that we're in a position to ramp up another cycle of industrial economic "growth?" Or that we can continue the web of cruel rackets that passes for medical care in this country? When the Democratic Party re-nominates Obama, it will be sealing its death warrant, and it will be on its way to the same cosmic vacuum where the memory of the Whigs lingers on.

Meanwhile, the Republicans labor to convert themselves into the party of corn-pone Nazism with all their unconcealed lust to push everybody around under the plastic eagle rubrics of "Freedom" and "Liberty." Look at the dismal lineup of morons, hypocrites, and religious fanatics arrayed for the Iowa caucus: a doctor who is also a creationist!? A leveraged buyout artist! A grifter fresh from K Street! A lady Christian theocrat wholly owned by the "dominionist" New Apostolic Reformation cult! A George W. Bush imitator showing symptoms of early onset senility! The whole posse is preoccupied with things supernatural. And being so dedicated to things unreal, they're the prime representatives of the suburban clusterfuck, who will do anything to keep that obsolete machine running, even if it means national suicide, because they lack the brains to understand where history is taking us and what the mandates of reality are shouting at us about the urgent need to reorganize American life. They are also the vassals of corporate despotism - where the Democrats are mere footservants.

They masquerade as "job creators," but they promote the off-shoring of every activity that corporate America can shed in its quest for ever-greater executive compensation. The lip-service they pay to "freedom" is belied by their intent to control everybody's personal life, commoditize the public interest, and sell out their grandchildren's future for a few extra rounds of golf.

I think this gang, too, will be sent packing by the mobs of 2012. I have a nagging intimation that some third party candidate will emerge. The two personalities I keep seeing in that role are Howard Dean and Michael Bloomberg. Both of them are imperfect, but both of them are clear-headed and action-oriented, and I have a feeling that both of them are stewing in the background over the spectacle of idiocy, inertia, and dithering they see at every political compass point. Maybe somebody else will crawl out of the woodwork. I've said before in the weekly blog that conditions could deteriorate so badly that a Pentagon general might have to step into national leadership just to keep the grocery stores supplied with basic rations - but that is an outcome in my personal asteroid belt of probabilities.

Whatever party ends up running things, and whomever fronts it, is going to be in for a helluva wild ride The USA is diving into an economic depression that will make the 1930s look like a Busby Berkeley production number. Compressive contraction will have its way with us, whatever Ben Bernanke thinks. There will simply be less activity of the kinds we're used to - Big Box shopping sprees, hamburger sales, theme park visits, house closings, you name it - than our hypertrophic system requires to keep its own destructive momentum going. Instead, the whole thing will just topple over, inert, like a 99-cent gyroscope giving into the forces of entropy. There will be a lot of bewildered, angry, dispossessed people from sea to shining sea. Not a few of them will "act out," that is, start breaking things, stealing things, targeting easy prey, hurting bystanders, and even tangling with police. Personally, I don't believe in the internment camp meme so popular among the doomer paranoiacs, but surely a lot of people will be cooling their heels in some slammer - while many other miscreants will just get away with crimes against persons and property.

The global banking system was on death-watch all through 2011. Somehow the various doctors in the central banks and finance ministries were able to muster enough accounting legerdemain to give the appearance of a system still showing a pulse. But in a compressive debt deflation, there are only so many accounting tricks you can pull off as money (and wealth) literally disappears down a cosmic worm-hole. In Europe, the process has moved from the margins toward the center. The people of Greece, Portugal, Ireland, Spain, Italy, Belgium will have less income, fewer government services, lost wages and pensions, less comfort than they have had for a couple of generations. Meanwhile, France is drowning in bad paper and the German banks are choking on it. There is really only one plausible outcome and that is default. The reckoning of the bondholders is at hand. Everybody will get poorer simultaneously - and if not, there will be not just regime change but civil war and revolution. The fantasy of a fiscal union in Europe is impossible because it means two things: that Germany will have to issue orders to everybody else; and that Germany would have to pick up the tab for everybody else while telling them what to do. Both are intolerable and implausible. Let's just think of the Euro experiment as an interesting side effect of the peak energy era... now drawing to a close.

These professional economists with their jabber about QEs and "financial repression" and bond-term "twists" and debt-to-GDP ratios are missing the point. The advanced industrial nations will not be re-jiggered onto any "growth" runway. Rather, we're entering the rutted wagon-road of de-industrializing and un-advancing. What awaits us in a "time-out" from hyperbolic technological progress. Forget about Ray Kurzweil's nanobot nirvana. That is not in the cards. Instead, wrap your mind around life in an economy organized around farming, with a much sparser distribution of big urban centers, and far fewer people over-all. Don't imagine for a moment that your grandchildren will be zinging across the landscape in electric cars sampling one theme park after another while "net-working" with "friends" on cyborg social networks implanted in their brain jel-lies. Think of them grooming their mules in the summer twilight. Anyway, you get the picture: everything that the finance ministries and treasuries and central banks are affecting to do is mere shadow theater performed in support of wishful thinking.

The question, then, is what kind of hardship and disorder will attend our journey out of the industrial era into post-technological age we are entering. Will we just turn the world into a Michael Bay movie and blow everything up? Or will we make some graceful descent and retain what is really best about the human spirit?

2012 will be the year of internal strife in these "advanced" nations, of peo-ple fighting over the table scraps of modernity among their own, in their own backyards, a desperate sorting out of the remnants. I don't think we'll see fight-ing between the European nations until the internal conflicts are resolved and that will take a few years.

The hot-spots for 2012 are very likely to be in the Middle East. You already know that. What could be more obvious than the tinderbox character of that region? Islamic extremism is poised to take over governments (and armies) in Egypt, Syria, Libya, possibly Algeria, and probably Pakistan. Iran lost its mind decades ago and seems determined to dominate the region by means of a strat-egy that can only get it into trouble (and perhaps the whole world if it goes really badly). Saber-rattling is one thing; making an actual move something else. Block the Straits of Hormuz? Not if you don't want Teheran to turn into an ash-tray. That may happen anyway if Iran rattles a nuclear saber. Germany, France, Britain, and Italy, all struggling with terrible problems at home, would breathe a sigh of relief if the mullahs were chastened. The chatter around the Web about an Israeli preemptive attack never ceases. But it is a possibility.

Oh, and don't forget Turkey. Formerly the "sick man" of Europe, Tur-key has become strangely resurgent, prompting some recollections that the Ot-toman Empire actually administered over much of the Middle East until 1914, and not with complete incompetence, either. They just sort of imploded from empire fatigue, which is not the worst way to go down, if history is taking you there anyway. But empires come back, too, and what passes for Turkey today is a polity that in one incarnation or another has been around since the ancient Greek days, and was, for quite a long while, Rome Release 2.0.

Don't be surprised if some hostilities break out between Turkey and Iran, since a battleground named Iraq lies between them. Iraq is a basket-case despite an immense reserve of oil under its sands, and having had the US military baby-sit it for eight years. The last American combat units left Iraq this fall, but there are still plenty of US soldiers there, maintaining our garrisons and keeping an eye on things. The question is: can they control what the Kurds do in the north, and whatever meddling Iran engages in around the Basra oil region in the South? These American support troops remaining in Iraq could find themselves looking like a ham-and-cheese sandwich between a lot of crusty mischief north-and-south. The Turks have already had a dustup or two with Syria lately - Syria occupies a big wedge between Turkey, Iraq and the Mediterranean Sea - and Turkey will take a dim view of that nation falling into the hands of Islamic extremists if Assad gets booted.

All bets are off in Egypt. Anything can happen there.

The dangerous position of Israel vis-à-vis all these quarreling players is probably as bad as it has been in two generations. An attack by a neighbor or getting caught in a crossfire between neighbors would stimulate a lusty response, and perhaps World War Three. As if the world needed this added aggravation. It makes my kishkas ache just to think about it. Sometimes I wonder why the whole Israeli nation doesn't just pack up and move to Nebraska.

2012 is the year that China proves to be a mortal nation and rolls over with a very bad case of the vapors. Their banking system is a sham. Their property bubble is a fiasco. Their government has no formal legitimacy and will install a new leadership group this year, while exports crash and mass factory layoffs happen. There will be a lot of pissed off people in China, and they may express themselves politically in ways that have seemed unthinkable for decades. The aura of social control looms large in China, but an aura is a light garment not recommended for stormy political weather. 2012 could be the year that China begins its journey into a "Balkanized" collection of smaller autonomous parts, which is the big fat trendline for all the nations of the world, including the USA.

It is hard to think about the bizarre case of India, a nation with one foot in the modern age and the other in a colorful hallucinatory dreamtime. Their climate-change related problems are doing heavy damage to the food supply. Their groundwater is almost gone. The troubles of the wobbling global economy will take a lot pep out of their burgeoning tech and manufacturing sectors. It wouldn't be surprising if these travails prompted distracting hostilities with its failed-state neighbor, Pakistan. Pakistan, with its inexhaustible supply of Islamic maniacs could easily start a rumble with some crazy caper like the Mumbai hotel assault of two years ago, but this time India would answer with a heavy cudgel, perhaps even a nuclear sortie designed to neutralize Pakistan's dangerous toys at a stroke. And that would be that. Like cleaning out an annoying neighborhood crack house. It's not a very appetizing scenario, but what else can you do about failed states with nuclear bombs?

Turning to Japan....That sore beset kingdom is suffering all the blowback of modern times at once: the Godzilla syndrome up in Fukushima; a demographic collapse; an imminent bond crisis; the collapse of export market partners; and a long, agonizing death spiral of its banks. I stick by a prediction I tendered back in March, after the deadly tsunami: Japan will decisively opt for a return to pre-industrial civilization. Why not? The rest of the world will be dragged kicking and screaming to the same place. Let Japan get there first and enjoy the advantage of the early adapter - back to an economy of local, hand-made stuff, rigid social hierarchy, folkloric hijinks in whispering bamboo groves, silk robes, and frequent time outs for the tea ceremony.

Russia? The big bear might have just sat out another decade and enjoyed its remaining fossil fuel supply, but the temptation to project power is a demanding habit, so they make all sorts of noises about watching Iran's back - though mutual hatred abounds - and generally rushing into the power vacuum occupied by a US with dwindling mojo. There were stirrings of political discontent just few weeks ago, after the rigged early rounds of national elections, and who knows where that will lead. Vlad Putin has held things together there impressively after the meltdown of the 1990s, but apparently the tranquil veneer is thin. Except for two big cities, the sprawling nation is broke and decrepitating, with little to offer the world but oil and gas - not an inconsiderable offering, but one with certain limits especially as they drain their oil fields for export cash. The rule of law is also pretty sketchy there. The government, as ever, is a kind of gangster affair, only this time one that allows some people to get really rich, not just connected. Their 70-year experiment with Marxian dogma has probably put them off ideology for a few centuries to come, which means less money spent on prisons for people with independent thoughts and more for call girls and home furnishings. I imagine that Putin will maintain his grip through the year. The Russians will appreciate relative order more when they see a few other countries devolve into internal conflict.

I don't see much action around South America this year. Some Americans are already fleeing to Argentina. Perhaps they'll enjoy it, but there is always the menace of property confiscation, and worse. Brazil will continue to appear vibrant while it grows more population, shoving it toward eventual ruin. They will see setbacks in the development of their deep-sea oil due to an international shortage of investment capital.

Mexico's fortunes depend on its oil industry, Pemex, which faces remorseless depletion. Revenue from oil production and (dwindling) exports can't hope to keep up with continuing population growth (and ever more poverty). These trends suggest a continued loss of control for the central government and more territorial fighting among the drug gangs and other criminal mafias. As long as all those loose heads roll on the south side of the Rio Grande the US will just tut-tut off to the side. But if the gangs get bold and start venturing cross border to make mischief we will make like Woodrow Wilson did and send the regular army down to spank them. It would be a satisfying diversion for that portion of the US demographic that enjoys Ultimate Fighting on TV, though it won't get them their job back at the Pontiac plant.

The global oil picture is not so reassuring. The fragility of our supply is simply unnoticed by commuters enjoying Lady Gaga on their iPods. Meanwhile, our politicians retail fantasies of endless domestic reserves, which is total horse shit. Global exports are in remorseless decline, apart from geopolitical fissures and strains that could just paralyze allocation cold. If a hot war breaks out in the Middle East, you'll see the American supermarket shelves empty in three days. Won't that be fun. Note, too: the manias over shale oil and shale gas will reveal themselves as just more bubbles in a long cavalcade of bubbles, and both will begin to founder on a shortage of investment capital. The shale plays will prove to have been a national self-esteem-building program, not any part of an energy policy.

The abiding question as we turn the corner into the New Year is: how come Jon Corzine is still at large? (Not to mention Angelo Mozilo, plus the entire executive floor of Goldman Sachs, and about 5000 other assorted Wall Street grifters still on the loose.) There is plenty of dire talk that the collapse of MF Global, and the shenanigans around its demise involving the evaporation of segregated accounts, has gravely and permanently damaged the entire investment industry, but especially the commodities funds, who can no longer depend on the Chicago Mercantile Exchange to honestly clear trades and regulate behavior. The whole affair, and the thundering silence from the oval office, makes Barack Obama seem not just inept but somehow complicit in the looting of America. As if he needs another mark of discredit in his record of consistent fumbling. There are signs that a lot of people who still have something resembling money invested in various funds will go to cash in the weeks ahead, including under-the-mattress style. The distrust and paranoia is palpable now, with the frenzies of Yuletide bygone for another year. After all, why trust banks, especially the TBTF monsters. Such a mass move could take the starch even out of highly manipulated equity markets.

Nemesis may have her day, though. Jamie Dimon might have just gone a swindle too far for the fates to ignore him another year. JP Morgan looks to be in a peck of trouble for its role in the confiscation of MF Global accounts, not to mention its hijinks in the precious metals markets. The impudence of these rascals! In a nation when all sorts of people are murdered every day for little more reason than being in the wrong place at the wrong time, is it not a wonder that some poor swindled Grampa with nothing left to live for has not tossed a Molotov cocktail through the window of a Wall Street watering hole known to be frequented by banking poobahs? Perhaps this sort of action awaits us in 2012.

Longtime readers of this blog know how much I love predicting the Dow Jones Industrial Average to crash down to 4000 every year. I never disappoint - though I am often disappointed. In 2011, the SP index managed the delightful trick of finishing a fraction below its previous January kickoff. The stock markets have churned in range-bound purgatory for a decade while the price of a jar of pickles has multiplied four-fold. Applying the calculus, and given the pickle-DOW differential, I'd say my call was actually pretty good. In any case, this year I change the tune slightly: I predict the DJIA will go to 4000, with the catch that the number is only a way-station to 1000, which it will hit in 2014. We may be short of snow here in the Northeastern US - thanks to La Nina - yet not short of confidence that the mills of the Gods grind slowly, but grind exceedingly fine.

Finally, look for the publication of my next book round July 2012, a non-fiction work titled *Too Much Magic: Wishful Thinking, Technology and the Fate of the Nation...* from The Atlantic Monthly Press. In a week, I begin work on *World Made By Hand* 3.

Good luck to you in 2012, and report any suspicious characters adorned with ear-plugs, quetzel feathers, and carrying obsidian knives to your nearest office of Homeland Security.

Boilerplate Bio:

James Howard Kunstler says he wrote *The Geography of Nowhere*, "Because I believe a lot of people share my feelings about the tragic landscape of highway strips, parking lots, housing tracts, mega-malls, junked cities, and ravaged countryside that makes up the everyday environment where most Americans live and work."

Mr. Kunstler is author of eight other novels including *The Halloween Ball, An Embarrassment of Riches*. He is a regular contributor to the New York Times Sunday Magazine and Op-Ed page, where he has written on environmental and economic issues.

Mr. Kunstler was born in New York City in 1948. He graduated from the State University of New York, Brockport campus, worked as a reporter and feature writer for a number of newspapers, and finally as a staff writer for *Rolling Stone Magazine*. In 1975, he dropped out to write books on a full-time basis.

He has lectured at Harvard, Yale, Columbia, Dartmouth, Cornell, MIT, RPI, the University of Virginia and many other colleges, and he has appeared before many professional organizations such as the AIA , the APA., and the National Trust for Historic Preservation.

He lives in Saratoga Springs in upstate New York.

APPENDIX H: NYE LAVALLE: FRAUDULENT ... ASSIGNMENTS

We are more than pleased to present work from Nye Lavalle, who discovered the depth of Securities Fraud, and began investigating and publishing on the subject in the mid-nineties. No one was listening. He has stayed true to his task. Read this as a partial guide to what happened in the Wall Street Mortgage Securitization industry.

This is part of story of what happened to multi-millions of homeowners with mortgages issued since 2000. This is the who, what, when, where, how and why.

Nye presents detailed forensic evidence exposing <u>exactly</u> what was done to most loans as they went from origination (at the escrow closing table) through the Securitization process up to the present day. He estimates as high as 90% of all mortgages since 2000 were in fact Securitized through Wall Street, based in knowing and witting failure of disclosure and misrepresentation to the borrower by the originators and up the chain to the Investment Bankers. This falls within the legal construct of Fraudulent Inducement. Absolutely establishing legal grounds to Confront Fraudulent Housing Debt. Text below is taken from an Affidavit submitted to an actual Court as "evidence" by an "expert witness" (Nye Lavalle) in support of a wrongful foreclosure action brought by a homeowner.

Report On Fraudulent & Forged Assignments Of Mortgages & Deeds In U.S. Foreclosures

By Nye Lavalle

Dedication Throughout America, countless millions of American homeowners have been unlawfully foreclosed upon via fraudulent means. For over fifteen years, I have dedicated my life and journey towards the protection of American families, investors, and taxpayers. Until the past few years, few, except family, friends, and some trusted colleagues, gave credence to the warnings I cried out. My motivation wasn't money, but justice, safety, and protection of the American Dream that so many Americans sought and attained.

Sadly, as you will read in this report, I was right in virtually all of my warnings. I have no regrets except that I could not do more. I pray and feel for all those victimized and can only say that I did all I could and wished I could have done more. However, the tides are changing and the light is coming that will shine on the evil of greed and arrogance.

BACKGROUND

1. I make this report based upon facts personally known by me and my investigation, research, review, and analysis of evidence provided in the many lawsuits I have testified in and assisted lawyers with; gathered from other advocates and

lawyers; thousands of other lawsuits; hundreds of thousands of papers, reports, and documents I have read, reviewed, and researched as well as filings filed with the Securities and Exchange Commission (SEC) available and retrievable at the Edgar database.

2. My analysis, statements, opinions, and findings are only as accurate as the information and data provided from the evidence presented and the sources of information used in my research and investigation.

3. Recently, there has been a plethora of court rulings, pleadings, and even civil and criminal investigations surrounding fraudulent and forged assignments of mortgages, deeds to secure debts, and deeds of trust across America. In fact, a Google search for mortgage assignment fraud returns over 700,000 hits with movies, examples, and court rulings relating to such frauds and abuses.

4. As an consumer/investor advocate and activist, I first identified this fraudulent assignment scheme in the mid to late 90s when various servicers were conducting judicial and non-judicial foreclosures in their names, rather than the real-party-in-interest and true owner and equitable holder of borrower's promissory notes.

5. One employee of a major servicer, EMC Mortgage a unit of JP Morgan Chase told me that you need to sue the lawyers, they are all in on it meaning the scam and scheme of fraudulent and unlawful foreclosures being conducted in the name of servicers who had no real ownership or interest in the note and thus no right or authority to conduct a foreclosure.

6. As I referenced above, mortgage assignment fraud is getting a lot of attention by state Attorney General offices, U.S. attorneys, Secretary of States, and both state and federal judges.

7. I shall highlight for this honorable Court a few examples of recent investigations, decisions, rulings, and orders across America in the following sections of this report:

Recent National & Mortgage Industry News Into Criminal & Civil Investigations Surrounding Fabricated, Forged, & Fraudulent Assignments By Foreclosure Lawyers, Servicers, & Vendors 8. As shown above and herein, there is increased judicial, state, and federal scrutiny of the fraudulent foreclosure and assignment schemes that are receiving increasing national and local media attention as in a recent article in the St. Petersburg Times evidencing that even the notaries are involved in the abuses. The following comments in a story by Kate Berry in the National Mortgage News ... stated the following:

a. The backlash is intensifying against banks and mortgage servicers that try to foreclose on homes without all their ducks in a row. Because the notes were often sold and resold during the boom years, many financial companies lost track of the documents. Now, legal officials are accusing companies of forging the documents needed to reclaim the properties. Recently, the Florida Attorney General's Office said it was investigating the use of bogus assignment documents by Lender Processing Services Inc. and its former parent, Fidelity National Financial Inc. And a federal judge in Florida has ordered a hearing to determine whether M&T Bank Corp. should be charged with fraud 2 http://www.tampabay.com/news/business/realestate/when-bryan-j-bly-became-nb-did-he-know-what-he-was-signing/1103508 after it changed the assignment of a mortgage note for one borrower three separate times.

b. Mortgage assignments are being created out of whole cloth just for the purposes of showing a transfer from one entity to another, said James Kowalski Jr., an attorney in Jacksonville, Fla., who represents the borrower in the M&T case. Banks got away from very basic banking rules because they securitized millions of loans and moved them so quickly, Kowalski said.

c. In many cases, Kowalski said, it has become impossible to establish when a mortgage was sold, and to whom, so the servicers are trying to recreate the paperwork, right down to the stamps that financial companies use to verify when a note has changed hands. Some mortgage processors are simply ordering stamps from stamp makers, he said, and are using those as proof of mortgage assignments after the fact.

d. Such alleged practices are now generating ire from the bench. The court has been misled by the plaintiff from the beginning, Circuit Court Judge J. Michael Traynor said in a motion dismissing M&T's foreclosure action with prejudice and ordering the hearing.

e. In a notice on its website, the Florida attorney general said it is examining whether Docx, an Alpharetta, Ga., unit of Lender Processing Services, forged documents so foreclosures could be processed more quickly.

These documents are used in court cases as 'real' documents of assignment and presented to the court as so, when it actually appears that they are fabricated in order to meet the demands of the institution that does not, in fact, have the necessary documentation to foreclose according to law, the notice said.

f. Docx is the largest lien release processor in the United States working on behalf of banks and mortgage lenders. Lender Processing Services, which was spun off from Fidelity National two years ago, did not return calls seeking comment Tuesday. The company disclosed in its annual report in February that federal prosecutors were reviewing the business processes of Docx. The company said it was cooperating with the investigators.

g. This is systemic, said April Charney, a senior staff attorney at Jacksonville Area Legal Aid and a member of the Florida Supreme Court's foreclosure task force. Banks can't show ownership for many of these securitized loans, Charney continued. I call them empty-sack trusts, because in the rush to securitize, the originating lender failed to check the paper trial and now they can't collect.

h. In Florida, Georgia, Maryland, and other states where the foreclosure process must be handled through the courts, hundreds of borrowers have challenged lenders' rights to take their homes. Some judges have invalidated mortgages, giving properties back to borrowers while lenders appeal. In February, the Florida state Supreme Court set a new standard stipulating that before fore-closing, a lender had to verify it had all the proper documents. Lenders that cannot produce such papers can be fined for perjury, the court said.

i. Kowalski said the bigger problem is that mortgage servicers are working in a vacuum, handing out foreclosure assignments to third-party firms such as LPS and Fidelity. There's no meeting to get everybody together and make sure they have their ducks in a row to comply with these very basic rules that banks set up many years ago, Kowalski said. The disconnect occurs not just between units within the banks, but among the servicers, their bank clients and the lawyers.

....

10. I have been investigating, reporting on, and testifying against the fraudulent and abusive practices, of LPS and its prior gestations and incarnations from Fidelity National Financial and All-Tel.

11. I have reviewed thousands of pages of manuals, documents, marketing materials, website info, pleadings, and information regarding LPS, Fidelity National Financial and various subsidiaries and affiliates related to these companies, including Sedgwick CMS.

12. In many thousands of instances, I can testify to the fact that these companies engage in the wide-scale practice of spoliation and fabrication of evidence in state and federal court cases across the nation.

13. In my opinion, nothing any of these companies place onto a document, assignment, affidavit, filing with a court, or pleading can be relied upon by any party or court without a complete forensic audit verifying and validating not only each fact or information stated on the documents, but the lawful signature and authorities of each person placing their mark or signature upon each document, including the notary itself on notarized documents.

14. I have personally witnessed many thousands of intentional and fraudulent misrepresentations made by LPS, Fidelity, law firms in their network, and their clients. I have also seen them change records, redact and alter records, and destroy evidence and records to conceal and cover-up the frauds and abuses of their companies, employees, lawyers, and clients. To validate my point and conclusions I offer the following facts below...

15. LPS is now under a federal criminal investigation by the U.S. attorney's office for the middle district of Florida for alleged false, fraudulent, and forged assignments of mortgages, deeds of trusts, and deeds to secure debt used by the foreclosure mill law firms3and their servicer clients in an attempt to establish standing and authority to foreclose and recreate chains-of-titles to mortgages and promissory notes that have been intentionally and admittedly lost and/or destroyed to conceal the fact that the real and lawful owner of such promissory notes. ....

We are able to analyze your situation, and make appropriate referrals. A form exists on our blog to originate contact − begin the conversation. But, first you must educate yourself. You've read the book, now read the blog. Then contact us through the blog. www.UseForeclosureLaw.com.

APPENDIX J: NASSIM TALEB: THE BLACK SWAN

Nassim Taleb's remarkable book *The Black Swan: The Impact of the Highly Improbable,* was the #1 Highest Selling Nonfiction book published in 2007 on Amazon for all of 2007, 17 weeks on the NYT Bestseller list, 78 weeks on the NYT extended list, & 15 months on the Business Week list, plus London Sunday Times, Germany, Switzerland, China, Italy, Brazil, etc.

Education: MBA from Wharton, Ph.D. from the University of Paris

Academic: Distinguished Professor of Risk Engineering, NYU-Polytechnic Institute, Visiting Professor, London Business School, & co-director of the **Decision Science Laboratory**. Dean's Professor in the Sciences of Uncertainty University of Massachusetts at Amherst, Fellow & Adjunct Professor of Mathematics at the Courant Institute of Mathematical Sciences of New York University. Affiliated faculty: Wharton School Financial Institutions Center, Honorary member, Edinburgh Generation Science Club; member, Advisory Board of the Centre for Integrative Thinking at the Rotman School of Management at the University of Toronto, etc.

We ask: *Is Nassim Taleb the smartest person on the planet these days?* Could be. We're not smart enough to tell. You can read his opinions and random thoughts, at FooledByRandomness.com.

By Nassim Taleb

For the last 12 years, I have been telling anyone who would listen to me that we are taking huge risks and massive exposure to rare events. I isolated some areas in which people make bogus claims – epistemologically unsound. The Black Swan is a philosophy book (epistemology, philosophy of history & philosophy of science), but **I used banks** as a particularly worrisome case of epistemic arrogance – and the use of "science" to measure the risk of rare events, making society dependent on very spurious measurements.

To me a banking crisis – worse than what we have ever seen – was unavoidable and NOT A BLACK SWAN, just as a drunk and incompetent pilot would eventually crash the plane. And I kept receiving insults for 12 years!" [Emphasis added.]

Brief Quotes From the Black Swan (written between: 2003-2006) that the IMBECILES did not want to hear:

"Globalization creates interlocking fragility, while reducing volatility and giving the appearance of stability. In other words it creates devastating Black Swans. We have never lived before under the threat of a global collapse. Financial Institutions have been merging into a smaller number of very large banks. Almost all banks are interrelated. So the financial ecology is swelling into gigantic, incestuous, bureaucratic banks – when one fails, they all fall….

"Banks hire dull people and train them to be even more dull. If they look conservative, it's only because their loans go bust on rare, very rare occasions. But (...) bankers are not conservative at all. They are just phenomenally skilled at self-deception by burying the possibility of a large, devastating loss under the rug. [Emphasis added.]....

"The government-sponsored institution Fannie Mae, when I look at its risks, seems to be sitting on a barrel of dynamite, vulnerable to the slightest hiccup. But not to worry: their large staff of scientists deemed these events "unlikely."

"Once again, recall the story of banks hiding explosive risks in their portfolios. It is not a good idea to trust corporations with matters such as rare events because the performance of these executives is not observable on a short-term basis, and they will game the system by showing good performance so they can get their yearly bonus....

The Achilles' heel of capitalism is that if you make corporations compete, it is sometimes the one that is most exposed to the negative Black Swan that will appear to be the most fit for survival....

"The giant firm J. P. Morgan put the entire world at risk by introducing in the nineties RiskMetrics, a phony method aiming at managing people's risks, causing the generalized use of the ludic fallacy, and bringing Dr. Johns into power in place of the skeptical Fat Tonys. (A related method called "Value-at-Risk," which relies on the quantitative measurement of risk, has been spreading.)

"Please, don't drive a school bus blindfolded."

[**Editor's Note:** We urge you to read this book and quite literally grow your brain. Here's the link to <u>Amazon.</u>]

Opacity: What We Do Not See

Quick Footnotes (generally working notes not interesting enough to make it to my next book). Note that there is nothing lowly technical in this page –my technical notes are _here_ . Once again, I beg you to avoid sending me the list of typos. [**Editor's Note:** We picked the following notes, and Nassim graciously allowed us to print them here.]

7 Knowledge as Self-Deception, November 2, 2005. I used to think that people treat their knowledge as personal property, something to protect, a hard-earned investment to guard against the disorderly and A Platonic truth. Robert Trivers made me realize that perhaps the entire business of knowledge came just as a tool for self-deception. We may have acquired the desire to know things first so we could fool ourselves –others perhaps, but ourselves first. No matter where I look, the curse of the Platonic fold shows up –that exact boundary that is far worse than pure disorder. Deceit is worse than disorder.

20 What I am Not Saying. Rome, Sep 29, 2006. I am not saying that we tend to always underestimate rare events. We sometimes overestimate them, or, developing phobias, overestimate some specific rare events (while ignoring others). My real idea is that the <u>more remote the event, the less we know about its probability</u>. The consequences of underestimation can be large –but not the opposite. We cannot evaluate some risks, so it is best not to take them (buy protection, or avoid them).

21 Crossing the Street Blindfolded –From The Black Swan, October 2, 2006. Many middlebrows have asked me over the past twenty years: "how do you Taleb cross the street given your extreme risk consciousness?" or the more foolish: "you are asking us to take <u>no</u> risks." Of course I am not advocating total risk phobia (as I matter of fact I encourage a class of 'convex" risk-taking): all I will be showing you is how to avoid crossing the street <u>blindfolded</u>.

104- Nothing Wrong with (Natural) Bubbles. Bubbles are not a problem – we move by fads (cycles of fads-squeezes) and there is no reason to rectify human nature. However, equity bubbles are benign (particularly when they are not fueled by debt). Consider that the internet craze left us so much better off (and consider that companies incapable of borrowing 5 million from the bank could manage to raise a billion at an IPO). Debt bubbles are not benign – leverage induces nonlinearities. There is an asymmetry: the equity owner gets almost all the positive uncertainty, the debt holder gets the negative. In my Fourth Quadrant problem (f. International Journal of Forecasting) I show that we need to "decomplexify" financial exposures and linearize them to face the switch into Extremistan. Apparently, Mediterranean cultures did not like debt but slowly relaxed the interdicts on lending and borrowing (except for Islamic Banking).

Stocks have Ponzi characteristics. People discuss "value" in stocks as if it were something tangible – beyond a mere opinion, and a public opinion at that. Listed stocks are not "self-liquidating" – at least not in any realistic investment horizon; an investment in the market is largely a bet on what some other idiot will think of the investment in a few years, assign "value" to it, or invent a convincing and contagious narrative. It is simply psychology of the other idiot. This makes anyone investing for "hard" value extremely vulnerable. Most people who act conservative in their regular business become suckers from listening to the news.

My Central Idea. People miss the obvious and get sophisticated with the useless details. I was at Balthazar three times in the past week. The last time I was having dinner with someone who was rehashing points from book reviewers saying (as a compliment) that I masterfully glued together ideas ideas from a variety of sources across philosophy, psychology, mathematics, economics, etc. [Of course, if I am saying obvious things, how come they did not see my obvious (and obviously stated) consequence that the current economic system would collapse?] Then I realized that people miss the obvious, here my central idea – they get a lot of things from my books but not the fundamental idea. Sadly,

NOBODY thought of my central idea before. Sadly, otherwise we would not be here.

My central idea in The Black Swan is that: rare events cannot be estimated from empirical observation since they are rare. We need an a priori model representation for that; the rarer the event, the more the dependence on aprorism. Further, we do not care about probability (if an event happens or does not happen); we worry about consequences (how much total wealth or total destruction will come from it). Given that the less frequent the event, the more severe the consequence (just consider that the 100 year flood is more severe, and less frequent, than the 10 year flood), our estimation of the CONTRIBUTION of the rare event is going to be massively faulty (contribution is probability times effect; multiply that by estimation error); and nothing can remedy it. So the rarer the event, the less we know about its role – and the more we need to make it up with an extrapolative, generalizing theory. Hence model error is more consequential in the tails and some representations ARE MORE FRAGILE than others. Then there are the SUBPLOTS: ...

1) I ground the idea into reality with epistemology/the philosophy of induction (to which it is remotely related), psychology (hindsight bias), psychology of risk, model error (Ludic fallacy), strong apriorism (Platonicity), the fact that people can't predict rare events and spin stories – and are more confident with rare events, ironically, the charlatanism in economics [institutionalized bullshit – nobody checked the track record], etc.

2) I also set up a domain separation (Mediocristan-Extremistan) and a decision separation (simple binary yes-no payoff or complex, expectation based) and have to worry about expectation-based decisions in Extremistan, THE FOURTH QUADRANT.

3) I set up an agenda to de-fragilize the world from the 4th Quadrant and make people more robust to negative Black swans and exploit positive Black Swans.

4) I made a living by hunting for fragility to the 4th Quadrant by people ignorant of it – and I was dead CERTAIN that the current economic system would collapse violently and unpredictably, and that Banks would go bust IN UNISON [next prediction almost everything else fragile will follow].

I am now setting up a program to help humanity formulate decisions under ignorance by changing the world in such a way as to make our forecast errors inconsequential – how to change the world for it to allow for our ignorance; the exact opposite of the enlightenment program. We should make our structures less complex (less debt) to face complexity from globalization & the net, etc.

People find a frame (skepticism,, empiricism, bullshitism), then try to squeeze an idea into a category. No, it is NOT Hume's problem of induction (which, incidentally, is not Hume's); it is NOT Mill's problem; it is CERTAINLY NOT Popper's falsification (it was more intelligently dealt with by Menodotus) and it is NOT about the dichotomy risk and uncertainty; it has little to do with Austrian Economics (except that they believe in fundamental uncertainty); it is not about power laws (I used it as a technical tool and used chaos theory to show the fragility of nonlinear modelization in the tails). Nobody before has examined my problem in the history of thought, let alone systematize the idea of decision-making under certain classes of ignorance.

APPENDIX I: MICHAEL THOMAS: THE BIG LIE

Our feature author and "expert witness" here is Michael M. Thomas, a true New York City *Raconteur*, intellectual leader, expert financial writer and novelist. Critically his thirty years on Wall Street, and, the fact that he was a Managing Director and Partner at Lehman Brothers, particularly qualifies him to make the comments and assessments below. Take heed, we have this article from a Master of Interpretation of modern history – also, an Honest Wall Street Insider. How rare! It's fitting we end these Appendices chapters with our senior writer, the one who was there and witnessed the Criminalization of Wall Street.

The Big Lie

By Michael M. Thomas

Wall Street has destroyed the wonder that was America.

Imagine a vast field on which a terrible battle has recently been fought, the bare ground cratered by fusillade after fusillade of heavy artillery, trees reduced to blackened stumps, wisps of toxic gas hanging in the gray, and corpses everywhere.

A terrible scene, made worse by the sound of distant laughter, because somehow, on the heights commanding the dead zone, the officers' club has made it through intact. From its balconies flutter bunting, and across the blasted landscape there comes a chorus of hearty male voices in counterpoint to the wheedling of cadres of wheel-greasers, the click of betting chips, the orotund declamations of a visiting congressional delegation: in sum, the celebratory hullabaloo of a class of people that has sent entire nations off to perish but whose only concern right now is whether the '11 is ready to drink and who'll see to tipping the servants. The notion that there might be someone or some force out there getting ready to slouch toward the buttonwood tree to exact retribution scarcely ruffles the celebrants' joy.

Ah, Wall Street. As it was in the beginning, is now, and hopes to God it ever will be, world without end. Amen.

Or so it seems to me. It was in May 1961 that a series of circumstances took me from the hushed precincts of the Metropolitan Museum of Art, where I was working as a curatorial assistant in the European Paintings Department, to Lehman Brothers, to begin what for the next 30 years would be an involvement—I hesitate to call it "a career"—in investment banking. I would promote and execute deals, sit on boards, kiss ass, and lie through my teeth: the whole megillah. In consequence of which, I would wear Savile Row and carry a Hermès briefcase. I had Mme. Claude's home number in Paris and I frequented the best clubs in a half-dozen cities. But I had a problem: I was unable to develop the anti-communitarian moral opacity that is the key to real success on Wall Street.

I had my doubts from the beginning. A few months after I started to work downtown, I ran into an old friend from college and before, a man later to become one of New York's most esteemed writers and editors.

"So," he asked, "how do you like what you're doing now?"

"I like it quite a lot," I said. And this was true: these were new frontiers for me, the pace was lively, the money was good enough ($6,500 a year), and there was so much to learn. But there was one aspect of Wall Street that I found morally confusing if not distasteful: "There's one thing that bothers me, though. It's this: on the one hand the New York Stock Exchange has sent its president, the estimable G. Keith Funston, out into the countryside, supported by an expensive, extensive advertising campaign, to exhort the proletariat to Own your share of America! As if buying 50 shares of IBM or GM in 1961 is as much of a civic duty as buying a $100 war bond in 1943."

I then added, "But here's the thing. At the same time as Funston's out there doing his thing, if you ask any veteran Wall Street pro how the Street works, the first thing he'll tell you is: The public is always wrong. Always." I paused to let that sink in, then confessed, "I have to tell you, I have trouble squaring that circle."

And that was back when Wall Street was basically honest, brought into line thanks in part to Ferdinand Pecora's 1933 humiliation of the great bankers of the Jazz Age and even more so because of the communitarian exigencies forced on the nation by war. From Pearl Harbor to V-J Day, greed was definitely not good, and that proscriptive spirit lingered on right up to 1970, when everything started to change, and the traders began their long march through our great houses of finance, with the inevitable consequence that the Street's moral bookkeeping grew more and more contorted, its corruptions more elaborate, its self-interest less and less governable. What someone has called the "Greed Wars" began.

But now, I think, the game is at long last over.

As 2011 slithers to its end, none of the major problems that led to the crisis point three years ago have really been solved. Bank balance sheets still reek. Europe day by day becomes a financial black hole, with matter from the periphery being sucked toward the center until the vortex itself collapses. The Street and its ministries of propaganda have fallen back on a Big Lie as old as capitalism itself: that all that has gone wrong has been government's fault. This time, however, I don't think the argument that "Washington ate my homework" is going to work. This time, a firestorm is going to explode about the Street's head—and about time, too.

It's funny; the Big Lie has a long pedigree. A year or so ago, I was leafing through Ron Chernow's indispensable history of the Morgan financial interests, and found this interesting exchange between FDR and Russell Leffingwell, a Morgan partner and Washington fixer, a sort of Robert Strauss of his day. It dates from the summer of 1932, with FDR not yet in office:

"You and I know," wrote Leffingwell, "that we cannot cure the present deflation and depression by punishing the villains, real or imaginary, of the first post war decade, and that when it comes down to the day of reckoning nobody gets very far with all this prohibition and regulation stuff." To which FDR replied: "I wish we could get from the bankers themselves an admission that in the 1927 to 1929 period there were grave abuses and that the bankers themselves now support wholeheartedly methods to prevent recurrence thereof. Can't bankers see their own advantage in such a course?" And then Leffingwell again: "The bankers were not in fact responsible for 1927–29 and the politicians were. Why then should the bankers make a false confession?"

This time, I fear, the public anger will not be deflected. Confessions, not false, will be exacted. Occupy Wall Street has set the snowball rolling; you may not think much of OWS—I have my own reservations, although none are philosophical or moral—but it has made America aware of a sinister, usurious process by which wealth has systematically been funneled into fewer and fewer hands. A process in which Washington played a useful supporting role, but no more than that.

Over the next year, I expect the "what" will give way to the "how" in the broad electorate's comprehension of the financial situation. The 99 percent must learn to differentiate the bloodsuckers and rent-extractors from those in the 1 percent who make the world a better, more just place to live. Once people realize how Wall Street made its pile, understand how financiers get rich, what it is that they actually do, the time will become ripe for someone to gather the spreading ripples of anger and perplexity into a focused tsunami of retribution. To make the bastards pay, properly, for the grief and woe they have caused. Perhaps not to the extent proposed by H. L. Mencken, who wrote that when a bank fails, the first order of business should be to hang its board of directors, but in a manner in which the pain is proportionate to the collateral damage. Possibly an excess-profits tax retroactive to 2007, or some form of "Tobin tax" on transactions, or a wealth tax. The era of money for nothing will be over.

But it won't just end with taxes. When the great day comes, Wall Street will pray for another Pecora, because compared with the rough beast now beginning to strain at the leash, Pecora will look like Phil Gramm. Humiliation and ridicule, even financial penalties, will be the least of the Street's tribulations. There will be prosecutions and show trials. There will be violence, mark my words. Houses burnt, property defaced. I just hope that this time the mob targets the right people in Wall Street and in Washington. (How does a right-thinking Christian go about asking Santa for Mitch McConnell's head under the Christmas tree?) There will be kleptocrats who threaten to take themselves elsewhere if their demands on jurisdictions and tax breaks aren't met, and I say let 'em go!

At the end of the day, the convulsion to come won't really be about Wall Street's derivatives malefactions, or its subprime fun and games, or rogue trading, or the folly of banks. It will be about this society's final opportunity to rip away the paralyzing shackles of corruption or else dwell forever in a neofeudal

social order. You might say that 1384 has replaced 1984 as our worst-case scenario. I have lived what now, at 75, is starting to feel like a long life. If anyone
asks me what has been the great American story of my lifetime, I have a ready
answer. It is the corruption, money-based, that has settled like some all-
enveloping excremental mist on the landscape of our hopes, that has permeated
every nook of any institution or being that has real influence on the way we live
now. Sixty years ago, if you had asked me, on the basis of all that I had been
taught, whether I thought this condition of general rot was possible in this country, I would have told you that you were nuts. And I would have been very
wrong. What has happened in this country has made a lie of my boyhood.

There should be more to America, Gore Vidal has written, than who pays
tax to whom. It has been in Wall Street's interest to shrivel our sensibilities as a
nation, to shove aside the verities of which General MacArthur spoke at West
Point—duty, honor, country—in favor of grubby schemes and scams and "car-
ried interest" calculations. Time, I think, to take the country back.

Author's Bio:

After a career as a curator at the Metropolitan Museum of Art, **a partner at
Lehman Brothers** and an independent financial consultant and investor, he
began writing novels in 1978.

He has published seven novels, written innumerable articles and reviews,
contributes occasional commentary to Forbes.com, and beginning in 1987,
wrote a weekly column for *The New York Observer*, "Midas Watch."

Books: Three of his Best Seller's are: Someone Else's Money, Love and
Money, Hard Money. Link to his books on Amazon, click here.
http://www.amazon.com/s/ref=sr_tc_2_0?rh=i%3Astripbooks%2Ck%3AMichae
l+M.+Thomas&keywords=Michael+M.+Thomas&ie=UTF8&qid=1326318959
&sr=1-2-ent&field-contributor_id=B000AP9WMW

This essay was published in Newsweek International's Special Edition, 'Issues 2012,' on sale from December 2011-February 2012. It was also published at
the   DailyBeast.com.
http://www.thedailybeast.com/newsweek/2011/12/25/wall-street-has-destroyed-
the-wonder-that-was-america.print.html

APPENDIX K: STATE BY STATE FORECLOSURE LAWS

State	Process Begins (Months)	Redemption Period (Days)	Security Instrument	Foreclosure Action
Alabama	2-3	365	Mortgage	Non-Judicial
http://www.foreclosure.com/statelaw_AL.html?rsp=22342				
Alaska	3-4	365	Deed of Trust	Non-judicial
http://www.foreclosure.com/statelaw_AK.html?rsp=22342				
Arizona	3	30-180	Deed of Trust	Non-judicial
http://www.foreclosure.com/statelaw_AZ.html?rsp=22342				
Arkansas	3	365	Mortgage	Judicial/ Non-Judicial
http://www.foreclosure.com/statelaw_AR.html?rsp=22342				
California	4	365	Deed of Trust	Non-judicial
http://www.foreclosure.com/statelaw_CA.html?rsp=22342				
Colorado	6	75	Mortgage/Deed of Trust	Non-judicial
http://www.foreclosure.com/statelaw_CO.html?rsp=22342				
Connecticut	2-5	Court Decides	Mortgage	Strict Foreclosure
http://www.foreclosure.com/statelaw_CT.html?rsp=22342				
Delaware	7-10	None	Mortgage	Judicial
http://www.foreclosure.com/statelaw_DE.html?rsp=22342				
District of Columbia	2	None	Deed of Trust	Non-judicial
http://www.foreclosure.com/statelaw_DC.html?rsp=22342				
Florida	5	None	Mortgage	Judicial
http://www.foreclosure.com/statelaw_FL.html?rsp=22342				

Georgia	2	None	Mortgage/Deed of Trust	Non-judicial
http://www.foreclosure.com/statelaw_GA.html?rsp=22342				
Hawaii	11	None	Mortgage	Judicial/ Non-Judicial
http://www.foreclosure.com/statelaw_HI.html?rsp=22342				
Idaho	5	365	Mortgage/Deed of Trust	Non-judicial
http://www.foreclosure.com/statelaw_ID.html?rsp=22342				
Illinois	12	365	Mortgage/Deed of Trust	Judicial
http://www.foreclosure.com/statelaw_IL.html?rsp=22342				
Indiana	9	None	Mortgage	Judicial
http://www.foreclosure.com/statelaw_IN.html?rsp=22342				
Iowa	4-6	20	Mortgage/Deed of Trust	Non-Judicial
http://www.foreclosure.com/statelaw_IA.html?rsp=22342				
Kansas	7-8	365	Mortgage	Judicial
http://www.foreclosure.com/statelaw_KS.html?rsp=22342				
Kentucky	6	365	Mortgage/Deed of Trust	Judicial
http://www.foreclosure.com/statelaw_KY.html?rsp=22342				
Louisiana	6-9	None	Mortgage	Judicial
http://www.foreclosure.com/statelaw_LA.html?rsp=22342				
Maine	9	90	Mortgage	Judicial
http://www.foreclosure.com/statelaw_ME.html?rsp=22342				
Maryland	2	Court De-cides	Mortgage/Deed of Trust	Judicial
http://www.foreclosure.com/statelaw_MD.html?rsp=22342				
Massachusetts	3	None	Mortgage	Judicial
http://www.foreclosure.com/statelaw_MA.html?rsp=22342				
Michigan	8	30-365	Mortgage	Non-judicial

http://www.foreclosure.com/statelaw_MI.html?rsp=22342				
Minnesota	**4**	**1825**	**Mortgage**	**Non-judicial**
http://www.foreclosure.com/statelaw_MN.html?rsp=22342				
Mississippi	**3-4**	**None**	**Deed of Trust**	**Non-judicial**
http://www.foreclosure.com/statelaw_MS.html?rsp=22342				
Missouri	**2**	**365**	**Deed of Trust**	**Non-judicial**
http://www.foreclosure.com/statelaw_MO.html?rsp=22342				
Montana	**5-6**	**None**	**Mortgage/Deed of Trust**	**Non-judicial**
http://www.foreclosure.com/statelaw_MT.html?rsp=22342				
Nebraska	**4-6**	**None**	**Mortgage/Deed of Trust**	**Judicial**
http://www.foreclosure.com/statelaw_NE.html?rsp=22342				
Nevada	**4**	**None**	**Deed of Trust**	**Non-judicial**
http://www.foreclosure.com/statelaw_NV.html?rsp=22342				
New Hamp-shire	**3**	**None**	**Mortgage**	**Non-judicial**
http://www.foreclosure.com/statelaw_NH.html?rsp=22342				
New Jersey	**9**	**10**	**Mortgage**	**Judicial**
http://www.foreclosure.com/statelaw_NJ.html?rsp=22342				
New Mexico	**6**	**30-270**	**Mortgage**	**Judicial**
http://www.foreclosure.com/statelaw_NM.html?rsp=22342				
New York	**15**	**None**	**Mortgage**	**Judicial**
http://www.foreclosure.com/statelaw_NY.html?rsp=22342				
North Caro-lina	**3-4**	**None**	**Deed of Trust**	**Non-Judicial**
http://www.foreclosure.com/statelaw_NC.html?rsp=22342				
North Dakota	**5**	**180-365**	**Mortgage**	**Judicial**
http://www.foreclosure.com/statelaw_ND.html?rsp=22342				

Ohio	7	None	Mortgage	Judicial
http://www.foreclosure.com/statelaw_OH.html?rsp=22342				
Oklahoma	6-7l	None	Mortgage/Deed of Trust	Judicial
http://www.foreclosure.com/statelaw_OK.html?rsp=22342				
Oregon	5	180	Mortgage/Deed of Trust	Non-judicial
http://www.foreclosure.com/statelaw_OR.html?rsp=22342				
Pennsylvania	10	None	Mortgage	Judicial
http://www.foreclosure.com/statelaw_PA.html?rsp=22342				
Puerto Rico	2-3	None	Mortgage	Judicial
http://www.foreclosure.com/statelaw_PR.html?rsp=22342				
Rhode Island	2	None	Mortgage	Non-judicial
http://www.foreclosure.com/statelaw_RI.html?rsp=22342				
South Caro-lina	6	None	Mortgage	Judicial
http://www.foreclosure.com/statelaw_SC.html?rsp=22342				
South Dakota	5	30-265	Judicial	Judicial
http://www.foreclosure.com/statelaw_SD.html?rsp=22342				
Tennessee	2	730	Mortgage/Deed of Trust	Non-judicial
http://www.foreclosure.com/statelaw_TN.html?rsp=22342				
Texas	3	None	Mortgage/Deed of Trust	Non-judicial
http://www.foreclosure.com/statelaw_TX.html?rsp=22342				
Utah	5	Court De-cides	Mortgage/Deed of Trust	Non-judicial
http://www.foreclosure.com/statelaw_UT.html?rsp=22342				
Vermont	9	180-365	Mortgage	Judicial
http://www.foreclosure.com/statelaw_VT.html?rsp=22342				
Virginia	2	None	Deed of Trust	Non-judicial

http://www.foreclosure.com/statelaw_VA.html?rsp=22342				
Washington	**5**	**None**	**Mortgage/Deed of Trust**	**Non-judicial**
http://www.foreclosure.com/statelaw_WA.html?rsp=22342				
West Virginia	**4**	**None**	**Mortgage/Deed of Trust**	**Non-judicial**
http://www.foreclosure.com/statelaw_WV.html?rsp=22342				
Wisconsin	**5**	**365**	**Mortgage**	**Judicial**
http://www.foreclosure.com/statelaw_WI.html?rsp=22342				
Wyoming	**2**	**90-365**	**Mortgage/Deed of Trust**	**Non-Judicial**
http://www.foreclosure.com/statelaw_WY.html?rsp=22342				

AUTHOR'S BIO

Author, Ken "Postman" Kappel was known solely as "The Postman" for his first book on the foreclosure disaster: *Choose Foreclosure: the Case For Walking Away.*

Background:

Licensed Real Estate Sales Agent in California, current.

The Homeowners Economist, web site, where he wrote accurately on the economy (2004-2006), and how it would affect residential homeowners and investors.

LampLight Communications Inc. NYC, while pursuing a writing career in NYC he owned and operated an incorporated expert word processing and training consultancy. He did work for: Goldman Sachs, Drexel Burnham, Morgan Stanley, Lehman Brothers, Solomon Brothers, Prudential-Bache Capital Funding, Merrill Lynch; law firms including Simpson Thacher & Bartlett, Baker & McKenzie; White & Case, Mound Cotton & Wollan, Bower & Gardner, and other "White Shoe" firms.

Resolution Trust Company. In NYC, as a sub-sub-contractor for the RTC's principal law firm, he designed an automated discrete loan document processing system, and processed 180 loan document packages that were executed in a three day period for commercial real estate purchases worth hundreds of millions of dollars.

KribKram Series. As a Microsoft Certified Systems Engineer and Certified Trainer, he wrote a series of study guides to enable individuals to pass rigorous technical examinations to obtain various Microsoft Certifications.

Design Implementation. Owner. Small construction company. Marin County, CA.

LIFE Magazine, Associate Merchandising Director, NYC

KTVU-TV, Assistant Sale Promotion Director, Oakland, CA .

Eugene Daily Emerald, Advertising Manager, Eugene, Oregon.

While completing his senior year as a Journalism major at the University of Oregon, he worked nearly full time at the campus daily newspaper.

BIBLIOGRAPHY

Allen, Gary. *None Date Call It Conspiracy.* California: Concord Press. 1971.

Bagdikian, Ben H. *The Media Monopoly.* Boston: Beacon Press, 1983.

Batra, Dr. Ravi. *Greenspan's Fraud.* New York: Palgrave MacMillan, 2005.

Batra, Dr. Ravi. *The New Golden Age: The Coming Revolution Against Political Corruption and Economic Chaos.* New York: Palgrave MacMillan, 2007.

Bitner, Richard, *Confessions of a Subprime Lender, An Insider's Tale of Greed, Fraud & Ignorance,* New York, John Wiley & Sons, 2008.

Bonner, William and Wiggin, Addison. *Empire of Debt: The Rise of an Epic Financial Crisis.* New York: John Wiley & Sons, 2006.

Brezezinski, Zbigniew. *The Grand Chessboard: American Primacy and Its Geostrategic Imperatives.* New York: Basic Books, 1997.

Brin, David. *The Postman.* New York: Bantam, 1985.

Broder, David S. *The Changing of the Guard.* New York: Simon & Schuster, 1980.

Campbell, Robert M. *Timing the Real Estate Market.* San Diego: The Campbell Method, 2004.

Chernow, Ron. *Alexander Hamilton.* New York: The Penguin Press, 2004.

Chernow, Ron. *The House of Morgan.* New York: Atlantic Monthly Press, 1990.

Chomsky, Noam, Herman Edward S. *The Washington Connection & Third World Fascism.* New York: South End Press, 1979.

Copeland, Vince. *The Built-In U.S. War Drive.* New York: World View Publishers, 1980.

Coppes, Charles H. *American's Financial Reckoning Day: How You Can Survive America's Monetary and Political Delcine in the 21st Century.* Lincoln, NE: iUniverse, 2007.

DeGrasse, Robert W. Jr., Council on Economic Priorities Report. *Military Expansion Economic Decline.* New York: M.E. Sharpe, Inc., 1983.

deMause, Lloyd, *Reagan's America.* New York: Creative Roots, Inc., 1984.

Duncan, Richard. *The Dollar Crisis: Cause, Consequences, Cures.* Singapore: John Wiley & Sons, 2003.

Ellis, Joseph, J., *American Sphinx: The Character of Thomas Jefferson.* New York, Vantage. 1996.

Ehrenreich, Barbara, *This Land is Their Land,* New York, Metropolitan, Henry Holt, 2008.

Faber, Marc. *Tomorrow's Gold: Asia's Age of Discovery.* Hong Kong: CLSA Books, 2002.

Ferris, Paul. *The Master Bankers.* New York: William Morrow & Co., Inc./Plume, 1984.

Fleckenstein, William A., with Sheehan, Frederick. *Greenspan's Bubble: The Age of Ignorance at the Federal Reserve.* New York: McGraw Hill, 2008.

Galbraith, John Kenneth. *The Age of Uncertainty.* Boston: Houghton Mifflin Co., 1977.

Greenspan, Alan. *The Age of Turbulence: Adventures in a New World.* New York: The Penguin Press, 2007.

Greider, William. *Secrets of the Temple: How the Federal Reserve Runs the Country.* New York: Simon and Schuster, 1987.

Hartmann, Thom. *Screwed: The Undeclared War Against the Middle class ... And What We Can Do About It.* San Francisco: Berrett-Koehler Publishers, Inc., 2006.

Hartmann, Thom. *Unequal Protection: The Rise of Corporate Dominance and the Theft of Human Rights.* USA: Rodale Inc., 2002.

Hartmann, Thom. *We The People: A Call To Take Back America.* Portland, Core-Way Media, Inc. 2004.

Hayek, F.A. *The Road to Serfdom.* U of Chicago Press, 1994.

Hazlitt, Henry, *Economics in One Lesson,* New York, von Mises Institute, Three Rivers Press, 2008.

Henwood, Doug. *Wall Street: How it Works and for Whom.* New York: Verso, 1997.

Huntington, Samuel E. *The Clash of Civilizations: Remaking of World Order.* New York: Touchstone/Simon & Schuster, 1996.

International Forum on Globalization Report. *Alternatives to Economic Globalization.* San Francisco: Berrett-Koehler Publishers Inc., 2002.

Jones, David M. *The Politics of Money: The Fed Under Alan Greenspan.* New York: NY Institute of Finance/Simon & Schuster, 1991.

Josephson, Matthew, *The Robber Barons: The Great American Capitalists.* New York: Harcourt, Brace & World Inc., 1962.

Kaplan, Robert D. *Warrior Politics: Why Leadership Demands A Pagan Ethos.* New York: Vintage Books, 2002.

Kelly, Kevin. *New Rules for the New Economy.* New York: Penguin Books, 1998.

Kennedy, Paul. *The Rise and Fall of the Great Powers.* New York: Random House, 1987.

Klein, Naomi. *The Shock Doctrine.* New York: Metropolitan Books/Henry Holt and Company, Inc, 2007.

Lakoff, George. *Moral Politics: What Conservatives Know That Liberals Don't.* Chicago: The University of Chicago Press, 1996.

Lakoff, George. *Whose Freedom? Battle Over American's Most Important Idea,* New York, Picador, Farrar, Straus and Giroux, 2006.

Lapham, Lewis. *Theater of War.* New York: The New Press, 2002.

Levitt, Steven D., and Dubner, Stephan J. Dubner. *Freakonomics, A Rogue Economist Explores the Hidden Side of Everything.* New York, William Morrow, 2005.

Lewis, Michael. *Liar's Poker: Rising Through the Wreckage on Wall Street.* New York: Norton/Penguin, 1989.

Lundberg, Frederick. *The Rich and The Super Rich: A Study in the Power of Money Today.* New York: Lyle Stuart, Inc., 1968.

Marrs, Jim. *Rule by Secrecy.* New York: Harper-Collins, 2000.

Marshall, Stephan, *Wolves in Sheep's Clothing: The New Liberal Menace in America.* New York: The Disinformation Company, Ltd., 2007.

Mayer, Martin. *The Fed.* New York: Simon & Schuster/Free Press, 2001.

Mehrling, Perry, G. *Fischer Black: And the Revolutionary Idea of Finance.* Hoboken, John Wiley and Sons, Inc. 2005.

Mehrling, Perry, G. *The Money Interest and the Public Interest.* Cambridge, MA: Harvard University Press, 1997.

Mills, James. *The Underground Empire.* New York, Doubleday & Co., Inc., 1986.

Minsky, Hyman P. *Some Collected Papers from Bard College,* http://www.bard.edu, 1991-1996.

Muolo, Paul & Padilla, Mathew, *Chain of Blame: How Wall Street Cause the Mortgage and Credit Crisis,* New York, John Wiley & Sons, 2008.

Noory, George & Birnes, William, *Worker in the Light,* New York, TOR, Doherty Associates, 2006.

Palast, Greg. *The Best Democracy Money Can Buy.* New York, Plume/Penguin, 2002.

Perkins, John. *Confessions of an Economic Hit Man.* San Francisco: Berrett-Koehler Publishers, Inc., 2004.

Pilger, John. *The New Rulers of the World.* New York: Verso, 2002.

Pizzo, Stephen; Fricker, Mary; and Muolo, Paul. *Inside Job: The Looting of America Savings and Loans.* New York: McGraw Hill, 1989.

Quindlen, Ruthann. *Confessions of a Venture Capitalist: Inside the High-Stakes World of Start-up Financing.* New York: Warner Books, 2000.

Rothbard, Murray N. *The Case Against the Fed.* Auburn AL: Ludwig von Mises Institute, 1994.

Rubin, Robert E. & Weisberg, Jacob. *In An Uncertain World.* New York: Random House, 2003.

Ruppert, Michael C. *Crossing the Rubicon: The Decline of the American Empire At The End Of The Age of Oil.* British Columbia: New Society Publishers, 2004.

Smith, Roy C., *The Global Bankers.* New York: Dutton, 1989.

Soros, George, *The Alchemy of Finance: Reading the Mind of the Market.* New York: John Wiley & Sons, 1987.

Soros, George. *Soros on Soros: Staying Ahead of the Curve.* New York: John Wiley & Sons, Inc., 1995.

Stormer, John A., *None Dare Call It Treason.* Missouri: The Liberty Bell Press, 1964.

Suskind, Ron. *The Price of Loyalty: George W. Bush, the White House and the Education of Paul O'Neill.* New York: Simon & Schuster, 2004.

Sutton, Antony, C. *The Federal Reserve Conspiracy.* Boring, OR: CPA Book Publishers, 1995.

Talbot, John, R. *The Coming Crash In the Housing Market.* New York: McGraw Hill, 2003.

Taleb, Nassim, Nicholas. *The Black Swan: The Impact of the Highly Improbable.* New York: Random House, 2007.

Vidal, Gore. *Perpetual War for Perpetual Peace.* New York: Thunder's Mouth Press/Nation Books, 2002.

The Internet and The Press

Clearly this book is not conventional. It has been enriched by articles in the press (many quoted herein), but moreover by the Internet and the access it provides to so much information never available before.

Since 2003 we have accumulated, read and been informed by literally thousands of economic based articles and opinions that were only available on the Internet. Below we've listed individuals who have been important to our learning over time. Thank all of you for the information, news and interpretation.

Abelson, Alan	Lavalle, Nye	Saxena, Puru
Ash, Adrian	Lemaire, Eric	Schiff, Peter
Auerback, Marshall	Liu, Henry C.K.	Shedlock, Mish
Baker, Dean	Maudlin, John	Shiller, Robert
Baum, Caroline	McCarthy, Ed	Shostak, Frank
Black, Esq., Bill	McHugh, Robert	Simon, Ruth
Bonner, Bill	Merk, Axel	Smith, Charles Hugh
Brown, Esq., Ellen	Minsky, Hyman P.	Smith, Yves
Calculated Risk	Mogambo Guru	Soros, George
Cockburn, Alex	Murphy, Bill	Spengler
Corrigan, Sean	Noland, Doug	Tanta
Das, Satyajit	Norris, Bruce	Taleb, Nassim
Denning, Daniel	North, Gary	Taylor, Jay
Escobar, Pepe	Nystrom, M. P.	Tice, David
Faber, Marc	Patrick	Toscano, Rich
Fitts, Catherine Austin	Paul, Ron	Turk, James
Fleckenstein, Bill	Pomboy, Stephanie	Tustain, Paul
Forysth, Randall	Richebächer, Kurt	Ure, George
Hanson, Mark	Roach, Stephen	Wakefield, Doug
aka "Mr. Mortgage"	Roberts, Paul Craig	Walker, Susan
Hewitt, Mike	Rockwell, Lew	Weisbrot, Mark
Hudson, Chad	Roubini, Nouriel	Whitney, Mike
Hutchinson, Martin	Rubino, John	Wiggins, Addison
Janszen, Eric	Said, Carolyn	Williams, John
Kunstler, James	Santelli, Rick	Willie, Jim
Krowne, Arron	Saunders, Chris	Wolf, Martin
Krugman, Paul	Saville, Steve	Many More

INDEX

www.ingramcontent.com/pod-product-compliance
Lightning Source LLC
Chambersburg PA
CBHW022053210326
41519CB00054B/326